FURNESS-HOULDER LINES

SIR CHRISTOPHER FURNESS 1852–1912

FOUNDER

FURNESS-HOULDER LINES

by

N.L. MIDDLEMISS

SHIELD PUBLICATIONS LTD
NEWCASTLE UPON TYNE
GREAT BRITAIN

ISBN 1 871128 07 2

Published by Shield Publications Ltd,
7, Verne Road, North Shields.
Printed by Smith Settle, Ilkley Road, Otley.

CONTENTS

1. FURNESS LINE.

2. HOULDER LINE.

AUTHOR

Norman Lea Middlemiss was born at South Shields in 1945 and was educated at Tynemouth High School and Newcastle University, graduating with an Honours degree in Mathematics in 1966. Since then he has worked as a Systems Analyst and Computer Consultant, writing software for a wide variety of applications. Systems of a maritime nature that he has seen to completion include the Seawolf missile system as carried by the Type 22 and Type 23 frigates, and the first shipyard computerised production planning system in the world for the Southwick shipyard of Austin & Pickersgill Ltd, Sunderland, home of the very successful 'SD14' 'Liberty' replacement tramp. He also lectures on Computing at Colleges and was formerly the Senior Lecturer in Computing for Ferranti Ltd at Bracknell, training Royal and foreign naval officers and crews in computer systems. The author has had several articles published in the magazines 'Ships Monthly' and 'Sea Chest', the magazine of his local World Ship Society Tyneside branch of which he was a founder member in 1960. He is the author of:-

'GATHERING OF THE CLANS'-'HISTORY OF THE CLAN LINE STEAMERS'
'PRIDE OF THE PRINCES' - 'HISTORY OF THE PRINCE LINE'
'TRAVELS OF THE TRAMPS' -'TWENTY TRAMP FLEETS' Vols. I and II
'THE BRITISH TANKERS' - 'THE STORY OF BP'
'THE ANGLO-SAXON/SHELL TANKERS'
'FRED. OLSEN/BERGEN LINE'

ACKNOWLEDGEMENTS

'UNDER THE FURNESS FLAG' by A.J. Henderson published by the company in 1951.
'50 YEARS OF SHIPOWNING' by A.J. Henderson published by Syren & Shipping in 1941.
'ONE HUNDRED YEARS OF HOULDERS' by Edward F. Stevens published by the company in 1950.
'SEA HAZARD' published by Houlders Brothers & Co. Ltd in 1947.
'THE SAGA OF MANCHESTER LINERS' by Robert B. Stoker published by Sea Breezes in 1985.
'THE FLAG OF THE SOUTHERN CROSS' by Frank C. Bowen published by Shaw,Savill & Albion Co. Ltd in 1947.
'SHAW,SAVILL & ALBION - POST-WAR FORTUNES OF A SHIPPING EMPIRE' by Richard P. de Kerbrech published by Conway in 1986.
'SHIPBUILDERS OF THE HARTLEPOOLS' by Bert Spaldin published by Hartlepool Borough Council in 1985.
'THE RED DUSTER AT WAR' by J. Slader published by Kimber in 1988.
'THE LOG' - Company House magazine.
Furness,Withy & Co. Ltd records held in National Maritime Museuem, Greenwich. Company Annual Reports and Accounts.
I am indebted to the help and information provided by John B. Hill, Marine Superintendent for Houlder Brothers & Co. Ltd and Chief Marine Superintendent for Furness,Withy(Shipping) Ltd until 1985. Thanks also to Richard Alexander,Alan Tennent,Richard Greenwood, Anna Robinson, and Barbara Jones of Lloyds Register of Shipping, and Tyne & Wear Museums Services for their help.

LIST OF ILLUSTRATIONS

53. PACIFIC NORTHWEST of 1954 was sold to Greece in 1971.
54. ROWANMORE of 1956 was sold in 1973 [A.Duncan].
55. PACIFIC STRONGHOLD of 1958 was sold to Greece in 1971 [J.K.Byass]
56. PACIFIC EXPORTER of 1957 in British Columbia in 1970 [J.K.Byass]
57. MANCHESTER TRADER of 1955 ex WESTERN PRINCE.
58. MANCHESTER FAME of 1959 became CAIRNGLEN in 1965 [A.Duncan].
59. MANCHESTER PROGRESS of 1967 was rebuilt for containers.
60. CAIRNESK of 1926 seen at Newcastle was taken over in 1928.
61. CAIRNGOWAN of 1952 arriving in the Tyne. [M.Donnelly]
62. CAIRNDHU of 1952 waiting to dry-dock at Wallsend [T.Rayner]
63. AKAROA of 1914 of Shaw,Savill was taken over in 1933 [V.H.Young]
64. SALAMANCA of 1948 of P.S.N.C. was taken over in 1965 [A.Duncan]
65. LOCH GARTH of 1947 of Royal Mail Line was taken over in 1965.

66. THORPE GRANGE of 1889 ex INDRAMAYO purchased by Houlder in 1901.
67. URMSTON GRANGE of 1894 was sunk as a blockship at Scapa.
68. SUTHERLAND GRANGE of 1907 ex GUARDIANA [M.Lindenborn].
69. CAPE TRANSPORT of 1910 was scrapped in Italy in 1933 [F.W.Hawks].
70. INDIAN TRANSPORT of 1910 was sold to Greece in 1929 [F.W.Hawks].
71. QUEENSLAND TRANSPORT of 1913 was sold to Greece in 1934.
72. ORANGE RIVER of 1914 was sold to Greece in 1934 [E.Johnson].
73. OAKLANDS GRANGE of 1912 was sold to Greece in 1934.
74. BARONESA of 1918 of Furness-Houlder Argentine Line [F.W.Hawks]
75. MARQUESA of 1918 pictured in the Thames in 1936 [A.Snook].
76. EL ARGENTINO of 1928 became a war loss on 26.7.1943.
77. DUNSTER GRANGE of 1928 became a crab fish factory ship.
78. IMPERIAL TRANSPORT of 1931 lost her bow half in 1940 [A.Duncan]
79. LYNTON GRANGE of 1937 became a war loss on 28.12.1942.
80. LANGTON GRANGE of 1942 ex EMPIRE PENNANT [M.Cassar].
81. URMSTON GRANGE of 1942 ex EMPIRE PIBROCH [A.Duncan].
82. BARTON GRANGE of 1944 ex EMPIRE BALFOUR [A.Duncan].
83. ARGENTINE TRANSPORT of 1944 ex SAMTYNE [A.Duncan].
84. CONDESA of 1944 was scrapped in Italy in 1962.
85. DUQUESA of 1949 was scrapped in Italy in 1969 [T.Rayner]
86. OSWESTRY GRANGE of 1952 was sold to Greece in 1971.
87. QUEENSBURY of 1953 of Alexander Shipping Co. Ltd
88. ORELIA of 1954 sailing from the Tyne [M. Donnelly].
89. OREGIS aground at Tynemouth on 10.3.1974 [M.Donnelly].
90. WESTBURY of 1960 was sold in 1978.
91. SWAN RIVER of 1959 served the Group for 12 years.
92. ROYSTON GRANGE of 1959 was gutted by fire in 1972 [J.K.Byass].
93. HARDWICKE GRANGE of 1960 was sold in 1977.
94. JOULE of 1965 was purchased in 1973.
95. HUMBOLDT of 1968 was sold in 1984 [J.K.Byass].
96. LORD KELVIN of 1978 was sold in 1987 [A.Duncan].

INTRODUCTION

Christopher Furness, the founder, formed Furness,Withy & Co. Ltd on 16th September,1891 in West Hartlepool by integrating his already extensive fleet of Canadian/U.S.A. traders with his Withy shipyard. He enjoyed managing ships, and the new shipping company could hardly fail to make money - enjoying the inherent flexibility of owning a shipyard. He obtained new ships more cheaply than his rivals, and could also lay keels for his own fleet for later sale 'off-the-peg' to prospective shipowners at a handsome profit. Christopher was the past master in the art of the take-over of shipping companies, building up one of the largest and greatest GROUP of shipping companies in the world. A large tramp fleet was owned between the years 1900 - 1920; after which the Group became noted for world-wide liner operations.

Another shipping empire - Houlder - plays an important and underrated part in the success of the Furness story. Houlder Brothers & Co. Ltd was formed by the brothers Edwin Savory Houlder and Alfred Houlder in 1856. An Australian service was started by chartering and purchasing American clippers. The service for which the company became famous - meat home from the Plate - was begun in 1884, and their first owned steamer was built in 1890. The Plate route was run alongside the Australia/New Zealand route until the latter was sold off in 1912. Furness,Withy & Co. Ltd obtained around one-third of the Houlder shares in 1911, and steadily built up their holding until total ownership was achieved in 1974. Unlike the Furness family, who moved out of shipowning in 1919, the Houlder family remain today as shipping men to their very core in a world in which high finance might seem to reign supreme.

Furness,Withy & Co. Ltd obtained control of Shaw,Savill & Albion Co. Ltd in 1933, and Pacific Steam Navigation Company and Royal Mail Line in 1965 - creating the largest British shipping Group of the time. An interchange of ships between companies then became widespread - a practice of which Furness had been early exponents - for taxation purposes by using up unused depreciation allowances. The Group was purchased twice between 1980 and 1990, first by C.Y. Tung of Hong Kong and recently by Hamburg-Sud, and the Furness Group survives intact today to continue into a second century of operations. The Furness subsidiaries fleet lists, with the exception of Manchester Liners, are taken from the date of majority-share control.

Norman L. Middlemiss

Newcastle-upon-Tyne

August,1991

CHAPTER 1.

FURNESS LINE

Christopher Furness, the founder, was the son of John Furness, who had been born at Myton in Yorkshire in 1808 and came to Stranton in Hartlepool to work on the Hartlepool Railway as a coal trimmer. He married Averill, a local girl, and they set up home in Ramsey's Buildings in New Stranton overlooking the Old Town Wall. The population of Hartlepool at this time was only 2,000. Their first two sons were named Thomas and John, and they then moved to Haverton Hill where they had four more children: Mary,Stephen,Wilson and Alfred. Early in 1851 they returned to live in New Stranton, and there in 1852 was born to them another son - Christopher Furness - youngest of seven children.

The eldest child, Thomas, was 16 years old when Christopher was born and was already well established in a shop in Lynn Street selling groceries when Christopher left school. Later Thomas became a wholesaler and commission agent importing eggs,cheese and butter from the Continent, and ran two coasting brigs - ASTLEY of 204 tons and WILLIAMS of 184 tons - for this purpose. WILLIAMS was a sailing ship known as a snow and had been built back in 1812, trading for 70 years until 1882. The wooden brig ASTLEY was the first ship registered in the name of Christopher Furness in 1876, and traded until 1880.

Christopher at the age of 18 in 1870 had sailed to the Continent when an outbreak of war between Germany and France had appeared imminent. There were many ships laden with grain in Swedish and Danish ports, and he reckoned that if war broke out prices would rise, so he made large purchases of grain and when the war came he made large profits.

1.1. CANADA/U.S.A. SERVICES

Christopher was made a partner in his brother's business of Thomas Furness & Co. in 1872, and encouraged by his success was eager to expand. He established contacts in North America for the supply of cheap food to supplement their usual Continental supply. In 1877 Thomas Furness & Co. began a steamer service between West Hartlepool and Eastern seaboard Canada/U.S.A. ports. The chartered HECLA owned by Messrs. Herskind arrived at Hartlepool in November, 1877; and VALETTA owned by William Gray arrived in December,1877 with produce purchased by their residing agents in Canada and the U.S.A.

The brothers then resolved to run steamers of their own and ordered two from the shipyard of William Gray in West Hart-

lepool. The first, CHICAGO, was launched in April,1878 and they
envisaged a fortnightly arrival in West Hartlepool, and made the
necessary arrangements to obtain a regular supply of outward
general cargo. Boston was the Eastern seaboard port chosen to ship
the produce, which was conveyed there from Chicago and Canada. The
American railway companies gave highly favourable terms, their
object being to encourage trade between Boston and the North of
England. The entire cost of bringing over a cargo from Boston and
delivering it to their warehouses in West Hartlepool was no more
than the landing charges at Liverpool and the carriage to West
Hartlepool.

A large trade in pigs was envisaged from Chicago - but
the first steamer of that name was a great disappointment to
Christopher as she was wrecked within 24 hours of leaving Hartlepool for the U.S.A. on the Haisbro' sands. Such an ill-omened
start on his first venture into steamer owning would have deterred
lesser men, but chartered steamers continued to deliver the produce necessary for the business - MELITA brought in 300 tons of
lard and 400 tons of bacon in July,1878. The lard was rough and
needed rendering, and was then put into bladders and marketed at
West Hartlepool. Thomas Furness & Co. had a contract for supplying
all the prisons in Durham,Yorkshire,Northumberland and Lancashire
with oatmeal,barley,rice,Indian meal etc. to the quantity of 50
tons every 14 days. They imported 1300 tons of oatmeal from
America every month.

In October,1878 the second owned steamer AVERILL, named
after their mother, sailed from Boston with provisions,live cattle
and dead meat. The cattle pens were on the upper deck, and there
was plenty of accomodation for passengers. AVERILL was a steamer
of 1690 grt and 1095 net tons with two decks; length 260 feet,
beam 34 feet and depth 23 feet. The fo'c'stle was 32 feet in
length and poop 26 feet and double bottoms extended for 181 feet
of her length. The compound interacting engines were supplied by
North East Marine Engineering Co. Ltd,Sunderland. She traded until
21st June,1883 when wrecked at Ingonish(CB) while on a voyage from
Barrow to Montreal with steel rails.

Other steamers followed from Gray of West Hartlepool -
BRANTFORD CITY of 1880 and YORK CITY of 1881. Thomas, however,
was not happy away from his groceries while Christopher enjoyed
managing ships. Moreover he had revolutionary ideas about the
integration of regional industries which were so ambitious he
probably scared his elder brother. Thus in 1882 when Christopher
was 30 years old the partnership was dissolved and the ships were
taken over by Christopher while Thomas took the grocery side of
the business. Christopher began in business on his own account
from an office in Victoria Terrace,West Hartlepool. In Hartlepool
at this time were talented, capable men such as William Gray
making a fortune out of shipbuilding, and others such as the Bell
brothers who made a good living out of steel and iron manufacture
- Christopher himself was doing quite well out of running a fleet

of ships, but he could see the advantages of integrating all
these profitable ventures into one huge business.

He began in 1883 by purchasing an interest in Edward
Withy's Middleton shipyard, reaping the benefit from building
some of his own ships such as GOTHENBURG CITY of 1884 and WASH-
INGTON CITY of 1885. The latter was the first steamer with triple
expansion engines in the Furness fleet. Thomas Richardson built
this engine with cylinder dimensions of 23,37 and 60 inches and
36 inch stroke and pressure of 145 lb. In 1884 Edward Withy
emigrated to New Zealand and Christopher purchased a further,con-
trolling interest in the yard. Edward Withy had been a man of
progressive ideas when he took over the former Denton yard in
1869 to form Withy,Alexander & Co. His younger brother Henry
served under him at the yard, and in 1873 Henry left the yard to
gain further experience at Fairfield on the Clyde and in South
America, returning in 1878 to assume full responsibility for the
yard. After the formation of Furness,Withy & Co. Ltd in 1891,
Christopher left control of the yard in the capable hands of
Henry Withy.

NEWCASTLE CITY was launched at the Withy yard in October,1882 and started a direct Newcastle/New York service with a
branch office opened on Newcastle Quayside. DURHAM CITY of 1882
and 3092 grt traded for many years to Canada/U.S.A. and had the
distinction of carrying the first cargo of frozen meat from the
United States to Britain. She was brigantine rigged and 314 feet
in length - a big ship for the time. At the end of 1882 the
Furness fleet consisted of the snow WILLIAMS and 6 steamers:-
AVERILL, BOSTON CITY, YORK CITY, BRANTFORD CITY, DURHAM CITY
and NEWCASTLE CITY. The town of Brantford, Ontario was the first
overseas branch of the provision business of Thomas Furness &
Co., and the ship named after the town - BRANTFORD CITY - was
wrecked on 10th August,1883 near Little Harbour(NS) while on a
voyage from London to Halifax and Boston with general cargo. Her
name was perpetuated in the telegraphic address of the company,
and later as the name of Group agents.

The following year brought the addition of the sisters
RIPON CITY and WETHERBY - three island types of 2100 grt from
William Gray. WETHERBY was lost 10 years later off Cape Hatteras
in December,1893 while on a voyage from Fernandina to Rotterdam
with phosphates. STOCKHOLM CITY was launched in 1884 and joined
YORK CITY and BRANTFORD CITY in the London/Halifax/Boston service. Sisters GOTHENBURG CITY and LINCOLN CITY joined in the same
year 1884 and were of 300 feet length and 2600 grt. GOTHENBURG
CITY lost her propeller in 1885 when 10 days out of London bound
for Boston. The Master decided to turn round and use her brigan-
tine-rigged sails, and after taking on more stores from another
ship, eventually made into Falmouth unaided some 33 days later.
STOCKHOLM CITY had a serious fire while bound from Manchester to
Newport News in December,1897. Her bridge, chartroom, part of the
spar deck, and lifeboats and stores were destroyed together with
hull damage. Her Master did well to reach his destination unaided

without charts or navigational instruments, and temporary repairs were made at Newport News to allow a return home.

ULUNDA and DAMARA were purchased on the stocks in 1895/96 and traded on the Halifax/U.K. service until scrapped in 1910. At this time the London firm of Adamson & Ronaldson, who ran a competing service to Boston from London, began acting as London agents for Christopher. Their Robert E. Burnett had seen BRANTFORD CITY moored at Deptford cattle market, and he wrote to Christopher asking if he was interested in some new business for his ship. This offer was accepted in order to provide additional cargo to supplement the outward general cargo and the homeward produce for Thomas Furness & Company. R.E. Burnett replaced the original Boston agent on 1st December,1884 establishing a Furness office at 130,State Street,Boston; and he was elected to the Furness board on 27th June,1905 and served as a director throughout the Furness family-directed era until they sold off their shipping shares and business in 1919. A sailing card of 1885 is shown below, note that the houseflag flown by the early Furness steamers was a Union Jack carrying in the centre a blue 'F' superimposed upon a white square with a blue border. This flag continued to be used until a Royal Navy commander ordered it to be hauled down in Canadian waters, on the grounds that it was not permissible to use the Union Flag for such a purpose. The design was then changed to a blue flag with a white 'F', which continued to be flown until 1946.

In 1887 both YORK CITY and NEWCASTLE CITY were lost: YORK CITY was wrecked on Faro Island in Sweden on 22nd December, and NEWCASTLE CITY was wrecked off Nantucket Island a day later while on a voyage from Newcastle to New York with general. The new BALTIMORE CITY joined in 1888 together with NEW BOROUGH, named after the 'new' borough of the Hartlepools from William Gray. TRURO CITY was a new steamer completed by the Sunderland SB Co. Ltd in 1889, and she was to have a very long career after her sale by Christopher to Norwegian owners in 1890. As the BISP of

Norway she succumbed to a torpedo from U23 in the North Sea on 4th January,1940 while on a voyage from Sunderland to Andalsnes. Christopher was very active in the second-hand market at this time, buying BLANCHE, PLEIADES, SCANDINAVIA, SULTAN, BARON HAMBRO,ST. LOUIS,CENISIO,DUART CASTLE and TAYMOUTH CASTLE. SULTAN was abandoned at sea in March,1889 to the south of New- foundland in position 42 N, 57 W while on a voyage from Norfolk (Va) to London. None of the purchased ships lasted long in the fleet,the sisters DUART CASTLE and TAYMOUTH CASTLE of 1877/78 were purchased from D. Currie & Co. Ltd,London and were sold to Pickford & Black of London in 1892.

Agreement was reached in 1890 with the Canadian Government for an annual mail subsidy for a direct London to Halifax(NS) and St. John(NB) service. This mail subsidy was renewed until 1913. Halifax(NS) became the hub of the Canadian services, with some cargo trans-shipped there for Canadian ports. HALIFAX CITY and ST. JOHN CITY with clipper bows and beautiful figureheads ran between Halifax(NS), St. John(NB) and St. John's(NF).

TYNEDALE had been completed at Stockton in 1889 as INCH- ARRAN for Liverpool owners. She was purchased in 1890 and was the first Furness ship to be registered at the new Furness London office at 5/6 Billiter Avenue. Her sister TYNEHEAD was completed new for Christopher in September,1890 and they were to trade for him until 1897 when sold to J. Holman & Sons,London. However TYNE- DALE as FURTOR was abandoned later that year on 27th July in the Atlantic while on a voyage from St. John's(NF) to Barry with timber, and TYNEHEAD as MISTOR was sunk at anchor in collision in Cardiff Roads while on a voyage from Newport to Malta with coal. By the summer of 1891 Christopher had a fleet of 18 new and second-hand steamers, and he was about to bring to fruition the first step in his grand scheme to integrate the shipowning, ship- building, coal, iron and steel and engineering industries of the North East.

1.2 FURNESS,WITHY & CO. LTD

The limited liability company was incorporated on 16th September,1891 at Baltic Chambers,Surtees Street,West Hartlepool with a nominal capital of £700,000 in 7,000 shares of £100 each of which all but £5,000 was paid-up. This was actually an amalga- mation of three existing companies:-

Christopher Furness,W. Hartlepool with branches at Boston, Baltimore & Chicago.
Christopher Furness & Co. of London
Edward Withy & Co.,West Hartlepool

The directors were the three directors of the Withy shipyard, namely:-

                Christopher Furness
                Henry Withy
                R.W. Vick

and   Robert B. Stoker
                George L. Wooley
                Thomas King

The first shareholders were:-

Christopher Furness	5402 shares
Thomas Furness & Co.	165 shares
Stephen W. Furness	20 shares
Henry Withy	603 shares
R.W. Vick	613 shares
Robert B. Stoker	20 shares
George W. Sivewright	1 share
T. Ayrton	4 shares
G. Craggs	100 shares
W.A. French	3 shares
C.W. Harrison	32 shares
J. Houlton	12 shares
J.M. Winspear	5 shares
G.L. Woolley	20 shares

**1891
FURNESS
CARD**

J.J.C. Warwick was appointed as first Company Secretary. George William Sivewright was appointed Manager of the Withy yard and dry-dock at this time under Henry Withy as Managing Director. He was also a partner in the local shipowning company of Sivewright, Bacon & Co. of West Hartlepool, and his sister Jenny was married to John Furness.

Christopher Furness, trading as C. Furness & Co. contributed assets valued at £233,048 including shares in six steamship companies, as well as the following 18 steamers plus shares in another 18:-

BOSTON CITY	NEW BOROUGH
DURHAM CITY	BLANCHE
RIPON CITY	DAMARA
STOCKHOLM CITY	TAYMOUTH CASTLE
GOTHENBURG CITY	DUART CASTLE
WASHINGTON CITY	OTTAWA
BALTIMORE CITY	CENISIO
HALIFAX CITY	TYNEDALE
WETHERBY	TYNEHEAD

The three partners of Edward Withy & Co. brought in assets of £158,963 plus shares in one steamship company and in three steamers. The total assets were £392,011 and the issued capital was £695,000; thus the difference of £302,989 was the value placed on the 18 ships and shares in another 21 steamers taken over. The Furness,Withy & Co. Ltd fleet at set-up thus consisted of 18 ships of 43,897 tons together with shares in another 21

steamers and seven steamship companies. There was to grow from
this nucleus the greatest SHIPPING GROUP in the world, which
purchased and took over hundreds of other companies.

1.3 EXPANSION AND SUBSIDIARIES 1893 - 1907

During this time of rapid development, Christopher kept
building and purchasing tonnage. CALCUTTA CITY was launched at
the Withy shipyard in March,1891 but was sold and completed the
following month as MELBRIDGE for United S.S. Co. Ltd (T.Temper-
ley),London. Another sister to CALCUTTA CITY was ordered by
Christopher but completed in 1891 as WILDCROFT for F. Woods of
London. The name CALCUTTA CITY was also proposed for other
steamers that were sold shortly before keel-laying or while on
the stocks. This naturally stemmed from the inherent flexibility
enjoyed by the new company as it owned a shipyard and could sell
new ships 'off-the-peg' to prospective shipowners at a handsome
profit. WELLDECK was launched for Christopher at the Irvine yard
in Hartlepool in 1891 and, as her name implies, was a well-deck
steamer of 4350 dwt. She was sold and completed as INCHDUNE for
Hamilton,Fraser & Co. Ltd,Liverpool, who also exchanged two old
iron screw steamers in the deal with Christopher: INCHGARVIE and
INCHULVA.

Furness Line began trading to St. John's(NF) in 1891/92, and
some years later became associated with the Allan Line in the
provision of a joint service from Liverpool known as the Furness
Allan Line. The Furness vessels after calling there proceeded to
Halifax only, while the Allan Line ships sailed to Halifax and
Philadelphia. A Canadian Government mail subsidy for Furness was
agreed in 1898 for this route and was renewed until 1913. The
route was strengthened in 1898 by the purchase of two ships and
the goodwill of the Canada & Newfoundland S.S. Co. Ltd.

However by far the most important event of 1893 was the setting up of the first subsidiary - CHESAPEAKE & OHIO S.S. CO. LTD.
- to maintain a service between the Virginia railway terminal of
Newport News and the ports of Liverpool and London. A trio of
identical clipper-bowed triple-expansion powered steamers of
around 5000 dwt were completed that year by the company shipyard -
APPOMATTOX,CHICKAHOMINY and GREENBRIER. A further trio of slightly
larger clipper-bowed steamers was completed later that year by
Alexander Stephen & Sons Ltd,Glasgow as RAPPAHANNOCK,SHENANDOAH
and KANAWHA. All were equipped to carry many cattle, having a
water distillation plant for their bovine passengers. They were
fitted with double derricks and six steam winches, and were rigged
as pole-masted schooners with telescopic masts for transit of the
soon to be completed Manchester Ship Canal. All six were given
Virginia river names and buff funnels with a white band bearing
the entwined letters C and O and a black top. The houseflag was
red with a white diamond bearing the letters C and O in black.
They were financed by the issue that year of £200,000 5%
debentures issued to the public by Furness,Withy & Co. Ltd.

1. NEWCASTLE CITY of 1882 was wrecked off Nantucket in 1887.

2. ALMERIANA of 1889 in the Bristol Gorge.

3. VENANGO of 1891 in the Bristol Gorge.

4. QUEEN WILHELMINA of 1898 with clipper bow and figurehead.

5. RAPIDAN of 1898 of Chesapeake & Ohio S.S. Co. Ltd.

6. AUSTRIANA of 1901 of British Maritime Trust Ltd [E.Johnson].

7. MALINCHE of 1906 was sold in 1913 [E.Johnson].

8. FERNANDINA of 1908 was sold in 1922.

9. CUNDALL of 1908 in the Bristol Gorge.

10. COLLINGWOOD of 1905 at Bristol. [B.J.Bryant].

11. HARLINGEN of 1909 was renamed PETER PAN in 1912.

12. BOLIVIANA of 1900 at Fowey. [A.B.Deitsch].

13. PENNINE RANGE of 1903, purchased in 1910.[E.Johnson].

14. SOUTH POINT of 1912 was a war loss on 27.3.1915 [W.S.P.L.]

15. CASTLE EDEN of 1914 in the Bristol Gorge.[A.Duncan].

16. HAMBLETON RANGE of 1914 was sold in 1923.[F.W.Hawks].

RAPPAHANNOCK was one of the earliest ships to be fitted with radio, and enabled her to go to the assistance of the emigrant ship VOLTURNO, on fire in the Atlantic, and rescue some of her passengers. The West Hartlepool trio traded to Newport News and Norfolk(Va) until sold in 1902 together with CARLISLE CITY of 1894 to Elders & Fyffes Ltd of banana fame. RAPIDAN of 1898 was built for the Chesapeake & Ohio company by the company shipyard, and at the time of her construction she was one of the largest cargo ships afloat at 7474 gross tons. She was sold to Houlder Brothers in 1901 becoming their HAVERSHAM GRANGE but was lost at sea on 23rd October,1906 after fire had broken out 800 miles off the Cape of Good Hope while on a voyage from New York to Australia with general. The other trio and all subsequent ships built for the Chesapeake & Ohio were transferred to Furness,Withy & Co. Ltd in 1907, and the C & O was wound up. The tugs that berthed these ships at Newport News belonged to the Chesapeake & Ohio Railroad of Cleveland,Ohio and they had a most amusing symbol on their blue funnels of a cat gazing at a yellow moon!

During 1894/96 several interesting steamers were purchased or built by Furness,Withy & Co. Ltd. The most important were ANTWERP CITY,CARLISLE CITY,HALIFAX CITY,ST. JOHN CITY and LONDON CITY from Sunderland and Clyde yards. Christopher found work for LONDON CITY shortly after her launch in February,1896, and she was completed three months later as MEGANTIC for the new Wilsons & Furness - Leyland Line Ltd. This company was formed in London by an association of Thomas Wilson,Sons & Co. Ltd,Hull; Frederick Leyland & Co. Ltd,Liverpool; and Furness,Withy & Co. Ltd. The three companies owned the entire share capital of £550,000 equally, and among the directors were the well-known names of Wilson,Ellerman and Furness attending board meetings in London from August,1896. Among the other non-Furness ships operating the joint service were ALEX-ANDRIA,LONDINIAN,BOADICEA,BOSTONIAN,CAMBRIAN,CLEOPATRA and VIC-TORIA. VICTORIA was launched at the Withy yard by Lady Furness in August,1897 and was of 8150 dwt with ten bulkheads,seven holds and 'tween decks, where 850 head of cattle and horses could be stabled. She could carry 120 first-class passengers at a speed of 13 knots, and was not only the largest vessel built at Hartlepool at that time but was also impressive-looking, being fitted with four masts.

The new Furness - Wilson - Leyland company supplied a weekly steamer service with Wilson ships from London to New York, and another with Furness ships from London to Boston. Prior to this there had been a Furness-Leyland service; and Christopher had purchased three old Leyland ships in 1894: BAVARIAN, BULGARIAN and ISTRIAN but they were quickly sold for scrap. However another Liverpool-owned ship ST. RONANS was purchased in 1894 and traded for four years for Furness on the regular Boston/London service in cattle, grain and general cargo. She was an iron ship with four masts, and was lost shortly after her sale to Danish owners at Freshwater Point(NF) while on a voyage from New York to Copenhagen with general on 1st June,1899. The Furness - Wilson - Leyland enterprise was highly successful, and secured an American mail

contract, the New York service being eventually bought up by
American interests and the Atlantic Transport Line, when the
pasenger ships of the latter company were taken over by the United
States Government.

The business of the company was rapidly expanding, and still
further capital funds were necessary. On 1st July,1896 a subscrip-
tion list was opened for the issue of £450,000 of 4.5% mortgage
debentures of £100 each, at a premium of 5%. At this point were
owned, or partly-owned, 62 ships with interests in Frederick
Leyland & Co. Ltd, Atlantic & Eastern S.S. Co. Ltd, and a
controlling share in the Chesapeake & Ohio S.S. Co. Ltd. The money
was used to purchase a controlling share in the British Maritime
Mortgage Trust Ltd, which in the following year became simply
BRITISH MARITIME TRUST LTD. This company had been established in
1888 to assist approved shipowners to build tonnage on the
security of sound mortgage, but under Christopher Furness tramp
tonnage was chartered to regular liner companies, or bought and
sold to them, as a result of which the beginnings of an extensive
fleet of tramps was constructed and successfully operated. Two
were taken over in 1896 - STRAITS OF MENAI and CYNTHIANA - both
nearly new and registered under Glasgow owners. The suffix 'IANA'
was then adopted by Christopher for the tramp tonnage operated by
the British Maritime Trust Ltd. Robert B. Stoker managed these two
steamers and MEDIANA of 1897 for Christopher before going across
to Manchester from Hartlepool to take charge of the new Manchester
Liners Ltd in 1898. The funnels colours of the British Maritime
Trust Ltd fleet were yellow with a broad blue band; the houseflag
was yellow with a white diamond in the centre bearing the letters
B.M.T.

The liner routes in operation by Furness ships in 1898 were:

1.   London/Boston weekly each way jointly with Leyland.

2.   London/Halifax(NS)/St. John(NB) fortnightly under subsidy
     mail contract with the Canadian Government.

3.   Liverpool/St. John's(NF)/Haliax(NS) fortnightly under subsidy
     mail contract with the Canadian Government.

4.   Tyne/New York fortnightly.

5.   Montreal/U.K. or Continent during the St. Lawrence open
     season.

Christopher had entered the U.K. passenger and cargo coastal
services in 1895 with the purchase of EDITH,OPORTO,PLATO,ALBERT
and ZEBRA mostly from Thomas Wilson,Sons & Co. Ltd, Hull. These
were to provide weekly services from West Hartlepool to London and
from Antwerp to London. Sunderland was added to the North East
ports in 1896, and in 1903 a new weekly service was commenced from

the Tyne to London using ZEBRA and the recently purchased BUCCAN-
EER of 1890. The Tyne/London service was ripe for expansion and in
1904 Furness,Withy & Co. Ltd coastal interests amalgamated with
the long-established competition - the Tyne Steam Shipping Co.
Ltd; Tees Union Shipping Co. Ltd; and the Free Trade Wharf Company
to form **Tyne-Tees Steamship Co. Ltd**. The Tyne Steam Shipping Co.
Ltd had been formed as a joint-stock company on 1st July,1864 and
started with 10 screw-propelled iron steamships totalling 4,594
tons. The Tyne/London service capacity was greatly extended in
1910 by the new STEPHEN FURNESS of Tyne-Tees Steamship Co. Ltd,
carrying 250 first-class and 120 second-class passengers. After
1904, Furness coastal ships were not registered under the parent
company, Furness,Withy & Co. Ltd, and in 1910 a service was
inaugurated between Kirkcaldy and London, and this later absorbed
the older and rival line run by the Kirkcaldy Shipping Company. A
year later the London Welsh Steamship Co. Ltd with services to
South Wales ports with ships with names beginning 'LADY' was purchased; eventually these were sold off to Coast Lines Ltd in 1924.

Christopher was knighted in 1895, having just lost his seat
in the House of Commons as Liberal M.P. for Hartlepool to Thomas
Richardson, the marine engine-builder. Christopher had defeated
Sir William Gray at the 1891 election by 293 votes out of 9,000
votes cast. In 1892 he defeated Thomas Richardson by only 76
votes out of 9,000 cast. Thomas was also knighted, and both
rivals contested the seat in the 1900 parliamentary election. Sir
Christopher beat Sir Thomas by nearly 2,000 votes out of 11,000
votes cast. In 1906 Sir Christopher was returned unopposed and in
1910 he beat a London politician W.G. Howard Gritten by 800 votes
out of 12,000 votes cast. This was disputed, and in the resultant
by-election Sir Christopher won by 160 votes. He was raised to a
peerage in 1910 taking the title Lord Furness of Grantley.

In 1898 Sir Christopher obtained control of long-established
West Hartlepool Steam Navigation Company, forming a limited
liability company with the same name with a capital of £500,000
on 2nd March,1899. Sir Christopher was elected chairman and J.E.
Guthe became managing director, the other directors being Stephen
W. Furness, Joseph F. Pease and Sir Edward T. Gourley who at that
time was M.P. for Sunderland. The fleet consisted of 20 vessels
at this time and orders for two more were placed with Irvine's
(owned by Furness) which were completed as the 6600 dwt sister
tramps POLAMHALL and HENDONHALL. The new Middleton yard-built
tramp DALTONHALL was purchased by Sir Christopher at this time
for his own fleet and traded for the next 15 years. Services
operated by W.H.S.N. included Hartlepool to Gothenburg and
Hamburg in addition to tramping. In 1902 a joint service to the
Persian Gulf from Manchester,Cardiff and London with Bucknall
Line and Strick Line was started. However, Sir Christopher sold
his shareholding in the company in 1904 to J.E. Guthe, and
resigned from the Board together with Stephen W. Furness and
Joseph F. Pease.

Business was still expanding, and in 1899 Furness,Withy &
Co. Ltd paid a dividend of 5%, with shipowning and shipbuilding
being just two of at least eleven distinct sources of revenue.
The policy of the company was clearly stated by Sir Christopher
at the A.G.M. of 1899:-

'The policy of your Board of Directors for many years past
has been to declare regular and fixed dividends ..... this policy
the Board proposes to continue,so that during periods of depression they can (with their large reserves and liquid investments)
continue to pay the same dividends during the lean years as they
have deemed it prudent to pay during the more prosperous times'.
These other sources of revenue in the North East were:-

SHIPBUILDING
In 1897 Sir Christopher had acquired the Hartlepool shipyard of Robert Irvine & Company, giving it a new title:-

Irvine's Shipbuilding & Drydock Co. Ltd.

David G. Irvine, second son of the founder, became managing
director with Sir Christopher as Chairman and Henry Withy,R.W.
Vick and Stephen W. Furness on the Board. The Irvine yard had a
capacity of around 20,000 tons of ships/year, which was increased
when modernised soon after by Christopher by 20-ton travelling
steam cranes to handle larger steel plates. Meanwhile, the existing Withy Middleton yard production was greatly increased by ex-
tending the launching ways to 450,550 and 700 feet in length, and
by converting the yard to electrical power to handle large steel
plates of 70 feet length and 64 inches wide from the Consett Iron
Company. A 380 feet long graving dock was built to dry-dock ships
up to 7000 dwt with the total cost of these improvements in the
neighbourhood of £60,000, and put the yard in a position to
double its capacity to around 50,000 tons of ships/year. In 1909
both the yards were operated under the Irvine title and were then
sold off during WWI. In 1911 the two yards completed 62,620 tons
of shipping and built tonnage for such well-known companies as
The Clan Line Steamers Ltd,Allan Line,Strick Line, Holland-
America Line and Hamburg-America Line. Christopher also had large
shareholdings in the Northumberland Shipbuilding Co. Ltd at
Howdon-on-Tyne; and Smiths Dock Co. Ltd at Middlesbrough; and
Palmers Iron Shipbuilding Co. Ltd,Jarrow.

MARINE ENGINEERING
Christopher was astute enough to realise he needed control
of an existing marine engine builder to provide engines for his
new ships, and an opportunity occurred in 1896 to acquire Westgarth,English & Co. and Teesside Engine Works Co. at Middlesbrough. These were renamed Sir Christopher Furness,Westgarth &
Co. Ltd but their capacity was limited, and Sir Christopher's
long cherished plans for the integration of North East industry
were beginning to take shape. In 1900 he formed Richardsons,
Westgarth & Co. Ltd out of:-

Thomas Richardson & Co. Ltd,Hartlepool
William Allan & Co. Ltd,Sunderland
Furness,Westgarth & Co. Ltd,Middlesbrough.

therebye acquiring a large section of the existing North East
engine-building capacity.

IRON AND STEEL

Sir Christopher purchased interests in iron and steel manufacture out of his shipping profits. In 1898 he merged three iron
and steel companies Moor Steel & Iron Works; Stockton Malleable;
West Hartlepool Steel & Iron Co. Ltd into:-

South Durham Steel & Iron Co. Ltd

In 1899 Sir Christopher bought Attwood's old Weardale Company
from Baring Brothers and formed the Weardale Steel,Coal & Coke
Co. Ltd with a capital of £1.025M. The Weardale steelworks at
Tudhoe near Spennymoor were old and could not stand up to foreign
competition so Sir Christopher purchased for £120,000 the share
capital of the Cargo Fleet Iron Company at Middlesbrough. These
works had been standing since 1864 and were obsolete but they
occupied a magnificent site with frontage on the Tees and with
ironstone mines within a few miles. A new Cargo Fleet Iron
Company was incorporated in 1904 with a share capital of £1M.
Sir Christopher installed new Talbot steel furnaces with larger
capacity, as well as rebuilding the rest of the works with modern
pig-iron blast furnaces, a by-product coking plant and rolling
mills capable of producing over 130,000 tons each of coke,pig-
iron and steel/year. The Cargo Fleet works was kept separate from
the South Durham company, but the two combined had a considerable
iron and steel making capacity.

COLLIERIES

Hartlepool had first exported coal in 1835, and due to the
expanding trade of the early railways and the growing coal trade
the Victorian new town of West Hartlepool was laid out in the
1840s. The combined Hartlepools were a major coal-exporting port
at this time, with Sir Christopher owning several collieries to
the west of Hartlepool near Bishop Auckland and to the north near
Easington. The coal was moved into Hartlepool for shipment by the
Stockton & Darlington Railway, the Clarence Railway and the
Hartlepool Railway & Dock Company, who also owned the Swainson
Dock,Jackson Dock,West Dock and Coal Dock.

INSURANCE

Sir Christopher entered the insurance market in 1900 seeing
possibilities of reduced bills for his ever increasing fleet. He
founded the Economic Insurance Company along with Robert B.
Stoker, and J.E. Guthe of the West Hartlepool Steam Navigation
Co. Ltd. This then expanded to cover all the insurance needs of
the Furness - Houlder empire, and the company Furness - Houlder
Insurance was eventually sold out of the Group in the 1970s.

However the biggest event in Furness shipowning interests in 1898 was the issuing of a prospectus on 5th May,1898 by Sir Christopher of the new <u>Manchester Liners Ltd.</u> The new Manchester Ship Canal had opened to traffic on 1st January,1894, and for the last two years Furness Line ships had called at 'cottonopolis' with general cargoes from Canada. Sir Christopher had agreed to take up £50,000 worth of ordinary shares in the company if Manchester interests could raise £200,000. Manchester businessmen then obtained subsidies and support from the Canadian Government, Canadian Pacific Railways and Chicago interests. The first directors of Manchester Liners Ltd were:-

Sir Christopher Furness	Chairman
Alderman Southern	Director Manchester Ship Canal
Sir Edward Jenkinson	Director Manchester Ship Canal
Sir Richard Mottram	Salford businessman
C. Schiff	Businessman trading to S.America

Robert B. Stoker was asked by Sir Christopher to go across to Manchester from Hartlepool to take charge of the new company. Robert had been born in the North East in 1859, and had been given a 500 ton coaster to manage by his father, a Newcastle shipowner, in 1876 at the age of 16 years. He also joined a Liverpool sailing ship company in the North Atlantic trade which then moved into steamers of which he became the manager. By the time he was 23 years of age his name was well-known in shipping circles, and in that year of 1882 Christopher invited Robert to become one of his aides, Christopher being 30 years of age at this time. He worked for three months in the Furness West Hartlepool office and then later in 1882 moved up to Newcastle to open a new Furness office there for the new Tyne/New York service. The American railways were expanding and there were westbound cargoes on offer from the Tyne with railway lines, pig and bar iron, and coal. Homeward cargo included grain,flour, apples,live cattle and meat.

In 1890 Robert B. Stoker was asked to go to London to open the new Furness office to take over operations there, which had been looked after by Adamson and Ronaldson up to this time. By now Robert had increased his own personal fleet by the 3500 dwt tramp SYDENHAM and the steamer KNUTSFORD. He was appointed Ship Director by Christopher in 1891 on the formation of Furness,Withy & Co. Ltd thus becoming Christopher's right-hand man and most trusted colleague. Robert saw great promise for the future of Manchester shipowning, and with the backing of Lancashire cotton and Manchester Ship Canal interests it flourished. Robert was more than able to manage the new fleet, which started with two purchased Johnston Line steamers (Johnston Line was later purchased by Furness,Withy) renamed MANCHESTER TRADER and MANCHESTER ENTERPRISE. He was thus left alone by Sir Christopher 'to get on with it', paying him a great compliment to his management skills. This was to be repeated time and again by later Furness takeovers of shipping companies, by allowing the management of the

company taken over to remain intact and conduct their own affairs
with Furness,Withy & Co. Ltd remaining as the holding company
only.

It was decided that Manchester Liners Ltd was to have a red
funnel of an orangey shade complete with black top and band. The
Furness funnels at this time were black, but then Sir Christopher
began to change his funnel colours to red. Robert Stoker objected
and the Furness funnels stayed black until the immediate pre-WWI
years when a white 'F' on a blue central band was added. After
the Furness family moved out of shipowning, Frederick Lewis
changed them in 1921 to black with a narrow and a broad red band,
the important distinction being the black base of Furness ships.
Although Manchester Liners Ltd was not majority financially-
controlled by Furness until 1970, when the stake was upped to
61.3%, it still belongs firmly in the Furness family of
companies.

Two British Maritime Trust Ltd tramps STRAITS OF MENAI and
CYNTHIANA were chartered by Robert B. Stoker for the new company
on formation to supplement the two Johnston Line steamers, which
had been on charter to Elder,Dempster from Avonmouth and were
converted for the carriage of 450 head of cattle by the fitting
of pens in the 'tween decks. The new company expanded in a few
months into the New Orleans and Galveston trade handling 13
cargoes of cotton totalling 62,258 bales. A Manchester - Boston
service was also started and the B.M.T. tramps GLORIANA,ITALIANA
and CYNTHIANA were chartered for this purpose.

A further £300,000 of 5% Preference shares of £10 each in
Furness,Withy & Co. Ltd were issued in September,1898 bringing
the capital of the company up to £1M. They were offered at a
premium of 10% reflecting the prosperity of the company at that
time. The capital of the company was further increased to £1.5M
in 1901.

Two fine cargo-liners with good passenger accomodation came
into service on the London - Halifax(NS) route in 1900/01 - EVAN-
GELINE and LOYALIST. They had a very long 120 feet bridge structure with two decks for passengers, and had the appearance of
yachts with clipper-bows and bowsprit and having crossed yards on
their foremast. The figurehead of EVANGELINE was a representation
of the Nova Scotian heroine of that name, while that of LOYALIST
was a Canadian with levelled musket. Triple expansion engines
gave a good turn of speed, and a quick passage together with
first-class accomodation attracted many passengers. Lamport &
Holt wanted two such cargo-liners to inaugurate a passenger
service between New York,Brazil and the Plate, and they made a
very good offer for the two sisters in 1902 which was accepted.
EVANGELINE became TENNYSON, and LOYALIST became BYRON and they
remained in Lamport & Holt service until sold in 1922, although
rarely going south of Santos after 1907 as larger liners had come
into service. Furness,Withy & Co. Ltd replaced them with two Clan
Liners, renaming them EVANGELINE and LOYALIST, and two further

Clan Liners were also purchased and named ST. JOHN CITY and LONDON CITY.

Gulf Line Ltd was purchased in 1902 with services from Australia and South Africa to the U.K., and a service to West Coast of South America. The company had been formed in 1899 by an amalgamation of Greenock Steamship Company and the Gulf Line Association,Greenock with a capital of £120,000. Things had not gone well for the new company, and Sir Christopher was able to buy a large block of shares at a low price to gain control of eight more ships. These had names beginning 'GULF', but under Sir Christopher a nomenclature ending in 'O' was favoured, but as the company also went in for tramping some tramps with names ending 'IANA' were chartered or transferred later to Gulf Line Ltd. ORISTANO was the first trading vessel to pass through the Panama Canal from the Atlantic to the Pacific when the Canal was opened in 1914. The West Coast South America service was run in conjunction with the Nautilus S.S. Co. Ltd of Sunderland with ships whose names ended in 'BRANCH'. A second ORISTANO was launched in 1924 at the Doxford yard in Sunderland but was sold and completed for Silver Line. Gulf Line Ltd was wound up in 1928 and the remaining ships either transferred to Furness,Withy & Co. Ltd or, as was the case with ARIANO and COMINO, sold to Continental owners.

In 1906 the capital of Furness,Withy & Co. Ltd was increased to £2M and, in the same year, the Atlantic trade of the **Neptune Steam Navigation Co. Ltd** of Sunderland was taken over. A service was operated between Rotterdam and Baltimore with a call at the Tyne for bunkers. QUEEN WILHELMINA,RUNO and OHIO were taken over at this point of time, and the latter two were part of a package deal of six ships sold to the Holland-America Line in 1909 which had some far reaching effects on both companies. The goodwill of the Neptune Line was also sold but it was stipulated that the Rotterdam agency for the Baltimore service should remain with Furness agents, Furness Shipping & Agency Co. of Rotterdam, while Furness,Withy & Co. Ltd should represent the Holland-America Line at U.S. Atlantic ports and undertake the stevedoring. This practice was continued up to the start of WWII with Furness,Withy offices representing Holland-America Line at Baltimore,Newport News,Norfolk(Va) and Philadelphia as well as in Canada. The other Furness ships sold to Holland-America Line in 1909 were BRANTFORD, ROTTERDAM,COMO and RAPALLO and were used to re-open their Rotterdam - Baltimore service. Three further ships were taken over from Neptune in 1906: VENANGO, TABASCO and DURANGO with clipper bows and were used on the Liverpool to Halifax(NS) service for many years.

While some new cargo-liner services were being developed, the emphasis of Furness,Withy & Co. Ltd changed to deep-sea tramping and the coal trades for the 20 years up to 1919. A very large programme of 35 good-sized tramps was completed mostly by company yards between 1897 and 1907:-

MEDIANA of 1897	CYNTHIANA of 1905
GLORIANA of 1898	ALBIANA of 1905
ITALIANA of 1898	MARIANA of 1905
RAPIDAN of 1898	SANDOWN of 1905
CEBRIANA of 1899	PERUVIANA of 1905
BOLIVIANA of 1900	ROANOKE of 1906
WYANDOTTE of 1900	RAPIDAN of 1907
POWHATAN of 1900	RICHMOND of 1907
ALLEGHANY of 1901	WASHINGTON of 1907
BIRMINGHAM of 1901	NEWPORT NEWS of 1907
POTOMAC of 1902	NORFOLK of 1907
EGYPTIANA of 1902	ADRIANA of 1907
ATHENIANA of 1902	ARABIANA of 1907
COMO of 1902	BRAZILIANA of 1907
INDIANA of 1902	GRACIANA of 1907
ORIANA of 1902	GUARDIANA of 1907
PERSIANA of 1902	ROTTERDAM of 1907

They had been built for the British Maritime Trust Ltd - controlled by Furness,Withy & Co. Ltd. Those without names ending in 'IANA' were either on charter to or completed for the Chesapeake & Ohio S.S. Co. Ltd or Gulf Line Ltd. Many were chartered out for periods such as two years or more to Robert M. Sloman of Germany, Hamburg-America Line and Watts,Watts & Co. Ltd,London. One tramp was completed as the engines-aft,dual oil/coal-fired tanker BEAUMONT in June,1903 by the company yard at Hartlepool but was retained by the builders until 1904 when sold to the Anglo-American Oil Co. Ltd,London and renamed SEMINOLE. Three more had been completed for the parent company Furness,Withy & Co. Ltd: SYLVIANA of 1898, GLORIANA of 1905 and the 'Turret' TUNSTALL of 1907.

1.4 LINER AND TRAMP COMPANY TAKEOVERS 1907 - 1914

The capital of Furness,Withy & Co. Ltd was further increased to £3.5M during 1907 with a fleet of 93 ships being controlled, the majority of these being tramps. The majority of the 40 ship fleet of the British Maritime Trust and Chesapeake & Ohio S.S. Co. Ltd were transferred to Furness,Withy & Co. Ltd ownership in 1907 with the remainder following at the end of 1909. The company was also taking delivery of some of the first of 26 colliers to be built during the years 1906/09. These had engines-amidships and were of three classes in the 2000 dwt - 3000 dwt range. They were suitable for the North East Coast and South Wales coal trades to London and South Coast ports, or Continental trades e.g. the Pomaron river iron ore trade from Spain. Many were to be sunk during WWII, and the last colliers to be built for the company were the 4500 dwt self-trimming ELDON and THROCKLEY of 1923. Many of the WWI survivors had had been sold to foreign owners in 1922, leaving these two new ones and THORNLEY of 1907 and ROUEN of 1909 to sail on until 1928 under the management of the Newcastle office on the North East Coast coal trade. The company withdrew from all coastal services in 1928.

The company was still eagerly looking for tramp companies
that were ready for take-over in the poor trading conditions of
1907. Sir Christopher had been interested for a number of years
in the **Hessler Shipping Co. Ltd**,West Hartlepool and their eight
small tramps which normally operated in the Baltic timber trades
and he acquired complete control in 1907. He added three more
tramps in 1909 when the **Laing Shipping Co. Ltd** went out of
business. This company had been started in 1903 in association
with Sunderland shipbuilder Sir James Laing & Sons Ltd but failed
owing to having undertaken a mail contract the conditions of
which were beyond their powers of performance. Another company
that failed was the Liverpool company of Eastern merchants and
shipowners **J.Marke Wood & Sons** in 1910. Their seven cargo
steamers, all engaged in the rice trade from the Orient, were
purchased by Sir Christopher but as most of the ships were old
none lasted more than three years in the Furness fleet.

The remaining tramps and entire assets and interests of the
Sunderland company,**Neptune Steam Navigation Co. Ltd,** were also
purchased during 1910 - these six all had names of hills with a
second word 'RANGE' :-

PENNINE RANGE	GRAMPIAN RANGE
NORFOLK RANGE	MALVERN RANGE
LOWTHER RANGE	SNOWDON RANGE

This nomenclature was to remain in the Furness fleet until
1924 when the last of 33 'RANGE's was sold off. As well as
tramping they were used on some of the Group's regular lines e.g.
MALVERN RANGE took the last sailing on the London to Newport News
service when it was discontinued in 1921. Many were lost during
WWI, and one nearly came to grief in an epic voyage in 1912.
SNOWDON RANGE had been built by Irvine's in 1906 and was a
typical 'three-island' tramp of 4500 dwt. On 22nd November,1912
she left Philadelphia with over 4000 tons of grain for Leith.
Capt. Ernest J. Dickinson was in command and the day marked the
commencement of a voyage which was to test his seamanship and
endurance to the full and secure for him and his crew an honour-
able place amongst the many who have fought the winter North
Atlantic when disabled. The first half of the voyage brought
severe and continuous gales during one of which the wheelhouse
and chartroom were stove-in by the heavy seas. But worse was yet
to happen for on 5th December,1912 the rudder broke and the tramp
became helpless in tremendous seas, which broke over her contin-
uously carrying away deck fittings and damaging lifeboats and the
superstructure. The tramp was eased somewhat by manoeuvring with
the engines and a staysail was set to steady her. As there was no
radio aboard, she had no means of communication with other ships
or with land. Great efforts were made to rig a jury rudder but
without success, and the tramp encountered gale after gale in her
helpless condition. The crew of 24 were undergoing terrible anx-
iety and hardship, and then when the first ship sighted on 19th
December nearly a month after leaving Philadelphia refused to tow
them owing to the weather, all looked lost. The Swedish master

had offered to take them off if they abandoned ship but Capt.
Dickinson was not prepared to comply. Grain was mixed with coal
to eke out the bunkers and satisfactory results were obtained.
New Years's Day 1913 brought the British steamer WELSHMAN on the
scene, and she succeeded in towing SNOWDON RANGE 500 miles to
Fastnet. Many times the tow-rope broke, and after a great
struggle the tramp was successfully handed over to tugs which
made for Queenstown. After still further adventures with parting
tow-ropes and twice being aground, Queenstown was finally reached
on 15th January - 54 days home from Philadelphia!

LOWTHER RANGE met with a different type of adventure in 1910
while on a voyage from Cardiff to Bombay with 6000 tons of coal.
She came up with the Austro-Hungarian TRIESTE at the end of June
disabled in the Indian Ocean with a broken tail shaft and lost
propeller. TRIESTE was a passenger ship owned by Austrian-Lloyd
and had left Trieste on 3rd June carrying passengers and a large
amount of bullion. She again had no radio for communicating her
predicament to shore, and LOWTHER RANGE commenced a tow which
lasted seven days in conditions anything but favourable. Capt.
J.R. Matthews and her crew strove hard and managed to tow TRIESTE
within 12 miles of Bombay when they met up with a fellow Austro-
Hungarian ship,CHINA. CHINA attempted to tow TRIESTE but the tow-
rope parted and she decided to return to Bombay with TRIESTE's
passengers and the news that she was safe. At 5pm on 2nd July
TRIESTE was anchored outside Bombay by LOWTHER RANGE after a long
and successful struggle. Capt. J.R. Matthews was awarded Lloyd's
Silver Medal together with the mate, second mate and three engineers including the Chief. Considerable salvage awards were made
and the Austrian Emperor personally sent thanks to Capt. Matthews
and a gold watch bearing the Royal Arms of Hapsburgs.

Also in 1910 the **Norfolk & North American S.S. Co. Ltd** was
purchased and brought a further large slice of the Virginia -
U.K. trade under the Furness flag. This company was also known as
the Point Line because of the fleet nomenclature ending in
'POINT' and had been incorporated in 1893 with Simpson,Spence &
Young as managers. Six steamers were taken over including four
sisters dating 1900, and two sisters built in 1899. Three more
sisters SOUTH POINT,WEST POINT and START POINT were completed for
the company at the Irvine yard in 1912, as well as another ship
which attained much fame for a different reason.

This was the small EAVESTONE and she was the first British
motorship when completed in 1912 at the Raylton Dixon yard at
Middlesbrough. She was given a 4-cylinder two stroke single
acting oil engine built at the Furness engine plant of Richardsons,Westgarth & Co. Ltd, Middlesbrough. This gave her a loaded
speed of 10 knots on her chosen route - the Pomaron river iron
ore trade from Spain. She was fitted with a stove pipe behind the
bridge to vent the exhaust gases. Although much valuable information of a technical nature was obtained during the next three
years, her engine was found to be too unreliable for smooth
running and in 1915 she was converted to a steamer with triple

expansion engines. Nevertheless, she was the forerunner of the large fleet of motorships subsequently owned by Furness. DOMINION MILLER built 10 years later proved successful, and the company were then able to accept the new form of marine propulsion.

Another small company which was under Furness control at this time was the **Agincourt Steamship Co. Ltd**,London whose ships traded to South America under charter to Lamport & Holt Ltd and were named after famous battles:- AGINCOURT,BALACLAVA,CORUNNA, DETTINGEN,EVESHAM and FLODDEN.

Expansion westwards from the St. Lawrence into the Great Lakes was achieved in 1911 by the purchase of a substantial holding in the **Richelieu and Ontario Navigation Company**, with which had previously been merged the Northern Navigation Company and the Niagara Navigation Company. This combination possessed the most extensive passenger and cargo services on the Great Lakes at this time.

Expansion into the lucrative South American meat trade was also achieved in 1911 by the purchase of around one-third of the shares of **Houlder Brothers & Co. Ltd**. This shareholding was gradually increased over the years until in December,1974 more than 80% were owned - the remaining 20% were then also automatically acquired giving total ownership. The enormous influence and contribution of Houlder Brothers to the Furness Group is fully documented in Chapter 2.

Lord Furness passed away on 10th November,1912 at the age of 60 years. 'Kitty' Furness had been a much-loved and respected figure in Hartlepool society, and all and sundry came to pay their last respects.

In 1912 Furness,Withy & Co. Ltd obtained control of the **Warren Line of Liverpool**, then known as the White Diamond Steamship Co. Ltd which had been registered on 19th July,1898 with a capital of £200,000. The business origins of Warren Line can be traced to the 1840s in competition with the Transatlantic trade of Samuel Cunard. The name Warren appeared in the shareholding for the first time in 1857 when the original owner went bankrupt, and George Warren, the Liverpool office manager, bought some of the sailing ships and then entered steam early in 1863 to make the company profitable. In 1902 the company came under the sole control of George Warren, son of the Liverpool manager. Furness, Withy & Co. Ltd renamed the company George Warren & Co(Liverpool) Ltd in 1912, and then floated the company Warren Line(Liverpool) Ltd in 1922. The ships taken over were the cargo-liner MICHIGAN and the passenger ships SACHEM,SAGAMORE and IOWA - the latter having no fewer than 5 masts and 10 holds built around the accomodation. SACHEM of 1893 had two of her decks fitted for transporting cattle, and the whole of the ship had been lit by electricity on completion, together with telescopic masts for transit of the Manchester Ship Canal. The old SACHEM was scrapped

in 1927 by which time the company ships were trading between
Liverpool,St John's(NF) and Halifax(NS) and Boston.

In the year before the outbreak of World War I some 28 deep-
sea tramps were sold out of the various Furness companies for the
high prices then being paid for second-hand tonnage including:-

GRAMPIAN RANGE,SNOWDON RANGE,MALVERN RANGE) Russian owners
CYNTHIANA,PERUVIANA,RICHMOND

CHEVIOT RANGE,CLEVELAND RANGE   ) Italian owners

COTSWOLD RANGE,CHILTERN RANGE   ) Norwegian owners

GLORIANA,ARABIANA,WASHINGTON,NEWPORT NEWS   ) Belgian owners

NORFOLK,TUNSTALL   ) Greek owners

ORIANA,POWHATAN,ALLEGHANY   ) Japanese owners

ATHENIANA   ) Swedish owners

WYANDOTTE   ) N.Zealand owners

NORFOLK RANGE,PENNINE RANGE   ) W. Seager,Cardiff

FELICIANA,POTOMAC   ) Sale & Co,London

BRAZILIANA   ) Sutherland,Newcastle

DALTONHALL   ) Liverpool owner

In addition, old ALMERIANA of 1889 was sent for scrap.

One addition to the fleet was the fine cargo-liner DIGBY completed at the Irvine yard in April,1913 for service on the Warren Line
route between Liverpool and North America. She had four holds with
seven watertight bulkheads, two masts with 12 derricks, a long bridge
structure with two decks for passengers above the weather deck and a
fine counter stern. Her triple expansion engines gave a speed of 12.5
knots on 42 tons of coal/day. Her hull was strengthened forward for
ice, and she was a real pioneer of cargo handling for she possessed a
side-loading port! Her holds were ventilated for the carriage of fruit
and dairy produce, and she had accomodation for 58 first-class and 32
second-class passengers. After war service as the French auxiliary
ARTOIS she was transferred in 1925 to the Caribbean service of the
Bermuda & West Indies S.S. Co. Ltd and renamed DOMINICA. She was sold
out of the Furness Group in 1936 to the United Baltic Corporation of
London, but she was to sail on for another 30 years before her loss by
capsize at Djakarta.

1.5 WORLD WAR I

A fleet of just over 100 ships was owned at the outbreak of war in August,1914 including 32 deep-sea tramps. The emphasis was now to switch from the Board room and possible take-overs to the ships at sea. Around one-quarter of the company collier fleet was requisitioned by the Government at 'Blue Book' rates introduced in 1915. The years 1911/14 had seen very high freight rates and profits for shipowners followed by a slight fall just prior to the onset of war, and the rate for requisitioned tonnage was to be that prevailing in 1914, and were not to be revised to keep pace with inflation. At the onset of host-lities freight rates soared and for those owners whose tonnage was not requisitioned enormous profits were made. So much so that an 'Excess Profits Duty' had to be introduced based on the excess over average profits made during any two pre-war years in the previous five years. The 'Excess Profits Duty' was fixed at 40% but was quickly doubled to 80%. No fewer than 38 of the company fleet were to be sunk by the enemy including eight as requisitioned colliers, with a further 10 from the Manchester Liners Ltd fleet, plus a further 12 from the Johnston Line fleet after they were taken over in 1916. The following list of losses were all as a result of submarine activity unless otherwise stated:-

27.3.1915	SOUTH POINT	60 miles West of Lundy Island.
28.4.1915	MOBILE	25 miles NW of Butt of Lewis.
8.5.1915	QUEEN WILHELMINA	20 miles SE of Longstone L.H.
23.6.1915	TUNISIANA	Off Lowestoft, beached at Barnard Sands.
26.9.1915	EASINGTON	Disappeared o.v. Sydney(CB) for St. John(NB),20 lost.
9.2.1916	CAMBRIAN RANGE	Sunk by MOEWE 610 miles SE of Cape Race.
28.3.1916	EAGLE POINT	100 miles WNW of Bishop Rock.
14.4.1916	SHENANDOAH	Mined/sunk 1.5 miles W of Folkestone,2 lost.
23.4.1916	PARISIANA	82 miles SW of Ushant.
8.10.1916	WEST POINT	46 miles ESE of Nantucket L.V.
26.10.1916	RAPPAHANNOCK	70 miles from the Scillies,37 lost.
26.1.1917	TABASCO	55 miles WNW of Skelligs.
3.2.1917	EAVESTONE	95 miles W of Fastnet,5 lost.
4.2.1917	TURINO	174 miles W of Fastnet,4 lost.
6.2.1917	CROWN POINT	55 miles W of the Scillies,7 lost.
3.3.1917	SAGAMORE	150 miles W of Fastnet.
9.3.1917	EAST POINT	9 miles SSE of Eddystone L.H.
28.3.1917	SNOWDON RANGE	25 miles W of Bardsey Island,4 lost.
19.4.1917	ANNAPOLIS	74 miles NNW of Eagle Island.
9.6.1917	EGYPTIANA	120 miles WSW of the Scillies.
10.6.1917	BAY STATE	250 miles NW of Fastnet.
12.6.1917	SOUTH POINT	30 miles SSW of Bishop Rock.
21.6.1917	ORTONA	140 miles SSW of Fastnet,1 lost.
22.7.1917	ROTA	7 miles SE of Berry Head,5 lost.
12.8.1917	ROANOKE	100 miles WNW of Butt of Lewis.
26.8.1917	DURANGO	50 miles NW of Barra Head.
2.10.1917	LUGANO	Mined/sunk 2 miles SW of Bull Point.
6.10.1917	BEDALE	25 miles SW of Mine Head,3 lost.
12.12.1917	CHARLESTON	30 miles W of the Smalls,Irish Sea.
28.12.1917	MAXTON	28 miles NNW of Malin Head,1 lost.

12.1.1918   WHORLTON   Near Owers L.V.,English Channel.
13.1.1918   RAPALLO   1.5 miles S Cape Peloro,Mediterranean,1 lost.
5.2.1918   CRESSWELL   18 miles NNE of Kish L.V.
7.2.1918   BEAUMARIS   2.5 miles NW of Longships L.V.
21.2.1918   CHEVIOT RANGE   25 miles S of Lizard, 27 lost.
4.3.1918   CASTLE EDEN   4 miles SSE of Inishtrahull L.H.,1 lost.
27.3.1918   ALLENDALE   52 miles SW of Lizard,1 lost.
20.4.1918   LOWTHER RANGE   20 miles NNW of South Stack Rock.
30.4.1918   CONWAY   38 miles SE Cape de Palos,Mediterranean.
4.9.1918   PENTLAND RANGE   Foundered off R. Plate with grain.
3.10.1918   WESTWOOD   5 miles WSW of Lizard,1 lost.

MANAGED VESSELS LOST:-
24.3.1918   WAR KNIGHT   In collision and then mined near Needles,32 lost.
16.10.1918   WAR COUNCIL   85 miles WSW of Cape Matapan.

MANCHESTER LINERS LTD:-
27.10.1914   MANCHESTER COMMERCE Mined & sunk off Tory Island,14 lost.
27.3.1916   MANCHESTER ENGINEER 20 miles SW of Conningbeg L.V.
18.1.1917   MANCHESTER INVENTOR 50 miles WNW of Fastnet.
27.4.1917   MANCHESTER CITIZEN 240 miles NW of Fastnet,1 lost.
4.6.1917   MANCHESTER TRADER   8 miles SE of Pantellaria Island,1 lost.
5.6.1917   MANCHESTER MILLER   190 miles NNW of Fastnet,8 lost.
29.7.1917   MANCHESTER COMMERCE 15 miles NNW of Cape Spartel,1 lost.
30.7.1917   MANCHESTER INVENTOR 80 miles NNE of Muckle Flugga.
16.8.1917   MANCHESTER ENGINEER 4.5 miles SE Flamborough Head.
22.1.1918   MANCHESTER SPINNER 33 miles SE of Malta.

JOHNSTON LINE LTD:-
26.10.1916   ROWANMORE   128 miles WNW of Fastnet.
7.2.1917   VEDAMORE   20 miles W of Fastnet,23 lost.
25.4.1917   SWANMORE   230 miles WNW of Fastnet,11 lost.
27.4.1917   DROMORE   140 miles NNW of Fastnet.
13.5.1917   JESSMORE   180 miles WNW of Fastnet.
31.7.1917   QUERNMORE   160 miles NNW of Tory Island,1 lost.
20.8.1917   INCEMORE   52 miles SSE of Pantellaria Island,1 lost.
25.8.1917   SYCAMORE   125 miles NW of Tory Island,11 lost.
26.8.1917   KENMORE   30 miles N of Inistrahull L.H.,5 lost.
16.12.1917   FOYLEMORE   22 miles SE of Lizard.
19.2.1918   BARROWMORE   53 miles WNW of Bishop Rock,25 lost.
22.9.1918   GORSEMORE   44 miles ESE of Cape Colonne, Gulf
                                of Taranto.

PRINCE LINE LTD:-
7.2.1917   CORSICAN PRINCE 3 miles E of Whitby,1 lost.
10.2.1917   JAPANESE PRINCE 24 miles SW of Bishop Rock.
23.2.1917   TROJAN PRINCE   5 miles NW of Cape Shershel,2 lost.
22.3.1917   STUART PRINCE   In St. George's Channel,20 lost.
12.5.1917   EGYPTIAN PRINCE 240 miles SSE of Malta.
21.7.1917   AFRICAN PRINCE 60 miles NNW of Tory Island.
31.7.1917   BELGIAN PRINCE 175 miles WNW of Tory Island,39 lost.
30.8.1917   EASTERN PRINCE 30 miles WSW of Eddystone L.H.,5 lost.
11.4.1918   HIGHLAND PRINCE 36 miles NE1/4E of Cape Bon,3 lost.

30.5.1918   ASIATIC PRINCE   190 miles SSE of Malta.

RIO-CAPE LINE LTD.
19.2.1918   GLENCARRON   47 miles ESE of the Lizard.
9.8.1918   GLENLEE   4 miles NE of Owers L.V.,1 lost.

A total of 325 brave men had died on Furness-owned ships in WWI

         Some of these losses and incidents deserve special
mention. The war was hardly two months old when during the night
of 26/27th October 1914 the outward-bound MANCHESTER COMMERCE was
sunk by a mine off Tory Island, giving her the dubious distiction
of being the first British ship mined and lost. One lifeboat was
launched and Capt. Pyle with other members of the crew were preparing another for launching when the ship sank only 7 minutes
after striking the mine. Those left on board had to jump into an
extremely rough sea and swim to the only lifeboat, but unfortunately Capt. Pyle and 13 others did not survive. It transpired
that a ship flying the Swedish flag had been seen behaving sus-
piciously in the area, and this ship was none other than the
Norddeutscher Lloyd liner BERLIN which had been fitted out as a
minelayer. On the day following the loss of MANCHESTER COMMERCE a
battleship was lost in the same minefield.

         CAMBRIAN RANGE was carrying 5500 tons of general home from
Baltimore when, just before midnight on 8/9th February,1916, the
eagle-eyed lookouts on the raider MOEWE spotted her 610 miles SE
of Cape Race. Her cargo was too valuable for her to be used as a
transport following a transfer of prisoners, so she was sunk and
her crew taken prisoner. She was the third ship to be sunk by
MOEWE that day.

         The tactics employed by merchantmen during 1915 had been to
pile on the coal and out-distance any threatening U-boat, and
HAMBLETON RANGE,START POINT and CROSSBY succeeded in this during
1915. Some of the larger vessels were then equipped with a gun at
the stern. On 4th June,1916 the recently purchased AUCHENBLAE was
in the Manchester Liners fleet as MANCHESTER TRADER sailing from
Suda Bay to Algiers in ballast under Capt. F.D. Struss when she
engaged a U-boat in a running gun battle before being sunk. Capt.
Struss and the Chief Engineer were each awarded the D.S.C., and
Capt. Struss was later in command in 1923 of MANCHESTER CIVILIAN
when made she several mercy voyages from the U.S.A. with relief
supplies for Japan following an earthquake. On 24th November,1916
EGYPTIANA put up such a good barrage of shells off Cape
Finisterre that she escaped unharmed from a marauding U-boat.

         Control of the **Johnston Line** fleet of Liverpool was obtained
in 1916, a partial shareholding having been purchased in 1914.
Their origins go back to 1873 and their traditional service to
Greece/Turkey and the Black Sea including the Crimea - indeed
their first ship was named CRIMEA. In 1880 a Transatlantic route
from Liverpool to Baltimore was started,and in the 1898s a nomen-

17. MENDIP RANGE of 1914 carrying engines.[A.Duncan].

18. WYNCOTE of 1907 in dry-dock at South Shields in WWI.

19. DOMINICA of 1913 ex DIGBY on Caribbean services [E.Johnson].

20. SACHEM of 1893 of Warren Line taken over in 1912.

21. STANMORE of 1914 of Johnston Line purchased in 1916.

22. WIGMORE of 1914 of Johnston Line. [J.Clarkson].

23. FORT HAMILTON of 1904 purchased in 1919 for Bermuda run.

24. FORT ST. GEORGE of 1912 purchased in 1919 for Bermuda run.

25. LONDON CITIZEN of 1918 ex VALEMORE [J.G.Callis].

S.S. LONDON EXCHANGE

26. LONDON EXCHANGE of 1921 ex PARISIANA.

27. LONDON CORPORATION of 1922 in the Thames [F.W. Hawks].

28. CHICKAHOMINY of 1921 became CORSICAN PRINCE [E.Johnson].

29. ALLEGHANY of 1922 became CASTILIAN PRINCE [E.Johnson].

30. AVIEMORE of 1920 was a war loss on 16.9.1939.

31. DROMORE of 1920 served the Group until 1955 [T.Rayner].

32. JESSMORE of 1921 ex PERUVIANA.

clature using the suffix 'MORE' came into force. Thirteen ships
were taken over in the deal by Furness,Withy & Co. Ltd but
management remained at Liverpool. 1917 was a black year for the
company with no fewer than 19 Furness-owned ships lost. In
addition both KERRY RANGE and LOWTHER RANGE were narrowly missed
by torpedoes in June and August,1917. GORSEMORE was similarly
missed in the Bristol Channel on 2nd May, and was then attacked
by gunfire from a U-boat on 26th June at the entrance to the
English Channel, one crew member being killed. She finally
succumbed to a torpedo on 22nd September,1918 in the Gulf of
Taranto while on a voyage from Barry to Taranto with coal.

The fleet continued to 'give' punishment as well as 'take'
it, and MANCHESTER PORT en route to Canada in June,1917 handed
out a heavy barrage of shells to beat off a U-boat. She had been
taken over by the Sea Transport in 1915 for a voyage to Egypt,
and later had delivered Admiralty coal to St. Vincent,Port
Stanley and Callao. Her brand-new fleetmate MANCHESTER DIVISION
under Capt. E.W.C. Beggs finally achieved the first 'kill' when
she rammed and sank a U-boat off Flamborough Head on her maiden
voyage from the company shipyard at Hartlepool to join convoy at
Plymouth at the end of September,1918.

Three replacements for the cargo-liner fleet of the Norfolk
& North American S.S. Co. Ltd and Gulf Line were obtained from E.
Nicholl & Co. of London. His WESTOE HALL,ALBERT HALL and BLAND
HALL became TURINO,SOUTH POINT and CORNISH POINT respectively
but both TURINO and SOUTH POINT succumbed to torpedoes during
1917, TURINO 174 miles W of the Fastnet and SOUTH POINT (the
second of this name to be lost) 30 miles SW 1/2 S of the Bishop
Rock. Four purchased vessels joined the Manchester Liners fleet
and were given the names of earlier losses, and subsequently
three of these were lost with two of them after only one voyage.

Prince Line Ltd owned by Sir James Knott was purchased for
£3M in December,1916 with a large fleet of 37 cargo-liners. Sir
James had started trading in Newcastle with one small old collier
brig named PEARL purchased for £186 in 1878, and had developed
services from Tyne,London and Antwerp to Central America, the
Plate,West Indies,Greece,Black Sea,Egypt,Syria together with
Italian emigrant services to New York and Central America, and
had also captured one-third of the coffee trade from Brazil up to
New Orleans and New York. He had decided to sell his fleet and
business assets and goodwill following the death of two of his
three sons with the eldest also presumed dead although in fact he
was a prisoner-of-war in Germany. He thus retired at the age of
61 years to his country estate at Close House to the west of Newcastle, setting up a Trust in memory of his dead sons and was to
philantropically give away half of his fortune to charity until
his death in 1934. Management of the fleet remained initially at
Newcastle, and in 1917 the 10-strong Glasgow fleet of J. Gardiner
& Co. Ltd with names starting with 'GLEN' was purchased and
transferred to a new floated company - Rio-Cape Line Ltd. In 1922
the remaining units of this fleet were given 'PRINCE' names, with

the Rio-Cape Line Ltd becoming a subsidiary of Prince Line Ltd.
The subsequent story of Prince Line Ltd is well documented by
this author in 'PRIDE OF THE PRINCES'.

The need for shipping became so desperate during the black
year of 1917 that overtures were made by the British Government
to the Portuguese concerning 72 German and two Austrian ships
bottled up in the harbours of Portugal and her overseas terri-
tories. The initial Portuguese response was unenthusiastic, they
were alarmed that such action would break their neutrality and
bring German reprisals. However Portugal was deprived of many of
the British calls at their ports and was thus unable to secure
supplies of coal,grain,sugar,cotton and meat. Thus decrees were
issued at the end of February,1916 proclaiming the requisitioning
of 63 German ships lying at Lisbon,Oporto,Setubal,Azores,Funchal,
Sao Vicente,Loanda and Mormugao. They were to be operated by
Transportes Maritimos do Estado(TME) and given Portuguese names.
On 12th August,1916 it was announced that 51 of the ships were to
be leased to the British Goverment with Furness,Withy & Co. Ltd
as managers of all 51 ships. Frederick Lewis, the Furness London
office manager and Deputy Chairman, was also serving as a
Shipping Controller in the Ministry of Shipping at this time.

Delivery was made to Casa Torlades, Furness,Withy's Lisbon
agents, of the first six ships in September,1916 with two large
cargo-liners sub-chartered to the French Government to take
troops and munitions to Salonika in Greece. The other four took
scarce fruit to South Wales and returned with coal; South Wales
ports became the assembly ports for 18 more transferred ships in
October and November,1916. The flagship of the TME fleet was the
former Norddeutscher Lloyd liner BULOW, renamed TRAZ OS MONTES,
and she had a varied career as a troopship under Furness,Withy
management during the war, and then repatriated troops to
Australia after the Armistice and made two voyages to the Far
East. At the other end of the scale a sailing ship came under
Furness,Withy management. She was the barque MAX formerly RICKMER
RICKMERS which was given the Portuguese name FLORES at Horta in
the Azores, and after war service became the sail training ship
SAGRES for the Portuguese Navy in 1924. The sailing ship GRACIOSA
arrived in the Tyne in July,1916 and SANTA MARIA in the Clyde a
month later and may have come under Furness,Withy oversight.

The rest of the German ships were transferred to Furness,
Withy management during 1917, the final total adding up to 41
ships. The careers of these during 1917 and 1918 were extremely
varied with French charters in the Mediterranean, Atlantic
voyages to Savannah and for the smaller ships trade to France and
Britain from Portugal as well as British coastal trading. War
losses amounted to 21 out of the 41, and the remainder were then
made full use of by Furness,Withy & Co. Ltd and the French Government at the end of the war. Transfer back to TME from charter
was a leisurely one during 1920; and several ships became
immobilised at British ports including SACAVEM at Hartlepool
while negotiations continued between TME and the company. The

last of the charters to return was INHAMBANE in April,1921 on the
Marseille to Beirut and Constantinople run for the French Government.

The company also became the 'owners' of 8 new Norwegian ships
building on the North-East coast during 1917/18. Four were two-
hold engines amidships colliers building for Fearnley,Eger of Oslo
but were registered under the company and operated by The Shipping
Controller as ALLENDALE,BEAUMARIS,HASLEMERE and KEIGHLEY. The
first two became war losses, but the others were returned to their
rightful owner in 1920 to become HOMLEDAL and GRAZIELLA respectively. The other four were cargo-liners completing at Sunderland,
with three for Wilhelm Wilhelmsen and one for A/S Gro(J.R. Olsen),
Bergen. These took the British names GLASTONBURY,ABERCORN,APPLEBY
and TENTERDEN and were registered under the Norfolk & N. American
S.S. Co. Ltd for operation by The Shipping Controller, and were
returned to their Norwegian owners in 1920 as SIMLA,MESNA,RINDA
and GRO.

An interesting group of 12 ships came under Furness,Withy &
Co. Ltd management during 1917. Some 20 standard Japanese-built
ships to four Japanese designs were purchased by the British
Government for management by Furness,Withy & Co. Ltd and Federal
Steam Navigation Co. Ltd. The first was delivered to Furness by
Kawasaki Dockyard in March,1917 and was a flush-decker of 9394 grt
named WAR KING. A twin-screw steamer she had six holds,two masts
with nine derricks plus another eight derricks on smaller posts.
The other 11 ships were delivered for management up to November,
1917 and nine were sisters to a smaller design of 5800 grt. These
were WARs QUEEN,PRINCE,COUNCIL,ADMIRAL,WOLF,LION,TIGER,HERO and
PILOT and were flush-deckers with 5 holds and two masts sporting
nine derricks. Triple expansion engines drove a single screw. The
other two, WAR SAILOR and WAR SOLDIER, were smaller versions of
WAR KING with twin screws. Four others were delivered for management by Federal, but the last remaining four were never built.
They were the subject of an interesting lawsuit in 1921. This was
decided in favour of Federal as the steel and other materials for
the ships had never been obtained by the Japanese builder due to a
steel embargo by the U.S.A. steelmakers on Japan at the end of the
war.

A large shareholding was purchased in **Kaye,Son & Co. Ltd** in
1918. Frederick Kaye had left Houlder Brothers & Co. Ltd in 1893
to form F. Kaye & Co. to manage steamers for the River Plate Fresh
Meat Company (later the British & Argentine Meat Co. Ltd) as well
as a coaling service,insurance agency and London agency of the
Prince Line River Plate service and later the Mediterranean
service. Kaye,Son & Co. Ltd was incorporated in 1905 and entered
shipowning in 1912. One tramp was owned when Furness,Withy & Co.
Ltd purchased shares, and the fleet was built up in the early
1920s by buying two Furness tramps in 1922 - MALVERN RANGE and
SIDLAW RANGE - as well as the Johnston Line STANMORE in 1923. Much
later in 1973 Kaye,Son & Co. Ltd was absorbed into the Furness,
Withy Group and their last ship, the tanker KAYESON of 47,900 dwt

and on charter to SHELL, was managed by Furness,Withy(Shipping) Ltd from 1977 until her sale in 1981 for use as a bunkering ship at Jeddah.

1.6 INTER-WAR YEARS

Marmaduke,second Lord Furness and only son of Sir Christopher Furness, had become Chairman of Furness, Withy & Co. Ltd on the death of his cousin Sir Stephen W. Furness M.P. in 1914. The second Lord Furness took personal charge of a new shipbuilding venture at Haverton Hill on the Tees, which was equipped for production by 1917 to help the war effort. Marmaduke also set up Cie Furness(France) in Paris to manage the Swiss merchant fleet during the war. However the extravagant personal and business lifestyle of the second Lord Furness, including long weekends on the French Riviera after motoring down from Paris with Lady Furness and a large number of guests, caused consternation with the Furness London office managers. A **'management buyout'** was mounted in the summer of 1919 and involved the purchase of all Furness,Withy & Co. Ltd shares in return for £6M of orders for the new Furness shipyard. In August/September 1919 the Furness family relinquished their shareholdings in the company with Marmaduke, Walter,Ethelbert,Einar and John Furness resigning from the Board and withdrawing completely from the company with no further direct interest. The ships that were completed in the £6M deal by the Furness family shipyard on the Tees - Furness Shipbuilding Co. Ltd - are detailed on the following page. The Furness family remained in control of the Tees shipyard, with descendant Stephen Furness as Chairman in the early post-WWII years. The last link between Furness,Withy & Co. Ltd and the yard was the building of the 168,000 dwt ore/bulk/oil FURNESS BRIDGE in 1971.

Frederick Lewis,who was manager of the London office and Deputy Chairman of the company became Chairman,and the other directors remaining were Robert E. Burnett, W.H. Beckenham,R.J. Thompson and H. Blackliston. The vacancies were filled by the appointment of N. Douglass(died 1926), Frank H. Houlder(died 1936),R.I. Dodsworth (died 1937),Sir John Esplen(died 1930),S.J. Forster and Walter C. Warwick. Frederick Lewis had started with the company as an office boy at the Hartlepool headquarters of Christopher Furness in 1883, and had then been transferred to the new London office in 1890 for training as an accountant. He was the godson of Christopher Furness, and worked under Robert B. Stoker in London and on Saturday mornings also delivered the mail to the Stoker home in Sydenham. Walter C. Warwick had joined the company on 1st January,1896 as an assistant to Frederick Lewis under Robert B. Stoker; and had been Managing Director of Houlder Brothers & Co. Ltd since July,1911 when a significant shareholding was acquired in that company.

In 1919 the capital of the company was increased to £5.5M, and in 1922 the Head Office was moved to Furness House,56 Leadenhall Street EC3 which also housed most of the subsidiaries, while Houlder Brothers were housed next door. The company had by now on its registers upwards of 10,000 shareholders of whom 90% had held their shares since the original allotment. Dividends had averaged 9.7% per annum before WWI, and in deciding to issue £2M of shares to shareholders on a share-for-share basis the management were making the issued capital more closely approximate the actual capital employed. The distribution of extra shares was only made possible by having reserves of £2M of which £1M had already been earned before the outbreak of war, and only the other £1M had come from 'war-profiteering'. Profit for the year 1920 amounted to £955,848 after tax, and a dividend on ordinary shares of 10% was paid plus a bonus of 5%. After transferring £300,000 to depreciation account this left £203,348 carried forward to the next year.

The new Furness family shipyard at Haverton Hill received some 16 orders for cargo-liners plus 2 colliers from Furness,Withy & Co. Ltd and its subsidiaries during the shipyards's first years of existence. These were:-

Furness,Withy & Co. Ltd   (4) TUNISIANA,PERSIANA,ITALIANA,BRAZILIANA (transferred shortly after completion to Prince Line as LANCASTRIAN,CORSICAN, ITALIAN and EGYPTIAN PRINCEs).

Norfolk & N.American S.S/ (5) LONDON MARINER,LONDON SHIPPER, Gulf Line Ltd/Neptune S.N.   LONDON MERCHANT,LONDON COMMERCE, Co. Ltd   LONDON IMPORTER.

Johnston Line Ltd   (4) KENMORE,QUERNMORE,SYCAMORE,TRAMORE.

Manchester Liners Ltd   (3) MANCHESTER REGIMENT,COMMERCE and CITIZEN.

The five 'LONDON' cargo-liners were completed in 1922/23 for a new fast cargo service operated between London,Philadelphia and New York returning via Halifax(NS) during the apple season. Two smaller ships were completed by Irvines shipyard with triple expansion engines - LONDON EXCHANGE and LONDON CORPORATION. The bigger quintet were given two steam turbines with single reduction gearing to a single screw. They were easily distinguished as they were given four very large goalpost masts for extra strength. Three acquired Prince Line names in 1928 - IMPERIAL PRINCE,ROYAL PRINCE and BRITISH PRINCE - although never actually registered under Prince Line. Four were sold to T. & J. Harrison of Liverpool in 1935 while the fifth went to the Admiralty as RELIANT. LONDON MERCHANT achieved immortality when as POLITICIAN she was wrecked on the Isle of Eriskay in Scotland on 4th February,1941 - later she became the subject of the classic Ealing film comedy 'Whisky Galore' in 1948.

In 1919 the company acquired the goodwill and assets of the **Quebec Steamship Co. Ltd** with their New York - Bermuda - Caribbean islands services. The three ships which commenced a New York - Bermuda service for the company were the BERMUDIAN of the Quebec company, renamed FORT HAMILTON, and FORT ST. GEORGE and FORT VICTORIA purchased from the Adelaide S.S. Co. Ltd,Australia as

WANDILLA and WILLOCHRA. FORT ST. GEORGE was employed during the slack season on the Bermuda route in the Saguenay river tourist trade, proving herself very popular there. For the operation of these three a new company was set up - Bermuda & West Indies Steamship Co. Ltd - and to add to the appeal of the naturally beautiful island of Bermuda the company laid-out a new 18-hole golf course. Three smaller ships - KORONA,PARIMA and GUIANA - established a New York service to the Leeward & Windward Islands, Trinidad and Guiana.

In the Autumn of 1920 the company purchased the goodwill and assets of the Trinidad Shipping & Trading Co. Ltd with their New York - Trinidad service and three steamers MARAVAL,MATURA and MAYARO. Various other profit-earning assets on Trinidad came with the deal, and a company office was opened at Trinidad under the charge of Hon. A. Fraser. The important feature of this acquisition was that it strengthened the Caribbean links purchased the previous year from the Quebec company. Subsequently the company established a ship-repair facility at Port of Spain,Trinidad as Furness Engineering(Trinidad) Ltd, and for a long time carried out voyage repairs afloat and dry-dock work on the Government slipway. During 1965 part of the U.S. Naval Base at Chaguaramas on the north-west tip of the island was made available to Furness - Smiths Dock(Trinidad) Ltd - jointly formed by the company and Smiths Dock Co. Ltd of North Shields. Small craft shipbuilding was undertaken together with the dry-docking in a floating dock of ships up to 11,200 tons displacement.

During 1920 the Johnston Line service to the Black Sea was strengthened by the acquisition of a company with specialist expertise in the Danube river trade. Watson & Youell had offices at Bucharest,Braila,Galatz,Sulina,Constantza and Oltenitza as a shipping agency but also had a merchant business which added to the volume of trade offering for Johnston Line, and also for Prince Line trading to Piraeus,Constantinople and Alexandria and other East Mediterranean ports.

Due to WWI the impetus to world trade of the opening of the Panama Canal had been retarded, but by 1921 rapid strides were being made to open up trade to the Pacific Coast regions of both U.S.A. and Canada from the U.K./Continent. Much refrigerated fruit as well as timber and grain were offering homewards, and the first ship to start the regular Furness service was MONGOLIAN PRINCE when she loaded in the Pacific in September,1921. This service later became fortnighly, and the new 'LONDON' ships were used as well as chartered-in Manchester Liners Ltd ships until purpose-built vessels took over. The company's first successful motorship DOMINION MILLER of 8960 dwt had been completed in February,1922 by the Doxford yard at Sunderland for the U.S. east coast trade of the Norfolk & North American S.S. Co. Ltd, but she was switched in 1923 to the Pacific service arriving at Los Angeles for the first time on 23rd May,1923 as PACIFIC COMMERCE. Two further sisters with split profiles followed for the Pacific service in March and

May,1924 from the Doxford yard - PACIFIC SHIPPER and PACIFIC
TRADER of 9500 dwt and service speeds of 11.5 knots.

A septet of fine twin-screw motorships entered the Pacific
trade from 1927. They were open-shelterdeckers with two continuous
tween decks and of these, the lower one with six compartments was
insulated for the homeward carriage of fruit. They had some
passenger accomodation in their very long extended bridge superstructure. A dozen derricks were positioned around the two masts
and a set of posts between numbers 1 and 2 holds. Blythswood SB Co.
Ltd at Glasgow received four of the orders in addition to others
from Prince Line at this time, and two went to the Deutsche Werft
yard at Kiel and the last came from the Burmeister & Wain yard at
Copenhagen. The engines reflected the yards' allegiances - the
Clyde-built ships had Kincaid engines from Greenock, and the
Continental yards manufactured their own oil engines. A loaded
speed of 13 knots was obtained on 20 tons of oil/day. PACIFIC
RELIANCE was the first of the sisters to appear on the Pacific
coast in October,1927.

7 PACIFIC CARGO-LINERS OF 10,000 DWT

Blythswood SB,Glasgow   (4) PACIFIC ENTERPRISE,PACIFIC RELIANCE,
                                PACIFIC EXPORTER,PACIFIC PIONEER.

Deutsche Werft,Kiel   (2) PACIFIC GROVE,PACIFIC PRESIDENT.

Burmeister & Wain,   (1) PACIFIC RANGER
Copenhagen

        The most noticeable difference of the class over their
elder running-mates was the introduction of the cruiser stern to
replace the counter stern. They had an extra hatch forward; with
the unbroken superstructure built around number 4 hatch, which
was trunked to the deck above. British shipbuilders were further
annoyed by three of the orders going to the Continent in addition
to the five the company had placed with the Deutsche Werft yard
in 1925 for the Rio-Cape Line subsidiary of Prince Line Ltd. The
ownership of the seven was divided between the parent company and
two subsidiaries: Norfolk & North American S.S. Co. Ltd and Gulf
Line Ltd. The German-built ships were longer by 15 feet, while
they and the Danish-built one could be distinguished from their
sisters by their bridges, which were one deck higher to give a
better view over the bows.

The former DOMINION MILLER was sold to British owners as
PACIFIC COMMERCE in 1936 and Ambrose,Davies & Matthews of Swansea
became her new managers. Thus a fleet of nine fast good-sized
cargo-liners ran a regular fortnightly service from the Pacific
coast in 1938. Only PACIFIC ENTERPRISE and PACIFIC EXPORTER were
to survive the holocaust of the next World War, and PACIFIC
ENTERPRISE was then unfortunate to be wrecked at Point Arena in
California on 8th September,1949. PACIFIC EXPORTER was sold to

Costa of Genoa in 1951 becoming his GIACOMO C until scrapped in 1959 when 21 years old.

Manchester Liners Ltd started the 1920s decade by having two Furness ships transferred to them from subsidiaries - START POINT and GRAMPIAN RANGE were renamed MANCHESTER PRODUCER and SPINNER respectively. The New Orleans service was resumed and the Baltimore service extended to serve Norfolk. In 1926, MANCHESTER PRODUCER lost her rudder in a gale while under the command of Capt. G.M. Mitchell on a homeward voyage near the Azores. Many cattle were lost due to the heavy seas breaking over her, and after many unsuccessful efforts at salvage she was finally towed home by the Dutch tug ZWARTE ZEE. REXMORE was transferred in from Johnston Line in 1929 to become MANCHESTER EXPORTER to maintain the American trade. In December 1929, MANCHESTER REGIMENT under Capt. Philip Linton steamed 160 miles through a gale to reach the sinking Glasgow tramp VOLUMNIA owned by Gow,Harrison. A lifeboat was launched to save the 45 doomed crew of the tramp, and on return home the King awarded the Silver Medal for Gallantry to 2nd Officer Downing, 3rd officer Espley, bosun Bromage and able seamen Stringer,Kearns,Chidlow,Manins and Ziegler who had manned the lifeboat.

In 1927 it was decided to develop the growing **New York - Bermuda** tourist trade by greatly increasing passenger capacity. An order had been placed with Workman,Clark & Co. Ltd,Belfast for a liner with accomodation for 616 first-class and 75 second-class passengers. She was named BERMUDA at her launch at Belfast on 28th July,1927 and was completed on 14th December,1927. Her maiden voyage from New York to Bermuda was on 14th January,1928. She was the first passenger ship to be fitted with four-cylinder Doxford oil engines driving four propellers. She had a short but dramatic career, catching fire at Hamilton in June,1931 and she was so badly damaged she had to be sent home to Belfast for repairs at her builders. However on 19th November,1931 shortly before the completion of repairs another serious fire occurred, gutting her completely and she sank at her berth. The wreck was sold to her builders by the company, and she was raised on 24th December,1931 to allow her engines to be removed before a final voyage to a scrapyard. Even this could not be completed, for en-route to Rosyth breakers in June,1932 the tug SEAMAN lost the tow, and the wreck ran aground on the appropriately named Badcall Islands in Eddrachilles Bay,Scotland and became a total loss.

Fortunately a running-mate had already been ordered from Vickers-Armstrong Ltd,Newcastle and launched into the water on 17th March,1931 as MONARCH OF BERMUDA. She was completed on 7th November,1931 after achieving nearly 21 knots on trials off Newbiggin. She was driven by large Fraser & Chalmers steam turbines linked to General Electric motors passing their power to four screws. She had two inordinately high masts and with her three funnels was just what was required to persuade Americans to holiday in Bermuda. She had accomodation for 830 first-class passengers, of which a few of the cabins could be converted to

house 31 second-class passengers. She proved a very great
success, helped even more by her prompt rescue of 71 survivors
from the burning American liner MORRO CASTLE off New Jersey on
8th September,1934 and an exact sister was ordered from Vickers-
Armstrong Ltd as a running-mate.

QUEEN OF BERMUDA was launched on 1st September,1932 at
Vickers-Armstrong Ltd Barrow yard and completed on 14th February,
1933. She had a similar interior layout as her sister, but
differed by having her mainmast sited further forward on the Sun
Deck and closer to the superstructure. She exceeded her sister's
speed on trials by achieving 21.07 knots. They were initially
registered at Hamilton but this was changed to London in 1937.
They maintained a regular peace-time service to Bermuda up to
1939 for the company in conjunction with the Hotel Bermudiana Co.
Ltd, which built three large hotels on the holiday island.

In 1928, the U.K. East Coast - Canada trade of the **Cairn
Line of Steamships Ltd,Newcastle** was purchased. The management
company of Cairns,Noble & Co. was purchased together with 85% of
Cairn Line shares. Sir William Joseph Noble then retired from his
Newcastle company and was made a director of Furness,Withy & Co.
Ltd in 1930. In the same year he took the title Lord Kirkley, and
retired to his country home, Kirkley Hall, seven miles north west
of Newcastle, purchased from the Ogle family in 1922. He had set
up Cairns,Young & Noble in 1883 on Newcastle Quayside with his
brother-in-law Thomas Cairns and Lindsay Young. Thomas Cairns had
started as an office boy with the Cape of Good Hope Steamship
Company, leaving in 1875 to join the Newcastle office of Davidson
& Charlton as a clerk. He became a partner in the following year
of Capt. B.B. Starks, shipbroker and merchant of Newcastle.

The first Cairn Line steamer was CAIRNGOWAN of 1883, which
was sold in 1909 to Swedish owners and then had a very long
career of 74 years until finally scrapped in 1957. Expansion from
the tramp trades into the Canadian trade led to the purchase just
before the death of Thomas Cairns in 1908 of the Thomson Line of
Dundee, bringing eight steamers including the former Blue Anchor
Line passenger ship WARRIGAL, used in the Australian emigrant
trade. Three fine passenger liners were then purchased for the
Canadian trade: CONSUELO from Wilson of Hull and two new Tyne-
built liners TORTONA and GERONA of 9111 grt. However the goodwill
of the Newcastle - Leith - Canada passenger service was sold to
Cunard in 1911 and the three liners became their ALBANIA,AUSONIA
and ASCANIA respectively. A fleet of nine good-sized cargo-liners
was purchased by Furness,Withy & Co. Ltd, and Lord Kirkley served
on the Furness Board until his death in 1935. The funnel colours
were changed after purchase in 1928 to red with a black top and
the white 'cairn' between two narrow white bands. The houseflag
then adopted was the blue and white chequered 'Betsy Norrie'
named after a lady of that name whose custom it was to make a
flag of this pattern and present one to each new Thomson sailing
ship!

In January,1929 C.T. Bowring & Co. Ltd sold their **Red Cross Line** (so called because of the Bowring funnel colours) passenger/ cargo services from St. John's(NF) to Halifax(NS) to New York to the Bermuda & West Indies S.S. Co. Ltd. ROSALIND and SILVIA maintained this service in summer together with the larger NERISSA of 5583 grt,which in winter maintained a New York - Bermuda service. ROSALIND and SILVIA were both of pre-war vintage, and SILVIA had originally been Danzig registered. C.T. Bowring had signed a contract with W. Hamilton & Co. Ltd,Port Glasgow on 3rd November, 1925 for the construction of NERISSA within 7 months. She was to have accomodation for 200 passengers and was launched on time on 31st March,1926; and was ready at the end of May to take passengers aboard after very fast work by Hamilton.

SILVIA was sold in 1934 but the other two stayed in service for Furness until two new ships were ready in January and April, 1936 - FORT AMHERST and FORT TOWNSHEND - from Blythswood SB Co. Ltd,Glasgow to replace ROSALIND and SILVIA. The two 'FORT's had accomodation for 100 passengers and were single screw triple expansion steamers with a speed of 13 knots. NERISSA was then used on the New York - Bermuda service all the year round.

On the last day of 1934, Warren Line lost its individual identity when the various Furness companies based in Liverpool amalgamated. Johnston Line Ltd and Neptune Steam Navigation Co. Ltd had been liquidated in November of that year and their assets taken over by Warren Line, which changed its name to **Johnston-Warren Lines Ltd**,Liverpool. The Johnston-Warren Transatlantic service was maintained at this time by the sister cargo-liners NEWFOUNDLAND and NOVA SCOTIA of 1925/26; and their Black Sea services by six steamers:- AVIEMORE,DROMORE,INCEMORE,JESSMORE, KENMORE and QUERNMORE.

Negotiations continued throughout 1934/35 between the Boards of **Shaw,Savill & Albion Co. Ltd**(SSA) and Furness,Withy & Co. Ltd after Furness had acquired a controlling interest in SSA in 1933. The rest of the SSA shares were acquired in 1935, the capital of SSA had stood at £700,000 with only £390,750 actually issued in 'B' preference shares and 'A' ordinary shares - Furness had acquired the right amounts of unissued capital to gain control. Since 1910, 44% of SSA had been owned by White Star Line with only Sir John Ellerman as the other major shareholder. In late 1926 Lord Kylsant of Royal Mail Group announced with effect from 1st January,1927 he had acquired White Star Line for £7M and thus SSA. In September,1931 Lord Kylsant was arrested and tried for issuing a misleading prospectus in 1928 - he was jailed for one year and the White Star Line crashed around him.

The shipping companies involved in the Kylsant crash were all most important to the nation, and the receivers and liquidators of Royal Mail separated them into individual units until they could be sold or stand alone themselves again. SSA survived and took over the White Star Australian services and the beautiful CERAMIC

together with Aberdeen Line - giving them full title to sisters
MATAROA and TAMAROA, as well as THEMISTOCLES and EURIPIDES
and the cargo ships HERMINIUS,HORATIUS,MAMILIUS - renamed
WAIMANA,KUMARA and MAMARI.

As a further part of the disentanglement, SSA with P&O,NZSC,
Orient Line and Furness,Withy & Co. Ltd acquired the **Aberdeen &
Commonwealth Line** for £500,000. As the largest shareholders SSA
became managers of the five large 'BAY' passenger ships serving
Australia: ESPERANCE BAY,HOBSONS BAY,JERVIS BAY,LARGS BAY and
MORETON BAY. As SSA was now owned by Furness,Withy & Co. Ltd these
five liners were effectively Furness majority-owned. ESPERANCE BAY
was then purchased outright by SSA in 1936 to replace IONIC and
sent to the Clyde for refit from which she emerged as ARAWA.
HOBSONS BAY was then renamed ESPERANCE BAY.

Furness,Withy & Co. Ltd allowed SSA to retain its individual
identity as well as leaving the management intact, a sensible
policy as they knew their own trade better than anyone. The Furness
empire now included:-

Parent company	U.K./Europe - Pacific Coast U.S.A/Canada; London - Philadelphia - New York returning via Halifax(NS) in summer.
Manchester Liners Ltd	Manchester - Eastern U.S.A.; Manchester - U.S. Gulf
Houlder Line	South American meat trade
Johnston-Warren Lines	Transatlantic service; Black Sea services.
Prince Line/Rio Cape Line	Round the World service; U.S.A./South Africa; Eastern Mediterranean services; New York - Brazil - Argentina
Bermuda & West Indies	New York - Bermuda; New York - Trinidad; St. John's(NF) - Halifax(NS) - New York
Shaw,Savill & Albion	U.K. - New Zealand & Australia

1.7 WORLD WAR II

Some 78 deep-sea passenger and cargo-liners were owned at
the outbreak of war on 3rd September,1939 including a new
flagship for the Australian service of Shaw,Savill & Albion Co.
Ltd. This was **DOMINION MONARCH** completed by Swan,Hunter & Wigham
Richardson Ltd at Wallsend-on-Tyne for a new service to Australia
and New Zealand via the Cape. Her maiden voyage departed from
Southampton on 17th February,1939 and at times her Doxford oil

engines kept up 20 knots, taking just under 24 days to complete the outward voyage. During her third outward voyage war was declared but she continued on her designed service until requisitioned in August,1940 as a troopship. Converted at Liverpool she then took a full load of troops to Port Said and then out to Australia, where she embarked more troops for the Middle East and retraced her route to Liverpool via Port Said. She then made a round voyage to Australia and New Zealand going out via Cape Town and returning via Panama. She then embarked troop reinforcements for Singapore and then was ordered to dry-dock there to overhaul her engines in spite of the Japanese advance from the north. The native labour was withdrawn as the air-raids intensified but Cheif Engineer Gibson and his men contrived to put the engines back together again and she just cleared the port before the Japanese arrived. Returning home via Panama she then made a number voyages with troops to Bombay and then on to Australia, and at the end of the war was on Transatlantic trooping.

CERAMIC remained on the Australian service via the Cape until requisitioned in February,1940 as a troopship. In the Autumn of 1942 she completed an extensive refit at Liverpool and left with 378 passengers and 279 crew under the command of Capt. H.C. Elford for Australia, but on the 6th December was torpedoed and sunk by U515 with only one survivor.

ARAWA was requisitioned as an Armed Merchant Cruiser in New Zealand on 24th August,1939 and was sent to patrol the China station. Her first trooping voyage was in January,1942 to Durban for the Middle East campaign, and was present at the North Africa landings and finished the war on Transatlantic trooping. Three of her four 'BAY' class sisters, ESPERANCE BAY,JERVIS BAY, and MORE-TON BAY were also armed with 6-inch guns as A.M.C.s, and JERVIS BAY was to be sunk by the pocket battleship ADMIRAL SCHEER in the defence of convoy HX84 from Halifax(NS) to the U.K. on 5th November,1940. Hopelessly out-gunned by six modern 11-inch long-range guns, Capt. E.S. Fogarty Fegen sacrificed himself and 198 of his crew to allow most of the 38-ship convoy of tramps and cargo-liners including the Furness PACIFIC ENTERPRISE and one liner to escape. No finer bravery has ever been shown in the annals of the war at sea.

MONARCH OF BERMUDA was converted into a troopship in November,1939 and was a unit of convoy TC1 in the following month with Canadian troops, sailing from Halifax(NS) in company with five other liners with a total of 7,400 men and arriving safely in the Clyde. She was then used to transport troops to Harstad in the Lofoten Islands to the east of Ofotfjord and Narvik during the occupation of Northern Norway on 15/16th April,1940 in company with REINA DEL PACIFICO and the Polish BATORY. During the week of 4th - 10th,June some 14 transports including MONARCH OF BERMUDA evacuated the survivors from Narvik and Harstad. She was later used to transport troops out to the Middle East via Free-town,Cape Town and Durban. She was carrying American troops at the landings in Les Andalouses Bay to the west of Oran in

November,1942 and was damaged by a hit on the Sun Deck by a 7.6" shell, killing one crew member. She made three more troop runs to North Africa, and carried the 59th Assault flotilla from the Middle East for the first Sicily landings on 10th July,1943. Her sister, QUEEN OF BERMUDA, gave good service as an A.M.C. with her third dummy funnel removed in 1940 and was not converted into a troopship until later in 1943, being used for Transatlantic voyages with American and Canadian troops.

The smaller passenger-cargo liners such as **TAMAROA** and **MATAROA** were used as transports from the end of 1940, particularly to South Africa and troops were then transhipped there for the Middle East permitting the sisters to call at the Plate for meat on the way home. The first voyage of TAMAROA was to the Middle East and then on to New Zealand to load meat for the return home nearly six months later. The full list of Group losses is now given, all being torpedoed and sunk unless otherwise stated:-

Furness,Withy & Co. Ltd:-
4.3.1940   PACIFIC RELIANCE   19 miles from Longships L.V.
12.10.1940 PACIFIC RANGER   East of Rockall.
2.12.1940 PACIFIC PRESIDENT South of Iceland, all crew lost.
30.4.1941 NERISSA Off N.W. Ireland,83 crew & 124 passengers lost.
   2.1942   MANAQUI Missing o.v. Loch Ewe - Kingston,all crew lost.
29.7.1942 PACIFIC PIONEER   160 miles ESE of Halifax(NS).
16.10.1942 CASTLE HARBOUR   Off Trinidad, 9 lost.
12.4.1943 PACIFIC GROVE   In Mid-Atlantic, 11 lost.

Johnston-Warren Line:-
16.9.1939 AVIEMORE Western Approaches, 23 lost.
16.9.1940 INCEMORE Wrecked on Anticosti Isle,St. Lawrence.
19.2.1941 JESSMORE N. Atlantic collision with BARON HAIG.
28.11.1942 NOVA SCOTIA Troop Transport, NE of Durban, 863 lost.
13.9.1943 NEWFOUNDLAND Hospital Ship at Salerno, 15 lost.

Manchester Liners:-
4.12.1939 MANCHESTER REGIMENT N. Atlantic collision, 9 lost.
26.9.1940 MANCHESTER BRIGADE Off N.W. Ireland, 58 lost.
25.2.1943 MANCHESTER MERCHANT Mid-Atlantic, 36 lost.
9.7.1943   MANCHESTER CITIZEN Off W. Africa, 15 lost.

Cairn Line:-
30.10.1939 CAIRNMONA Off Peterhead, 3 lost.
17.1.1940 CAIRNROSS Mined 8 miles from Mersey Bar L.V.
22.10.1940 CAIRNGLEN Wrecked at Marsden,South Shields.

Shaw,Savill & Albion:-
3.12.1939 TAIROA   S. Atlantic by GRAF SPEE, crew captured.
1.5.1940   MATAKANA   Wrecked at Plana Cays,Bahamas.
5.11.1940 JERVIS BAY Homeward HX84 convoy, 199 lost.
20.11.1940 MAIMOA   Indian Ocean by raider PINGUIN,crew captured.
25.12.1940 WAIOTIRA   N. Atlantic homeward voyage.
17.1.1941 ZEALANDIC   N. Atlantic outward voyage, 73 lost.
3.6.1941   MAMARI Wrecked off Norfolk disguised as HMS HERMES.

29.6.1942   WAIWERA   Near Azores on homeward voyage, 8 lost.
13.8.1942   WAIRANGI   Operation Pedestal Malta convoy.
13.8.1942   WAIMARAMA   Operation Pedestal Malta convoy, 83 lost.
6.12.1942   CERAMIC   North Atlantic, 656 lost.

Shaw,Savill Managed vessels:-
13.8.1942   EMPIRE HOPE   Operation Pedestal Malta convoy.
21.2.1943   EMPIRE TRADER Ex TAINUI   North Atlantic.

Prince Line:-
14.12.1940 WESTERN PRINCE   300 miles S of Ireland, 15 lost.
17.2.1941 SIAMESE PRINCE   Mid-Atlantic, 67 lost.
3.4.1941   NORTHERN PRINCE   Bombed/sunk off Crete,
6.4.1941   CYPRIAN PRINCE   Bombed at Piraeus, 4 lost.
6.12.1941 WELSH PRINCE   Mined/sunk E of Cromer.
29.5.1942 NORMAN PRINCE   W of Martinique, 16 lost.
12.4.1943 LANCASTRIAN PRINCE Mid-Atlantic, 45 lost.
11.11.1943 INDIAN PRINCE   Aerial torpedo 25 miles NE of
                               Oran, 1 lost.

Rio-Cape Line:-
16.3.1941 SARDINIAN PRINCE   Battlecruisers to SE of Cape Race.
20.5.1941 JAVANESE PRINCE   185 miles NW of Butt of Lewis,2 lost.
12.6.1941 CHINESE PRINCE   280 miles WNW of Malin Head,45 lost.
20.9.1941 CINGALESE PRINCE   Mid-Atlantic to SW of Freetown,56 lost.
26.9.1941 BRITISH PRINCE   Air attack E of Hornsea.
17.3.1942 SCOTTISH PRINCE   Off Cape Palmas,Liberia, 1 lost.

A total of 1,078 brave men had died in Furness-owned ships in WWII.

Most of the Furness Pacific and Prince Line Round the World
cargo-liners were taken off their normal routes at the commencement of hostilities and switched to the North Atlantic run. Over
two million tons of cargo were carried on this route alone by
Furness,Withy operated ships, and a total of 7.5 million tons for
routes including the Middle East was handled by the New York
stevedoring company owned by the company. FORT AMHERST and FORT
TOWNSHEND remained on their route between New York and St. John's
(NF) via Halifax(NS), each completing 100 round voyages and both
survived the war.

AVIEMORE of 1920 was the first Group loss on 16th September,
1939 in outward convoy OB4 from Liverpool to North America. She
started to sink immediately after being struck by two torpedoes
and 23 lives were lost. CAIRNMONA of Cairn Line had crossed the
Atlantic with a full cargo of wheat from Montreal in HX5 from
Halifax and then rounded the north of Scotland in the North Sea
section of that convoy. Off Rattray Head she was torpedoed and
sunk by the coastal attack U-boat U13. TAIROA under Capt. W.B.S.
Starr was homeward-bound from the Australia when attacked on 3rd
December,1939 and was forced to surrender after being hit by 59
shells. Several had been killed or seriously wounded and the
remainder were captured and put on the oiler ALTMARK, being
rescued in a Norwegian fjord by HMS COSSACK. MAIMOA under Capt.

H.S. Cox was similarly shelled and sunk by a raider, this time PINGUIN, in the Indian Ocean on 20th November,1940. Shaw,Savill were later to lose two owned ships - WAIRANGI and WAIMARAMA - and the managed EMPIRE HOPE in the desperate Operation Pedestal convoy to relieve Malta on 13th August,1942 with 83 lost from WAIMARAMA.

MANCHESTER REGIMENT under Capt. W.E. Raper was proceeding westward without lights on 4th December,1939 when she was in collision with the P.S.N.C. troopship OROPESA - detached from an eastbound convoy for special duty - unfortunately with the loss of 9 lives. Capt. F. Clough and 57 crew of MANCHESTER BRIGADE died when she was torpedoed off N.W. Ireland on 26th September, 1940. MANCHESTER PROGRESS under Capt. J. Barclay towed the disabled Morel tramp FOREST of Cardiff several hundred miles to the safety of Iceland in 1942 without naval escort. MANCHESTER DIVISION under Capt. H. Hancock was en-route to Cape Town when diverted to lift the 43 crew and 21 passengers of the beached DUNEDIN STAR, stranded on an isolated beach near Saldanha Bay. The Blue Star liner had hit a submerged object close to the shore on 29th November,1942. Commodore F.D. Struss was rescued from the water on 25th February,1943 after MANCHESTER MERCHANT had been torpedoed and sunk but 36 of his crew were not so lucky.

Capt. Smith and all of the crew of PACIFIC PRESIDENT perished when she was torpedoed and sunk in homeward HX90 in the 'black pit' of the central Atlantic which at that time in December,1940 had no air cover. Her sister PACIFIC RANGER had been lost two months earlier to East of Rockall in HX77, and PACIFIC RELIANCE had taken two torpedoes amidships when 19 miles from Longships L.V. bearing 352 degrees on a voyage from London to Liverpool on 4th March,1940. Both crews were saved as were those on board the outward-bound PACIFIC PIONEER when she was torpedoed and sunk 160 miles ESE of Halifax(NS) on 29th July,1942.

The disaster that befell NERISSA was particularly gruesome. She was 35 miles West of St. Kilda homeward-bound with 175 passengers, a crew of 106 and 6 gunners aboard on 30th April,1941. She was torpedoed by U552 when a full gale was blowing, making it difficult to launch the lifeboats and 124 passengers and 83 crew were drowned. The commander of U177 did not realise when he torpedoed the Johnston-Warren NOVA SCOTIA off Durban on 28th, November,1942 that he was sending 650 Italian prisoners-of-war to an early grave. Her sister NEWFOUNDLAND under Capt. Wilson was clearly marked as a Hospital ship and fully illuminated as laid down by the Geneva Convention during the landings at Salerno, yet this meant nothing to the enemy as two radio-controlled aerial torpedoes were launched at her, killing 23 medical staff but fortunately there were no wounded personnel aboard.

Lord Essendon,Group Chairman (formerly Sir Frederick Lewis) died during 1944, having played a role of almost comparable importance during his 61 years with the company to that of Sir Christopher Furness, the founder. He had been knighted in 1927 and honoured by a barony in 1932 taking the title Lord Essendon. Sir Ernest H. Murrant, a director since 1924 and Deputy Chairman since 1936, succeeded Lord Essendon and served until 1959. During the war Sir Ernest was the Middle East representative of the Ministry of War Transport with offices in Cairo and thus obtained first-hand knowledge of the Mediterranean trade of Prince Line and Johnston-Warren Line.

1.8 POST-WWII REBUILDING 1945 - 1965

Most of the company passenger liners continued trooping and repatriaton duties through 1945/46, and then required extensive overhauls before restarting their long-interrupted services. MONARCH OF BERMUDA returned to the Tyne for renovation at the end of 1946, but suffered a disastrous fire on 24th March,1947 and was almost totally destroyed, but fortunately her turbines and electric motors suffered little damage, and she was sold to the Ministry of Transport for rebuilding at Southampton into the Australian emigrant carrier NEW AUSTRALIA. Her sister QUEEN OF BERMUDA did, however, restart the New York - Bermuda service in February,1949. A replacement was ordered immediately for the 'MONARCH' from Walker Naval Yard on the Tyne and was launched on 27th July,1950 as the smaller OCEAN MONARCH of 13581 grt but still able to accomodate 414 first-class passengers. Parsons geared turbines drove twin screws on trials on 23rd March,1951 at a speed in excess of her service speed of 18 knots, and she salied from New York on 3rd May,1951 on her first voyage with holidaymakers for Bermuda.

Shaw,Savill & Albion Co. Ltd were left with six passenger liners: DOMINION MONARCH,ARAWA,MATAROA,TAMAROA,THEMISTOCLES and AKAROA. DOMINION MONARCH was sent to her builders yard of Swan, Hunter & Wigham Richardson Ltd at Wallsend in August,1947 and emerged 15 months later with accomodation for 508 passengers in first class only. ARAWA spent the latter part of 1945 repatriat-ing released P.O.W.s from Black Sea ports and Istanbul to Mar-seilles. She was then sent to Newcastle for refitting, and like all the company liners emerged with accomodation for one class only. She was the first to restart, sailing from London on 7th February,1946 for New Zealand via Panama with first-class accom-odation for 274 passengers. Her surviving sisters ESPERANCE BAY (ex HOBSONS BAY),MORETON BAY and LARGS BAY returned to Australian service during 1948 for Aberdeen & Commonwealth Line with the company as managers with accomodation for 514 tourist-class pass-engers. Sisters MATAROA and TAMAROA returned to service during 1948 each with accomodation for 380 passengers. AKAROA, built for the Aberdeen Line in 1914 as EURIPIDES, was reconditioned at Wallsend in 1947 for further service carrying 198 tourist-class passengers and sailed on until scrapped in Belgium in 1954. THEM-ISTOCLES of 1910 had completed 79 round voyages to Australia and was laid-up on the Fal, but did not return to service and was sent for scrap to the Clyde.

33. PACIFIC SHIPPER of 1924 served the Pacific until 1950.

34. PACIFIC ENTERPRISE of 1927 stranded in California in 1949.

35. PACIFIC RELIANCE of 1927 became a war loss on 4.3.1940.

36. PACIFIC PRESIDENT of 1928 became a war loss on 2.12.1940.

37. PACIFIC GROVE of 1928 became a war loss on 12.4.1943.

38. PACIFIC EXPORTER of 1928 in Manchester Ship Canal.

39. NOVA SCOTIA of 1927 in the Mersey. [B.Fielden].

40. BERMUDA of 1927 had a short, ill-starred career [E.Johnson].

41. MONARCH OF BERMUDA of 1931 – classic liner [B.Fielden].

42. QUEEN OF BERMUDA of 1933 was scrapped in 1967 [B.Fielden].

43. ROSALIND of 1911 purchased in 1929 from Red Cross Line.

44. JESSMORE of 1941 ex EMPIRE FAITH of Johnston-Warren Line

45. HEATHMORE of 1945 a C1–M–AV1 type.

46. PACIFIC IMPORTER of 1943 ex SAMTREDY.

47. NOVA SCOTIA of 1947 of Johnston-Warren Line.

48. PACIFIC FORTUNE of 1948 was sold in 1965 [F.R.Sherlock].

49. FORT AVALON of 1949 was sold in 1960.

50. SYCAMORE of 1950 became MERCHANT PRINCE in 1965.

FURNESS BERMUDA LINE, T.S.S. "OCEAN MONARCH"

51. OCEAN MONARCH of 1951 was finally gutted by fire in 1981.

52. PACIFIC RELIANCE of 1951 was scrapped in 1971 [F.R.Sherlock].

53. PACIFIC NORTHWEST of 1954 was sold to Greece in 1971.

54. ROWANMORE of 1956 was sold in 1973 [A.Duncan].

55. PACIFIC STRONGHOLD of 1958 was sold to Greece in 1971 [J.K.Byass]

56. PACIFIC EXPORTER of 1957 in British Columbia in 1970 [J.K.Byass]

57. MANCHESTER TRADER of 1955 ex WESTERN PRINCE.

58. MANCHESTER FAME of 1959 became CAIRNGLEN in 1965 [A.Duncan].

59. MANCHESTER PROGRESS of 1967 was rebuilt for containers.

60. CAIRNESK of 1926 seen at Newcastle was taken over in 1928.

61. CAIRNGOWAN of 1952 arriving in the Tyne. [M.Donnelly]

62. CAIRNDHU of 1952 waiting to dry-dock at Wallsend [T.Rayner]

63. AKAROA of 1914 of Shaw,Savill was taken over in 1933 [V.H.Young]

64. SALAMANCA of 1948 of P.S.N.C. was taken over in 1965 [A.Duncan]

A motley collection of 10 aging cargo-liners with Maori names except for COPTIC of 1928 also returned to service. EMPIRE GRACE was purchased to become WAIRANGI alongside her sisters WAIPAWA and WAIWERA. Two new classes of cargo-liner were then ordered to appear on the Australian/New Zealand service from 1947. The White Star naming system ending in 'IC' was to be restarted.

7 PASSENGER/CARGO-LINERS OF 12,000 DWT

Cammell Laird,Birkenhead	(3) CORINTHIC,CERAMIC,PERSIC.
Harland & Wolff Ltd,Belfast	(3) ATHENIC,RUNIC,SERVIC.
Swan Hunter,Wallsend	(1) GOTHIC.

PERSIC,RUNIC and SERVIC had the same hull but did not carry passengers, and entered service during 1949/50, two years after the passenger quartet. CORINTHIC was ready first in April,1947 followed by ATHENIC three months later. Six steam turbines gave a service speed of 17 knots, and her holds included large refrigerated capacity. The spacious accomodation for 85 first-class passengers was in 53 cabins of which 36 were single-berth, while 23 had the luxury of their own private bathroom. There was fluorescent lighting in all public rooms, and those of the CORINTHIC were inspected by the King during a private visit at London Docks in October,1950.

Shortly afterwards it was announced from Buckingham Palace that one of the quartet had been selected for use as a Royal Yacht for the proposed Royal Commonwealth Tour. The latest ship, GOTHIC of December,1948 was chosen and painted white - as was CERAMIC which was standby Royal Yacht. The alterations to GOTHIC were carried out at the Cammell,Laird yard,including dividing the ship's dining room into two, in readiness to receive the Royal furniture when required. It was then announced that Princess Elizabeth and the Duke of Edinburgh were to go on Tour as the King was in poor health. GOTHIC was at Mombasa on 5th February, 1951 to embark the Royal couple,but the Tour was cancelled the next day on the King's death and the Royal couple returned home.

The Tour was re-scheduled for the end of 1953 and would start in Jamaica with a cruise through the Pacific islands to New Zealand and Australia and on to Ceylon and Aden. The Royal apartments were refurbished on the Mersey, and after trials GOTHIC sailed under Capt. David Aitchison for Jamaica, arriving on 21st November,1953. Visits to Suva and Tonga, Auckland, Wellington and Bluff,Sydney,Hobart,Melbourne,Townsville,Cairns,Mackay,Adelaide and Fremantle. Next stop was Cocos Island en-route to Colombo, and the Royal Tour ended at Aden on 28th April,1954 where the Queen and Duke of Edinburgh disembarked and flew to Entebbe. GOTHIC sailed for Malta where the Royal furniture was transferred to the new Royal Yacht BRITANNIA.

CORINTHIC and ATHENIC had their passenger accomodation removed in 1965 and arrived for scrap at Kaohsiung at the end of October,1969. GOTHIC had suffered a bad fire on 1st August,1968 some 300 miles E of New Zealand while on a voyage from Bluff to Panama. It had started in the officers' smoke room and seven people died. She returned to Wellington with a completely burnt out bridge, and arrived back at Liverpool on 10th October,1968 where repairs were effected so that she could make one more cargo-only round voyage. She arrived at Kaohsiung for scrap on 13th August,1969. CERAMIC lasted the longest of the four passenger ships, arriving at Tamise in Belgium in June,1972 for scrap. The cargo-only RUNIC came to an unfortunate end on Middleton Reef some 120 miles N of Lord Howe Island on 19th February,1961 while on a voyage from Brisbane to Auckland. She was hard aground and the Newcastle tramp BRIGHTON stood by until tugs could arrive. All salvage attempts failed and she was declared a constructive total loss in March,1961. Her hull rusted very slowly, and her unmistakeable outline can still be seen today at the spot where she ploughed to a halt.

The cargo-fleet of Shaw,Savill & Albion Co. Ltd was also replaced:-

7 CARGO-LINERS OF 12,500 DWT

Harland & Wolff,Belfast	(2) CEDRIC,CYMRIC.
Fairfield,Glasgow	(1) DORIC.
Hawthorn Leslie,Hebburn	(1) DELPHIC
Vickers-Armstrong,Tyne	(1) CANOPIC.
Swan Hunter,Wallsend	(1) CRETIC.
Cammell Laid,Birkenhead	(1) CARNATIC.

These good-looking ships entered service between 1949 and 1957. All were given oil engines - the first pair, DORIC and DELPHIC, received Doxford while the others received B&W type oil engines. DORIC and DELPHIC were very popular on the Australian and New Zealand coasts in a social capacity. The 'C' class had six hatches served by an array of 22 derricks plus a 70-tonner at No. 2 hatch, and a 25-tonner at no. 5 hatch. The deck officers were at the forward end of the boat deck and the engineers were on the outside of the engine room casing on the same deck. The petty officers and crew were accomodated below on bridge deck. CYMRIC,CRETIC and CARNATIC were transferred to Royal Mail in 1973 following the acquisition of Royal Mail shares in 1965, and renamed DURANGO,DRINA and DARRO respectively. CANOPIC was to last the longest, however, following her sale to Roussos Brothers in 1975 she was renamed CAPETAN NICOLAS and was laid-up at Piraeus from 26th December,1981 until her last voyage to the breakers yard at Aliaga in September,1986.

It was clear also that the cargo-liner fleets of the other Furness subsidiaries would take time to replace. The parent company **Pacific Service to U.S.A./Canada** was left with only PACIFIC ENTERPRISE and PACIFIC EXPORTER. The first named was unfortunately wrecked at Point Arena in California on 8th September,1949; and four standard 'Liberties' and one 'Victory' were pressed into service from 1947. PACIFIC EXPORTER was sold to Costa of Genoa in 1951, and her replacements had started to come into service in 1948:-

6 PACIFIC CARGO-LINERS OF 11,750 DWT

Vickers-Armstrong,Tyne   (4) PACIFIC RELIANCE,PACIFIC NORTHWEST, PACIFIC ENVOY,PACIFIC STRONGHOLD.

Blythswood SB,Glasgow   (1) PACIFIC FORTUNE.

Sir James Laing,Sunderland (1) PACIFIC UNITY.

The class was delivered over a ten-year period starting with PACIFIC FORTUNE and PACIFIC UNITY in 1948. PACIFIC RELIANCE entered service in December,1951 and the standard types had all been sold off or transferred to Prince Line by the time the next - PACIFIC NORTHWEST - was completed in 1954. PACIFIC ENVOY and PACIFIC STRONGHOLD were the last pair completed on the Tyne in April and July,1958 and although very similar to the first pair could be distinguished by their six sets of kingposts as against the topmasts fitted to the 1948 pair. All had two complete 'tween decks, the lower of which was fully insulated for the carriage of between 132,000 - 162,000 cu ft of refrigerated fruit. From 1947, the Furness Pacific ships ran in conjunction with T.& J. Harrison service to the West Indies, resulting in a big increase in cargo planning and loading work. The original pair were sold off in 1964/65, but the other four were kept going until 1971 and the last trio completed were sold to N. Papalios of Piraeus and his Aegis Shipping Group.

The Transatlantic service of **Johnston-Warren Line** from Liverpool to St. John's(NF) was restarted in 1947/48 with two new sisters NOVA SCOTIA and NEWFOUNDLAND from the Vickers-Armstrong Ltd Walker Naval Yard in Newcastle, built to replace ships of the same name lost in the war. They were single-screw turbine vessels with a service speed of 15 knots and plenty of passenger accom- odation on three decks for 155 passengers. Four holds were served by ten derricks on two masts and a pair of posts in front of the bridge, the unbroken superstructure was built around no. 3 hatch which was trunked to the deck above. They were sold to the Dominion Navigation Co. Ltd(H.C. Sleigh),Liverpool in 1962/63 and renamed FRANCIS DRAKE and GEORGE ANSON respectively for Australian services. DROMORE was the only survivor on the Black Sea service, and she was joined by the purchased EMPIRE FAITH in 1946 to become JESSMORE, and the German prize LEVANTE to become

OAKMORE, and a 6000 dwt C1-M-AV1 type from war surplus U.S. fleets to become HEATHMORE.

The Johnston-Warren new replacements started to appear in 1950, being part of a six-ship order for the Group as a whole:-

6 MEDITERRANEAN CARGO-LINERS OF 4600 - 4900 DWT

Burntisland SB   (6) SYCAMORE,SCOTTISH PRINCE,EGYPTIAN PRINCE, BEECHMORE,PINEMORE,BLACK PRINCE.

SYCAMORE was completed first for Johnston-Warren in February,1950 with a capacity for 4625 dwt of cargo and accom- odation for 12 passengers. The second ship completed in November, 1950 but was taken on charter by Shaw,Savill & Albion Co. Ltd for five years as AFRIC for a new cargo service between Mombasa, Durban,Cape Town and Australian ports. The third joined Prince Line in January,1951 as EGYPTIAN PRINCE and the next pair joined Johnston-Warren in October,1954 and June,1955 as BEECHMORE and PINEMORE. BLACK PRINCE completed the sextet in March,1955. Except for SYCAMORE they had 4-cylinder oil engines manufactured by Hawthorn,Leslie & Co. Ltd at their Newcastle engine plant and the ships were towed down the East coast to the Tyne for their insta- llation. SYCAMORE,BEECHMORE and PINEMORE finally joined the Prince Line fleet in 1965 as MERCHANT PRINCE,ENGLISH PRINCE and AFRICAN PRINCE respectively.

The Johnston-Warren Line Black Sea services described above were terminated in 1969/70 and the vessels sold off, this left Johnston-Warren with a pair of 7500 dwt Burntisland-built sisters of 1964/65 - NEWFOUNDLAND and NOVA SCOTIA - on the Transatlantic service. They had engines placed in the three quarters-aft pos- ition and were fitted with three deck cranes and two sets of posts. They were twice chartered because of their refrigertated capacity by Shaw,Savill & Albion Co. Ltd - renamed CUFIC and TROPIC - and joined another similar Johnston-Warren Liner of 1959 which had always been on charter to Shaw,Savill as MYSTIC. MYSTIC was sold off after the Beeching axe of November,1970.

The Transatlantic service of **Cairn Line** from Newcastle and Leith was left with only two survivors from the war: CAIRNVALONA of 1918 and CAIRNESK of 1926. The standard type EMPIRE SNOW with her war-economy transom stern was then purchased in 1946 and renamed CAIRNAVON. The post-war Cairn Line rebuilding programme consisted of three ships:-

3 CAIRN LINE CARGO-LINERS OF 9400 - 10700 DWT

W. Gray,Hartlepool   (2) CAIRNGOWAN,CAIRNDHU.

Burntisland SB   (1) CAIRNFORTH.

CAIRNGOWAN was the fourth ship of that name to enter service when completed in May,1952, as was her sister CAIRNDHU when she joined in September,1952. They were single-screw vessels powered by three Parsons Marine double reduction turbines taking steam from two oil-fired water tube boilers of the Babcock & Wilcox type. The whole engine installation was carried out by the builders Central Marine Engine Works at Hartlepool. CAIRNFORTH was larger when completed in November,1958 at Burntisland and she was given a 4-cylinder Doxford oil engine manufactured in New-castle by Hawthorn,Leslie & Co. Ltd. All three were chartered into the Manchester Liners fleet in 1965, but the sisters return-ed in 1966 to resume their original names whereas CAIRNFORTH did not resume hers in 1969 when she came off charter, being trans-ferred to Royal Mail instead to become their LOMBARDY.

Manchester Liners Ltd fared slightly better being left with 8 ships from the war holocaust:-

MANCHESTER DIVISION of 1918	MANCHESTER CITY of 1937
MANCHESTER EXPORTER of 1918	MANCHESTER PROGRESS of 1938
MANCHESTER COMMERCE of 1925	MANCHESTER TRADER of 1941
MANCHESTER PORT of 1935	MANCHESTER SHIPPER of 1943

MANCHESTER EXPORTER was sold in January,1947 a month before the first of the post-war replacements:-

4 MANCHESTER CARGO-LINERS OF 9,500 DWT

Blythswood SB   (2) MANCHESTER REGIMENT,MANCHESTER MERCHANT

Cammell Laird   (2) MANCHESTER SPINNER,MANCHESTER MARINER

MANCHESTER REGIMENT had been launched by the wife of the Colonel of the Manchester Regiment on 16th October,1946. She was powered by the same machinery that had been used for all Manchester Liners since MANCHESTER PORT of 1935 - three steam turbines single reduction geared to a single screw. MANCHESTER MERCHANT joined in 1951, MANCHESTER SPINNER in 1952 and MANCH-ESTER MARINER in 1955; but the decision to enter the Great Lakes trade down the length of Lake Ontario to Toronto had been taken earlier in 1950. Two four-hold engines amidships ships were specially designed for this service, and after leaving the builders yard at Birkenhead in 1952 MANCHESTER PIONEER and MANCHESTER EXPLORER were the first British ships to trade on Lake Ontario. They were subsequently joined by a purchased Norwegian ship in 1953 - renamed MANCHESTER PROSPECTOR - and by two engines-aft German-built ships in 1956, MANCHESTER VANGUARD and MANCHESTER VENTURE. The idea of a service linking one inland port to another caught the imagination of Canadian businessmen and the service prospered.

Two further engines-aft Manchester Liners were completed on the Wear in 1959 - MANCHESTER FAITH and MANCHESTER FAME. The

FAITH was first completed in March,1959, and achieved fame by
beating a large crowd of ships waiting to enter the new St.
Lawrence Seaway. Prior to the official opening of the Seaway the
master of MANCHESTER FAITH had brought his ship alongside a small
passenger vessel on board which was Kenneth Stoker, Chairman of
Manchester Liners and son of Robert B. Stoker - Ship Director of
Furness,Withy & Co. Ltd when Christopher Furness set up the
company in 1891. Also on board was the Chairman of Canadian
Pacific Steamships who was so impressed by MANCHESTER FAITH that
he ordered some sisterships. The MANCHESTER sisters were also
designed to participate in the fruit trade from the Canary
Islands or Mediterranean in winter. Tanks with special epoxy-
linings were fitted to carry edible oils and lard. The export
grain trade from the Prairies to Chicago and Milwaukee and other
inland Lakes ports and then via deep-sea ships such as those
operated by Manchester Liners Ltd was then developed after the
opening of the St. Lawrence Seaway.

The passenger services of **Shaw,Savill & Albion Co. Ltd** were
separated from the cargo service by the arrival of the new
engines-aft passenger-only SOUTHERN CROSS in March,1955 to run
alongside DOMINION MONARCH in a new 'Round the World' service.
SOUTHERN CROSS had been launched by the Queen on 17th August,1954
and had accomodation for 1160 tourist-class passengers with a
crew of 410 and was scheduled to make four voyages/year - two
westbound and two eastbound at her service speed of 20 knots. Her
spacious decks and grey hull with eau-de-nil colour superstructure soon made her a favourite with passengers. When DOMINION
MONARCH was pensioned off in 1962, she was replaced by a larger
but similar sister to SOUTHERN CROSS - continuing the stellar
names she was christened NORTHERN STAR at her launch at Walker
Naval Yard,Newcastle by Queen Elizabeth the Queen Mother on 27th
June,1961. NORTHERN STAR had accomodation for 1436 tourist-class
passengers, and was scheduled to pass her earlier sister at sea
twice a year.

The advent of the container on American services in 1956 did
not prevent Shaw,Savill & Albion Co. Ltd bringing new conventional break-bulk cargo-liners into their fleet. The 'A' class of
five smaller German-built ships had been completed between 1957
and 1960:-

5 NEW ZEALAND CARGO-LINERS OF 9400 DWT

Bremer Vulcan,Vegesack   (5) ARABIC,AFRIC,ARAMAIC,ALARIC,
                               AMALRIC.

All the holds of the 'A' class were non-refrigerated and
three were forward of the squat funnel and two aft, and there
were deep tanks for the carriage of edible oils(tallow),vegetable
oil,dry cargo or water ballast were fitted on either side of the
shaft tunnel below no. 4 hold. There were 16 derricks of 3- or

10-ton capacity with a 70-tonner on the foremast and a 25-tonner
on the mainmast. German-built 9-cylinder M.A.N. oil engines were
easier to specify for installation at Vegesack to give a service
speed of 17 knots. AMALRIC was completed in November,1960 with
three holds forward of the superstructure and one aft, and
LAURENTIC and ZEALANDIC completed in 1965 by Alexander Stephen &
Sons at Glasgow were based on this design although fitted with
Stulcken heavy-lift masts. ARABIC,AFRIC and ARAMAIC were
transferred to South American routes in 1968, becoming OROYA,
ORITA and OROPESA of P.S.N.C. with ARABIC and ARAMAIC being
briefly used on the Furness Pacific service as PACIFIC RANGER and
PACIFIC EXPORTER in 1970.

Four larger cargo-liners of the 'I' class were completed between
1959 and 1961:-

4 NEW ZEALAND CARGO-LINERS OF 14,000 DWT

Cammell,Laird,Birkenhead (1) IONIC.

Vickers-Armstrong,Tyne   (1) ILLYRIC.

Harland & Wolff,Belfast   (1) ICENIC.

A. Stephen,Glasgow   (1) IBERIC.

They had long bridge-structures although carried no passengers and had large,pear-shaped funnels. The six holds were
served by 22-ton derricks with a 50-tonner on the foremast and a
25-tonner on the mainmast. They were powered by a single turbo-
charged 8-cylinder B&W oil engine manufactured by Harland & Wolff
Ltd at Belfast to give a service speed of 17 knots. The four 'I'
class cost £10M and originally had black hulls before adopting
the grey of the six-hold MEGANTIC and MEDIC, completed by Swan,
Hunter at Wallsend in 1963. This pair differed by having an extended fo'c'stle taking in no. 1 hatchway, and the bridge deck
amidships was extended aft to combine with the poop and form an
extra 'tween deck. Two edible oil tanks were fitted for the
carriage of 450 tons of tallow, and the 7-cylinder B&W - H&W oil
engine was uprated to give a service speed of 18 knots.

Sir Ernest H. Murrant retired as Chairman of Furness,Withy &
Co. Ltd on 31st March,1959 after a career with the company of 57
years, having joined as an office boy in 1902. He was succeeded
as Chairman by Frank Charlton, and then by Sir Errington Keville
from 1st August,1962. Sir Errington had been made a Director of
Shaw,Savill & Albion Co. Ltd in 1941 at the age of 40 years
rising to become Deputy Chairman. He joined the Board of Furness,
Withy & Co. Ltd in 1950 and was knighted in the same year of 1962
as his appointment as Chairman. He served in this capacity until
1968 and was also Chairman of the General Council of British
Shipping in 1961.

However, the event that was to change completely British
liner shipping occurred in 1965 when **Overseas Containers Ltd**
(O.C.L.) was formed by Furness,Withy & Co. Ltd, Ocean Steamship
Co. Ltd(Blue Funnel),British & Commonwealth Shipping Co. Ltd(Clan
Line and Union Castle Line) and P.& O. Ltd. The first O.C.L.
service was between U.K. and Australia, and six ships capable of
carrying 1130 containers were ordered to enter service in 1969. A
19-acre terminal was readied at Tilbury and ports of call were to
be Fremantle,Melbourne and Sydney with feeder services to
Tasmania and other Australian ports. The cost of the six ships,
construction of terminal facilities, purchase of containers was
in excess of £42M. Things would never be the same again!

1.9 RATIONALISATION 1965 - 1980

The Group owned some 64 cargo-liners in 1965 on the world-
wide services of Manchester Liners,Cairn Line,Furness Pacific,
Johnston-Warren Line,Prince Line and Shaw,Savill & Albion Co.
Ltd. To this large total were added a further 28 cargo-liners on
the West Indian,Pacific Coast U.S.A./Canada and East & West coast
of South America of **Royal Mail Line and Pacific Steam Navigation
Co. Ltd.** An offer of purchase by Furness,Withy & Co. Ltd was
accepted by Royal Mail Line of the remaining majority of their
shares, a fair-sized holding having been taken in 1937. Pacific
Steam Navigation Co. Ltd had been acquired by Royal Mail Line in
October,1938 but the Liverpool staffs were kept separate although
a single Board had been created.

An 'umbrella' management company was created in 1965 - **Furness
Ship Management Ltd** - to manage Furness,Withy; Johnston-Warren ;
Prince Line; P.S.N.C., and Royal Mail although still spread between
Liverpool,Manchester and London. Manchester Liners was managed
independently from Manchester;Cairn Line was managed from Newcastle
and Shaw,Savill & Albion Co. Ltd from London, also independently.

The Transatlantic service of Manchester Liners Ltd was the
first to be containerised in the Group, with the arrival on
service of the 12039 grt MANCHESTER CHALLENGE in November,1968
between the container terminals at Manchester and Montreal. She
had a total capacity of 500 containers of 20 feet length, with
the majority in her cellular guides below deck and the rest on
deck where some 40 feet containers could also be handled. She was
one of a class of four:-

4 MANCHESTER CONTAINER SHIPS OF 12,000 DWT

Smiths Dock,M'bro   (4) MANCHESTER CHALLENGE,MANCHESTER COURAGE,
                         MANCHESTER CONCORDE,MANCHESTER CRUSADE.

The COURAGE and the CONCORDE joined the service in 1969 with
the CRUSADE following up in 1971. The CHALLENGE and the COURAGE

served for 10 years before being sold off to Hong Kong owners,
and the other pair served until 1982. The conventional MANCHESTER
MILLER of 1959 and MANCHESTER PROGRESS were converted to cellular
container ships in 1970/71 by Smiths Dock Co. Ltd at Middlesbrough when the last of the break-bulk cargo-liners, some less
than five years old, were sold off as redundant.

Next to enter service were the OCL container ships on
the Australia/New Zealand service during 1969:-

6 AUSTRALIA/NEW ZEALAND CONTAINER SHIPS OF 29100 DWT

Howaldtswerke,Kiel   (4) BOTANY BAY,DISCOVERY BAY,
                                 ENCOUNTER BAY,FLINDERS BAY.

Blohm & Voss,Hamburg (1) MORETON BAY.

Upper Clyde SB   (1) JERVIS BAY.

      BOTANY BAY was owned by Furness,Withy & Co. Ltd and
JERVIS BAY by Shaw,Savill & Albion Co. Ltd. P & O owned DISCOVERY
BAY and MORETON BAY, Ocean(Blue Funnel) owned FLINDERS BAY, and
British & Commonwealth owned ENCOUNTER BAY through their Australian trade subsidiary of Scottish Shire Line. JERVIS BAY of Shaw,
Savill was launched on 3rd May,1969 at Glasgow and like all her
sisters measured 746 feet in length overall with a breadth of 100
feet and a tonnage of 26876 grt. Two Swedish manufactured Stal-
Laval geared turbines give her a service speed of 22 knots with
all her 1530 TEU (20 foot equivalent units) container capacity
utilised of which 304 TEU were refrigerated for the meat trade. A
green hull and a black funnel carrying the OCL logo completed
their bulky,business-like appearance. The containers were stacked
six high, four below deck and two above and later 40 foot
containers were carried. A crew of 35 to 40 was carried on the
fortnightly service with anticipated turn-rounds of 48 hours
and when all were operational the service increased to a
sailing every 10 days.

      It was obvious a complementary break-bulk service would
also be needed into the early 1970s to allow users to become
accustomed to the packing and unpacking of containers. However
with a very large fleet of cargo-liners at their disposal it is
difficult to justify the ordering of the 13680 dwt sisters MAJ-
ESTIC and BRITANNIC - the latter was completed in December,1967 -
when some 9180 TEU of container capacity was also on order. The
axe was thus even heavier when it finally fell on 23 break-bulk
cargo-liners owned by the Group in November,1970.

      The **Passenger Services** run by the Group in 1965 were
also to undergo severe rationalisation followed by total extinct-
ion by the end of 1975. The take-over of Royal Mail Line in 1965

brought into the fold the much-loved and well-patronised cruise liner ANDES of 1939. She had been launched on 7th March,1939 at the Harland & Wolff yard at Belfast as their flagship for the Southampton - Rio de Janeiro - Buenos Aires service, but was not able to take a centenary sailing of the founding of the company on 26th September,1939 due to the war, and instead proceeded to Liverpool in her peace-time colours for conversion into a troop-ship. After distinguished service which included carrying the Norwegian Government in exile back to Oslo in May,1945 she was reconditioned at Belfast during 1946/47. She finally took her first commercial sailing on her intended route on 22nd January, 1948 with accomodation for 528 passengers. She was sent for rebuilding as a cruise liner to the De Schelde yard at Flushing in 1959 and entered cruising on 10th June,1960 with accomodation for 480 passengers in one class. She sailed on her final cruise in April,1971 and arrived back at Southampton on 3rd May flying a paying-off pennant nearly 100 feet long - a yard for every year of her 31 years of service. Her total mileage as troopship, mail express and cruise liner came to 2.75 million miles and had taken her to every part of the world. After a turn-round at Southampton of 48 hours she sailed for the breakers torch at Ghent.

However three other Royal Mail passenger/cargo liners of 20300 grt with a history of unprofitability were also brought into the Group. AMAZON,ARAGON and ARLANZA had been introduced on to the London - Rio de Janeiro - Buenos Aires service in 1960 at a cost of £12.6M, and were then transferred to Shaw,Savill routes to Australia/New Zealand in 1968. Since Shaw,Savill had abandoned the concept of the mixed passenger/cargo-liner in the 1950s there was no way the trio could make a profit; why they were trans-erred remains a mystery of Group decision making. Renamed AKAROA, ARANDA and ARAWA respectively, financial common sense finally returned in the cuts of November,1970 and the three 'white elephants' were sold off to Norwegian owners for conversion into car carriers.

The New York - Bermuda holiday trade of QUEEN OF BERMUDA and OCEAN MONARCH had been a very profitable one, and the 'QUEEN' had been sent to the Harland & Wolff yard at Belfast in October, 1961 for modernisation. She was then reconstructed with a new bow, given new air-conditioning and new boilers and a single modern funnel to replace her three existing ones. She resumed the Bermuda service alongside OCEAN MONARCH in April,1962 but was retired four and a half years later and arrived at Faslane on 6th December,1966 for scrapping. OCEAN MONARCH was also laid-up at the same time on 22nd September,1966 on the Fal when the Group pulled out of the Bermuda trade. She found a buyer in August,1967 as a cruise liner for the Bulgarian Balkanturist and was renamed VARNA for Eastern Mediterranean cruises. She finally met her end on 28th May,1981 when gutted by fire off Ambelaki while awaiting modifications for the summer season. The fire had started in her boiler room but soon destroyed her superstructure and she capsized on her side on 1st June,1981 off Kynosoura.

The Round-the-World passenger service of Shaw,Savill & Albion Co. Ltd taken by the near-sisters SOUTHERN CROSS and NORTHERN STAR did not begin to feel the overwhelming competition of the long-haul jet aircraft until the late 1960s. This was reflected in the seven-cruise programme of NORTHERN STAR from Southampton in the summer of 1969, while SOUTHERN CROSS was chartered for a cruise to Tokyo that year from Australia. SOUTHERN CROSS had been designed in the early 1950s and her air-conditioning was primitive with toilets,baths and showers in communal ladies and gents RAF-style ablutions; and it was obvious if the Group were to seriously attack the U.K. cruise market total air-conditioning and en-suite facilities were needed. It was decided to purchase the Tyne-built EMPRESS OF ENGLAND from Canadian Pacific Steamships for £5M and convert her to a cruise ship instead. She was renamed OCEAN MONARCH and sailed on 11th April,1970 for one voyage to South Africa and Australia before making a 38-day cruise to Japan in connection with EXPO-70. She was then sent for a £4M conversion into a cruise ship at the Cammell,Laird yard at Birkenhead on return. Her cargo holds were removed and all her cabins for 1372 passengers were updated during the 12-month refit and she arrived back at Southampton on 19th September,1971.

All three Shaw,Savill passenger liners were marketed during the last quarter of 1971 under the Shaw Savill Sea Spectaculars banner, but SOUTHERN CROSS was withdrawn from service in early 1972 at Southampton. She was sent to the Fal for lay-up before finding a buyer willing to convert her into a cruise liner. This was carried out at Piraeus where her cabins were refurnished, carpeted and fitted with private bath and toilet facilities. Re-named CALYPSO she became a very popular cruise ship, a role she continues to play up to the present day. While a certain amount of market share of the U.K. cruise market was won by NORTHERN STAR and OCEAN MONARCH, the latter sailed out of Sydney on Pacific cruising during the whole of 1973, and the boilers of NORTHERN STAR began to malfunction with a cruise in June,1974 aborted at Tunis and her passengers flown home at great expense. It fell to Lord Beeching of British Rail fame and Group Chairman since 1st September,1972 to perform another of his famous axes and chop the Group cruise operation in 1975, reflecting:-

'Ships such as NORTHERN STAR and OCEAN MONARCH inspire a strong sentimental attachment and I am sure many of our share-holders will regret their passing just as we do. Nevertheless, it must be said that from a financial point of view their disposal gives rise to nothing but a sigh of relief. They have become a loss-making worry and there could be no surer way of improving the profitability of Shaw,Savill than by withdrawing them'

OCEAN MONARCH sailed from Southampton in June,1975 to the breakers at Kaohsiung, followed by NORTHERN STAR in November. Lord Beeching had succeeded John MacConochie as Chairman, and in turn was succeeded as Chairman in 1975 by Sir James Steel, the Lord Lieuteneant of Tyne & Wear. Sir James had spent many years

in control of his Sunderland-based family iron and steel business
- Steel Group Ltd - and had been knighted in 1967.

The mass sale of cargo-liners in November,1970 was followed
by the transfer of similar ships to routes that had not been containerised e.g. three 'C' class of Shaw,Savill were transferred
in 1972 to Royal Mail Line and used on the Plate meat trade. OCL
and ACT container ships displaced Shaw,Savill conventional cargo-
liners first out of Australia and then out of New Zealand. In the
ensuing trade redistribution the N.Z.S.C. was allocated the New
Zealand to Far East route; Blue Star from West Coast U.S.A. to
New Zealand and Shaw,Savill the New Zealand to West Indies route.
CEDRIC made two voyages on this route in 1974/75, and the Johnston-Warren sisters NEWFOUNDLAND and NOVA SCOTIA of 1964/65 were
chartered again as CUFIC and TROPIC for the route in 1975/76. Two
Danish-owned reefers fitted with deck guides for good container-
carrying capability on deck had been purchased and renamed LIMPS-
FIELD and MAYFIELD in 1973, having previously been on charter to
the company. This pair were then sent for conversion into full
container ships by Smiths Dock Co. Ltd at North Shields in 1976
in readiness to start a full container service between U.S.
Gulf/West Indies to New Zealand in November,1976; LIMPSFIELD
emerged with the less embarassing name of LINDFIELD.   The last
conventional break-bulk sailing from London to New Zealand was
taken by LAURENTIC of 1965 on 29th April,1977.

Shaw,Savill & Albion Co. Ltd then combined with Bank Line
from 1st January,1978 to form Bank & Savill Ltd for the Australia
and New Zealand to the West Indies/U.S. Gulf. MAYFIELD and LIND-
FIELD, each with their 260 container capacity of which 158 were
refrigerated, plus other chartered-in tonnage handled this until
two new fully containerised ships of 762 TEU capacity were ready
from North East Coast yards in 1980 - DUNEDIN and WILLOWBANK -
fine purpose-built container ships with cellular guides and 358 of
their containers were refrigerated.   There were seven holds, five
forward of the machinery space and two aft; and nos. 2,3,4 and 5
had cellular guides for 20-foot containers, while No. 6 hold had
portable guides to switch between 20-foot and 40-foot containers.
The remaining holds, nos 1 and 7, could handle containers, and
palletised or break-bulk cargoes as required. DUNEDIN was the last
ship launched at the famous Walker Naval Yard at Newcastle on 15th
February,1980, and she attained a speed of 20.8 knots on trials in
June,1980 from a 6-cylinder 2SCSA B&W type oil engine built by
Harland & Wolff Ltd,Belfast. A crew of 29 was carried each with a
single-berth cabin and shower/W.C. WILLOWBANK was launched into
the Tees four days later on 19th February at South Bank and was
accepted into service on 16th July,1980. A German-built container
ship of similar size was completed for The Shipping Corporation of
New Zealand Ltd as NEW ZEALAND CARIBBEAN for the same service at
this time. Calls were made at Melbourne, Sydney,Lyttelton,New
Plymouth and then on through Panama to Puerto Cabello
(Venezuela),Port of Spain,Bridgetown,Fort France (Martinique),
Kingston(Jamaica),Vera Cruz,Houston and New Orleans.

Following the acquisition of **Royal Mail Line and Pacific Steam Navigation Company** in 1965 the Group began a policy of re-appraising American routes and tonnage. In 1968 the Royal Mail route to West Coast U.S.A./Canada was merged with the Furness, Withy one and PACIFIC ENVOY of 1958 became LOCH RYAN. She re-gained her name in 1970 when LOCH GOWAN of Royal Mail was sold for scrap. Two former Shaw,Savill ships, ARABIC and ARAMAIC,were transferred to this route and took the traditional names of PACIFIC RANGER and PACIFIC EXPORTER respectively. However they were transferred back to South American routes in 1970 when the service was abandoned at the end of 1970, and the remaining Furness,Withy PACIFIC class of the 1950s together with LOCH LOYAL of Royal Mail were sold off to Papalios of Piraeus and his Aegis Group.

The traditional break-bulk cargo-liner services of Royal Mail to the West Indies/Venezuela and the East Coast of South America plus those of Pacific Steam Navigation Company to the West Coast of South America were ripe for rationalisation. Heavy competition with Continental shipping companies together with unsettled political conditions throughout South America made this imperative. By 1971/72 the last of the Royal Mail post-WWII cargo-liners had been sold off and a consortium formed to operate the Central American services, with the East Coast Brazil/Plate service taken by three aging Shaw,Savill 'C' class transferred to Royal Mail - and complementary to the Houlder Line service to the Plate. The P.S.N.C. through service to the West Coast via the West Indies was then modernised. POTOSI and COTOPAXI had been built to a Clan Line design in the 1950s, and were the last of the conventional West Coast cargo-liners to be sold off in 1972 leaving only ORCOMA of 1966 on service. This was in readiness for the entry into service in 1973 of the first of three new sisters with hold container capability and fitted with deck guides for deck container handling - ORBITA,ORDUNA,ORTEGA. They had four holds with one behind the superstructure and were fitted with Vele swinging derricks to handle the 300 containers of 20 foot length. They had unmanned engine room operation and 8-cylinder 2SCSA B&W type oil engines by J.G. Kincaid of Greenock gave 18 knots service speed. A monthly service had been envisaged but soon capacity voyages were being realised and a three week service was instituted together with chartered-in semi-container tonnage. ORBITA was sold in April,1980 to the Chilean company of Cia Sud Americana de Vapores, Valparaiso; ORDUNA was renamed BEACON GRANGE at the end of September,1982 and was sold to Cenargo Ltd in 1984 for Falkland Islands services; ORTEGA was given the traditional Royal Mail name of ANDES in April,1980 and sold off in August,1982.

Two further engines-aft semi-containerships were completed for the route in 1978 - OROYA and OROPESA - with a capacity of 536 containers of 20 foot length loaded through nine hatches into five holds as well as stacked on deck. Nine sets of electric derrick cranes were fitted, eight of 22 tons capacity and of 100 tons capacity to serve nos. 3 and 4 hatches which were each 63

feet long. The weather and 'tween deck hatch covers were electro-
hydraulic folding - all at the touch of a button. A crew of 41
each had single-berth cabins with private shower/W.C. and there
was a swimming pool,gymnasium and hobbies room. OROPESA was sold
on 25th May,1984 to Cenargo Ltd for Falklands Islands services as
MERCHANT PRINCIPAL; and OROYA was handed over to the Nigerian
Green Line at Hamburg on 9th September,1986 to become their YINKA
FOLAWAYO but has since joined her sister in the Cenargo fleet as
MERCHANT PREMIER.

Exactly 100 years after Christopher Furness had placed his
first order for two small steamers for his Transatlantic trade
the Group formed a fully-integrated management company - **Furness,**
Withy(Shipping) Ltd - on 12th July,1977. In truth,however, there
was very little liner shipping left to manage. Two large container ships, BOTANY BAY and JERVIS BAY, plied the container route to
Australia/New Zealand; five container ships plied between Manchester and Montreal; plus three semi-container ships to the West
coast of South America, ORBITA,ORDUNA and ORTEGA. Two short-sea
traders were on charter to Prince Line for service to Malta and
the Eastern Mediterranean;two cargo-liners built for the Johnson-
Warren Transatlantic trade, NOVA SCOTIA and NEWFOUNDLAND, had
twice been on charter to Shaw,Savill & Albion Co. Ltd as TROPIC
and CUFIC respectively and were near the end of their careers
with the Group. NEWFOUNDLAND was sold later in 1977, and NOVA
SCOTIA went to Booker Line in 1978.

One interesting venture was the introduction of three
engines-aft multi-purpose 9200 dwt ships for operation in South
East Asia and Australian waters. ROEBUCK was completed at the
Pusan yard of Dae Sun SB & Eng. Co. Ltd,Korea in late 1976 for a
new Group company - **Dee Navigation** - and was named after the ship
which took the explorer Capt. William Dampier along the northern
coast of Australia in 1699. Two further sisters, RIVERINA and
RAVENSWOOD, completed the trio with their green funnels with a
black top and a central white band and they had four holds served
by four swinging Vele derricks. A Series III 'SD14' from the
Southwick, Sunderland home of Austin & Pickersgill Ltd was
launched on 28th February,1979 for Shaw,Savill but took a Royal
Mail name DERWENT and wore their colours of yellow funnel with a
black top. DERWENT and the three Dee Navigation sisters had all
been sold by 1982.

As the past master in the art of the takeover, Furness,
Withy(Shipping) Ltd was in for some of the same treatment itself
over the next decade - twice being purchased outright!

1.10 NEW OWNERS

On the evening of 13th February,1980 Furness,Withy(Shipping) Ltd received a takeover bid from one of the most powerful shipping men in the world - C.Y. Tung of Hong Kong. He offered £4.20/share through his Kenwake Holdings Ltd, a wholly-owned subsidiary of the gigantic world-wide container company **Orient Overseas Containers (Holdings) Ltd.** This offer was accepted by the Furness Board on 17th March,1980 having received assurances that the Group would retain its British character and management, with vessels sailing under the British flag and manned by British officers and crews.

Chao Yung Tung was in his late 60s at the time of the offer, and was small in stature but big on the world shipping scene. He had been born at Shanghai before WWI and had started his career in coastal shipping, and by the age of 24 years was vice-president of the Tientsin Shipowners Association. After the wreckage of WWII he moved to Hong Kong to rebuild his fleet with one 10,000 dwt ship. In 1954 he purchased FORDSDALE of 1924, completed at Sydney(NSW) for the Commonwealth Government Line,Australia and subsequently taken over by Shaw,Savill & Albion Co. Ltd., keeping her for five years before sending her for scrap to Osaka. By 1972 he controlled a massive fleet of 71 large bulkers and tankers including VLCCs and one container ship - ORIENTAL EXPRESS - plus the largest liner in the world SEAWISE (C.Y.'s) UNIVERSITY, the former Cunard QUEEN ELIZABETH and subsequently destroyed by fire in Hong Kong harbour later that year. The container operation was then developed into one of the largest in the world - Orient Overseas Container Line - with a fast Europe/Far East route and a Middle East service; a stake in a Far East/Australia consortium through OOCL; and a third ownership of the DART Container Line. In the mid-1970s he handed over the day-to-day running of the business to his sons C.H. Tung and C.C. Tung, his eldest son C.H. Tung handling the subsequent negotiations with Furness,Withy (Shipping) Ltd.

John E. Keville as Chief Executive of Furness,Withy(Shipping) Ltd and Sir Brian Shaw, Chairman of the Group, looked forward to working in a much larger Group with world-wide interests and potential. However with hindsight the Tung dynasty can best be summed up as a clinical dissection of the Furness Group in the face of ever falling freight rates. Those parts that proved useful and complementary to Tung operations e.g. the new Manchester Liners container ships were transferred into his OOCL operation, whereas those parts that were unprofitable were ruthlessly cut. The Tung Group was backed with unlimited money via the Hong Kong & Shanghai Bank, and subjected the Group to a most concentrated assault from which it was lucky to survive. Sir Brian Shaw had been trained as a lawyer and then joined Pacific Steam Navigation Company in 1957, becoming their company secretary in 1960 and was made a director of Furness,Withy & Co. Ltd in 1973 and Managing Director in 1977 and then Chairman in 1979. John E. Keville had joined from the Houlder side and his career is given in Chapter 2.

DART Container Line had been established in the late 1960s as an international grouping of the interests of the Bristol City Line, Compagnie Maritime Belge(Lloyd Royal) SA,Antwerp and Clarke Traffic Services Ltd,Montreal. Three sisters of 1535 TEU capacity had been completed in the following year: DART ATLANTIC, DART AMERICA and DART EUROPE with the first two from the Walker Naval Yard of Swan Hunter Shipbuilders Ltd and the last from the Cockerill yard in Hoboken. Bristol City Line had subsequently been taken over by Bibby Line of Liverpool, and the Canadian Clarke interests had been purchased by C.Y. Tung with the similar sized DART CANADA of 1978 managed through his Hong Kong office.

In the early 1980s a dramatic freight rate-cutting battle was in progress between the Eurocanadian CAST Group and its large bulker/container operation and the more established 'big three' North Atlantic container operators: Furness,Withy(Shipping) Ltd via Manchester Liners Ltd, DART Container Line, and Canadian Pacific. Eurocanadian CAST had designs on taking over Manchester Liners and/or Furness,Withy(Shipping) Ltd before the Tung bid,and had a 37.6% ordinary shareholding in Manchester Liners Ltd, which was then purchased by C.Y. Tung after his Furness bid had been accepted. Eurocanadian CAST then used this money to purchase seven OBOs, and placed orders with Korean and Yugoslavian yards for two OBOs and six container/bulk ships of 1500 TEU to expand their container fleet. Cut-throat rate cutting by Eurocanadian CAST and their breakaway management company Sofati Line forced the 'big three' into long Board room meetings as to how best to handle this competitor in the long term. The solution of course was to band together, and in October,1981 a new co-ordinated weekly service from the Walton Container Terminal at Felixstowe to Montreal was started by MANCHESTER CHALLENGE, the former DART AMERICA; and CP AMBASSADOR, the former DART ATLANTIC; and CANADIAN EXPLORER, the former DART CANADA; and DART EUROPE.

This meant the end of Manchester Liners Ltd usage of both Manchester Terminal and Greenock Terminal, and the setting up of an office at Felixstowe. The existing Manchester container ships were sold off with the 1977 pair of MANCHESTER VANGUARD and MANCHESTER VENTURE then switched to Tung services or put out on charter. After being ice-strengthened for winter operation the large DART ships established a weekly service each way between Hamburg,Antwerp,Felixstowe,Le Havre and Montreal. DART Container Line also ran a service into New York via Halifax(NS); the latter town naturally became worried about the effects of the new DART direct service with Canadian cargo into the St. Lawrence, and brought political pressure to bear on Canadian National Railways (CNR), which had a large shareholding in CAST. An option for CNR to increase its holding in CAST was turned down and they began distancing themselves from CAST. The result was that CAST went bankrupt in 1983, from which the receivers and banks managed to salvage CAST(1983) Ltd, which reached agreement with the 'big three' on freight rates.

In April,1982 C.Y. Tung died, but his policy of integrating and reducing the services of Royal Mail Line,Pacific Steam Navigation Company,Houlder Line and the Mediterranean services of Prince Line and Manchester Liners continued. In January,1982 Royal Mail as partners in the four-company STREAMLINE consortium from Liverpool to the Caribbean/East Coast Central America began ro-ro and multi-purpose services. Houlder Line and Royal Mail offered chartered slots in container ships plus conventional services to Brazil and the Plate. Pacific Steam Navigation Company was preparing for a fully-containerised through service to the Caribbean,Colombia(Pacific),Peru and Chile in 1984. ORDUNA of 1973 had been transferred to the Plate and renamed BEACON GRANGE and her two sisters had been sold; OROPESA of 1978 was sold on 25th May,1984 to Cenargo Ltd for Falklands Islands services leaving only her sister OROYA on the West Coast S. America. The giant 2145 TEU container ship ANDES entered service by sailing direct across the Pacific from the builders yard at Ulsan to load at Antofagasta, arriving on 17th May,1984. She had been built to operate as one of seven ships on the EUROSAL (Europe South America Line) service. A B&W type oil engine by the builder Hyundai gave her a service speed of 18.5 knots, and her enormous container capacity could be handled into her forward holds by a 40-ton gantry crane. She has six holds with no. 1 for dangerous cargoes, nos. 2,3,4 and 6 allowing bulk copper in the bottom with TEUs on top, and no. 5 hold is refrigerated for 254 TEUs for the carriage of bananas. All holds are strengthened for fork-lift truck operation. A bow thruster ensures continuous operation in port entry, and the gantry crane is used in S. American ports without container cranes. Single cabins with good facilities are provided for all 24 crew.

ANDES was completed some 700 tonnes short of her contracted dwt and this could not be corrected by the builder, thus the Group were compensated by Hyundai. Her sisters on the West Coast South America route are BO JOHNSON of the Axel Johnson Line of Sweden - later owned by Laser Line consortium of Nordstjernan Forvaltning A/B,Stockholm; NEDLLOYD CLEMENT and NEDLLOYD CLARENCE of the Nedlloyd Group of Rotterdam; HUMBOLDT EXPRESS of HAPAG of Germany; ISLA DE LA PLATA, the former CORDILLERA EXPRESS sold on completion in 1984 to Transportes Navieros Ecuadorianos(TRANSNAVE),Ecuador; and MAIPO of Compania Sud Americana de Vapores SA,Valparaiso. A further set of nine sisters was completed by Hyundai for the four member states of the United Arab Shipping Company fleets, to sail on other routes.

The Shaw,Savill container ship DUNEDIN arrived in the U.K. on 3rd April,1982 with a cargo of New Zealand refrigerated lamb to mark the centenary of the first such cargo. One hundred years before a ship of the same name had sailed east from New Zealand and rounded Cape Horn and arrived in the Thames on 24th May,1882 after a passage of 98 days. She had an early Hall refrigerating machine cooling some 140 tons of refrigerated cargo on board - 4460 sheep,449 lambs and 22 pigs. The container ship had 16,000 tons of cargo including 358 refrigerated containers holding some

145,000 carcasses and 9,000 cartons of meat and 5,000 cartons of
butter! In June,1984 the partnership between the Bank Line and
Shaw,Savill ended and DUNEDIN was then switched from the New
Zealand - West Indies service to Australia/New Zealand to Pacific
coast U.S.A. carrying Californian citrus produce to the Antipodes
on charter to New Zealand Shipping Corporation.

Since Manchester LIners Ltd was now 100% owned by Tung and
Furness,Withy(Shipping) Ltd, this was an opportunity to bring
together the Mediterranean services of Prince Line and Manchester
Liners Ltd. The entry of Manchester Liners into the Mediterranean
had been in 1968 when Prince Line decided to withdraw their Manchester services and were also thinking of closing the Mediterranean services, which operated from London. Manchester Liners
then purchased the Manchester loading agents of Prince Line -
Gough & Crosthwaite - and were given North West England loading
rights to the Mediterranean. Small ships were chartered to cream
off the trade from competitors, and following the closure of the
Johnston-Warren service to Greece and the Black Sea decided to
put in a regular service to Greece from Manchester - much to the
annoyance of their Furness colleagues - to assist the homeward
cargo from their Beirut trade. Competition with Ellerman began to
get too hot at the end of the 1970s, and they decided to co-oper-
ate and take business from other competitors instead of from each
other. Ellerman then fed Manchester Liners with cargo from Portugal, and by taking further trade from other foreign competitors
forced one of these out of business.

Thus in 1982 the Mediterranean services of Prince Line and
Manchester Liners were merged to become **Manchester-Prince Line.**
The Prince Line service had been operated since 1979 by two container ships of 288 TEU of which 50 were refrigerated - CROWN
PRINCE and ROYAL PRINCE. These had been completed at the Walker
Naval Yard of Swan Hunter Shipbuilders Ltd with Doxford oil
engines to give a service speed of 15 knots. They had an advanced
Loadmaster computer to allow forward planning and stowage of the
containers, which could be stacked three high on deck. In June,
1982 ROYAL PRINCE was involved in the rescue of British subjects
from war-torn Beirut, picking them up from the small port of
Jounieh to the North. Manchester-Prince Line through services
from Malta were then terminated at Piraeus and other ports until
the battles at Beirut subsided two months later.

In July,1983 a combined Mediterranean service was started by
Manchester-Prince/Ellerman/Zim Israel with a service from the
North-West ports of Ellesmere Port and Dublin, and another from
London. Ellerman and Zim Israel already operated from Ellesmere
Port but for Manchester Liners it was the sad end of all services
to the Port of Manchester. CROWN PRINCE was renamed MANCHESTER
CROWN and in addition to her sister ROYAL PRINCE - renamed CITY
OF OPORTO - the service used three of their Ellerman 4200 dwt
sisters plus Zim and chartered vessels. The two Prince Line
sisters were sold off in 1985 to Far East interests for service
on the 15-day container route between Bangkok and Hong Kong as

THAI AMBER and THAI JADE. The service continues to the present day with chartered German-owned Manchester-Prince container ships as well as Ellerman vessels.

The last Shaw,Savill ship, DUNEDIN, was sold in early 1986 to Hamburg-Sud D.G. and renamed MONTE PASCOAL for the East Coast South America trade. A prophetic sale if ever one could be found, but the reason for her sale can be found in the Group Annual Report to the end of 1986, where a deterioration in trading results was largely due to reduced cargo volumes in the liner trades and the corresponding decline in agency commission earnings; a severe downturn in offshore activities reflected by a collapse in the drilling and diving market following a steep fall in the price of oil in early,1986; plus problems resulting from the sale of the drilling rig SHELF DRILLER to a German company. Group profit after tax had slumped from £2.02M in 1982 to a loss of £1.17M in 1986 on turnover down from £255M to £183M.

Shipping had moved back into profit but had been dragged down by the collapse of the oil drilling market. The Houlder Offshore activities are outlined in Chapter 2. The ultimate Tung holding company was now Orient Overseas(Holdings) Ltd,Hong Kong - effective from 27th January,1987 - which successfully concluded a business and financial restructuring agreement dividing the Furness,Withy Group into two parts:-

1. FURNESS,WITHY(SHIPPING) LTD
Major shipping operations and container terminals plus stevedoring,freight forwarding etc.

2. FURNESS,WITHY(INVESTMENTS) LTD
Offshore support,drilling services,insurance broking and gas ship operations. This company was a former subsidiary of the Furness,Withy Group but which now became directly owned by OOHL. The seven Houlder offshore and drilling companies are outlined in Chapter 2.

In March,1987 the second of two gigantic 173,000 dwt ore-carriers for British Steel Corporation came into service under the management of the company. IRONBRIDGE is a sister of BRITISH STEEL, delivered by the same builder - Harland & Wolff Ltd at Belfast - in October,1984. This pair are the largest bulk-carriers ever built in Europe, and are fitted with a new type of fuel-efficient oil engine. The Group had previous experience of managing large ore-carriers for British Steel, having managed ABBEY of 118,000 dwt since 1979. Painted rust red and with blue funnels carrying the British Steel logo these leviathans make an impressive sight when fully loaded.

At the start of the decade on 1st January,1990 the Furness, Withy(Shipping) Ltd companies were:-

Furness,Withy & Co. Ltd
Furness,Withy(Chartering) Ltd

Furness,Withy(Terminals) Ltd
Furness,Withy(Australia) Pty Ltd
Furness,Withy(Agency) Ltd
Brantford International Ltd
Manchester Liners Ltd
DART Manchester Liners Ltd
Manchester Liners Containerline Ltd
Tynedale Shipping Co. Ltd
Coquet Shipping Co. Ltd
Walton Container Terminal Ltd,Felixstowe
Shipping Investment Trust Ltd
Pacific Steam Navigation Company Ltd
Prince Line Ltd
Gough & Crosthwaite Ltd - Container chartering
Golden Cross Line - Container chartering
Royal Mail Line   - Hotels
Shaw,Savill & Albion Co. Ltd - Warehousing

The new business interests of Royal Mail and Shaw,Savill & Albion Co. Ltd will bring a smile to the faces of the countless thousands of former serving seafarers of these two great British shipping companies.

On 17th October,1990 an offer by **Hamburg-Sud A.G.** of Germany of $130M for Kenwake Ltd - owner of Furness,Withy(Shipping) Ltd and subsidiary of Orient Overseas(Holdings) Ltd - was accepted by C.H. Tung. Hamburg-Sud is part of the Oetker Group involved in container operations from Northern Europe to the East Coast of South America and New Zealand; and from the Mediterranean to New Zealand. The fleet includes the new 33,000 dwt sisters CAP TRAF-ALGAR,CAP POLONIO and CAP FINISTERRE capable of carrying 1900 TEU of containers, plus the slightly smaller MONTE ROSA and MONTE CERVANTES - all five on East Coast South American services to Brazil and the Plate. The Columbus Round-the World operations and Deutsche Nah-Ost Line are also part of Hamburg-Sud, which also manages Europe Paraguay Line and Rotterdam-Zuid Amerika Lijn.

Horst Schomburg, Chairman of Hamburg-Sud, welcomed Furness, Withy(Shipping) Ltd into the Hamburg fold by recalling the equally long history of Hamburg-Sud since 1871 and their take-over by the Oetker Group in 1954. Hamburg-Sud and Furness,Withy (Shipping) Ltd are thus heavily involved in container operations to both the East and West coast of South America. Hamburg-Sud further strengthened its hold on the South American trade by the purchase in June,1991 of Laser Line from Nordstjernan Forvaltning A/B,Stockholm with six container ships including BO JOHNSON on the West Coast and ROSA BLANCA and ROSA TUCANO on the East Coast. Cost-cutting and the elimination of the duplication of agents in South American and Mediterranean ports will be the order of the day in the future. ANDES continues to trade on the West Coast service, but everything as always depends on a reasonable return from freight rates.

CHAPTER 2.

HOULDER LINE

Edwin Savory Houlder was the son of a Sussex landowner and commenced in business in 1853 as a ship and insurance broker and forwarding agent at the age of 25 years at 6, St. Benet's Place, Gracechurch Street,London EC3. It was not long before his brother Alfred joined him as Houlder Brothers & Company in 1856, trading from 146, Leadenhall Street. Together they then turned their attention to shipping, first by chartering tonnage such as the famous American clipper RED JACKET of 460 tons. Her cargo for Canvas Town - then the name of the camp settlement which later became Melbourne - was insufficient even for this small ship so a part-cargo was loaded for Port Jackson - now Sydney(NSW). The outbreak of the American Civil War in 1861 was the brothers' opportunity to enter shipowning,as many American owners preferred to sell their ships in Europe rather than continue to trade them in the hazardous conditions of war. GOLDEN HORN,GOLDEN CITY and EAGLE SPEED were purchased in 1861 while the GOLDEN SUNSET, GOLDEN CLOUD and GOLDEN FLEECE were chartered. EMPRESS and LUCIBELLE and GLENDOWER were purchased in 1863, followed by their largest sailing ship ever - GOLDEN SEA of 1418 gross tons - completed by Oliver of Quebec in July,1864 for American owners and purchased by Houlder Brothers & Co. in 1865. Another Houlder brother - Augustus Frederick joined the business as a partner in 1867.

2.1 AUSTRALIAN TRADE

These sailing ships established a fortnightly service from London to Port Phillip near Melbourne using a combination of owned and chartered ships leaving on the 11th and 25th of each month; a similar service left on 7th and 21st of each month for Newcastle(NSW),Twofold Bay,Queensland and New Zealand. Passenger fares to Sydney(NSW) were 50 guineas, and 60 guineas to New Zealand, providing you 'brought your own bed,lamp,cutlery,cups, plates,saucers,water can and washing basin'!

Normally these sailing ships carried between 35 and 40 saloon and cabin passengers, but occasionally carried many more e.g. troops and coolies. EMPRESS carried 305 Officers and men to New Zealand in 1863; GOLDEN CITY 103 passengers in 1863 to Auckland from London; EAGLE SPEED 354 passengers from Liverpool to Melbourne in 1857 and 191 passengers from London to Auckland in 1864, and had 300 coolies on board when lost in 1865. GOLDEN SEA carried 478 Chinese coolie emigrants from Hong Kong to New Zealand in 1871, and 365 passengers to New Zealand from London in 1874. GOLDEN SEA was sold in that year to Shaw,Savill & Albion Co. Ltd.

A problem with the development of the Australian trade was the almost non-existent homeward-cargo, as Australia in the early days was concerned solely in establishing itself and had very little, if anything, to export. This was solved by developing the phosphate,guano and coconut trade from the Pacific Islands. The brothers leased a number of Pacific islands from the Government to provide enough homeward cargo. This became a money-spinner later when high-grade phosphate rock was discovered at Ocean Island and Nauru in 1899, and companies such as Pacific Island Ltd and later Pacific Phosphate Ltd provided excellent charters from the Pacific Commissioners for Houlder ships for many years.

By 1869 the brothers undertook large contracts for the carriage of coal to the South African and Indian Governments for railway use. For many years Houlders were practically the only supplier of coal to the Cape Government Railways. Sailing ships and later steamers were chartered in London to carry coal from South Wales to Cape Town and Durban - the yearly contract for Cape Town was 120,000 tons and 70,000 tons for Durban. This business continued until the Durban coalfields were opened up and a home supply of coal for the Cape Government was obtained. An agreement was reached with competitors in 1877 to regulate the trade to Cape Town,Algoa Bay and East London.

Also in 1877 Houlder Brothers & Co. were admitted as founder members of the Australian Owners & Brokers Association. Other members included Shaw,Savill & Albion Co. Ltd; Trinder,Anderson & Co. Ltd; Devitt & Moore and Galbraith & Co. Ltd. Alfred Houlder died in 1878 in Hawaii while engaged in the development of the copra trade after a volcano erupted causing everyone to run for their lives, and as he was a sufferer from a weak heart the sudden exertion killed him. In 1878 Edwin Savory Houlder, his wife and children, moved into 'The Grange' at Sutton in Surrey, and this explains the adoption of the suffix 'GRANGE' for Houlder ships. However no explanation is ever given as to why a Maltese cross was adopted as the company houseflag.

The iron barque QUEEN OF THE NORTH, built by Pile of Sunderland in 1865, was purchased in 1879. The company now ceased to charter the 'GOLDEN' sailing ships as faster Scottish-built iron clippers were then available: CAIRNBULG,WASDALE, several 'LOCH' ships and BRILLIANT, the latter establishing an unbroken record for a round voyage to Sydney(NSW). Passenger accomodation on these fast Australian wool clippers was built into the 'tween decks of the ships, with cheap fares of 12 guineas being offered to Australia. Steamers owned by W. Lund & Sons Ltd started to be chartered from around 1886: DELCOMYN,HUBBUCK,MURRUMBIDGEE,WOO-LLOOMALOO and WARRIGAL of 1893. Houlder Brothers & Co. acted in conjunction with Trinder,Anderson & Co. Ltd as freight and loading brokers for the Lund ships, which later were operated under the Blue Anchor Line banner. WARRIGAL was merged into the Cairn Line fleet in 1908 when Thomson of Dundee was taken over by Cairn, but had a short Cairn Line career as she was sunk on 20th May 1908 off the Wolf Lighthouse in collision with the British

steamer JAPANIC while on a voyage from Montreal to London with
livestock and general. The Blue Anchor Line fleet was taken over
by P. & O. in 1911.

DUNEDIN owned by Shaw,Savill & Albion Co. Ltd had carried
the first cargo of refrigerated meat home from the Antipodes in
1882, and as these refrigerated machines became more widely
available a homeward trade in refrigerated meat from Australia
was established. As shipowners were unwilling to foot the cost of
these new machines, it was the responsibility of the shipper to
install them at their own expense into the steamers.

Edwin Savory Houlder admitted his son Frank into the
business in 1881 at the age of 14 years followed by Maurice at
the age of 16 years in 1886, together with two nephews, Alfred
and Augustus. The increase in the business merited the purchase
of steam tonnage for their own ownership, and orders were placed
with Wigham,Richardson & Co. Ltd on the Tyne and Raylton,Dixon &
Co. on the Tees for two steamers with an insulated capacity of
70,000 cu. ft. HORNBY GRANGE and OVINGDEAN GRANGE entered service
in February and March,1890 at a cost of £40,000 each, raised by
forming single-ship limited companies with a capital of £40,000
divided into £100 shares. They each had twin funnels with fore-
masts crossed by yards so that sails could be used if necessary.
Fast sailing ships were still being chartered by the company to
Australia at this time e.g. the famous four-masted clipper CLUNY
CASTLE owned by Donald Currie. The steamer CONSTANCE was purchased in 1893 from Furness,Withy & Co. Ltd and renamed ELSTREE
GRANGE, and these three Houlder steamers were some of the first
to load from Manchester to Melbourne and Sydney(NSW) after the
opening of the Manchester Ship Canal in 1894.

Also in 1894 the first refrigerated meat contract was made
with the Queensland Meat Export Agency for the carriage of meat
from Brisbane and Townsville. This contract was for 600 tons/
month from each port and was soon raised to 1,200 tons/month. A
contract was also made to ship refrigerated meat from Gladstone
in Queensland, and the company also obtained an interest in the
Northern Territory in Arnheim Land. The Bowen Meat Company was
acquired in 1895 and the new URMSTON GRANGE of November,1894 was
fitted for the carriage of meat from their Works, which opened in
May,1896. By February,1897 some 24,000 cattle carcasses had been
transported home in Houlder Brothers steamers. A regular service
from the Queensland ports of Bowen,Gladstone,Townsville and
Brisbane was instituted to supplement the one from Sydney(NSW)
and Melbourne.

Houlder owned and chartered ships were being used for a
variety of homeward cargoes from around 1898, including 160,000
tons of nickel ore/annum from New Caledonia to Glasgow and Le
Havre, and supplemented the copra trade from the Pacific Islands.
DENTON GRANGE of 1897 and SOUTHERN CROSS, purchased in 1899, were
used to transport Australian troops to the Boer War in South
Africa in 1899 and bring them home again. A contract was made in

1902 for the despatch of 12 steamers from New Zealand to South Africa to carry horses, cattle,general cargo and a total of 100,000 carcasses of mutton for the South African military authorities. URMSTON GRANGE of 1894 carried deep-sea cable to Guam at this time, returning with copra.

At the turn of the century a contract was made with the New Zealand Government by Houlder and the Federal S.N. Co. Ltd for a service from New Zealand and Australia to South Afica. A three-year contract was obtained in 1904 for the carriage of refrig-erated meat from Gladstone to Sydney(NSW),London,Cape Town and Durban at roughly monthly intervals. On the outbreak of the Russo-Japanese war in 1904 the company transported 10,000 horses from Australia to Japan, and OVINGDEAN GRANGE was used to trans-port stores from Vladivostock to Port Arthur. In 1905, EVERTON GRANGE carried 1,585 horses from Melbourne and Sydney to Kobe and Hiroshima in the orlop and 'tween decks with the fodder in the lower holds. The ship's refrigerator plants were brought into operation to keep the holds cool in the tropics. She was capable of carrying 130,000 cattle carcasses as well as general cargo, and had twin propellers powered by triple expansion engines. Her 'midships shell plates were 65 feet long and weighed 6 tons each, and her holds were equipped with steam fire equipment.

In 1906 the Federal-Houlder-Shire Line commenced joint regular sailings between Australia,New Zealand and South Africa and the U.K. The Scottish Shire Line was later taken over by Clan Line in 1918. OSWESTRY GRANGE running on the joint service carried a cargo of 50,000 cartons of apples home from Hobart in 1908. EVERTON GRANGE carried meat home from Australia throughout 1909, and OSWESTRY GRANGE carried 400 emigrants in third class accomodation to Queensland and returned with meat in that year. Assisted passages were then being offered by the Australian Goverment on Federal-Houlder-Shire ships and four-masted OSWESTRY GRANGE was again prominent in this trade in 1911. Allan Hughes of Birt, Potter & Hughes, owners of refrigerated ships, and Chairman and principal shareholder of Federal, had always maintained good working relationships with Houlders and the Scottish Shire Line but this was to fade after the take-over of Federal by the New Zealand Shipping Co. Ltd at the end of 1911. EVERTON GRANGE was sold to New Zealand Shipping Co. Ltd on 24th December, 1911 as part of an agreement wherebye Houlders disposed of a large part of their Australian interests and rights in Federal-Houlder-Shire from April,1912. DRAYTON GRANGE,OSWESTRY GRANGE and RIPPING-HAM GRANGE then joined the the N.Z.S.C. fleet.

2.2 PLATE MEAT TRADE

The chartered steamer MEATH brought the first Houlder meat home from the Plate to London in January,1884. A contract had been made with the River Plate Fresh Meat Company (later British & Argentine Meat Co. Ltd) to carry meat from their Campana Works. MEATH and WEXFORD ran under charter to Houlder to London and Antwerp until 1886. Edwin Savory Houlder had earlier visited the

Argentine to size up the trade, taking along with him on the trip
his sons Frank and Maurice. The port of Buenos Aires was under
construction at this time and Houlder ships transported all the
necessary material for this work in 1883, and further cement and
coal for extensions in 1887. A Capt. Jenkins was attached to the
company agents at Buenos Aires to oversee business at this time,
and then a Houlder office was opened in 1890 at Buenos Aires.

More cement,granite,dock gates,coal and construction material was shipped out to complete the harbour works at Buenos
Aires in 1891/92. The twin-funnelled HORNBY GRANGE was first ship
into the new South Dock at Newport in South Wales on 6th June,
1893 as the company were beginning to build up a Plate/South
Wales trade. URMSTON GRANGE of 1894 carried 20,000 hard-frozen
sheep from Magellan Straits to London during 1896, the shipment
being made from a hulk at Puerto Delgada. HORNBY GRANGE made a
similar shipment from the Falkland Islands. The sheep were killed
on shore and the carcasses transported to the ship by her own
lifeboats!

Houlder Brothers & Co. Ltd was incorporated as a company
with limited liability in 1898 with £20,000 each in ordinary and
preference shares, and £125,000 in debenture stock. The Houlder
family converted their interests into £133,330 of shares in the
new company. In 1899 the various single-ship limited liability
companies were formed into Houlder Line Ltd with a capital of
£500,000 and the fleet was then:-

> HORNBY GRANGE of 1890
> OVINGDEAN GRANGE of 1890
> URMSTON GRANGE of 1894
> LANGTON GRANGE of 1896
> DENTON GRANGE of 1896
> ELSTREE GRANGE of 1892
> ROYSTON GRANGE of 1897
> BEACON GRANGE of 1898
> RIPPINGHAM GRANGE of 1898
> SOUTHERN CROSS of 1899

As can be seen from this list, Edwin Savory Houlder started
the practice of naming the fleet after the initial letters of
HOULDER BROTHERS and this was carried right through to the last
'GRANGE' - the North East Coast collier OSWESTRY GRANGE - which
hauled down the Maltese cross houseflag for the last time on 6th
August,1985 at Oxelosund in Sweden. It must be borne in mind that
Houlder Brothers & Co. Ltd were, and remained, as managers of
Houlder Line Ltd and all subsequent subsidiaries which were set
up. The relative sizes of the Plate and Australian trades of the
company can be visualized from a sailing card dated 8th
September,1900 in which 32 vessels were fixed for Buenos Aires, 18
for New Orleans, 14 for Australia, 7 for Fiume and 5 for Montreal.
The small MALTESE CROSS of 1490 grt with engine-aft was completed
at Londonderry for the fleet in October,1900 but was sold seven
months later to Australian owners.

The directors including Maurice C. Houlder, who was appointed to the Boards in 1901/02, took a close interest in the provision of horses and remounts for the British Army in connection with the Boer War. This included visits to Argentina with remount officers to obtain horses. Maurice C. Houlder was appointed Inspector of Ships engaged in carrying remounts on behalf of the War Office and Imperial Yeomanry. His plans for horse stabling in ships were subsequently adopted as the Admiralty standard pattern fittings.

RAPIDAN was purchased from Furness,Withy & Co. Ltd in 1901 and renamed HAVERSHAM GRANGE, but had a short career being burnt-out at sea 800 miles from the Cape of Good Hope on 23rd October, 1906 while on a voyage from New York to Australia with general. Capt. J. Bennett was appointed master of the new DRAYTON GRANGE in 1901, and he was later to become Marine Superintendent for the company for over 20 years. INDRAMAYO of 1889 was purchased from Glaswegian owners to become THORPE GRANGE also in 1901.

The death of Edwin Savory Houlder occurred at the Annual General Meeting of the company on 29th July,1901 at the Cannon Street Hotel in London. His unfortunate passing was the result of differences of opinion as to the direction of the company and the A.G.M. was a very stormy affair. His son Maurice C. Houlder was appointed to the Boards, and Ebenezer Cayford, who had been instrumental in developing the Pacific Islands trade, was made Chairman.

2.3 EXPANSION AND SUBSIDIARIES 1902 – 1914

The **Empire Transport Co. Ltd** was formed in 1902 to indicate the world-wide nature of the company trades and took over the HAVERSHAM GRANGE (formerly RAPIDAN) of 1898. OSWESTRY GRANGE was completed in this year for Houlder Line Ltd, and the new EVERTON GRANGE in August,1903 for the Empire company. EVERTON GRANGE was used on the Australian service and carried a large number of passengers.

Expansion in the Argentine/Uruguay meat trade continued with several important contracts with meat processing companies during 1903/4:-

1. La Blanca Company. Exports from Bahia Blanca/Buenos Aires.

2. Sansinena Meat Company. Exports from Bahia Blanca/Buenos Aires at 1600 tons/week.

3. Frigorifo Uruguayo. Exports from Montevideo, the whole output of this company was to be carried at 3/4 weeks intervals, amounting to around 1500 tons of hard frozen beef/month.

4.   South American Export Syndicate. Exports from Rio Seco
      Works,Punta Arenas in Magellan Straits, amounting to
      their whole production.

GUARDIANA of Furness,Withy & Co. Ltd was purchased in 1909
and renamed SUTHERLAND GRANGE, having been completed in 1907 by
Palmers at Jarrow for the British Maritime Trust Ltd. ROYSTON
GRANGE made a fast passage of 28 days from Buenos Aires to Liverpool at this time, and DRAYTON GRANGE another fast passage in 29
days from Montevideo to London, calling at Avonmouth. Other U.K.
ports used included Southampton and the Tyne.

The Empire Transport Co. Ltd was greatly expanded by the
addition of ten new ships between the middle of 1910 and the end
of 1911:-

                  EMPIRE TRANSPORT
                  BRITISH TRANSPORT
                  CANADIAN TRANSPORT
                  CAPE TRANSPORT
                  INDIAN TRANSPORT
                  NATAL TRANSPORT
                  AMERICAN TRANSPORT
                  ARGENTINE TRANSPORT
                  AUSTRALIAN TRANSPORT
                  NEW ZEALAND TRANSPORT

Disputes between the owning Houlder family members and
others had continued and culminated in 1911 by Augustus Frederick
Houlder and Alfred Henry Houlder and others selling their share-
holding - about one-third of the total - to Sir Christopher
Furness and Furness,Withy & Co. Ltd. They then resigned from the
Boards together with C.F. Hartridge and they were replaced by
Frank H. Houlder,Stephen W. Furness,Frederick W. Lewis, Walter C.
Warwick,Robert E. Burnett with Maurice C. Houlder retaining his
seat. Joint managing directors were now:-

                  Frederick W. Lewis
                  Stephen W. Furness
                  Walter C. Warwick

Walter C. Warwick took charge of all departments of the
company, and under his guidance the period of dissent was brought
to an end. He was later made Chairman and continued in this
capacity until January,1962. Frank H. Houlder was appointed
Chairman of the Empire Transport Co. Ltd with the top managers of
Furness,Withy & Co. Ltd joining as directors (See Chapter 1).

Furness,Withy & Co. Ltd formed the **British & Argentine Steam
Navigation Co.** Ltd in 1911 to operate in association with the
Houlder fleet, and long-term freight contracts were entered into
with the Argentine/Uruguay meat processing companies for the
transport of chilled and frozen meat. Furness had previously been

trading with refrigerated ships between Canada and South Africa in association with Elder,Dempster,and when this was discontinued their refrigerated ORIANA and WYANDOTTE plus the purchased CHASE SIDE (renamed EL CORDOBES) found employment to Argentina. Orders for three new refrigerated ships - EL URUGUAYO,LA ROSARINA, LA NEGRA - were placed and shares in the Argentine Cargo Line (A.C.L.) were purchased. A.C.L. had been formed in 1908 with Birt,Potter & Hughes as managers to purchase two ships - LA BLANCA and EL ARGENTINO - from the bankrupt Anglo-Argentine Shipping Company(J. & E. Hall Ltd). An agreement was made by Birt,Potter & Hughes with Furness,Withy & Co. Ltd and Manchester Liners Ltd to run their GUARDIANA and MANCHESTER CITY in conjunction with the A.C.L. ships. In 1912, Birt,Potter & Hughes assigned the manage-ment of the A.C.L. to Furness,Withy & Co. Ltd, and the working of the A.C.L. was incorporated into that of the new British & Argentine S.N. Co. Ltd.

LA BLANCA and EL ARGENTINO were chartered by the British & Argentine S.N. Co. Ltd from A.C.L. and managed by Houlder Brothers. In addition other refrigerated ships joined the Houlder Line Ltd fleet:-

> EL PARAGUAYO of 1912
> LA CORRENTINA of 1912
> LYNTON GRANGE of 1912
> DENBY GRANGE of 1912
> OAKLANDS GRANGE of 1912
> ROUNTON GRANGE of 1913
> OLDFIELD GRANGE of 1913

A contract was signed in 1913 to ship the whole output of Soc. Explotadora del Tierra del Fuego at Puerto Bories Works in Last Hope Inlet,South Patagonia. This contract was only possible by pioneer work by Capt. McCamley, Marine Superintendent for the company, who surveyed and charted the treacherous Kirk Narrows. EL CORDOBES is believed to have shipped the first meat shipment to Lisbon from Buenos Aires during 1913. The Empire Transport Co. Ltd signed contracts with the Pacific Phosphate Company during 1913 to provide six steamers/year carrying phosphate from Ocean Island in the Pacific to Stettin. New steamers entered this fleet during 1913/14:-

> QUEENSLAND TRANSPORT
> VICTORIAN TRANSPORT
> TASMANIAN TRANSPORT
> AFRICAN TRANSPORT
> OCEAN TRANSPORT
> IMPERIAL TRANSPORT
> PACIFIC TRANSPORT
> NEW ZEALAND TRANSPORT
> ROYAL TRANSPORT
> EGYPTIAN TRANSPORT
> PANAMA TRANSPORT

In 1914 the Empire Transport Co. Ltd had a fleet of 19 steamers totalling 150,810 dwt. The company relinquished sailings to South Africa at this time but continued to act as loading brokers for Bucknall Line and others.

The **British Empire Steam Navigation Co. Ltd** was formed in early 1914 with Frank H. Houlder as Chairman; Marmaduke, second Lord Furness; Frederick W. Lewis; Maurice C. Houlder; Walter C. Warwick; W.H. Smith and E. Levy as Directors. It took delivery of the folowing 10 steamers during 1914/15:-

> ORANGE RIVER
> BRISBANE RIVER
> CLUTHA RIVER
> SAGAMA RIVER
> DERWENT RIVER
> SWAN RIVER
> PENNAR RIVER
> GAMBIA RIVER
> FRASER RIVER
> MERSEY RIVER

An office was opened in Port Moresby,Papua New Guinea to handle the lumber trade of the Papua Co. Ltd, and auxiliary ketches and cutters were purchased to transport the lumber out to the waiting Houlder ships. The coral reefs in the channel to the port were blasted with gelignite during World War I.

2.4 WORLD WAR I.

Some of the fleet had been armed with 4.7" guns on the stern during 1913 at the instigation of Winston Churchill, and the gun on LA CORRENTINA went into action at once when she met up with the armed merchant cruiser KRONPRINZ WILHELM, a converted liner, on 7th October,1914 some 320 miles East of Montevideo. LA CORREN-TINA was quickly disabled,captured and sunk. It was fortunate that only one vessel - VICTORIAN TRANSPORT - was captured in port at Stettin in August,1914 in connection with the phosphate ship-ments to that port.

All the refrigerated ships of Houlder Line Ltd and its associate companies were requisitioned in June,1915 by the Board of Trade, and many of the general cargo ships were requisitioned by the Admiralty. LYNTON GRANGE had been intercepted by the German cruiser DRESDEN before the outbreak on 6th August but was released. The full list of subsequent losses to enemy submarines unless otherwise stated is now given:-

Late 1914 URMSTON GRANGE   Sunk as a blockship at Scapa.
7.10.1914 LA CORRENTINA   Raider KRONPRINZ WILHELM.
4.9.1915   NATAL TRANSPORT 40 miles W of Gavdo Island,S. Crete.
26.5.1916 EL ARGENTINO   Mined/sunk 7 miles SSE of Southwold.

11.4.1917   IMPERIAL TRANSPORT 140 miles NW1/2W of Alexandria.
16.4.1917   BRISBANE RIVER   140 miles W of Gibraltar.
14.6.1917   NEW ZEALAND TRANSPORT 8 miles SE of Serphopulo Isle.
7.7.1917   CONDESA 105 miles W of Bishop Rock on her maiden voyage
            home from the Plate.
3.9.1917   LA NEGRA   50 miles SSW of Start Point.
27.9.1917   SWAN RIVER   27 miles NNW of Oran.
23.11.1917 LA BLANCA   10 miles SSE of Berry Head.
11.12.1917 OLDFIELD GRANGE   30 miles NE of Tory Island.
25.6.1918   AFRICAN TRANSPORT   3 miles N of Whitby.
23.8.1918   AUSTRALIAN TRANSPORT Off Bizerta.
24.10.1918 DENBY GRANGE   In collision with WAR ISLAND
                                in convoy.

        NATAL TRANSPORT could not out-distance U34 while on a voyage
from Bombay to Liverpool with general and was sunk by gunfire to
become the first company loss to U-boats. The twin-funnelled
BUTESHIRE, completed by Hawthorn,Leslie & Co. Ltd in 1893, was
purchased in 1915 and renamed BOLLINGTON GRANGE - the third twin-
funnelled ship in the fleet. She was transferred in the following
year to Furness-Houlder Argentine Line Ltd as CANONESA, and on
1st May,1918 was torpedoed and damaged off Worthing by UB57. She
was beached and subsequently refloated and towed to Southampton
and abandoned to H.M. Government. They sold her to Union Cold
Storage Ltd(Blue Star Line,managers) who repaired her as
MAGICSTAR, and she was eventually scrapped at Inverkeithing in
1930. LA ROSARINA used her gun to good effect to escape a U-boat
off S. Ireland on 17th April,1915.

        Furness-Houlder Argentine Line Ltd had been formed in June,
1914 to provide tonnage for an additional contract. An agreement
was reached with Furness,Withy & Co. Ltd in April,1916 to
centralise the superintendence of the British & Argentine S.N.
Co. Ltd and A.C.L. ships with the Houlder ships and divide the
costs annually. Three ships joined Furness-Houlder Argentine Line
Ltd under Houlder management in 1916:-

CANONESA   See BOLLINGTON GRANGE above.

ABADESA   A new ship laid down by Sir Raylton Dixon at Middles-
           brough as DOMINION MILLER for Norfolk & North American
           S.S. Co. Ltd(Furness,Withy & Co. Ltd) but transferred
           while still on the stocks. She was transferred in 1934
           to Houlder Line Ltd to become ELSTREE GRANGE.

CONDESA   A new refrigerated ship built by Earle's of Hull. She
           was torpedoed and sunk by U84 on 7th July,1917 when 105
           miles West of the Bishop Rock on her maiden voyage home
           from the Plate to Falmouth with frozen meat.

        EL ARGENTINO was outward bound from Hull to the Plate
on 26th May,1916 when she hit a mine off Southwold laid by UC1
and sank. Eight ships were lost during the black year of 1917
with four going to the bottom in the Mediterranean. Three crew

died when NEW ZEALAND TRANSPORT under Capt. Edward Grant was
torpedoed and sunk in the Aegean on 14th June while on a voyage
from Port Talbot to Mudros with coal. Capt. Grant was then
appointed to the command of EGYPTIAN TRANSPORT, but she was
torpedoed on New Years Day,1918 in the Mediterranean and five
lives were lost. Capt. Grant received Lloyd's Silver Medal for
bravery when beaching his ship, which was later refloated and
repaired. As at 30th June, the Houlder fleet stood at 43 ships,
of which:-

    15 Refrigerated ships were on requisition to Board of Trade.
    22 General cargo ships were on requisition to the Admiralty.
    1 was interned at Stettin.
    4 were on time-charter.
    1 was on the open freight market.

    Capt. Pope had won the D.S.O. in connection with an earlier
incident, and was presented to the King during 1917 when he
visited London Docks to watch meat being unloaded. Frank H.
Houlder gave permission for a private code to be used for
telegraph messages to avoid sending in 'clear', after consul-
ation with Admiral Brownbridge, the Senior Naval Censor. Four
refrigerated sister ships joined Furness - Houlder Argentine
Lines Ltd in 1918:-

    DUQUESA from Irvine's at West Hartlepool.
    BARONESA from Sir Raylton Dixon at Middlesbrough.
    MARQUESA from W. Hamilton at Port Glasgow.
    PRINCESA from Alexander Stephen at Glasgow.

    These were twin-screw ships powered by two triple-expansion
engines. They had six holds with nos. 2,3 and 4 hatches being
part of a very long raised central structure, and two masts and
two sets of posts carried a fine array of 16 cargo derricks. Also
two German ships, SALATIS and MERA, which had been seized by the
Uruguayan Government in 1914 at Montevideo, were chartered to the
British Government under Houlder management. As TREINTA -Y-TRES
and RIO NEGRO they were returned to the Uruguayans in 1920. The
final casualty of the war was DENBY GRANGE of 1912, which was
sunk by collision in convoy on 24th October,1918 with the new
cargo ship WAR ISLAND.

2.5 INTER-WAR YEARS.

    The surviving fleet of Houlder Brothers & Co. Ltd stood
at 39 ships at the end of the war, distributed between:-

Houlder Line Ltd	11 ships
British Empire S.N. Co. Ltd	6 ships
Empire Transport Co. Ltd	13 ships
Furness-Houlder Argentine Lines Ltd	9 ships

The twin-funnelled HORNBY GRANGE of 1890, the first steamer in
the fleet, was sold to Spanish owners in 1919 together with

ELSTREE GRANGE of 1892. The Furness family withdrew all connect-
ions with Houlder Brothers by the resignation of Marmaduke,second
Lord Furness, in 1919/20 as a director of the various Boards. The
requisitioned ships were slow to return to company control, a
fact that was hard to accept by the joint managing directors
Walter C. Warwick and Frederick W. Lewis. However a standard 'G'
class meat carrier was purchased from the Government in 1919 and
launched as CANONESA on 6th March,1920 at the Belfast yard of
Workman,Clark & Co. Ltd.

These 'G' class standard meat-carriers were the best and
largest standard ships of WWI, and the fastest with a top speed
of 13 knots. Some were twin-screw, some single-screw for the
frozen meat trade from the Plate, Australia and New Zealand. They
had five holds with no. 3 hold between bridge and funnel and the
plated-in midships structure of the Houlder-designed ships was
absent. When sold to private owners they were given varying
amounts of refrigerated space, the largest being that of CANONESA
with 457,000 cu. ft. Many were sold to Royal Mail Line, British
India, New Zealand Shipping Corporation, and White Star Line with
three later sold out of these fleets to The Clan Line Steamers
Ltd in the 1930s as CLAN COLQUHOUN ex GALLIC, CLAN FARQUHAR ex
DELPHIC, and CLAN ROBERTSON ex OTAKI. CANONESA completed trials
on 4th November, 1920 and joined Furness-Houlder Argentine Lines
Ltd under Houlder management.

New Houlder offices were opened in Buenos Aires,Montevideo,
Santos and Rio de Janeiro in the early 1920s with Edifico Houlder
in Buenos Aires being the grandest. BEACON GRANGE of 1899 was
wrecked at the entrance to Rio Gallegos while entering with coal
from Newport News on 6th September,1921. She was replaced in the
Houlder Line Ltd fleet by the new HARDWICKE GRANGE from W.
Hamilton & Co. Ltd,Port Glasgow in the following month. In 1924
the company was engaged in carrying large shipments of railway
materials and cement under contract to South America. The first
motor ship in the fleet was UPWEY GRANGE of 1925 completed by the
Fairfield SB Co. Ltd at Govan with two 12-cylinder 2SCSA oil
engines also manufactured at the yard. THORPE GRANGE had the
distinction in 1925 of being the first company ship to discharge
chilled meat at Southampton.

PANAMA TRANSPORT opened a new direct service between Manchester and the Plate in 1927. On 25th October,1927 Mrs. Walter
C. Warwick launched the motorship DUNSTER GRANGE at the Fairfield
yard as a sister to UPWEY GRANGE. She was to be the only 'GRANGE'
to escape destruction in WWII. On 30th June,1928 OCEAN TRANSPORT
was lost in a hurricane off Ocean Island while engaged in the
phosphate trade. In the same year the company entered the tanker
trades with the motor tanker CARONI RIVER for the British Empire
S.N. Co. Ltd from Blythswood SB Co. Ltd,Glasgow. She had a raised
catwalk from the 'midships bridge structure to the engineers
accomodation right aft, but no catwalk from the bridge to the
fo'c'stle! She was delivered on 25th October,1928 for charter to
SHELL but stranded at Curacao on 21st December,1928 but was

65. LOCH GARTH of 1947 of Royal Mail Line was taken over in 1965.

66. THORPE GRANGE of 1889 ex INDRAMAYO purchased by Houlder in 1901.

S.S. "URMSTON GRANGE"

67. URMSTON GRANGE of 1894 was sunk as a blockship at Scapa.

68. SUTHERLAND GRANGE of 1907 ex GUARDIANA [M.Lindenborn].

69. CAPE TRANSPORT of 1910 was scrapped in Italy in 1933 [F.W.Hawks].

70. INDIAN TRANSPORT of 1910 was sold to Greece in 1929 [F.W.Hawks].

71. QUEENSLAND TRANSPORT of 1913 was sold to Greece in 1934.

72. ORANGE RIVER of 1914 was sold to Greece in 1934 [E.Johnson].

73. OAKLANDS GRANGE of 1912 was sold to Greece in 1934.

74. BARONESA of 1918 of Furness-Houlder Argentine Line [F.W.Hawks]

75. MARQUESA of 1918 pictured in the Thames in 1936 [A.Snook].

76. EL ARGENTINO of 1928 became a war loss on 26.7.1943.

77. DUNSTER GRANGE of 1928 became a crab fish factory ship.

78. IMPERIAL TRANSPORT of 1931 lost her bow half in 1940 [A.Duncan]

79. LYNTON GRANGE of 1937 became a war loss on 28.12.1942.

80. LANGTON GRANGE of 1942 ex EMPIRE PENNANT [M.Cassar].

81. URMSTON GRANGE of 1942 ex EMPIRE PIBROCH [A.Duncan].

82. BARTON GRANGE of 1944 ex EMPIRE BALFOUR [A.Duncan].

83. ARGENTINE TRANSPORT of 1944 ex SAMTYNE [A.Duncan].

84. CONDESA of 1944 was scrapped in Italy in 1962.

85. DUQUESA of 1949 was scrapped in Italy in 1969 [T.Rayner]

86. OSWESTRY GRANGE of 1952 was sold to Greece in 1971.

87. QUEENSBURY of 1953 of Alexander Shipping Co. Ltd

88. ORELIA of 1954 sailing from the Tyne [M. Donnelly].

89. OREGIS aground at Tynemouth on 10.3.1974 [M.Donnelly].

90. WESTBURY of 1960 was sold in 1978.

91. SWAN RIVER of 1959 served the Group for 12 years.

92. ROYSTON GRANGE of 1959 was gutted by fire in 1972 [J.K.Byass].

93. HARDWICKE GRANGE of 1960 was sold in 1977.

94. JOULE of 1965 was purchased in 1973.

95. HUMBOLDT of 1968 was sold in 1984 [J.K.Byass].

96. LORD KELVIN of 1978 was sold in 1987 [A.Duncan].

refloated,repaired and back in service in early 1929. A similar sister of around 11,000 - 12,000 dwt was completed by the same yard for the Empire Transport Co. Ltd in 1931 as IMPERIAL TRANSPORT. She proceeded from the builders yard to lay-up in Holy Loch and remained there for two years before sailing on her maiden voyage. She was later to have many adventures during WWII including losing her bow half and being twice torpedoed.

EL ARGENTINO was launched on 12th January,1928 at the Fairfield yard for the British & Argentine S.N. Co. Ltd with Furness,Withy & Co. Ltd as managers. Later in 1936 when the British & Argentine company was wound up she was transferred to Furness-Houlder Argentine Lines Ltd with Houlder Brothers & Co. Ltd as managers. During 1929 a serious collapse in the Plate homeward freight rates occurred, and AMERICAN TRANSPORT,CAPE TRANSPORT, INDIAN TRANSPORT and ROYAL TRANSPORT were sold to foreign owners. CAPE TRANSPORT had to be seized back from her Greek buyer due to non-payment of the balance of her purchase price. THORPE GRANGE was sold in 1930 for scrap, with profits plummeting by 1932 to only £40,000 making it necessary for the reserves to be called upon during the Depression. On a brighter note DUNSTER GRANGE had the honour of carrying the Royal cars for the visit of the Prince of Wales and Prince George to South America in 1931. She also carried an unusual cargo of galvanised iron sheets in September,1933 to South America to make barriers against the locust pest that was plaguing the country. HARDWICKE GRANGE carried a cargo of apples from Seattle to the U.K. at this time - the total on board was estimated at 27.82 million! In 1933 the following tonnage was disposed of:-

Houlder Line Ltd:	LYNTON GRANGE,SUTHERLAND GRANGE.
British Empire S.N. Co. Ltd:	DERWENT RIVER,SAGAMA RIVER.
Empire Transport Co. Ltd:	BRITISH TRANSPORT,CANADIAN TRANSPORT, EGYPTIAN TRANSPORT,PACIFIC TRANSPORT, TASMANIAN TRANSPORT,PANAMA TRANSPORT, VICTORIAN TRANSPORT.

Five of these were sold for scrap in an effort to remove the older,uneconomic ships from the overburdened freight markets. In September,1933 ORANGE RIVER was still laid-up in River Blackwater at Tollesbury alongside the Furness ships LONDON CITIZEN, LONDON CORPORATION,LONDON EXCHANGE,LONDON MERCHANT, BRITISH PRINCE,IMPERIAL PRINCE and ROYAL PRINCE. In 1934/35 there were more disposals:-

Houlder Line Ltd:	OAKLANDS GRANGE,ROUNTON GRANGE.
Empire Transport Co. Ltd:	RHODESIAN TRANSPORT,QUEENSLAND TRANSPORT.
British Empire S.N. Co. Ltd:	GAMBIA RIVER,ORANGE RIVER.

However by 1935 there were signs that the depression was lifting, and three ships SALADO,SEGURA and ZAPALA were purchased from the Buenos Aires Great Southern Railway Co. Ltd and renamed ROYSTON GRANGE,LANGTON GRANGE and OVINGDEAN GRANGE - however the first two were 'WAR' standard ships dating from 1918/19 which were only kept for a year to fulfil an additional contract. ARGENTINE TRANSPORT was completed by Blythswood SB Co. Ltd in this year, but was transferred to Prince Line in 1936 to become their RHODESIAN PRINCE and then transferred back to Houlder in 1937 to become OSWESTRY GRANGE.

The Chairman, Frank H. Houlder, died at his ranch in Argentina on 21st January,1935 aged 68 years, and was succeeded by Lord Essendon (Sir Frederick Lewis) as Chairman of the principal companies. Frank H. Houlder was the son of Edwin Savory Houlder and had joined the business in 1881 and subsequently travelled abroad extensively making many valuable contacts for the company. In latter years he had spent much time at the ranch, Estancia Houlder, where he died.

EL PARAGUAYO of 1912 was sold for scrap in 1936, and contracts signed for the building of two new ships, LYNTON GRANGE and BEACON GRANGE. LYNTON GRANGE was the smaller of the two from the Blythswood yard, while BEACON GRANGE of 10119 grt was the first ship ordered from the Hebburn yard of Hawthorn,Leslie & Co. Ltd. She was a twin-screw refrigerated motor ship powered by two 4SCSA oil engines from the builder's factory in Newcastle and was delivered on 4th May,1938. Most of the post-WWII company orders went to Hawthorn,Leslie & Co. Ltd. The Houlder fleet stood at 16 ships on the outbreak of war in September,1939 distributed as:-

Houlder Line Ltd: 8 ships.

British Empire S.N. Co. Ltd: 1 tanker.

Empire Transport Co. Ltd: 1 tanker.

Furness-Houlder Argentine Lines Ltd: 6 Refrigerated ships.

2.6 WORLD WAR II.

The Houlder fleet and the sea-going staff suffered heavy losses during WWII, amounting to 11 owned ships and 4 managed ships lost together with 114 brave men. In addition to these, IMPERIAL TRANSPORT was twice torpedoed, losing her bow half on the first occasion, and twice repaired. The old-timer ROYSTON GRANGE, completed in 1918 as WAR BISON as a 'WAR' B type, was the first to go. She had reached the Western Approaches under Capt. A.G.P. Mead on a voyage from Buenos Aires to Liverpool with grain and general when torpedoed in the engine room on 25th November, 1939. Her engine room filled rapidly with water and she went down about 15 minutes after the torpedo struck. All 36 crew plus their pet monkey were picked up by the Lamport & Holt ROMNEY and landed

at Swansea. Brian Gaffney, a member of the crew who had already
been torpedoed five times in WWI, was awarded the British Empire
Medal for bravery. The full list of losses to submarine activity
unless otherwise stated is now given:-

25.11.1939	ROYSTON GRANGE	50 miles SW of Scillies.
20.1.1940	CARONI RIVER	Mined/sunk off Falmouth.
8.8.1940	UPWEY GRANGE	200 miles NW of Donegal,36 lost.
21.9.1940	CANONESA	W of Ireland,1 lost.
18.12.1940	DUQUESA	Captured on Equator, mid-way between Dakar and Pernambuco by ADMIRAL SCHEER,crew taken prisoner. DUQUESA sunk on 18.2.1941.
12.2.1941	OSWESTRY GRANGE	Near Azores by ADMIRAL HIPPER,5 lost.
27.4.1941	BEACON GRANGE	Near Faeroes,2 lost.
3.5.1941	ELSTREE GRANGE	Sunk by land mine at Liverpool,7 lost.
12.6.1942	HARDWICKE GRANGE	450 miles N of San Juan(PR),3 lost.
28.12.1942	LYNTON GRANGE	Mid-Atlantic.
26.7.1943	EL ARGENTINO	Bombed/sunk off Portuguese coast, 4 lost.

Managed vessels:-

27.10.1942	ANGLO-MAERSK	Near Canary Islands.
21.11.1942	EMPIRE STARLING	E of Barbados.
28.12.1942	EMPIRE SHACKLETON	Mid-Atlantic,37 lost.
27.2.1945	SAMPA	10 miles N of Ostend, 15 lost.

114 brave men died in Houlder ships.

The manner in which the owned ships were lost is now described:-

CARONI RIVER under Capt. R.S. Grigg had left Falmouth for defen-
sive armament trials including paravane tests when she struck a
mine in nos. 1 and 2 main cargo tanks. Efforts were made to beach
her but she sank by the stern within two hours, heeling over to
port in 10 fathoms of water.

UPWEY GRANGE under Capt. W.E. Williams was homeward bound from
Buenos Aires with frozen meat when hit by two torpedoes on the
port side causing major devastation to the engine room and stern
of the ship and she sank 19 minutes later. 36 crew had died in
the blast and the survivors were picked up by a trawler three
days later.

CANONESA under Capt. F. Stevenson was homeward bound from
Montreal to Manchester with a full,frozen cargo when torpedoed in
the engine room on the starboard side, flooding both engine and
boiler rooms,blasting no. 4 hatch and a lifeboat into the air and
wrecking the mainmast. Fortunately all but one man was picked up
from the remaining lifeboats.

DUQUESA under Capt. L. Bearpark was homeward bound from the Plate
and had just passed the Equator when a warship began to overhaul
her from astern. This turned out to be ADMIRAL SCHEER and the RRR

raider message and description was sent off by radio to Sierra
Leone before a German boarding party captured her. DUQUESA was
not sunk and her crew were first accomodated on the battleship
before being transferred to the tanker NORDMARK. DUQUESA was then
used as a storeship in the South Atlantic, and her name was
planned to be changed to HERZOGIN but she was sunk by explosive
charges by the Germans on 18th February,1941 before the change
took place.

OSWESTRY GRANGE under Capt. E. Stone was homeward bound from
Rosario with grain when attacked by rapid shelling from the heavy
cruiser ADMIRAL HIPPER. Capt. Stone and 4 others were drowned in
transferring from a damaged,sinking lifeboat to another boat,
which was picked up by a British ship and the 37 survivors were
landed at Madeira.

BEACON GRANGE under Capt. A.B. Friend sailed from Loch Ewe for
Buenos Aires in ballast and commenced zig-zagging. However she
was hit by three torpedoes on the starboard side, and the crew
managed to escape in two lifeboats and were adrift for two days
and six days repectively. The U-boat surfaced to finish off the
wreck with gunfire and a fourth torpedo.

ELSTREE GRANGE had left Liverpool Docks to anchor in the Mersey
when she was hit by a parachute mine and sank. The wreck was
later raised and beached.

HARWICKE GRANGE under Capt. T. McNamara was sailing between
Newport News and Trinidad in the Caribbean when hit by two
torpedoes which damaged two lifeboats. The crew got away in the
remaining four boats with the U-boat surfacing to obtain the
ship's name. Capt. McNamara and his boat drifted for 13 and a
half days before arriving at Monte Christi in Dominica; the mate
and 15 men arrived in their boat at San Nicolas,Haiti; the second
mate and 22 men landed at Neuvitas,Cuba; and the third mate and
18 men landed at Turk's Island.

LYNTON GRANGE under Capt. R.S. Grigg was outward bound to South
Africa and the Middle East when hit by a torpedo in no. 1 hold.
As she was carrying 3,000 tons of explosives the order to abandon
ship was given immediately, and the crew were picked up by a
destroyer and landed at Ponta Delgada in the Azores.

EL ARGENTINO under Capt. F.W. Kent was outward bound to the Plate
and off the Portuguese coast when hit by a stick of five bombs in
nos. 5 and 6 holds dropped from a Focke Wulf aircraft flying at
10,000 feet. A fire was started at the stern, and the order to
abandon was given as she was starting to settle by the stern. One
crew member died in the bombing but the other 77 were rescued -
including Engineer Mallins, who had been torpedoed 8 times in WWI
and three times in WWII, two of these on the tanker IMPERIAL
TRANSPORT. Capt. W. Smail was in command of this tanker on the
first occasion when she left Scapa Flow for Trinidad on 10th
February,1940 and she was struck by a torpedo on the following

day, breaking in two in less than 5 minutes. All the officers who
were berthed amidships were able to get on the stern half before
she broke in two. The crew took to the boats but reboarded the
stern half the next day. The engines were restarted and the stern
half was steamed head-first until some 130 miles W of Cape Wrath.
The master and crew were advised to board a destroyer as a gale
was forecast and they were landed at Scapa Flow. The stern half
was later towed in and beached at Kilchattan Bay,Bute. A new
forepart was built at Greenock and the two halves were joined in
the Elderslie dry-dock. IMPERIAL TRANSPORT was again torpedoed on
25th March,1942 while on a voyage from the Tyne to Curacao in
convoy to E of Newfoundland. She took a heavy list to port and
appeared to be sinking - all the crew abandoned ship and were
picked up by a Free French corvette. As the tanker had not sunk a
skeleton crew of 6 together with 8 men from a British corvette
reboarded and managed to start the auxiliary machinery the next
day. The main engine then started and they arrived at St. John's
(NF) on the 29th.

However the punishment was not all 'take', as Houlder ships
'gave' it with their guns and on one occasion with depth charges.
DUNSTER GRANGE under Capt. R.A. Smiles left Liverpool in an
Atlantic convoy on 21st September,1940 and was joined by ships
from the Bristol Channel and Glasgow on the next day. The escort
left the convoy at 6 a.m. on the 25th and the Commodore hoisted
the signal 'Disperse Convoy'. This was the cue to attack by the
U-boats and the Donaldson SULAIRIA was torpedoed at 1020 hours
and sunk. The Blue Funnel EURYMIDON was also torpedoed but
remained afloat, and DUNSTER GRANGE then altered course and depth
charged the U-boat. While probably shaking their attacker the
action at least kept her under water and from doing further
damage to the convoy - although CORRIENTES,another Donaldson ship
was later torpedoed and sunk at midnight. This was believed to be
the first recorded occasion in which a merchant ship dropped
depth charges.

The managed **EMPIRE SHACKLETON** was also torpedoed and sunk in
the same convoy as LYNTON GRANGE on 28th December,1942. EMPIRE
SHACKLETON was Convoy Commodore ship with Vice-Admiral Egerton on
board, having loaded general cargo,ammunition and aircraft on the
Johnston-Warren Line berth at Liverpool for Halifax(NS). On three
consecutive evenings starting on the 26th the convoy was attacked
losing one ship on 26th, three ships plus a straggler on 27th,
and 13 ships on the 28th including both Houlder ships. EMPIRE
SHACKLETON was about the last ship torpedoed in the convoy when
struck in the forward holds. One boat was lowered and 11 crew
entered and fell astern and were rescued by the steamer CALGARY.
The crew remaining on board signalled their intention of proceeding to the Azores but she subsequently sank and two lifeboats
containing Vice Admiral Egerton and the rest of the crew were
picked up by H.M.S. FIDELITY. Unfortunately the Vice Admiral and
all but one crew member of EMPIRE SHACKLETON were then lost when
H.M.S. FIDELITY was lost by enemy action on New Years Day,1943.

The surviving owned Houlder ships at the end of the war were:-

DUNSTER GRANGE of 1928
BARONESA of 1918
MARQUESA of 1918
PRINCESA of 1918
IMPERIAL TRANSPORT of 1931

plus the new refrigerated motorships RIPPINGHAM GRANGE and CONDESA completed at the Hebburn yard of Hawthorn,Leslie & Co. Ltd in September, 1943 and April,1944 respectively.

2.7 POST-WWII REBUILDING 1945 - 1965.

Walter C. Warwick was made Chairman of all the principal Houlder companies on the death of Lord Essendon on 24th June, 1944. His nephew Cyril W. Warwick was appointed a director of Houlder Brothers & Co. Ltd, later becoming Deputy Chairman. John Maurice Houlder was appointed a director of Houlder Line Ltd, having first been made a director of Houlder Brothers & Co. Ltd in 1937 at the age of 21 years. He had served in the Army during the war and was Port Officer at Tobruk for part of the time where he was severely wounded. After convalescence he joined the Combined Operations staff at the War Office in London.

The pressing need for replacement ships was plugged in the short term by three managed 'Liberties': SAMPEP,SAMEARN and SAMTAMPA. SAMEARN was sold to the Claremont Shipping Company in 1947 and renamed CLAREPARK but remained on charter to Houlder. SAMPEP was returned to the U.S. Government in 1948, but SAMTAMPA was wrecked on Sker Point near Port Talbot on 23rd April,1947 after dragging her anchors in a gale while on a voyage from Middlesbrough to Newport in ballast. Unfortunately this resulted in the loss of the Mumbles lifeboat and the entire crew who had gone to the aid of SAMTAMPA. Three further 'Liberties' were purchased in 1947 to become ARGENTINE TRANSPORT,ELSTREE GRANGE and FRASER RIVER.

The standard 10,000 dwt EMPIRE BALFOUR, completed by Lithgow in 1944, was bareboat-chartered in 1946 and purchased in 1949 to become BARTON GRANGE. EMPIRE BUCKLER,EMPIRE PIBROCH and EMPIRE PENNANT were purchased in 1946 and renamed OVINGDEAN GRANGE, URMSTON GRANGE and LANGTON GRANGE respectively. The crew living space of all these standard ships was later converted to single-berth cabins with movable furniture, and they were to stay in the fleet until around 1960. The Canadian-built FORT BRANDON and FORT ASH were bareboat-chartered in 1946, and FORT ASH was purchased in 1950 to become ROYSTON GRANGE.

The refrigerated HORNBY GRANGE was launched by Mrs. Cyril W. Warwick at the Hebburn yard of Hawthorn,Leslie & Co. Ltd and was fitted with the first Doxford oil engines manufactured at their

Newcastle engine works. Delivered on 12th December,1946 she replaced BARONESA which was sold for scrap in Belgium. Her two sisters MARQUESA and PRINCESA were scrapped at Faslane and Blyth in 1948 and 1949, and replaced by a new DUQUESA launched by Mrs. Maurice C. Houlder and completed at Hebburn in March,1949. In sharp contrast to earlier twin-screw oil-engined refrigerated Houlder ships, DUQUESA was given double reduction geared turbines driving a single screw - obviously a dichotomy of opinion existed as to how these large meat carriers should be propelled at this time. She was one of the largest chilled meat carriers afloat at the time with nearly 600,000 cu. ft., a fact that was recorded in a BBC newsreel film made at the time. Old DUNSTER GRANGE was sold in 1951 to Finland as VAASA, and was to survive afloat until scrapped in 1974 in Japan after use as a crab fish factory ship.

In February,1947 the purchase of a controlling interest and management of the **Alexander Shipping Co. Ltd** was made, a smaller shareholding having been purchased in 1938. Sir Frank Alexander joined the Board of Houlder Line Ltd, and five standard 'EMPIRE's joined the Houlder fleet as BIBURY,CHARLBURY,EASTBURY,HOLMBURY and AYLESBURY plus one 'Liberty' - KINGSBURY. This company had previously been controlled by Capper,Alexander & Co. with a history that can be traced back to the last century with the first 'BURY' being SHREWSBURY from W. Gray & Co. Ltd at West Hartlepool in 1901. Sir Frank Alexander then retired shortly after the take-over to allow his elder son Charles G. Alexander (later Sir) to join the Board of Houlder Brothers & Co. Ltd in May,1948. Sir Frank Alexander died at his home, Norsted Manor in Kent, on 18th July,1959. Charles G. Alexander rose to become Deputy Chairman of Houlder Brothers & Co. Ltd, and his brother John became manager of the Houlder Liverpool office in 1950 and joined the Houlder Board in 1960.

OSWESTRY GRANGE had a much more modern,clean design when delivered in April,1952 by Hawthorn,Leslie & Co. Ltd at Hebburn. She was not refrigerated, and could carry 13400 dwt of cargo and four first-class passengers to the Plate at a speed of 12 knots from her four-cylinder Doxford oil engine.

The war hero tanker IMPERIAL TRANSPORT was sold to Norwegian owners in 1947, and orders placed for three tankers of 18,000 dwt and delivered from Clyde yards as:-

NEWBURY of 1951 for Alexander Shipping Co. Ltd
CLUTHA RIVER of 1952 for British Empire S.N. Co. Ltd
IMPERIAL TRANSPORT of 1953 for Empire Transport Co. Ltd

Ten or 15-year charters were obtained with SHELL, at the end of which they were sold to Greek and Finnish owners for further trading. Two further wholly-owned tankers of 18,000 dwt were completed on the Tyne - DENBY GRANGE of 1958 from Hawthorn,Leslie & Co. Ltd and ABADESA of 1962 from Swan,Hunter & Wigham Richardson Ltd. A joint venture with BP was formed in October,1958 and

named after the Warwick family - the Warwick Tanker Co. Ltd - and
two 37,000 dwt tankers were ordered from Hawthorn,Leslie & Co.
Ltd and Cammell,Laird & Co. Ltd. These were sisters of tankers in
the BP fleet and were delivered in 1960 as BRANDON PRIORY and
BIDFORD PRIORY respectively.

    Ore Carriers Ltd was set up jointly with BISCO in 1953 to
own six ore-carriers of 9500 dwt, then the largest size able to
enter Port Talbot in South Wales:-

6 PORT TALBOT ORE-CARRIERS OF 9500 DWT

W. Gray,West Hartlepool (6) ORELIA,OREOSA,OREPTON,
                              OREDIAN,OREGIS,OREMINA.

        The engines fitted to this class to provide a loaded
service speed of 12 knots were interesting. The first four completed were fitted with twin Gray-Polar 5-cyl 2SCSA oil engines as
no Doxford oil engines could be obtained. However the last pair,
OREGIS and OREMINA, did have single 5-cylinder Doxford engines
from the Newcastle factory of Hawthorn,Leslie & Co. Ltd. The last
of the sextet,OREMINA, was launched by Mrs James Huntly, the wife
of the Houlder Technical Director. They had four holds and were
on long-term charter to carry iron ore into British ports even
though OREOSA at one time carried the funnel colours of Sven
Salen of Stockholm. The first four were sold to Greek owners in
1971, and OREMINA was sold to Italian owners in 1974 as GENERALE
FEDERICO and was scrapped at Savona in 1985. However OREGIS was
sold to Houlder Offshore Ltd in 1974 for conversion into a diving
maintenance ship (See Section 2.8). OREOSA was sold on to Yugoslavian owners as PODGORICA, and finally arrived at Alang for
scrapping in March,1989 as ALMADEN.

    Two larger ore-carriers of 16830 dwt were ordered from
William Gray & Co. Ltd, and had the distinction of being the
largest ships ever built at Hartlepool. JOYA McCANCE was launched
by Lady McCance, wife of Sir Andrew McCance - a director of Ore
Carriers Ltd, in 1960 and was marginally longer than her near
sister MABEL WARWICK. Their beam was 69 feet 1 inch with the
maximum width of the locks at Hartlepool being 70 feet.

    The general cargo fleets of Houlder Line Ltd and Alexander
Shipping Co. Ltd were updated with six new near-sisters delivered
between 1953 and 1965:-

6 GENERAL CARGO SHIPS OF 12,500 DWT

Burntisland SB Co. Ltd   (5) QUEENSBURY,SHAFTESBURY,TEWKESBURY,
                              WESTBURY,TENBURY.

Bartram,Sunderland   (1) THORPE GRANGE.

All had five holds with three foward of the four-deck
high superstructure and two aft, except in the case of TENBURY of
1965 which had four holds forward and one aft. A fine array of
around 12 medium-to-heavy derricks were fitted with TENBURY also
having prominent deckhouses. Their main trade was grain home from
the Plate, and QUEENSBURY fouled her anchors with an Argentinean
ship at Rosario in September,1962 causing a slight collision and
dents to her port bow. Engines again varied with THORPE GRANGE,
SHAFTESBURY,TEWKESBURY and WESTBURY having Doxford oil engines;
QUEENSBURY had twin Gray-Polar oil engines; and TENBURY had a
Sulzer oil engine. They were sold out of the Group in the early
1970s with WESTBURY lasting the longest before going to Greeks in
1978 as DIAMANDO. All have now either been scrapped or lost due
to marine causes.

The Houlder refrigerated fleet was updated with two new
ships during 1959/60 - ROYSTON GRANGE and HARWICKE GRANGE - from
the Hebburn yard of Hawthorn,Leslie & Co. Ltd. They could carry
435,000 cu. ft. of refrigerated cargo and 12 first-class
passengers. Two double reduction steam turbines drove a single
screw to give 16 knots service speed. The pair were distinctly
handsome ships in comparison to the old,high-sided and box-like
refrigerated ships. This pair had good lines of flair with
extended and streamlined superstructures and funnels. They had
six holds with nos. 4 and 5 hatches trunked through two decks of
cabins. They differed here also in that no. 5 hatch was trunked
through an extra deck in the case of ROYSTON GRANGE.

HARDWICKE GRANGE stood by the heavily-listing German ore-
carrier KREMSERTOR in January,1966, which later sank. ROYSTON
GRANGE saved the lives of the fire-ravaged small Spanish cargo
ship MORCUERA in a merciful rescue on 14th February,1965 near the
Ile de Batz off the French coast. However the hand of fate was
not to augur so well for ROYSTON GRANGE and her crew when outward
bound from Buenos Aires to London on 11th May,1972 with a full
cargo of meat and butter. She collided in the Indio Channel near
Montevideo with the fully-loaded tanker TIEN CHEE of 18,000 dwt,
which was inward bound from Bahia Blanca to La Plata with crude
oil. The damaged tanker spewed blazing oil on to ROYSTON GRANGE
and her 63 crew including the wife and daughter of the Chief
Steward were horribly burnt to death. Ten passengers and the
Argentinean pilot aboard her also died, together with 8 members
of the tanker's crew - a total of 82 lives. ROYSTON GRANGE was
gutted and towed to Montevideo where the fire was extinguished.
She was listing heavily and was condemned for scrap, being towed
to Spain for the breaker's torch.

The Houlder refrigerated fleet was depleted in the 1960s by
the sale of RIPPINGHAM GRANGE in 1961, and CONDESA was chartered
from October,1960 as a storeship for frozen meat at Boulogne
until sent for scrap in June,1962. DUQUESA was transferred to
Royal Mail Line in 1968 and arrived for scrapping at Spezia in

August,1969. HORNBY GRANGE was transferred to Royal Mail Line in 1969 and renamed DOURO, continuing to trade to the Plate until she arrived for scrapping at Aviles in June,1972. HARWICKE GRANGE sailed on for Houlder Line Ltd until sold in 1977 and renamed JACQUES, and she too succumbed to the inevitable breaker's torch at Kaosiung in 1979.

The post-WWII fleet rebuilding was completed in 1959/60 by two general cargo ships of 13,100 dwt - SWAN RIVER with engines amidships for the British Empire S.N. Co. Ltd; and OCEAN TRANSPORT with engines-aft for Empire Transport Co. Ltd.

2.8 DIVERSIFICATION 1965 - 1990.

Cyril W. Warwick had been made Chairman on the retirement of his uncle Walter C. Warwick for health reasons on 31st January, 1962. Walter had started work with Furness,Withy & Co. Ltd on 1st January,1896 as an assistant to Frederick Lewis under Robert B. Stoker, and thus completed a magnificent 66 years service to the Group. He died on 20th May,1963 at his home in Hadley Wood. Cyril W. Warwick and John M. Houlder were both made Managing Directors of Houlder Brothers & Co. Ltd in 1957. John M. Houlder later became Chairman and Managing Director of the Boards in 1970, following the retirement of Cyril W. Warwick. John was the son of Maurice C. Houlder, who had died in 1955, and grandson of the founder Edwin Savory Houlder, and had become the first chairman of the Plate - Europe Freight Conference in 1961, having served on earlier committees since 1954. He was also made a director of Furness,Withy & Co. Ltd in 1954. The Houlder fleet at the end of 1965 stood at 26 conventional ships:-

Houlder Line Ltd: 3 Refrigerated ships
                                2 General cargo ships
                                1 tanker

Alexander Shipping Ltd: 5 General cargo ships
                                1 tanker

British Empire S.N. Co. Ltd: 1 General cargo ship
                                1 tanker

Empire Transport Co. Ltd: 1 General cargo ship
                                1 tanker

Furness-Houlder Argentine Line Ltd: 1 Refrigerated ship
                                1 tanker

Ore Carriers Ltd: 6 ore-carriers

Warwick Tanker Co. Ltd: 2 tankers

The only new trade of the previous 20 years was the iron-ore shipments into the U.K., and similar joint agreements had been entered into with BISCO by many other British tramp owners. The liner trade to the Plate was contracting, and ship sizes and new building costs were starting to increase alarmingly. A policy of diversification was now followed by the company, pioneering inno-vative high technology that augurred well for future profits:-

(1) SEABRIDGE CONSORTIUM World-wide very large bulker operation.
(2) OCEAN GAS TRANSPORT   Liquid petroleum gases/ethylene.
(3) NORTH SEA OIL FIELDS   Diving/Fire-fighting/Maintenance.

(1) SEABRIDGE CONSORTIUM.

The sizes and new building costs of bulk carriers were increasing rapidly in leaps, and in order to ensure a return on the money invested long-term charters would have to be negotiated with major shippers. This could best be done by banding together and thus in 1965 the Seabridge consortium was founded by:-

> Bibby Line
> C.T. Bowring
> H. Clarkson
> Hunting & Son
> Houlder Brothers
> Silver Line

Houlder Brothers & Co. Ltd ordered a 51,500 dwt bulker from Sunderland Shipbuilders Ltd for delivery in 1968. OROTAVA was chartered for 5 years to Seabridge and took the name OROTAVA BRIDGE in 1969. A larger 137,500 dwt bulker was later ordered from the same builder for delivery in 1972, and when launched on 3rd November,1971 ORENDA BRIDGE was the largest ship built on the Wear at that time. Her 5-year charter to Seabridge expired in 1977 and she was sold in 1978. OROTAVA continued to trade for Houlder until sold in 1980, having gained the traditional name of RIPON GRANGE in 1979. A third bulker was owned on a 50/50 basis with Hadley Shipping Co. Ltd, which shared the same offices as the company and had family links with Houlder and Furness,Withy & Co. Ltd. (See 'TRAVELS OF THE TRAMPS' Vol. I by this author). This was CLYDESDALE, built by Scotts of Greenock in 1967 and from 1969 operated in Seabridge as CLYDE BRIDGE until 1977, when Houlder purchased the Hadley 'half' ownership and renamed her DUNSTER GRANGE. She was sold out of the fleet in 1982.

Furness,Withy & Co. Ltd became joint partners in Sea-bridge with Houlder Brothers & Co. Ltd and ordered a 168,000 dwt OBO from the Furness yard at Haverton Hill for management by Houlder. FURNESS BRIDGE was the first of a class of six ill-fated sisters when delivered in 1971. Three of her sisters DERBYSHIRE and ENGLISH BRIDGE (Bibby),TYNE BRIDGE (Hunting) later encounter-ed severe structural problems that have been given widespread publicity. However FURNESS BRIDGE is still sailing in 1991 as OCEAN SOVEREIGN, as are her two former Norwegian-owned Thornhope Shipping Ltd sisters SIR JOHN HUNTER and SIR ALEXANDER GLEN -

Houlder-managed between 1975 and 1977. A smaller bulker of 120,000 dwt was then ordered by Furness,Withy & Co. Ltd from Harland & Wolff Ltd, Belfast and launched as WINSFORD BRIDGE on 1st October, 1973 for operation in Seabridge but she was completed as MOUNT NEWMAN on 7-year bare-boat charter to Australian National Line carrying iron ore from her namesake, Mount Newman.

(2) OCEAN GAS TRANSPORT CO. LTD

An agreement had been made in 1964 with a French company with previous experience in the carriage of liquid gas - GAZOCEAN SA of Paris - for joint operation of the small gas tanker AVOGADRO and the new slightly larger gas tanker JOULE completed that year at Nantes. An order was then placed with a shipbuilder that was both well-known to the company and had previous experience of building gas tankers - Hawthorn,Leslie & Co. Ltd at Hebburn. CLERK-MAXWELL was completed in 1966, and her cargo tanks had a metric capacity of 11751 cu. m. and a dwt of 9067 tons, the cargo coolant temperature being controlled by a large white-painted housing on deck in front of the bridge connected via much visible piping to the liquid cargo. A small goalpost mast was fitted on top of the bridge to complete the appearance of the first large deep-sea gas tanker built in Britain. She was registered under the Nile S.S. Co. Ltd but was later transferred to Ocean Gas Transport Co. Ltd. This company was formed jointly with GAZOCEAN, and the French company name was painted in large white letters on the hulls of the jointly-owned tankers.

Ocean Gas Transport Co. Ltd tankers had double markings on their funnels, with the Houlder Maltese cross side-by-side with the GAZOCEAN dolphin breathing flame on a blue disc. Later gas tankers had funnels too narrow for both devices to be displayed side-by-side, and so the dolphin was placed above the cross. The gas tanker fleet was added to by:-

1968	*HUMBOLDT of 5165 dwt	6247 cu.m.
1971	FARADAY of 24750 dwt	31215 cu.m.
1971	*CAVENDISH of 29500 dwt	40200 cu.m.
1973	*JOULE of 11355 dwt	11071 cu.m. Built in 1965.
1978	*LORD KELVIN of 28400 dwt	31243 cu.m.

* Jointly owned with GAZOCEAN

Cargos carried included anhydrous ammonia,propane,butane, propylene/butane mixtures,vinyl chloride,ethylene and naptha.

(3) NORTH SEA OILFIELDS.

In the early 1970s, a market existed for diving/fire-fighting/maintenance services to support the drilling rigs. A stable ship fitted with cranes for maintenance work and from where divers could safely enter the sea through a moonpool to work on the rigs was required - such a ship already existed in the fleet and was laid-up in the Fal - the ore-carrier OREGIS. She had led a mundane life from completion at Hartlepool in 1955 bringing iron ore from the orefields of the world to British

ports such as Port Talbot,Workington,Birkenhead,Tyne and Tees.
Her only moments of excitement occurred while bound from Lulea to
Port Talbot in November,1964 via the Kiel Canal she had struck
the lock gates at Brunsbuttelkoog; and when she had run aground
at Workington in December,1969. She arrived in the Fal on 15th
September,1971 and was towed round to the Tyne for conversion,
arriving at Smiths Dock Co. Ltd at North Shields on 6th April,
1973.

        The conversion of OREGIS took 12 months and as well as
the fitting of a moonpool in her double bottom amidships, a heli-
deck was built on to her fo'c'stle, a large white crane of 100
tons capacity was fitted amidships together with a pipe tensioning
structure to allow her to connect undersea pipelines. The conversion had cost £4M but a further £2M was to be needed for repairs
for disaster struck when she was leaving the Tyne for trials on
10th March,1974. Her engine stopped mid-way between the piers and
she drifted ashore on the Black Middens at Tynemouth. A local Tyne
tug NORTHSIDER also went ashore during refloating attempts, and
unfortunately a crew member of a Hull tug called in to help was
drowned. She was refloated on 8th April,1974 and towed back to
Smiths Dock for repairs which took 3 months. Her ownership
together with that of OREMINA had been transferred from Ore
Carriers Ltd to Vallum Shipping Co. Ltd on 24th July,1972, and
OREGIS was then transferred to Houlder Line Ltd on 7th May,1973.
Houlder Line Ltd was then renamed Houlder Offshore Ltd to allow
the Chairman, John M. Houlder, to move from shipping into offshore
work.

        Other Houlder developments during the period under
review included the purchase of the South American conference
rights and goodwill of the South American Saint Line in 1966.
THORPE GRANGE and the ore-carrier JOYA McCANCE were given traditional 'Saint' names of ST. MERRIEL and ST. MARGARET. However
both these Houlder 'Saint's had been sold off by 1976, ending a
history of such ships in the Plate trade which can be traced back
to the 1920s. A 15600 dwt engines-aft general cargo ship had been
launched as BANBURY for Alexander Shipping Ltd at Scotts yard at
Greenock. She was fitted with eight raised deck cranes to enable
deck timber and containers to be carried, and went into service
on the Australian coast as IRON BANBURY in 1972 having been
chartered by the Broken Hill Proprietary Co. Ltd.

        France,Fenwick & Co. Ltd had a long history in the North East
coal trade going back to the last century, and in 1972 were operating two colliers, a deep sea tramp and a new bulk carrier fitted
with gantry cranes operating in the STAR consortium. However they
were gradually withdrawing from shipping and the fleet was managed
by Houlder until sold to the Jessel finance Group in 1974. The
deep-sea tramp SHERWOOD was sold to Greek owners, and the bulk
carrier STAR PINEWOOD was sold to Fred. Olsen and his Blandford
Shipping Co. Ltd to become STAR BULFORD. However the two colliers
CHELWOOD and DALEWOOD were acquired separately by Houlder, and by
Hadley Shipping Co. Ltd to become OSWESTRY GRANGE and CYMBELINE

respectively. They then operated together in the North East coal
trade until ousted by three giant 22,000 dwt supercolliers owned
by the C.E.G.B. in 1985.

John Errington Keville was managing director of France,Fenwick
& Co. Ltd when their management was taken over by Houlder. John was
the son of Sir Errington Keville, a past Chairman of Furness,Withy
& Co. Ltd, who had obtained experience elsewhere in the shipping
industry before joining France,Fenwick & Co. Ltd. John M. Houlder
then brought John E. Keville onto the Houlder Boards as his succ-
essor on the shipping side while he concentrated on offshore work
as Chairman of Houlder Offshore Ltd. John E. Keville became Chief
Executive of the newly-created Furness,Withy(Shipping) Ltd in 1977.

Houlder Brothers & Co. Ltd had thus diversified into the
following trades in 1974:-

Plate liner service: 1 Refrigerated ship
                               2 General cargo ships

SEABRIDGE Consortium: 2 large bulkers with another jointly-
                               owned with Hadley Shipping Co. Ltd.

U.K. iron ore trade: 2 ore-carriers

North Sea diving: 1 vessel

Australian coastal: 1 General cargo ship

North-East coal trade: 1 collier

Tanker trades: 2 tankers

Ocean Gas Transport: 5 gas tankers

The refrigerated ship, HARDWICKE GRANGE, was transferred
from the ownership of Houlder Line Ltd in 1975 to that of Shaw,
Savill & Albion Co. Ltd; this allowed Houlder Line Ltd to be
renamed Houlder Offshore Ltd. OCEAN TRANSPORT and WESTBURY were
similarly transferred from the ownership of the Empire Transport
Co. Ltd and Alexander Shipping Co. Ltd to that of Shaw,Savill &
Albion Co. Ltd in 1976 but continued to sail to the Plate.

In 1977 a 'second-generation' diving/fire-fighting/mainten-
ance 'ship' came into service. This was the self-propelled semi-
submersible platform UNCLE JOHN, named after the Chairman and
Managing Director - John M. Houlder - who was awarded a C.B.E. in
1977 for services to transportation. John had previous experience
of semi-submersibles in the early 1970s when he organised the
technical staff of the first British company to undertake offshore drilling from a semi-submersible. UNCLE JOHN has a deck
work area of 20,000 sq. ft. supported by 6 legs positioned on two
pontoons, each of which has 3000 hp thrusters for forward motion

as well as transverse thrusters. It has two deck cranes of 100
tons and another of 15 tons for rig maintenance work and for
lifting the COMEX saturation diving system. This does the subsea
work e.g. oxy-electric cutting,concrete blasting,dredging,pipe
alignment and hyperbaric welding etc. It can operate with the
diving bell lowered in up to Force 6 winds, and can maintain
position for fire-fighting work until Force 12 is reached. UNCLE
JOHN was built at Oslo by Nylands Vaersted and named on 6th May,
1977, ownership being on the old style of 64ths with Houlder
having 43, Ellerman 15, and Ugland of Norway 6. She commenced
work in the Brent field on a 3-year contract to SHELL/ESSO coup-
ling underwater pipelines. Repairs and survey work was always
carried out at Smiths Dock Co. Ltd,North Shields and included an
amazing act of dry-docking, with each pontoon manoeuvred and
subsequently resting in adjoining dry-docks!

Furness,Withy & Co. Ltd had purchased the remaining Houlder
shares at the end of 1974 to give total ownership, and Houlder
thus became a part of the Tung empire after the takeover of
Furness in February,1980. At this time the Houlder fleet was:-

Bulk trades: 3 bulk carriers
                          1 General cargo ship

Tanker trades: 2 tankers

North East coal trade: 1 collier

North Sea oilfields: 1 vessel
                          1 platform

Ocean Gas Transport: 6 gas tankers

The bulker DUNSTER GRANGE, ex CLYDESDALE, was sold in 1982,
the other two were B26 types built by Austin & Pickersgill Ltd in
1976 - LYNTON GRANGE and UPWEY GRANGE - and were also sold in
1982. A larger bulker of 70,000 dwt was later purchased in 1980
and renamed ROUNTON GRANGE and lasted until sold in 1984. The
general cargo vessel BANBURY traded on the Plate liner service
after the end of her Australian charter in 1975, but she was sold
in 1982. The two tankers, ELSTREE GRANGE and HORNBY GRANGE, were
completed in 1979 by Harland & Wolff Ltd at Belfast and were sold
in 1985. The North Sea vessel OREGIS left the Tyne for scrapping
at Vigo in November,1982. The collier OSWESTRY GRANGE was thus
the last owned 'GRANGE' when she hauled down the Maltese cross
houseflag for the last time on 6th August,1985 at Oxelosund in
Sweden on hand-over to new owners.

A 'third-generation' diving support vessel was completed on
the Tyne by Swan Hunter Shipbuilders Ltd in June,1984. ORELIA has
a low profile with a barge type hull with a sloping,angular bow
and stern. She has six 6-cylinder Mirlees oil engines DR geared
to three propulsion shafts. A computerised dynamic positioning

system can keep her on station in all but the roughest of gales.
Her bridge is where one would expect it to be - up forward - and
she has two deck cranes each of 100 tons capacity for lifting the
saturation diving chambers and bells. Her deck area is 19,400 sq.
ft. with accomodation for 100 workers. She has powerful fire-
fighting and rescue equipment including 2 lifeboats for 132 survivors and 6 liferafts for another 120 survivors.

The fleet in 1986 was thus the platform UNCLE JOHN and
ORELIA plus four gas tankers of which CAVENDISH had anchored off
Guayaquil in Ecuador for use as a gas storage tanker on 4th
November,1985.

C.H. Tung completed a re-organisation of Furness,Withy & Co.
Ltd on 27th January,1987 in which the Houlder ships and interests
were transferred to Furness,Withy(Investments) Ltd - directly
owned by Orient Overseas(Holdings) Ltd,Hong Kong. The Houlder
companies were:-

> Houlder Offshore Ltd - offshore servicing
> Houlder Comex Ltd - offshore servicing
> Houlder Comex Diving Ltd - diving support
> Houlder Marine Drilling - rig operations
> Houlder Marine Services Ltd - diving support ships
> Houlder Offshore Engineering Ltd - design work
> Ocean Gas Transport Ltd - gas tankers
> Kingsnorth Marine Drilling Ltd - rig owners

In the North Sea, Stena of Sweden combined with Houlder to
form Stena Houlder Ltd and ORELIA became STENA ORELIA in 1989,
with Stena Houlder Ltd also taking over the Houlder 64ths in
UNCLE JOHN. The gas tankers were trading on South American
contracts with CAVENDISH back in service in 1989 with FARADAY,
and a new smaller HUMBOLDT was purchased in 1987 for the feeder
service to Ecuador. A third smaller JOULE was purchased from
Bibby in 1989 and is trading in the Mediterranean. UNCLE JOHN
continues to slip quietly from her moorings on the Tyne or at
Peterhead or other East Coast ports and head out to sea on
lucrative oil company charters - long may the most profitable
venture ever initiated by John M. Houlder CBE continue to do so!

VESSELS UNDER FURNESS or FURNESS,WITHY & CO. LTD OWNERSHIP.

F1. CHICAGO (1878) 1384g 1020n 255' x 34'
C 2-cyl by N.E. Marine Eng. Co. Ltd,Sunderland.
4.1878 Launched by W. Gray & Co.,West Hartlepool for Thomas
Furness & Co.,Hartlepool. 1878 Wrecked on Haisbro Sands on
maiden voyage to U.S.A.

F2. AVERILL (1878 - 1883) 1690g 1095n 260' x 34'
C 2-cyl by N.E. Marine Eng. Co. Ltd,Sunderland.
9.1878 Launched by W. Gray & Co.,West Hartlepool for Thomas
Furness & Co.,Hartlepool. 21.6.1883 Wrecked at Ingonish (CB)
o.v. Barrow to Montreal.

F3. BRANTFORD CITY (1880 - 1883) 2371g 1566n 280' x 39'
C 2-cyl by Blair & Co. Ltd,Stockton.
3.1880 Completed by W. Gray & Co.,West Hartlepool for Thomas
Furness & Co.,Hartlepool. 10.8.1883 Wrecked near Little Harbour
(NS) o.v. London to Halifax & Boston with general.

F4. YORK CITY (1881 - 1887) 2325g 1530n 280' x 40'
C 2-cyl by Blair & Co. Ltd,Stockton.
10.1881 Completed by W. Gray & Co.,West Hartlepool for Thomas
Furness & Co.,Hartlepool. 22.12.1887 Wrecked on Faro Island,
Sweden.

F5. BOSTON CITY (1882 - 1897) 2334g 1534n 280' x 40'
C 2-cyl by Blair & Co. Ltd,Stockton
2.1882 Completed by W. Gray & Co.,West Hartlepool for Thomas
Furness & Co.,Hartlepool. 1891 Reg. under Furness,Withy & Co.
Ltd. 1897 Sold to A/S Norman(Blom & Ohlsen),Fredrikshavn ren.
NORMAN. 1899 Sold to O. Banck,Helsingborg ren. ARLA. 1914 Sold to
W.A. Stranne,Gothenburg name u/ch. 1919 Sold to C. Hoffman
Bang,Copenhagen ren. ACACIA. 1924 Sold to Rederi A/B Cargo(B.
Carlstrom),Helsingborg ren. FREJ. 1934 B/U.

F6. DURHAM CITY (1882 - 1897) 3092g 2037n 314' x 43'
C 2-cyl by Blair & Co. Ltd,Stockton.
3.1882 Completed by W. Gray & Co.,West Hartlepool for Thomas
Furness & Co.,Hartlepool. 1891 Reg. under Furness,Withy & Co.
Ltd. 1897 Sold and broken up.

F7. NEWCASTLE CITY (1882 - 1887) 2129g 1384n 285' x 36'
C 2-cyl by T. Richardson & Sons,Hartlepool.
10.1882 Completed by Edward Withy & Co.,West Hartlepool for
Christopher Furness. 23.12.1887 Wrecked off Nantucket Island o.v.
Newcastle to New York with general.

F8. WETHERBY (1883 - 1893) 2129g 1381n 285' x 36'
C 2-cyl by Black,Hawthorn & Co.,Gateshead.
4.1883 Completed by W. Gray & Co.,West Hartlepool for Christopher
Furness. 1891 Reg. under Furness,Withy & Co. Ltd. 12.1893 Wrecked
off Cape Hatteras o.v. Fernandina to Rotterdam.

F9. RIPON CITY   (1883 - 1896) 2141g 1384n   285' x 36'
C 2-cyl by Blair & Co.,Stockton.
11.1883 Completed by W. Gray & Co.,West Hatlepool for Christopher
Furness. 1891 Reg. under Furness,Withy & Co. Ltd. 1896 Sold to
P. Viale di G.B.,Genoa ren. SILVIA. 1914 Sold to Conti,Giorgi &
Co.,Genoa ren. PINA. 1918 B/U.

F10. STOCKHOLM CITY (1884 - 1898) 2686g 1759n   300' x 40'
C 2-cyl by bldrs.
3.1884 Completed by Palmers,Jarrow for Christopher Furness. 1891
Reg. under Furness,Withy & Co. Ltd. 1898 Sold to A. Bensa fuP,
Genoa ren. CAROLINA P. 1901 Sold to G. Corvaja,Palermo ren.
ADELINA CORVAJA. 1902 Repurchased by A. Bensa ren. CAROLINA P.
8.1906 B/U.

F11. GOTHENBURG CITY (1884 - 1891) 2529g 1658n   301' x 38'
C 2-cyl by T. Richardson & Sons,Hartlepool.
1884 Completed by Edward Withy & Co.,West Hartlepool for Christopher Furness. His first passenger-carrying ship, although made
only one voyage as such. 6.1891 Wrecked near Blyth o.v. Montreal
to the Tyne with cattle,deals and general.

F12. LINCOLN CITY   (1884 - 1885) 2729g 1750n   301' x 40'
C 2-cyl by T. Richardson & Sons,Hartlepool.
1884 Completed by W. Gray & Co.,West Hartlepool for Christopher
Furness. 1885 Sold to T. Wilson,Sons & Co. Ltd,Hull ren. CHICAGO.
1898 Ren. SALERNO. 1901 Sold to Macbeth & Gray,Hull name u/ch.
1901 Sold to A/S Salerno(W. Wilhelmsen),Tonsberg name u/ch.
30.6.1905 Wrecked on Lichfield Shoal off Halifax(NS) o.v. Cadiz
to St. John(NB).

F13. DAMARA   (1886 - 1905) 1779g 1145n   275' x 35'
C 2-cyl by bldrs.
3.1885 Completed by A. Stephen & Sons,Glasgow for Christopher
Furness. 1891 Reg. under Furness,Withy & Co. Ltd. 7.2.1905
Wrecked off Musquodoboit o.v. Liverpool to Halifax.

F14. ULUNDA (1885 - 1890) & (1898 -1910) 1789g 1096g 275' x 35'
C 2-cyl by bldrs.
5.1885 Completed by A. Stephen & Sons,Glasgow for Christopher
Furness. 1890 Sold to Canada & Newfoundland S. S. Co. Ltd(J.
Hall,mgr),Halifax. 1898 Repurchased by Furness,Withy & Co. Ltd.
1910 Sold to Anglo-Hellenic S.S. Co. Ltd(A.A. Embiricos),Andros
ren. ELLI. 11.1911 B/U at Gateshead.

F15. WASHINGTON CITY (1885 - 1891) 2296g 1441n   285' x 36'
T 3-cyl by T. Richardson & Sons,Hartlepool.
9.1885 Launched and 10.1886 completed by Edward Withy & Co.,West
Hartlepool for Christopher Furness. First Furness triple expansion powered ship. 1891 Sold to Bennetts & Co.,Hartlepool name
u/ch. 1894 Sold to S.M. Kuhnle & Son,Bergen ren. FRAM. 26.10.1900
Stranded on Seaton Rocks near Blyth o.v. Kallundborg to Blyth in
ballast.

F16. KATIE (1886 - 1890) 2796g 1806n 321' x 40'
C 2-cyl by bldrs.
1880 Completed by A. Stephen & Sons,Glasgow for C.H.S. Schultz,
Hamburg. 1886 Purchased by Christopher Furness. 1890 Sold to J.&
M. Gunn & Co. ren. DUNKELD. 27.3.1895 Struck a derelict 28 miles
E of Lobos Island and sank o.v. Cardiff to Buenos Aires with
coal.

F17. MADURA (1887 - 1895) 2324g 1658n 309' x 36'
C 2-cyl by Blair & Co,Stockton. Tripled in 1890 by W. Allan & Co.
9.1873 Completed by Richardson,Duck & Co.,Stockton for Java Stoom
Maats,Amsterdam. 1887 Purchased by Christopher Furness. 1891 Reg.
under Furness,Withy & Co. Ltd. 11.1895 Foundered o.v. Hamburg to
Port Royal.

F18. BALTIMORE CITY (1888 - 1897) 2334g 1534n 290' x 39'
T 3-cyl by bldrs.
5.1888 Completed by A. Stephen & Sons,Glasgow for Christopher
Furness. 1891 Reg. under Furness,Withy & Co. Ltd. 7.1897 Wrecked
in Belle Isle Strait o.v. Montreal to Manchester with deals and
corn.

F19. FIRE QUEEN (1888 - 1890) 1220g 914n 249' x 26'
C 2-cyl by J. Jones & Co.,Liverpool.
10.1864 Completed by Pile,Spence & Co,Hartlepool for J. Pile and
J. Spence. 1866 Purchased by T.& J. Harrison Ltd,Liverpool. 1879
Sold to H. Swan,Newcastle. 26.5.1885 Sold by public auction at Le
Havre. 1887 Sold to R. Beveridge,London. 1888 Purchased by
Christopher Furness. 1890 Sold to W.F. Connor. 1890 Sold to F.
Anquetil & Son,Rouen ren. FERDINAND A. 11.12.1894 Wrecked at
mouth of Seine o.v. Spain to Rouen.

F20. NEW BOROUGH (1888 - 1895) 1795g 1169n 260' x 37'
T 3-cyl by Central Marine Eng. Works,Hartlepool.
1888 Completed by W. Gray & Co.,West Hartlepool for Christopher
Furness. 1891 Reg. under Furness,Withy & Co. Ltd. 4.1895 Stranded
but refloated and sold to Louisville & Nashville Railroad Co(M.H.
Smith),Pensacola ren. PENSACOLA. 1901 Sold to Southern Products
Co of New York ren. WILHELMINA. 7.1916 Sunk by collision in Rio
de Janeiro bay o.v. Newport News to Rio de Janeiro with coal.

F21. BLANCHE (1888 - 1892) 246g 147n 146' x 20'
I 2-cyl by bldrs.
4.1863 Completed by A.& J. Inglis,Glasgow for J. Weatherley,
London. Later Weatherley,Mead & Hussey. 1888 Purchased by
Christopher Furness. 1892 Sold to Osborn & Wallis,Hartlepool.
1902 B/U.

F22. PLEIADES (1888 - 1890) 2297g 1456n 343' x 35'
C 2-cyl by Maudslay,Sons & Field,London.
1873 Completed by A. Leslie & Co.,Hebburn as PLEIADES for Star
Nav. Co. Ltd,Liverpool. 1887 Sold to Marques de Campo,Cadiz ren.
GUATEMALA. 1888 Purchased by Christopher Furness as PLEIADES.
1890 Sold to R.F. Routh,Hartlepool. 1891 Sold to A. Trabotti,

Odessa ren. EMELIA. 1.1892 Foundered o.v. Cardiff to Constantinople with coal.

F23. SCANDINAVIA (1888 - 1890) 1138g 852n   258' x 26'
I 2-cyl by D. & W. Henderson,Glasgow. Compounded in 1876.
1865 Completed by C.& W. Earle,Hull as SIRIUS for Wilson & Co.,
Liverpool. 1868 Sold to Handyside & Co,Glasgow ren. COLUMBIA.
1869 Ren. SCANDINAVIA. 1874 Sold to Henderson Bros,Glasgow name
u/ch. 1888 Purchased by Christopher Furness. 1890 Sold to J.
Meek,Liverpool ren. SIRIUS. 1893 Sold to Oliver & Co,U.S.A. name
u/ch. 1894 Sold to C. Nelson,Hawaii ren. KAHULUI. 1898 Ren.
CLEVELAND. 10.1900 Wrecked at Cape Rodney 34 miles from Nome o.v.
Seattle to Nome with coal.

F24. SULTAN (1888 - 1899) 2525g 1899n   319' x 37'
C 2-cyl by Ravenhill,Eastons & Co.
3.1873 Completed by R.& H. Green,London as SULTAN for the
builders. 1880 Sold to Marques de Campo,Cadiz ren. ASIA. 1888
Purchased by Christopher Furness ren. SULTAN. 3.1889 Abandoned in
position 42 N, 57W to S of Newfoundland o.v. Norfolk(Va) to
London.

F25. BARON HAMBRO (1888 - 1889) 579g 367n   209' x 25'
C 2-cyl by C.& W. Earle,Hull.
1.1861 Completed by C.Lungley,London as BARON HAMBRO for Wilson &
Sons,Hull. 1880 Sold to W. Tulley & Co.,Hull. 1888 Purchased by
Christopher Furness name u/ch. 1889 Sold to Powley,Thomas &
Co.,Hartlepool name u/ch. 1889 Sold to E. Jenkins & Co., Hart-
lepool. 1895 Sold to Baron Hambro S.S. Co. Ltd(Jobson & Stally-
brass),Hartlepool. 1901 Sold to P.P. Gourgy,Odessa ren. TARAS
BOULBA. 1920 Sold to N. Methinity,Odessa ren. OLGA METHINITY.
1921 Ren. VERA GEELMUGDEN. 1922 Ren. NADINA. 1924 Sold to
P.Dounias,Constantinople ren. CANDILLI. 1931 Sold to Dr. Nihat,
Istanbul ren. ZUHAL. 21.6.1943 Driven aground by storm at Kara
Burnu on Turkish European Black Sea coast o.v. from Zonguldak
with coal,total loss.

F26. ST. LOUIS (1888 - 1889) 1862g 1213n   301' x 35'
C 2-cyl by C.D. Holmes & Co.,Hull.
7.1870 Completed by G.R. Clover & Son,Birkenhead for T.
Baker & Son,Cardiff. 1888 Purchased by Christopher Furness.
1889 Sold to Khoo Tiong Poh then Khoo Sin Thuak,Singapore
ren. CHEANG CHEW. Later sold to Nah Kim Seng,Singapore name
u/ch. 10.8.1911 Wrecked to E of Madura.

F27. TRURO CITY (1889 - 1890) 1006g 743n   210' x 30'
T 3-cyl by N.E. Marine Eng. Co. Ltd,Newcastle.
1889 Completed by Sunderland SB Co. for Christopher Furness. 1890
Sold to D/S Normandie(Meinich & Co),Christiania ren. NORMANDIE.
1900 Sold to Brusgaard & Kjosterud,Drammen name u/ch. 1914 Sold
to A/S Norli Thygo Sorensen,Christiania ren. NORLI. 1914 Sold to
Lie & Roer D/S A/S,Christiania ren. BISP. Later to D/S Baltic
(E.H. Rustad),Christiania. 4.1.1940 Torpedoed and sunk by U23 in
North Sea o.v. Sunderland to Andalsnes.

F28. DUART CASTLE   (1889 - 1892)   1839g 1180n   301' x 33'
C 2-cyl by bldrs.
7.1878 Completed by Barclay,Curle & Co.,Glasgow as ADJUTANT for
Seater,White & Co.,Leith. 1880 Sold to D. Currie & Co.,London ren.
DUART CASTLE. 1889 Purchased by Christopher Furness. 1891 Trans-
ferred to Furness,Withy & Co. Ltd. 1892 Sold to Pickford & Black,
London name u/ch. 1901 Ren. ORURO by Pickford & Black. 1925 B/U.

F29. TAYMOUTH CASTLE (1889 - 1892) 1827g 1172n   300' x 34'
C 2-cyl by bldrs.
3.1877 Completed by Barclay,Curle & Co.,Glasgow as TAYMOUTH
CASTLE for D. Currie & Co. Ltd,London. 1889 Purchased by
Christopher Furness. 1891 Reg. under Furness,Withy & Co. Ltd.
1892 Sold to Pickford & Black,London name u/ch. 1900 Ren. OCAMO
by Pickford & Black. 1914 Sold to Newport S.S. Co. Ltd,Halifax
name u/ch. 1921 B/U.

F30. TYNEDALE   (1889 - 1897) 2148g 1391n   272' x 39'
T 3-cyl by Blair & Co.,Stockton.
8.1889 Completed by Ropner & Son,Stockton as INCHARRAN for
Hamilton,Fraser & Co.,Liverpool. 1889 Purchased by Christopher
Furness & Co. ren. TYNEDALE. 1891 Reg. under Furness,Withy & Co.
Ltd. 1897 Sold to J. Holman & Sons ren. FURTOR. 27.7.1897 Aban-
doned in Atlantic o.v. St. John(NF) to Barry with timber.

F31. CENISIO   (1890 - 1891) 1431g 927n   222' x 36'
C 2-cyl by Konin Maats Scheldt,Flushing.
7.1867 Completed by Palmers,Jarrow for A.Cerruti,Genoa as CLEM-
ENTINA. 1875 Sold to Sivtori & Schiaffino,Genoa ren. CENTRO
AMERICA. 1884 Sold to Ponzone & Astengo,Genoa ren. CENISIO. 1888
Sold to F. Stumore & Co.,London. 1890 Purchased by Christopher
Furness as CENISIO. 1891 Reg. under Furness,Withy & Co. Ltd. 1891
Sold to Benchimol & Sobrinho,Lisbon ren. ELISA. 1895 Sold to
Empresa de Nav Cruzeiro do Sol,Lisbon ren. CRUZEIRO. 18.12.1895
Wrecked at Aracaju.

F32. TYNEHEAD   (1890 - 1897) 2258g 1462n   272' x 39'
T 3-cyl by Blair & Co.,Stockton.
9.1890 Completed by Ropner & Son,Stockton as TYNEHEAD for Christopher Furness & Co. 1891 Reg. under Furness,Withy & Co. Ltd.
1897 Sold to J. Holman & Sons ren. MISTOR. 1899 Sold to Anglo-
Grecian S.S. Co. Ltd(Mango,Doresa & Co),London name u/ch. 8.1900
Sunk by collision while at anchor in Cardiff Roads o.v. Newport
to Malta with coal.

F33. OTTAWA   (1891)   1719g 1107n   275' x 35'
T 3-cyl by bldrs.
2.1891 Completed by A. Stephen & Sons,Glasgow for Christopher
Furness. 9.1891 Transferred to Furness,Withy & Co. Ltd. 11.1891
Wrecked on Blonde Rock,Seal Island in Bay of Fundy(NS) o.v.
London to Halifax & St. John.

F34. CALCUTTA CITY   (1891)   2868g 1855n   314' x 41'
T 3-cyl by T. Richardson & Sons,Hartlepool.

3.1891 Launched as CALCUTTA CITY by E. Withy & Co. for Christopher Furness and 4.1891 completed as MELBRIDGE for United Steamship Co. (T.Temperley,mgr),London. 14.2.1907 Abandoned at sea in posn. 46 N, 9 W o.v. Cardiff to Montevideo with coal and coke.

F35. CUNDALL (1891) 4753g 2960n 399' x 47'
T 3-cyl by Wallsend Slipway Co. Ltd.
1891 Launched as CUNDALL for Furness,Withy & Co. Ltd by C.S. Swan & Hunter,Wallsend and 7.1891 completed as CHANCELLOR for T.& J. Harrison, Liverpool. 1901 Sold to R. Sloman,Hamburg ren. PALLANZA. 1906 Sold to Hamburg America Line,Hamburg name u/ch. 11.11.1915 Mined and sunk off River Ems.

F36. WELLDECK (1891) 2697g 1895n 314' x 39'
T 3-cyl by T. Richardson & Sons,Hartlepool.
1891 Launched as WELLDECK for Furness,Withy & Co. Ltd and completed as INCHDUNE for Hamilton,Fraser & Co.,Liverpool. 1899 Sold to Aznar y Cia,Bilbao ren. SOLLUBE. 1905 Sold to Cia Marit del Nervion(urquijo y Aldecoa),Bilbao ren. MAR-NEGRO. 1921 Sold to Fabrica de Mieres,Spain ren. ENRIQUE BALESTEROS. 1932 Ren. NUMA. 1938 Scrapped.

F37. INCHGARVIE (1892) 2814g 1706n 310' x 39'
C 2-cyl by R.&W. Hawthorn,Newcastle.
10.1882 Completed by Sir W.G. Armstrong,Mitchell & Co,Newcastle for Hamilton,Fraser & Co.,Liverpool. 1892 Purchased by Furness, Withy & Co. Ltd. 1892 Sold to Northumbrian Shipping Co. Ltd(L. Macarthy & Co),Newcastle name u/ch. 1900 Sold to Cie de Lloyd Franco-Africaine,Dunkirk ren. LEON REVELHAC. 1902 Sold to Dall Orso & Co,Spezia ren. DANTE. 1904 Sold to Inui Gomei Kaisha (I.Shinbei,mgr),Suma ren. KENKON MARU. 9.4.1925 Wrecked at Yerimosaki on Hokkaido while carrying logs.

F38. INCHULVA (1892 - 1893) 2229g 1453n 285' x 38'
C 2-cyl by Wallsend Slipway Co. Ltd.
2.1881 Completed by Sir W.G. Armstrong,Mitchell & Co,Newcastle for Hamilton,Fraser & Co.,Liverpool. 1892 Purchased by Furness,Withy & Co. Ltd. 1893 Sold to J.E. Guthe & Co. 2.11.1895 Wrecked off Isle of Santa Maria o.v. Cardiff to Acapulco with coal.

F39. CONSTANCE (1892 - 1893) See ELSTREE GRANGE H3

F40. MADRID (1892 - 1894) 2439g 1571n 316' x 36'
C 2-cyl by bldrs.
1873 Completed by T.R. Oswald & Co.,Sunderland as AURRERA for Olano & Co. later Olano,Larrinaga & Co.,Bilbao. 1880 Sold to Marques de Campo,Madrid. 1883 Ren. MADRID. 1888 Sold to W.S. Bailey,Hull name u/ch. 1892 Purchased by Furness,Withy & Co. Ltd. 1894 Sold to E. Morgan & Co. 5.1896 In port, damaged.

F41. AUSTRALIA (1893) 2252g 1455n 324' x 35'
C 2-cyl by D. & W. Henderson,Glasgow.

1870 Completed by R. Duncan & Co.,Port Glasgow as AUSTRALIA for Handyside & Co.,Glasgow.1875 Sold to Henderson Bros,Glasgow. 1893 Purchased by Furness,Withy & Co. Ltd. 5.1893 B/U.

F42.STRAITS OF BELLE ISLE (1893 - 1894) 2484g 1586n 320' x 38' C 2-cyl by C.D. Homes & Co.,Hull.
6.1870 Completed by R .Napier & Sons,Glasgow as LORD OF THE ISLES for Shaw,Maxton & Co,London. 1878 Shaw & Son. 1879 Shaw,Bushby & Co.,London. 1880 Purchased by E. Maclean & Co.,Glasgow ren. STRAITS OF BELLE ISLE. 1893 Purchased by Furness,Withy & Co. Ltd. 1894 Sold to N. Maclean,Glasgow name u/ch. 1894 Sold to Kita Ihei,Hiogo ren. HOKOKU MARU. 1901 Sold to S. Kurawara,Kobe name u/ch. 2.1904 Sunk at entrance to Port Arthur during Russo-Japan war.

F43. BULGARIAN (1894 - 1895) 3118g 2031n 400' x 37' C 2-cyl by J. Jack & Co.,Liverpool.
1870 Completed by Harland & Wolff,Belfast for J. Bibby,Liverpool. 1873 F. Leyland became mgr. 1889 Sold to W. Glynn, Liverpool. 1894 Purchased by Furness,Withy & Co. Ltd. 1895 B/U.

F44. BAVARIAN (1894 - 1895) 3030g 1976n 400' x 37' C 2-cyl by J. Jack & Co.,Liverpool.
1869 Completed by Harland & Wolff,Belfast for J. Bibby,Liverpool. 1873 F. Leyland became mgr. 1889 Sold to W. Glynn ,Liverpool. 1894 Purchased by Furness,Withy & Co. Ltd. 1895 Sold to T. Ward & Co. and broken up.

F45. ISTRIAN (1894 - 1895) 2963g 1906n 390' x 37' C 2-cyl by G. Forrester & Co.,Liverpool.
1867 Completed by Harland & Wolff,Belfast for J. Bibby, Liverpool. 1873 F. Leyland became mgr. 1889 Sold to J. Glynn & Son,Liverpool. 1894 Purchased by Furness,Withy & Co. Ltd. 1895 B/U.

F46. SAINT RONANS (1894 - 1898) 4457g 2916n 402' x 43' C 2-cyl by bldrs.
10.1881 Completed by Earle & Co.,Hull for British & Foreign S.S. Co Ltd(Rankin,Gilmour & Co),Liverpool. 1894 Purchased by Furness, Withy & Co. Ltd. 1898 Sold to A. Christensen,Denmark ren. ORION. 1.6.1899 Wrecked at Freshwater Point(NF) o.v. New York to Copenhagen with general.

F47. CUNDALL(2) (1894 - 190) 2390g 1534n 290' x 41' T 3-cyl by T. Richardson & Sons,Hartlepool.
10.1894 Completed by Furness,Withy & Co. Ltd for S.W. Furness. By 1900 Sold to Cia de Nav Olazarri (Garteiz y Mendialdua),Bilbao ren. OGONO. 18.8.1929 Sunk in collision with s.s. RYTON in North Sea o.v. Castro Urdiales to Middlesbrough with iron ore.

F48. ANTWERP CITY (1894 - 190) 3229g 2108n 340' x 42' T 3-cyl by W. Allan & Co. Ltd,Sunderland.
6.1894 Completed by J. Priestman & Co.,Sunderland for Furness, Withy & Co. Ltd. 1900 Sold to T. Bochenski & Co.,Odessa ren. LILIA. 1902 Sold to Massey & Co,Hull ren. ANTWERP CITY. 31.5.1911

Sunk by collision 66 miles off Ushant o.v. Hull to Savona with
coal.

F49. CARLISLE CITY (1894 - 1903) 3002g 1894n   345' x 41'
T 3-cyl by bldrs.
4.1894 Completed by William Doxford & Sons,Sunderland for Furness,
Withy & Co. Ltd. 1903 Sold to Elders & Fyffes ren. ORACABESSA.
1910 Sold to W. Garthwaite,Hartlepool name u/ch. 1916 Sold to Soc
Anon Martinelli,Rio de Janeiro ren. BELEM. 1925 Sold to Lloyd
Nacional,Rio de Janeiro name u/ch. and broken up at Rio do Sul in
1932.

F50. HALIFAX CITY   (1894 - 1900) 2141g 1377n   311' x 37'
T 3-cyl by bldrs.
2.1894 Completed by A. Stephen & Sons,Glasgow for Furness,Withy &
Co. Ltd. 1900 Sold to Sicilia Soc di Nav,Palermo later Soc.di Nav
Italia,Palermo ren. ETRURIA. 1929 B/U.

F51. ST. JOHN CITY (1895 - 1899) 2153g 1379n   311' x 37'
T 3-cyl by bldrs.
1.1895 Completed by A. Stephen & Sons,Glasgow for Furness,Withy &
Co. Ltd. 1899 Sold to Sicilia Soc di Nav,Palermo later Soc.di Nav
Italia,Palermo ren. PIEMONTE. 1925 Sold to Cia Transatlantica,
Palermo name u/ch. 1929 B/U.

F52. COVENTRY   (1895) 1773g 1044n   257' x 34'
T 3-cyl by T. Richardson & Sons,Hartlepool.
1883 Completed by Edward Withy & Co.,West Hartlepool for Sive-
wright,Bacon & Co.,West Hartlepool. 1895 Purchased by Furness,
Withy & Co. Ltd. 1895 Sold to THomas Gentles & Sons,South
Shields. 1896 Sold to Frederick Childs,Cardiff. 1898 Sold to E.
Jenkins & Co.,Cardiff. 1.10.1908 Stranded off Oporto Bar.

F53. LONDON CITY   (1896) 5532g 3613n   450' x 49'
T 3-cyl by bldrs.
2.1896 Launched as LONDON CITY by A. Stephen & Sons,Glasgow for
Furness,Withy & Co. Ltd and 5.1896 completed as MEGANTIC for
Wilsons & Furness - Leyland Line Ltd. 1898 Ren. ANGLIAN. 1914
Reg. under F. Leyland & Co. 10.6.1917 Torpedoed and sunk in posn.
49-22 N, 7-12 W o.v. Boston to London with general.

F54. EDITH   (1895) 609g 274n   218' x 25'
C 2-cyl by Earles Co. Ltd,Hull
1864 Completed by Henderson,Coulborn & Co.,Renfrew for G. Lawson,
Hull. 1895 Purchased by Furness,Withy & Co. Ltd. 11.1895 Sunk in
collision in Thames o.v. Ghent to London.

F55. OPORTO   (1896 - 1902) 580g 327n   201' x 26'
C 2-cyl by J. Jack & Co.,Liverpool.
3.1870 Completed by J. Reid & Co.,Pt. Glasgow for Coverley &
Westray,London. 1896 Purchased by Furness,Withy & Co. Ltd. 8.1902
Beached after collision, sold to R. Neugebauer & Co. Ltd.

F56. PLATO   (1895 - 189)   793g 518n   249' x 27'
C 2-cyl by C.D. Holmes & Co.,Hull.
1857 Completed as TIGER for Brownlow & Co.,Hull then T. Wilson,
Sons & Co,Hull. 1895 Purchased by Furness,Withy & Co. Ltd. 1897
Sold to C.B. Ellis,Hull name u/ch. 1899 Sold to T. Ronaldson & Co.
Ltd,Hull name u/ch. 1900 Sold to Antwerp S.S. Co. Ltd(J. Deffy,
mgr),Hull name u/ch. 12.1902 B/U.

F57. ALBERT   (1895 - 1897)   525g 198n   199' x 26'
C 2-cyl by Earle & Co.,Hull.
1856 Completed by C.& W. Earle,Hull for Italian owners as VIS-
CONDE DI ATTAGONIA. 1877 Sold to G. Lawson,Hull ren. ALBERT. 1895
Purchased by Furness,Withy & Co. Ltd. 1897 Sold to E.W. Sollas,
Hull name u/ch. 1907 Sold to New Hebrides Cie(E. Leclerc),Dieppe
ren. GUILLAUME LE CONQUERANT. 1908 Sold to F. Bruggiser,Porto
Ferraio ren. ELSA. 1911 Sold to Soc Anon Siderurgica di Savona,
Savona ren. EOLO. 1920 Sold to Soc. Anon. Ilva,Genoa name u/ch.
1925 B/U.

F58. ZEBRA   (1895 - 1903)   551g 351n   196' x 26'
C 2-cyl by C.D. Holmes & Co.,Hull.
1858 Completed by Brownlow & Pearson,Hull for T. Wilson,Sons &
Co.,Hull. 1895 Purchased by Furness,Withy & Co. Ltd. 1903 Sold
for B/U.

F59. SORRENTO   (1895)   2208g 1775n   301' x 35'
C 2-cyl by bldrs.
1878 Completed by Earle & Co.,Hull for T. Wilson,Sons & Co.,Hull.
1892 Sold to R. Sloman,Hamburg name u/ch. 1895 Purchased by
Furness,Withy & Co. Ltd. 7.1895 Sold to C.H. Garnett for B/U.

F60. MANNINGHAM   (1896)   1924g 1253n   286' x 36'
C 2-cyl by Wallsend Slipway Co. Ltd.
4.1880 Completed by Mitchell & Co.,Newcastle for Hamilton,Fraser &
Co.,Liverpool as INCHMAREE. 1890 Sold to Thompson S.S. Co.(V.T.
Thompson),Liverpool ren. MANNINGHAM. 1896 Purchased by Furness,
Withy & Co. Ltd but 5.1896 stranded,reloated and sold to Handelsbo
Solvesborg Skepps (O.Banck),Solvesborg(Sw) name u/ch. 1897 J.
Ingmansson now mgr. 21.2.1917 Torpedoed and sunk 25 miles N of
Ushant o.v. Penarth to St. Vincent,C.V.I. with coal.

F61. HARCALO   (1895 - 1896) 2401g 1477n   295' x 42'
T 3-cyl by G. Clark Ltd,Sunderland.
6.1895 Completed by W. Pickersgill & Sons Ltd,Sunderland as
HARCALO for Furness,Withy & Co. Ltd. 1896 Sold to J.& C. Harrison
Ltd,London name u/ch. 1898 Sold to Cia Bilbaina de Nav,Bilbao
ren. GANECOGORTA. 1908 Sold to Cia Maritima del Norvion(Urquijo y
Aldecoa),Bilbao ren. MAR-ADRIATICO. 14.2.1917 Torpedoed and sunk
in Bay of Biscay o.v. from Lisbon with copper.

F62. OREGON   (1895 - 1897) 3714g 2373n   361' x 40'
C 2-cyl by J.& J. Thompson,Glasgow.

12.1882 Completed by Charles Connell & Co.,Glasgow for Mississippi & Dominion S.S. Co. Ltd. Emigrant carrier from Italy to U.S.A. 1895 Purchased by Furness,Withy & Co. Ltd. 1897 B/U.

F63. SARNIA (1895 - 1897) 3728g 2400n 361' x 40'
C 2-cyl by J.&J. Thompson,Glasgow.
6.1882 Completed by Charles Connell & Co.,Glasgow for Mississippi & Dominion S.S. Co. Ltd. Emigrant carrier from Italy to U.S.A. 1895 Purchased by Furness,Withy & Co. Ltd. 1897 B/U.

F64. KIRKSTALL (1895 - 1896) 1831g 1162n 265' x 38'
T 3-cyl by Central Marine Eng. Works,Hartlepool.
9.1895 Completed by W. Gray & Co. Ltd,Hartlepool as KIRKSTALL for S.W. Furness; having been launched as LADY OLIVIA for Shipping Agency Ltd,London and sold while fitting out to J.R. Cuthbertson, Glasgow who in turn resold her to S.W. Furness. 1896 Purchased by J.E. Guthe. 30.3.1899 Purchased by West Hartlepool S.N. Co. Ltd. 1908 Sold to Kelvin Shipping Co. Ltd(H.Hogarth),Glasgow ren. BARON GARIOCH. 28.10.1917 Torpedoed and sunk 5 miles SE of Anvil Point by UC63 o.v. Calais to Liverpool in balast,2 lost.

F65. HEATHER BELL (1896 - 1897) 1253g 791n 230' x 33'
T 3-cyl by J.G. Kinciad & Co. Ltd,Greenock.
1896 Completed by Campbeltown SB Co. for Heather Bell S.S. Co. Ltd(J.Davidson),London. 1896 Furness,Withy & Co. Ltd became mgrs. 1897 Sold to A/S Verma(M. Pedersen),Mandal ren. VERMA. 1901 Sold to Meliton Gonzalez,Gijon ren. SEGUNDO, later to Rodriguez y Cerra,Gijon. 1916 Sold to Ferrer Peset Hermanos,Valencia ren. C. SORNI. 1917 Sold to Cia Transmeditteraneana,Valencia name u/ch. 1929 B/U.

F66. LONDON CITY(2) (1897 - 1900) 2487g 1576n 300' x 41'
T 3-cyl by Wallsend Slipway Co. Ltd.
1891 Completed by C.S. Swan & Hunter for Deutsche D/S Rhederei zu Hamburg as PRIOK. 1893 Sold to Cie de Nav Mixte,Marseilles ren. GUINEE. 1897 Purchased by Furness,Withy & Co. Ltd ren. LONDON CITY. 1900 Sold to Osaka Shosen Kaiska,Osaka ren. TAIHOKU MARU. Under Kita Nippon K.K. 1933 B/U.

F67. DAHOME (1898 - 191) 2470g 1552n 300' x 41'
T 3-cyl by Wallsend Slipway Co. Ltd.
2.1891 Completed by C.S. Swan & Hunter,Wallsend as LAWANG for Deutsche D/S Rederi of Hamburg. 1896 Sold to Cie de Nav Mixte, Marseilles ren. DAHOME. 1898 Purchased by Furness,Withy & Co. Ltd. 1910 Sold to Mihran Nakashian,Turkey ren KAISSERI. 1912 Captured by Italians in Tripoli War and scuttled.

F68. SYLVIANA (1898 - 1905) 4187g 2715n 360' x 48'
T 3-cyl by W. Allan & Co.,Sunderland.
5.1898 Completed by Craig,Taylor & Co.,Stockton for Furness, Withy & Co. Ltd. 1905 Captured by Japanese warships, taken as a prize ren. GOTO MARU. 1906 Sold to N. Hiroumi,Japan name u/ch. 8.11.1907 Left Hakodate o.v. to San Francisco and disappeared.

F69. GURLY (1898) 847g 442n 195' x 28'
Two T 3-cyl by Muir & Huston,Glasgow. 2-screw.
1891 Completed by Murdoch & Murray,Pt. Glasgow for J. Christensen,
Bergen. 1898 Purchased by Furness,Withy & Co. Ltd. 1898 Resold to
D/S Juno(J. Christensen) ren. JUNO. 1900 Sold to Cia Mexicana de
Nav., Veracruz ren. PORFIRIO DIAZ. 1902 Ren. CULIACAN. 1904 Ren.
PORFIRIO DIAZ. 1911 B/U.

F70. HOLGUIN (1898) 842g 442n 195' x 28'
Two T 3-cyl by Muir & Huston,Glasgow. 2-screw.
1890 Completed by Murdoch & Murray,Pt. Glasgow for J. Christensen,
Bergen. 1898 Purchased by Furness,Withy & Co. Ltd. 1898 Resold to
D/S Urania(J. Christensen) ren. HEBE. 1900 Sold to Cia Mexicana de
Nav.,Veracruz ren. BENITO JUAREZ. 1911 B/U.

F71. DALTONHALL (1899 - 1914) 3534g 2279n 338' x 45'
T 3-cyl by Furness,Westgarth & Co. Ltd,Middlesbrough.
6.1899 Completed by Furness,Withy & Co. Ltd,Hartlepool for West
Hartlepool S.N. Co. Ltd. 1899 Purchased by Furness,Withy & Co.
Ltd name u/ch. 1914 Sold to Oxton S.S. Co. Ltd(W. Roberts,mgr),
Liverpool. 1917 Sold to Commonwealth Government Line of Steamers,
Sydney(NSW) ren. AUSTRALSTREAM. 1918 Sold to Soc. Maritime Belge
ren. GENERAL DEGOUTTE. 1921 Sold to N.D. Rallias,Andros ren.
DIMITRIOS N. RALLIAS. 1936 B/U at Dunston-on-Tyne.

F72. FLORENCE (1900 - 1912) See Houlder H8

F73. EVANGELINE (1900 - 1902) 3900g 2525n 372' x 45'
T 3-cyl by bldrs.
10.1900 Completed by A. Stephen & Sons Ltd,Linthouse for Furness,
Withy & Co. Ltd. 1902 Sold to Lamport & Holt Ltd ren. TENNYSON.
1922 Sold to Soc. Anon. Comercial Braun & Blanchard,Chile ren.
VALPARAISO. 1932 B/U in Italy.

F74. LOYALIST (1900 - 1902) 3904g 2526n 372' x 45'
T 3-cyl by bldrs.
1.1901 Completed by A. Stephen & Sons Ltd,Linthouse for Furness,
Withy & Co. Ltd. 1902 Sold to Lamport & Holt Ltd ren. BYRON.
1922 Sold to Soc. Anon. Comercial Braun & Blanchard,Chile
ren. SANTIAGO. 1932 B/U in Italy.

F75. EVANGELINE(2) (1902 - 1911) 2268g 1473n 305' x 39'
T 3-cyl by bldrs.
21.4.1891 Launched and 5.1891 completed by A. Stephen & Sons,
Glasgow as CLAN MACKINNON for The Clan Line Steamers Ltd,Glasgow.
1902 Purchased by Furness,Withy & Co. Ltd ren. EVANGELINE. 1911
Sold to A. Embiricos,Greece ren. PELAGOS. 14.8.1912 Stranded off
Barry, subsequently refloated but found to be too badly damaged.
Sold to T.W. Ward Ltd and B/U at Morecambe.

F76. LOYALIST(2) (1902 - 1904) 2268g 1436n 305' x 39'
T 3-cyl by bldrs.
5.8.1891 Launched and 8.1891 completed by A. Stephen & Sons,
Glasgow as CLAN MACALISTER for The Clan Line Steamers Ltd,Glasgow.

1902 Purchased by Furness,Withy & Co. Ltd ren. LOYALIST. 27.9.1904
Wrecked at Freshwater Cove,Trepassey Bay,Newfoundland o.v. Halifax
(NS) to London with general.

F77. ST. JOHN CITY(2) (1902 - 1910) 2268g 1463n 305' x 39'
T 3-cyl by bldrs.
9.6.1891 Launched by Miss Constance Cayzer and 6.1891 completed
by A. Stephen & Sons,Glasgow for The Clan Line Steamers Ltd,
Glasgow as CLAN MACNAB. 23.12.1894 In collision with Russian
gunboat GREMIATSCHY in the Suez Canal. 1902 Purchased by Furness,
Withy & Co. Ltd ren. ST. JOHN CITY. 1910 Sold to Anglo Hellenic
S.S. Co.(A.A.Embiricos,mgr),Greece ren. PONTOS. 1915 Requisition
by Admiralty and scuttled as a blockship at Scapa Flow. 1922
Raised and B/U.

F78. LONDON CITY(3) (1903 - 1922) 2441g 1591n   324' x 38'
C 2-cyl by bldrs.
15.8.1882 Launched by A. Stephen & Sons,Glasgow as CLAN FORBES for
The Clan Line Steamers Ltd,Glasgow. 1903 Purchased by Furness,
Withy & Co. Ltd ren. LONDON CITY. 1910 Sold to Denaby and Cadeby
Collieries Ltd,London. 1920 Transferred to Denaby & Commercial Co.
Ltd,London. 1922 Sold to German breakers.

F79. BUCCANEER   (1902 - 190) 925g 653n   217' x 30'
T 3-cyl by bldrs.
5.1890 Completed by J. Scott & Co.,Kinghorn for Buccaneer S.S. Co.
Ltd(Tatham,Bromage & Co),London. 1902 Purchased by Furness, Withy
& Co. Ltd. 1904 To Tyne-Tees Steam Shipping Co. Ltd,Newcastle name
u/ch. 1925 Sold to C.H.E. Chase,Hartlepool name u/ch. 1925 Sold to
Riga Exchange Committee,Latvia ren. AGATHE. 1926 Sold to Baltische
D/S A.G.,Riga ren. HERMAN. 1929 Sold to Rudolf Stukalis,Riga ren.
ALBERT. 1933 B/U.

F80. WATERLAND   (1903 - 1921) 494g 267n   164' x 25'
T 3-cyl by McColl & Pollock,Sunderland.
3.1903 Completed by W. Dobson & Co. Ltd,Newcastle as WATERLAND
for Furness, Withy & Co. Ltd.1921 Transferred to Prince Line Ltd
ren. EGYPTIAN PRINCE. 1922 Sold to Khedivail Mail S.S. & Graving
Dock Co. Ltd(Lord E. Hamilton,mgr),London ren. RAMLEH. 1931 Sold
to Ovadia Israil Ovadia,Alexandria ren. LATEEF. 1946 Ren. RAMLEH.
1947 Sold to Trans Mediterranean Nav. Co,Alexandria ren. SHADWAN.
1986 Deleted from Register.

F81. GLORIANA(2)   (1905 - 1913) 3050g 2119n   325' x 47'
T 3-cyl by Richardsons,Westgarth & Co. Ltd,Hartlepool.
5.1905 Completed by Irvines SB & DD Co. Ltd,Hartlepool for
Furness,Withy & Co. Ltd. 1913 Sold to Antwerpsche Zeev. Maats.
(Mercantile & Shpg. Co. Ltd),Antwerp ren. REMIER. 1921 Sold to
Konan Kisen K.K.,Kobe ren. KENJO MARU. 1938 Amended to KENZYO
MARU. 12.6.1945 Torpedoed & sunk by U.S.S. SKATE in posn. 37-07N,
136-42E.

F82. ALMERIANA   (1906 - 1914) 2906g 1736n   324' x 40'
T 3-cyl by T. Richardson & Co.,Hartlepool.

1889 Completed by Raylton Dixon & Co.,Middlesbrough for W. Lund, London as ECHUCA. 1898 Sold to R.M. Sloman,Hamburg ren. CATANIA. 1904 Sold to D/S Union A.G.,Hamburg name u/ch. 1906 Purchased by Furness,Withy & Co. Ltd. ren. ALMERIANA. 1914 Sold to T.W. Ward Ltd for B/U.

F83. ANNAPOLIS (1906 - 1907) 2037g 1351n 284' x 35'
T 3-cyl by bldrs.
1889 Completed by Flensburger Schiffs. as DIANA for Hamburg Pacific D/S Linie (Kirsten,mgr),Hamburg. 1897 Sold to R.M. Sloman & Co., Hamburg ren. CAPRI. 1906 Purchased by Furness,Withy & Co. Ltd ren. ANNAPOLIS. 1907 Sold to Cie d'Armement Colonial, Marseilles ren. MANGORO then to Soc. des Pecheries de Kerguelen, Havre. 1915 Sold to New Transvaal Chemical Co. Ltd, Port Natal ren. ISLANDIA. 1916 Sold to Laurium Transport Co Ltd(L. Walford), London. 1924 Sold to D.F. Andreadis,Piraeus name u/ch. 1926 Sold to Rosina S.S. Co. Ltd(C. Dixon),London ren. SAINT PARASKEVI. 1928 Sold to Soc. de Gestion Maritime,Nantes ren. GUINEE FRANCAIS. B/U in 1934.

F84. HALIFAX CITY(2) (1906 - 1910) 2429g 1619n 320' x 40'
T 3-cyl by bldrs.
1895 Completed by S/A John Cockerill,Hoboken as JOHN COCKERILL for Soc. Cockerill,Antwerp. 1906 Purchased by Furness,Withy & Co. Ltd ren. HALIFAX CITY. 1910 Sold to Anglo-Hellenic S.S. Co. Ltd (A.A. Embiricos),Andros ren. SYRA. 1911 Sold to Soc. France-Mostaganemoise d'Armement,France ren. TIJDITT. 1916 Sold to Soc Anon des Acieries de Paris et d'Outreau,Boulogne ren. PARACIERS. 17.9.1917 Torpedoed and sunk 8 miles E of Spurn Head o.v. Tyne to Boulogne with coal.

F85. COLLINGWOOD (1905 - 1926) 1278g 816n 235' x 34'Collier
T 3-cyl by Richardsons,Westgarth & Co. Ltd,Sunderland.
10.1905 Completed by Osbourne,Graham & Co.,Sunderland for Furness,Withy & Co. Ltd. 1926 Sold to Halvorsen Shpg. Co A/S, Bergen ren. JERMLAND. 1947 Sold to Paulins Rederi A/B Ostra Nagu,Abo ren. NAGU. 1960 B/U.

F86. FARADAY (1906 - 1909) 892g 552n 214' x 28'
C 2-cyl by Ouseburn Eng. Works,Newcastle.
1873 Completed by T. & W. Smith,North Shields as FARADAY for G. Reid & Co.,Newcastle. 1875 Sold to Tyne Steam Shipping Co. Ltd, Newcastle name u/ch. 1904 To Tyne-Tees Steam Shipping Co. Ltd, Newcastle. 1906 Purchased by Furness,Withy & Co. Ltd. 1909 B/U.

F87. RIPON (1906 - 1912) 2965g 2070n 325' x 47'
T 3-cyl by Richardsons,Westgarth & Co. Ltd,Hartlepool.
9.1906 Completed by Irvines SB & DD Co. Ltd,Hartlepool for Furness, Withy & Co. Ltd. 1912 Sold to Scheeps. Maats. Gylsen (Mercantile & Shipping Co. Ltd),Antwerp ren. FRUITHANDEL 1916 Sold to Lloyd Royal Belge,Antwerp ren. GASCONIER. 20.8.1918 Mined and sunk off Udsire.

F88 - F115 Vessels transferred from British Maritime Trust,

and Chesapeake & Ohio S.S. Co. Ltd. See Appendices FB & FC.

F116. CRAMLINGTON (1907 - 1908) 1824g 1160n 275' x 40' Collier
T 3-cyl by Dunsmuir & Jackson Ltd,Glasgow.
1907 Completed by Greenock & Grangemouth D.D. Co. for Furness,
Withy & Co. Ltd. 10.1908 Sunk in collision at the mouth of the
Humber o.v. Tyne to Seville with coal.

F117. DAGENHAM (1907 - 1909) 1456g 930n 239' x 36' Collier
T 3-cyl by Richardsons,Westgarth & Co. Ltd.
9.1907 Completed by J. Crown & Son,Sunderland for Furness,Withy &
Co. Ltd. 4.1909 Wrecked in Cobo Bay,Guernsey o.v. Tyne to St.
Malo with coal.

F118. EASINGTON (1907 - 1915) 1387g 868n 240' x 36' Collier
T 3-cyl by bldrs.
5.1907 Completed by Palmers,Jarrow for Furness,Withy & Co. Ltd.
26.9.1915 Sailed from Sydney(CB) for St. John(NB) and disappeared.

F119. LUDWORTH (1907 - 1919) 1300g 783n 235' x 34' Collier
T 3-cyl by Richardsons,Westgarth & Co. Ltd,Sunderland.
1907 Completed by Blyth SB Co. Ltd for Furness,Withy & Co. Ltd.
1919 Sold to W.H. van der Zee,Smryna ren. HELENA(Dutch flag).
1937 Sold to Hamdi Selimoglu ve Serikleri,Istanbul ren. ATILLA.
1951 Reg. under Mehmet Kazanci ve Serikleri name u/ch. 1958 Sold
to Ahmet ve Mehmet Kosar Kolletif Sirketi ren. KOSAR. 1969 B/U.

F120. NORTON (1907 - 1922) 1825g 1135n 276' x 40' Collier
T 3-cyl by Richardsons,Westgarth & Co. Ltd,Middlesbrough.
1907 Completed by Greenock & Grangemouth Dkyd Co. Ltd,Grangemouth
as CORNWALL for Furness,Withy & Co. Ltd. 1908 Renamed NORTON.
1922 Sold to A.Bernstein,Hamburg ren. JOHANNA. 1927 Sold to J.
Jost,Flensburg ren. JUSTITIA. 1933 B/U at Flensburg.

F121. POMARON (1907 - 1922) 1809g 1127n 376' x 40' Collier
T 3-cyl by Richardsons,Westgarth & Co. Ltd.
1907 Completed by Grangemouth & Greenock Dkyd. Co. Ltd,Grangemouth
for Furness,Withy & Co. Ltd. 1922 Transferred to Johnston Line Ltd
ren. WRAYMORE. 1922 Sold to P. Danneberg,Riga ren. BIRUTA. 1950
Reg. under U.S.S.R.(Estonia & Latvia). 1954 Ren. SIGULDA. 1968
Deleted.

F122. RYHOPE (1907 - 1922) 1334g 695n 234' x 34' Collier
T 3-cyl by Richardsons,Westgarth & Co. Ltd,Sunderland.
8.1907 Completed by Blyth SB Co. Ltd for Furness,Withy & Co. Ltd.
1922 Sold to D/S A/S Kistentransport(T.Halvorsen,mgr),Bergen ren.
LYSLAND. 1951 Sold to R.Januzzi & G.Ursino,Naples ren. VOMERO.
1959 Sold to Lorenzo de Medici,Naples name u/ch. 1960 B/U.

F123. THIMBLEBY (1907 - 1915) 1865g 1152n 279' x 40' Collier
T 3-cyl by McColl & Pollock Ltd,Sunderland.
1907 Completed by Osbourne,Graham & Co.,Sunderland for Furness,
Withy & Co. Ltd. 1915 Sold to Kelvin Shipping Co. Ltd(H. Hogarth),
Glasgow ren. BARON KELVIN. 1923 Sold to British Invicta Shipping

Co. Ltd(Eggar,Forrester & Parker Ltd),London ren. L'INVICTA. 1923
Sold to T. Murao,Japan ren. TAKASAGO MARU. 1925 Sold to Asahi
Shokai K.K.,Japan. 1931 Sold to Sanbo Kisen Goshi Kaisha,Japan.
6.3.1932 Wrecked in fog on S.W. coast of Korea near Mokpo o.v.
Miike to Kunsan.

F124. WESTWOOD   (1907 - 1918) 1968g 1070n 275' x 40' Collier
T 3-cyl by Richardsons,Westgarth & Co. Ltd.
1907 Completed by Raylton Dixon & Co.,Middlesbrough for Furness,
Withy & Co. Ltd. 3.10.1918 Torpedoed and sunk 5 miles SW 1/2W
from Lizard o.v. Barry to Devonport with coal.

F125. WHORLTON   (1907 - 1918) 1469g 885n 239'x 36' Collier
T 3-cyl by Richardsons,Westgarth & Co. Ltd.
11.1907 Completed by J. Crown & Son,Sunderland for Furness,Withy
& Co. Ltd. 12.1.1918 Torpedoed and sunk by UB30 near Owers L.V.
in English Channel while on Admiralty service o.v. Dunkirk to
Southampton.

F126. TUNSTALL   (1907 - 1914) 3825g 2438n 350' x 50' Turret
T 3-cyl by bldrs.
4.12.1906 Launched by William Doxford & Sons Ltd,Sunderland for J.
Sunley & Co.,London as BILLITER,and 1.1907 completed as TUNSTALL
for Furness,Withy & Co. Ltd. 1914 Sold to Felix S.S. Co. Ltd(N.E.
Ambatielos),London. 1919 Ren. ARGOSTOLI. 1922 Sold to Sovereign
Shpg. Co. Ltd(F.J.Mundy),Cardiff ren. CARTHAGE. 1925 Sold to V.G.
Mantacas,Greece ren. MARIONGA MANTACA. 1927 B/U in Holland.

F127. CASTLE EDEN   (1908 - 1913) 1844g 1138n 276' x 40' Collier
T 3-cyl by Dunsmuir & Jackson Ltd,Glasgow.
1908 Completed by Greenock & Grangemouth Dockyard Co. Ltd,Greenock
for Furness,Withy & Co. Ltd. 1913 Sold to Kelvin Shipping Co. Ltd
(H.Hogarth),Glasgow ren. BARON BLANTYRE. 3.9.1917 Torpedoed and
sunk by U89 60 miles NW3/4W from Cape Finisterre o.v. Clyde to
Huelva with coal.

F128. CHARLESTON   (1908 - 1917) 1865g 1163n 279' x 40' Collier
T 3-cyl by McColl & Pollock,Sunderland.
1908 Completed by Irvines SB & DD Co. Ltd,Hartlepool for Furness,
Withy & Co. Ltd. 12.12.1917 Captured by UB65 and sunk by bombs 30
miles W of The Smalls o.v. Cardiff to Berehaven with coal.

F129. CUNDALL(3)   (1908 - 1922) 1851g 1120n 276' x 40' Collier
T 3-cyl by N.E. Marine Eng. Co. Ltd,Sunderland.
6.1908 Completed by Northumberland SB Co. Ltd,Howdon-on-Tyne for
Furness,Withy & Co. Ltd. 1922 Transferred to Johnston Line Ltd
ren. WILLOWMORE. 1922 Sold to Latvian Government(V.Parvalde,mgr)
ren. VENTA. 5.1.1940 Detained at Hamburg having called at Sassnitz
for investigation. 1945 Ren. UNDINE(Ge). 1947 Allocated to Ministry of Transport(Springwell Shpg. Co. Ltd) ren. VENTA. 1956 B/U.

F130. GRANTLEY   (1908 - 1922) 1869g 1154n 279' x 40' Collier
T 3-cyl by McColl & Pollock,Sunderland.

1908 Completed by Osbourne,Graham & Co. Ltd for Furness,Withy &
Co. Ltd. 1922 Sold to H.Harrison(Shpg) Ltd ren. KENNINGTON. 1924
Sold to D/S A/S Saima(Bergmann & Hammer A/S),Bergen ren. BLENDA.
1934 Sold to Rederi A/B Diana(Tore Ulff A/B),Finland ren. DIANA.
5.3.1944 Bombed and sunk off Schiermonnikoog o.v. Emden to Stockholm with coke,2 lost.

F131. PORTINGLIS   (1908 - 1922) 1867g 1164n 279' x 40' Collier
T 3-cyl by McColl & Pollock,Sunderland.
1908 Completed by Irvines SB & DD Co. Ltd,Hartlepool for Furness,
Withy & Co. Ltd. 1922 Transferred to Johnston Line, Liverpool ren.
WESTMORE. 1922 Sold to Seed Shipping Co. Ltd,Liverpool ren.
PHYLLIS SEED. 1924 Sold to Rederi A/B Gothia(G.Osterberg),
Trelleborg ren. PATRIA. 1936 Sold to Rederi A/B Amfritrite(Fanges
& Pahlsson),Helsingborg ren. TRITON. 1955 B/U.

F132. FERNANDINA   (1908 - 1922) 1851g 1146n 276' x 40' Collier
T 3-cyl by Richardson,Westgarth & Co. Ltd,Sunderland.
1908 Completed by Northumberland SB Co. Ltd for Furness,Withy &
Co. Ltd. 1922 Sold to A. Bernstein,Hamburg ren. FALKENSTEIN. 1933
Ren. FORDTRANSPORT IV. 1934 Ren. FALKENSTEIN. 1935 B/U.

F133. CANADIA   (1908 - 1909) 2413g 1525n   302' x 40'
T 3-cyl by bldrs.
3.3.1889 Launched and 1889 completed by Reiherst'g Schiffs at
Hamburg as STEINHOFT for D/S Rhederei Hansa,Hamburg. 1892 Purch-
ased by Hamburg America Line ren. CANADIA. 1905 Ren. REVEL. 1908
Purchased by Furness, Withy & Co. Ltd as CANADIA. 1909 Sold to
Anglo-Hellenic Shipping Co. Ltd (A.A. Embiricos), Andros ren.
MYRTOON. 1914 Sold to J. Castanie,Oran ren. GYPTIS. 1922 Sold to
Groupement Industriele de Charbons et de Transport,Havre ren.
VILLE DE NANCY. 1922/23 Served with Russian Volunteer Fleet. 1924
Scrapped.

F134. LANGDALE   (1909 - 1910) 3930g 2515n   366' x 47'
T 3-cyl by G. Clark Ltd,Sunderland.
11.1903 Completed by Sir J. Laing & Sons,Sunderland for Laing
Shipping Co.,Sunderland 1909 Purchased by Furness,Withy & Co.
Ltd.1910 Transferred to Furness Shipping & Agency,Rotterdam ren.
BEEKBERGEN. 1912 Reg. under Stoom Maats Indische Lloyd(J. van
Meel,mgr),Rotterdam. 1916 Ren. GAASTERLAND. 22.2.1917 Torpedoed
and sunk about 30 miles NW of Bishop Rock o.v. Amsterdam and
Falmouth to New York with corn and wheat.

F135. SWALEDALE   (1909 - 1910) 3658g 2348n   356' x 46'
T 3-cyl by G. Clark Ltd,Sunderland.
7.1897 Completed by Sir J. Laing & Sons,Sunderland as SWALEDALE
for Laing Shipping Co.,Sunderland,having been launched as ILE DE
LA REUNION. 1909 Purchased by Furness,Withy & Co. Ltd. 1910
Transferred to Furness Shipping & Agency,Rotterdam ren. RIJS-
BERGEN. 1912 Reg. under Stoom Maats Indische Lloyd(J. van Meel),
Rotterdam. 1920 Sold to Maats Bothnia(C. Goudriaan),Rotterdam
ren. RIJNSBURG. 1923 Sold to N.V. Scheeps Jan Smit,Rotterdam name
u/ch. 1924 B/U.

F136. WENSLEYDALE   (1909 - 1910) 3963g 2538n   366' x 47'
T 3-cyl by G. Clark Ltd,Sunderland.
6.1903 Completed by Sir J. Laing & Sons,Sunderland for Laing
Shipping Co.,Sunderland. 1909 Purchased by Furness,Withy & Co.
Ltd. 1910 Transferred to Furness Shipping & Agency,Rotterdam ren.
STEENBERGEN. 1912 Reg. under Stoom Maats Indische Lloyd(J. van
Meel,mgr),Rotterdam. 1917 Sold to Konink. Hollandsche Lloyd,
Amsterdam ren. DRECHTERLAND. 1932 B/U.

F137. APPENINE   (1909 - 1912) 3684g 2390n   347' x 51'
T 3-cyl by Richardsons,Westgarth & Co. Ltd,Hartlepool.
1909 Completed by Irvines SB & DD Co. Ltd,Hartlepool for Furness,
Withy & Co. Ltd. 1912 Transferred to Gulf Line Ltd. 4.3.1919
Wrecked in Witless Bay near St. John's(NF) o.v. Liverpool to St.
John's(NF) with general.

F138. HOWDEN   (1909 - 1913) 1013g 608n 210' x 33' Collier
T 3-cyl by Richardson,Westgarth & Co. Ltd,Sunderland.
1909 Completed by Osborne,Graham & Co.,Sunderland for Furness,
Withy & Co. Ltd. 1913 Transferred to Tyne-Tees Steam Shipping Co.
Ltd,Newcastle. 1928 Sold to D/S A/S Aslaug(D.K. Haaland),Haug-
esund ren. ASLAUG. 25.12.1929 Wrecked on Farallones Rocks,Bayona
o.v. Vestmann Islands to Vigo with cod.

F139. HARLINGEN   (1909 - 1922) 938g 545n 210' x 33' Collier
T 3-cyl by Richardson,Westgarth & Co. Ltd,Sunderland.
1909 Completed by Osborne,Graham & Co.,Sunderland for Furness,
Withy & Co. Ltd. 1912 Transferred to George V. Turnbull & Co.
Ltd,Glasgow ren. PETER PAN. 1916 Reg. under Furness,Withy & Co.
Ltd. 1922 Sold to Rederi A/B Sirius,Helsingborg ren. SIRIUS. 1922
Sold to Ensign Shipping Co. Ltd (G.J. Dunn),Newport ren. NEWBURN.
1927 Sold to D/S A/S Als(A. Vollmond),Copenhagen ren. FEDDY. 1940
Ministry of Shipping(W. Cory & Son Ltd). 5.4.1942 Sunk by
collision with H.M. ship off N. Ronaldsay o.v. Thorshavn to
Kirkwall & Methil in ballast, crew saved.

F140. AXWELL   (1909 - 1912) 1442g 784n 240' x 36' Collier
T 3-cyl by Richardson,Westgarth & Co. Ltd,Sunderland.
9.1909 Completed by J. Crown & Son,Sunderland for Furness,Withy &
Co. Ltd. 1912 Sold to Broomhill Collieries Ltd(Coates,Henry),
Newcastle name u/ch. 13.11.1917 Torpedoed and sunk by U B56 3
miles WSW of Owers L.V. o.v. Warkworth to Rouen with coal,2 lost.

F141. ASIANA   (1909 - 1910) 2993g 1867n   325' x 47'
T 3-cyl by Richardson,Westgarth & Co. Ltd,Hartlepool.
6.1909 Completed by Irvines SB & DD Co. Ltd,Hartlepool for Furness,
Withy & Co. Ltd. 1910 Sold to R.H. Holman,London ren. ROWTOR. 1914
Sold to G. Vergottis(Plisson & Co,mgr), Argostoli ren. EFTYCHIA
VERGOTTI. 1938 Sold to Soc. Europeen de Nav,Oran ren. CALVADOS. 1941
Sold to Cie des Bateaux a Vapeur du Nord,Marseilles ren TOURQUENNOIS
1943 Taken by Italy,ren. FERRARA. 8.1944 Sunk by aircraft at Genoa.
1947 Raised,repaired at Genoa and sold to Achille Lauro,Genoa ren.
POLINNIA. 19.4.1958 Arrived Savona for B/U.

F142. FELICIANA   (1909 - 1915) 4681g 2765n   380' x 49'
T 3-cyl by Richardson,Westgarth & Co. Ltd,Sunderland.
1909 Completed by Northumberland SB Co. Ltd,Howdon-on-Tyne for
Furness,Withy & Co. Ltd. 1911 Transferred to Gulf Line Ltd. 1915
Sold to Bay S.S. Co. Ltd(Sale & Co),London name u/ch. 21.4.1916
Torpedoed & Sunk by U19 67 miles NW 1/2N of Fastnet o.v. London
to Cardiff and New York in ballast.

F143. NAPOLIANA   (1909 - 1910) 3030g 1935n   325' x 47'
T 3-cyl by Richardsons,Westgarth & Co. Ltd,Hartlepool.
1909 Launched as NAPOLIANA by Irvines SB & DD Co. Ltd,Hartlepool
for Furness,Withy & Co. Ltd and completed as ARMSTOR for J.
Holman,London. 23.12.1912 Left New Orleans for Aalborg,Nakskov
and Esbjerg with oilcake and disappeared.

F144. PARISIANA   (1909 - 1910) 4823g 3084n   410' x 52'
T 3-cyl by Palmers Co. Ltd,Jarrow.
11.1909 Completed by Northumberland SB Co. Ltd,Howdon-on-Tyne for
Furness,Withy & Co. Ltd, having been laid down as NEW ZEALAND
TRANSPORT for Empire Transport Co. Ltd(Houlder Bros.,mgrs).
1.10.1910 Purchased by Empire Transport Co. Ltd name u/ch.
13.12.1910 Burned at sea in Indian Ocean in posn. 38 S 81 E o.v.
New York to Melbourne.

F145. ROUEN   (1909 - 1928) 1968g 1201n 279' x 40' Collier
T 3-cyl by McColl & Pollock,Sunderland.
1909 Completed by Irvines SB & DD Co. Ltd,Hartlepool for Furness,
Withy & Co. Ltd. 1928 Sold to Cie Mar Normandie(Heuzy et Chast-
ellain),Rouen ren. JEAN DE BETHENCOURT. 1936 Sold to Mooringwell
S.S. Co. Ltd,Cardiff ren. JEANNE M. 12.1938 Sunk by collision
near Lappegrund L.V. to N of Elsinore o.v. Stockholm to
Kristiansand in ballast.

F146. SAVANNAH (1909 - 1910)   See EMPIRE TRANSPORT HE1

**F147 - F159 Vessels transferred from British Maritime Trust Ltd,
and Chesapeake & Ohio S.S. Co. Ltd. See Appendices FB and FC.**

F160. ABANA   (1910 - 1912) 4189g 2709n   380' x 45'
T 3-cyl by bldrs.
4.1894 Completed by Palmers,Jarrow for J.M. Wood,Liverpool.
12.1898 Stranded but refloated. 1910 Purchased by Furness,Withy &
Co. Ltd. 1912 Sold to Y.Hachiuma,Dairen ren. TAMON MARU 15. 1916
Sold to Katsuda Shokai Goshi Kaisha ren. KAIHO MARU. 11.11.1916
Wrecked on Patras Reef near Hong Kong o.v. Moji to Rangoon with
coal.

F161. AMANA   (1910 - 1911) 3412g 2161n   350' x 45'
T 3-cyl by bldrs.
7.1895 Completed by Palmers,Jarrow for J.M. Wood,Liverpool. 1910
Purchased by Furness,Withy & Co. Ltd. 12.1911 Lost while on a
voyage from Leith to Philadelphia.

F162. ACARA   (1910) 4982g 2677n   380' x 47'
T 3-cyl by bldrs.
31904 Completed by Palmers,Jarrow for J.M. Wood,Liverpool. 1910
Purchased by Furness,Withy & Co. Ltd. 1910 Transferred to Furness
Shipping & Agency,Rotterdam ren. GRAMSBERGEN. 1914 Sold to
Holland-America Line ren. WAALDIJK. 1932 Sold to A. Lauro,Genoa
ren. ERCOLE. 20.7.1944 Mined and sunk off Leghorn. 1947 Raised &
traded by Lauro. B/U in 1953.

F163. ADANA   (1910) 3448g 2178n   350' x 45'
T 3-cyl by bldrs.
7.1897 Completed by Palmers,Jarrow for J.M. Wood,Liverpool. 1910
Purchased by Furness,Withy & Co. Ltd. 1910 Sold to G.M. Embiricos,
Andros ren. MILTIADES EMBIRICOS. 1.7.1917 Torpedoed & Sunk by
submarine in the Mediterranean.

F164. ANAPA   (1910 - 1912) 3541g 2251n   350' x 45'
T 3-cyl by bldrs.
2.1896 Completed by Palmers,Jarrow for J.M. Wood,Liverpool. 1910
Purchased by Furness,Withy & Co. Ltd. 1912 Sold K.Hashimoto,Dairen
ren. TENZAN MARU. 25.4.1920 Left Rosario and Montevideo on
17.5.1920 with wheat for Antwerp and disappeared.

F165. ASAMA   (1910 - 1913) 4217g 2671n   380' x 45'
T 3-cyl by bldrs.
12.1897 Completed by Palmers,Jarrow for J.M. Wood,Liverpool. 1910
Purchased by Furness,Withy & Co. Ltd. 1913 Sold to Dairen Towa
S.S. Co. Ltd,Dairen ren. ASAMA MARU. 1917 Taken by French Govt.
ren. LA CHAUSSADE. 13.8.1918 Torpedoed and sunk in Mediterranean
o.v. Port Talbot to Bizeta.

F166. AVALA   (1910 - 1913) 3751g 2388n   370' x 42'
T 3-cyl by Blair & Co.,Stockton.
1890 Completed by Ropner & Son,Stockton for J.M. Wood, Liverpool.
1910 Purchased by Furness,Withy & Co. Ltd. 1913 Sold to G.
Maggiolo fuA,Genoa name/uch. 24.3.1918 Torpedoed and sunk in
Atlantic o.v. New Orleans to Gibraltar.

F167. CHASESIDE   (1911)   See EL CORDOBES   Houlder HF4

F168. MESSINA   (1911 - 1912) 4270g 2757n   380' x 49'
T 3-cyl by Richardsons,Westgarth & Co. Ltd,Sunderland.
1911 Completed by Northumberland SB Co. Ltd,Howdon-on-Tyne for
Furness,Withy & Co. Ltd. 1912 Transferred to Gulf Line Ltd.
4.12.1919 Abandoned 520 miles E of St. John's(NF) o.v. St.
John(NB) to Antwerp.

F169. HOCHELAGA   (1911 - 1917) 4680g 2601n   375' x 52'
T 3-cyl by Richardsons,Westgarth & Co. Ltd,Middlesbrough.
1911 Completed by Sir Raylton Dixon & Co.,Middlesbrough for
Furness,Withy & Co. Ltd. 1917 Sold to Dominion Coal Co. Ltd,
Montreal name u/ch. 7.8.1930 Struck Bird Island,beached East
Point,Magdalen Islands,Gulf of St. Lawrence o.v. Sydney(CB) to
Quebec.

F170. LINGAN (1911 - 1917) 4676g 2603n 375' x 52'
T 3-cyl by Richardsons,Westgarth & Co. Ltd,Middlesbrough.
1911 Completed by Sir Raylton Dixon & Co.,Middlesbrough for
Furness,Withy & Co. Ltd. 1.1917 Sold to Dominion Coal Co. Ltd,
Montreal name u/ch. 1935 B/U.

F171. ALBIANA (1912 - 1913) 3607g 2297n 350' x 46'
T 3-cyl by G.Clark Ltd,Sunderland.
12.1898 Completed by W. Pickersgill & Sons Ltd,Sunderland as CORBY
CASTLE for Lancashire Shipping Co. Ltd(J.Chambers & Co),Liverpool.
1908 Sold to Braemount S.S. Co. Ltd(Sloan & Jackson),Glasgow ren.
BRAEMOUNT. 1912 Purchased by Furness,Withy & Co. Ltd ren. ALBIANA.
1913 Sold to Sale & Co.,London name u/ch. 1934 B/U.

F172. BALACLAVA (1912 - 1915) 4220g 2757n 360' x 48'
T 3-cyl by Richardsons,Westgarth & Co. Ltd),Sunderland.
6.1906 Completed by Northumberland SB Co. Ltd,Howdon-on-Tyne as
BALACLAVA for Agincourt S.S. Co. Ltd,London. 1912 Purchased by
Furness,Withy & Co. Ltd and chartered to Lamport & Holt Ltd. 1914
Ren. TUNISIANA. 23.6.1915 Torpedoed and sunk by UB16 off
Lowestoft o.v. Montreal to Hull with grain. Beached at Barnard
Sands,total loss.

F173. CORUNNA (1912 - 1914) 3810g 2456n 340' x 47'
T 3-cyl by Richardsons,Westgarth & Co. Ltd,Hartlepool.
12.1906 Completed by Furness,Withy & Co. Ltd,Hartlepool for
Agincourt S.S. Co. Ltd,London. 1912 Purchased by Furness,Withy &
Co. Ltd and chartered to Lamport & Holt. 2.1914 Transferred to
Furness Shipping & Agency,Rotterdam ren. TENBERGEN. 19.11.1916
Wrecked on South Rock,Vieille Noir near Ile de Quemenes o.v. Plate
to Rotterdam with maize.

F174. FLODDEN (1912 - 1914) 4211g 2711n 360' x 48'
T 3-cyl by Richardsons,Westgarth & Co. Ltd,Sunderland.
10.1907 Completed by Northumberland SB Co. Ltd,Howdon-on-Tyne for
Agincourt S.S. Co. Ltd,London. 1912 Purchased by Furness,Withy &
Co. Ltd and chartered to Lamport & Holt. 2.1914 Transferred to
Furness Shipping & Agency,Rotterdam ren. VRIJBERGEN. 1915 Sold to
Holland-America Line ren. POELDIJK. 1927 Sold to W. Schuchmann,
Bremerhaven ren. SCHWARZESEE. 1933 B/U.

F175. GRACIANA(2) (1912 - 1924) 3536g 2283n 361' x 46'
T 3-cyl by D. Rowan & Co. Ltd,Glasgow.
1903 Completed by C. Connell & Co.,Glasgow as SIERRA MORENA for
Sierra Shipping Co. Ltd(Thompson,Anderson & Co),Liverpool. 1912
Purchased by Furness,Withy & Co. Ltd ren. GRACIANA. 1924 Sold to
P. Margaronis & Sons,Piraeus ren. ANDREAS K. 3.1931 Stranded,
refloated and B/U.

F176. DIGBY (1913 - 1936) 3960g 2233n 351' x 50'
T 3-cyl by Richardson,Westgarth & Co. Ltd,Hartlepool.
4.1913 Completed by Irvines SB & DD Co. Ltd,Hartlepool as for
Furness, Withy & Co. Ltd . 1916 French Auxiliary as ARTOIS. 1919
Renamed DIGBY. 1925 Transferred to Bermuda & West Indies S.S. Co.

ren. DOMINICA. 1936 Sold to United Baltic Corporation,London ren.
BALTROVER. 1947 Sold to Hellenic Mediterranean Lines Co. Ltd,
Piraeus ren. IONIA. 1964 Sold to Ionia Shpg. Co. SA,Panama ren.
IONIAN. 26.7.1965 Touched bottom at wharf and capsized at
Djakarta. Total loss.

F177. VENICE   (1914 - 1922) 1869g 1161n   279' x 40'
T 3-cyl by Richardsons,Westgarth & Co. Ltd,Middlesbrough.
1914 Completed by Greenock & Grangemouth SB Co. Ltd,Grangemouth
for Furness,Withy & Co. Ltd. 1922 Transferred to Johnston Line
Ltd ren. WIGMORE. 1926 Sold to E. Erichsen ren. MAI. 1931 Sold to
O.& H. Holta,Norway ren. HERLEIK. 7.2.1941 Seized by Japanese
while unloading at Chingwangtao. 17.5.1942 Condemned as a prize
at Sasebo ren. YURIN MARU. 24.2.1945 Sunk by Allied forces.

F178. BEDALE   (1914 - 1917) 2107g 1265n   279' x 40'
T 3-cyl by Richardsons,Westgarth & Co. Ltd,Middlesbrough.
1914 Completed by North of Ireland SB Co. Ltd,Londonderry for
Furness,Withy & Co. Ltd. 6.10.1917 Torpedoed and sunk by U96 25
miles SSE of Mine Head o.v. Cardiff to Berehaven with coal and
stores.

F179. WINGATE   (1914 - 1922) 1911g 1152n   279' x 42'
T 3-cyl by N.E. Marine Eng. Co. Ltd,Sunderland.
1914 Completed by Osbourne,Graham & Co.,Sunderland as WINGATE for
Furness,Withy & Co. Ltd. 1922 Transferred to Johnston Line Ltd,
Liverpool ren. VEDAMORE. 1928 Sold to D/S A/S Eikland(I.M.
Skaugen),Oslo ren. ERLAND. 1939 Sold to F. Pajomagi,Tallinn ren.
NEEME. 3.1940 Damaged by ice and abandoned.

F180. CASTLE EDEN(2) (1914 - 1918) 1949g 1169n   283' x 40'
T 3-cyl by Richardsons,Westgarth & Co. Ltd,Hartlepool.
1914 Completed by Irvines SB & DD Co. Ltd,Hartlepool for Furness,
Withy & Co. Ltd. 4.3.1918 Torpedoed and sunk by U110 4 miles SSE
of Inistrahull L.H. o.v. Clyde to Lough Swilly with general and
coal.

F181. MOBILE   (1914 - 1915) 1950g 1165n   283' x 40'
T 3-cyl by Richardsons,Westgarth & Co. Ltd,Hartlepool.
1914 Completed by Irvines SB & DD Co. Ltd,Hartlepool for Furness,
Withy & Co. Ltd. 28.4.1915 Captured and sunk by U30 25 miles W of
Butt of Lewis o.v. from Barry with coal.

F182. PENSACOLA   (1914 - 1922) 2092g 1268n   279' x 40'
T 3-cyl by Richardsons,Westgarth & Co. Ltd,Sunderland.
7.1914 Completed by Osborne,Graham & Co.,Sunderland for Furness,
Withy & Co. Ltd. 1922 Sold to A. Cappel ren. CLAPTON. 1924 Sold
to D/S A/S Saima(Bergmann & Hammer A/S),Bergen ren. SAIMA. 1936
Sold to S.Synodinos,Piraeus ren. DANAPRIS. 20.4.1940 Sunk in Mediterranean due to war reasons.

F183. SOWWELL   (1914) 3771g 2430n 340' x 50'
T 3-cyl by Central Marine Eng. Works,Hartlepool.

7.1900 Completed by W. Gray & Co. Ltd,Hartlepool as KENLEY for
Mitre S.S. Co. Ltd(Middleton,Houlder & Co),London. 1913 Sold to
Atlantic Traders Ltd(Roth Bros),London ren. SOWWELL. 1914
Purchased by Furness,Withy & Co. Ltd. 1914 Sold to Galbraith,
Pembroke & Co. Ltd,London name u/ch. 19.4.1917 Torpedoed & sunk
170 miles SW of Gibraltar by U35 o.v. Sagunto to Clyde with iron
ore,21 lost.

F184. BOLDWELL   (1914) 3118g 1918n   325' x 48'
T 3-cyl by bldrs.
10.1901 Completed as VOORBURG for Stoom Maats,Amsterdam by
Nederland Scheeps Maats,Amsterdam. 1910 Sold to Franco-Ottoman
Shipping Co. Ltd(Roth Bros),London ren. BOLDWELL. 1914 Purchased
by Furness,Withy & Co. Ltd. 1915 Sold to Neilrose S.S. Co. Ltd
(Letricheaux & David),Swansea name u/ch. 1916 Sold to Byron S.S.
Co. Ltd (M. Embiricos),London name u/ch. 27.5.1917 Torpedoed and
sunk by UC20 35 miles NE of Linosa Island near Malta o.v. Tyne to
Alexandria with coal,3 lost.

F185. MAXTON   (1915 - 1916) See START POINT   FP9

F186. ALGERIANA   (1915 - 1917) See CEBRIANA   FB6

F187. ANNAPOLIS(2) (1915 - 1917) 4567g 2845n   380' x 51'
T 3-cyl by D. Rowan & Co. Ltd,Glasgow.
6.1911 Completed by W. Hamilton & Co.,Pt. Glasgow as LORD LONS-
DALE for S.S. Lord Kelvin Co. Ltd(J.Herron & Co),Liverpool. 1915
Purchased by Furness,Withy & Co. Ltd ren. ANNAPOLIS. 19.4.1917
Torpedoed and sunk by U61 and U69 74 miles NW 1/2 N of Eagle
Island in Atlantic o.v. Halifax(NS) to London with general.

F188. ROTA   (1915 - 1917) 2170g 1152n   310' x 45'
T 3-cyl by bldrs.
1915 Completed by Dunlop,Bremner & Co.,Glasgow for Furness,Withy
& Co. Ltd. 22.7.1917 Torpedoed & sunk by UB40 7 miles SE of Berry
Head o.v. Benisaf to Middlesbrough with iron ore.

F189. TAMAQUA   (1915 - 1924) 5191g 3318n   405' x 52'
T 3-cyl by D. Rowan & Co. Ltd,Glasgow.
7.1910 Completed by Napier & Miller Ltd,Glasgow as DEN OF GLAMIS
for C. Barries & Sons,Dundee. 1915 Purchased by Furness,Withy &
Co. Ltd ren. TAMAQUA. 1924 Sold to Yamashita Kisen Goshi
Kaisha,Dairen ren. GYOKOH MARU. 1938 Ren. GYOKO MARU. 23.2.1944
Wrecked on Ryuku Islands.

F190. WYNCOTE   (1915 - 1924) 4937g 3116n   400' x 52'
T 3-cyl by D. Rowan & Co. Ltd,Glasgow.
6.1907 Completed by C. Connell & Co.,Glasgow for C. Barrie &
Sons, Dundee as DEN OF RUTHVEN. 1915 Purchased by Furness,Withy &
Co. Ltd ren. WYNCOTE. 1924 Sold to Kintyre S.S. Co. Ltd(McMurchy
& Greenlees,mgrs),Liverpool ren. KINTYRE. 1929 Sold to E.L.
Michalitsianos,Argostoli ren. POLYMNIA. 1937 Sold to A.Puech,Le
Havre ren. SYDNEY. 1938 Seized by Franco's forces during Spanish
Civil War ren CORUNA. 1939 Transferred to Empresa Nacional

Elcano,Cadiz ren. CASTILLO SIMANCAS. 1952 Sold to Maritima
Madrilena,Cadiz ren JARAMA. 1960 Sold to A.R. Suardiaz,Gijon ren.
RIVADEMAR. 1963 Sold to Nav. Forestal Africana SA,Cadiz ren.
MUNISA. 28.4.1972 Abandoned as a total loss.

F191. LEXINGTON (1916 - 1924) 3974g 2541n 379' x 50'
T 3-cyl by N.E. Marine Eng. Co. Ltd,Newcastle.
12.1906 Completed by W. Dobson & Co. Ltd,Newcastle for Law,Leslie
& Co.,London as INVERTAY. 1916 Purchased by Furness,Withy & Co.
Ltd ren. LEXINGTON. 1924 Sold to Britain S.S. Co. Ltd(Watts,Watts
& Co), London ren. DENHAM. 1931 B/U in Italy.

F192. CONWAY (1916) 4003g 2591n 345' x 48'
T 3-cyl by Richardsons,Westgarth & Co. Ltd,Sunderland.
1.1901 Completed by Irvine SB & DD Co. Ltd,Hartlepool for Conway
S.S. Co. Ltd(L.R. Conner & Co),Hartlepool. 1916 Purchased by
Furness,Withy & Co. Ltd. 30.4.1916 Torpedoed & sunk 38 miles S
1/2E Cape Palos o.v. Genoa to Almeria in ballast.

F193. PARISIANA(2) (1916) See ARGENTINE TRANSPORT HE7

F194. ALLENDALE (1917 - 1918) 2153g 1268n 285' x 43'
T 3-cyl by McColl & Pollock Ltd,Sunderland.
12.1917 Completed by Osbourne,Graham & Co.,Sunderland as ALLENDALE
for The Shipping Controller, having been taken over for the war and
registered under Furness,Withy & Co. Ltd although Fearnley & Eger,
Oslo were the actual owners. 27.3.1918 Torpedoed and sunk 52 miles
SW of Lizard o.v. Ardrossan to Bordeaux with coal.

F195. BEAUMARIS (1917 - 1918) 2372g 1460n 290' x 44'
T 3-cyl by bldrs.
8.1917 Completed by J.T. Eltringham & Co.,Willington-on-Tyne as
BEAUMARIS for The Shipping Controller, having been taken over for
the war and registered under Furness,Withy & Co. Ltd although
Fearnley & Eger,Oslo were the actual owners. 7.2.1918 Torpedoed &
sunk 2.5 miles NW of Longships o.v. Cardiff to St. Nazaire with
coal.

F196. HASLEMERE (1917 - 1920) 2126g 1282n 285' x 44'
T 3-cyl by Richardsons,Westgarth & Co. Ltd,Sunderland.
1917 Completed by S.P. Austin & Son,Sunderland as HASLEMERE for
The Shipping Controller, having been taken over for the period of
the war and registered under Furness,Withy & Co. Ltd although
Fearnley & Eger,Oslo were the actual owners. 1920 Returned to
Fearnley & Eger ren. HOMLEDAL. 1935 Sold to A/S Salvesen(Jacob
Salvesen,mgr) ren. SPIND. 23.8.1941 Torpedoed and sunk by U564
and U552 off Portuguese coast o.v. Barry to Lisbon with coal.

F197. KEIGHLEY (1917 - 1920) 2150g 1301n 285' x 44'
T 3-cyl by Richardsons,Westgarth & Co. Ltd,Sunderland.
1917 Completed by Osborne,Graham & Co.,Sunderland as KEIGHLEY for
The Shipping Controller, having been taken over for the period of
the war and registered under Furness,Withy & Co. Ltd although
Fearnley & Eger were the actual owners. 1920 Returned to D/S

Garonne(Fearnley & Eger),Oslo ren. GRAZIELLA. 16.9.1943 Torpedoed
by British aircraft o.v. Fredrikstad to Berlevag and driven
ashore near Egersund.

F198. CRESSWELL   (1917 - 1918) 2829g 1761n   318' x 46'
T 3-cyl by Central Marine Eng. Works,Hartlepool.
2.1917 Completed by W. Gray & Co. Ltd,Hartlepool for Furness,
Withy & Co. Ltd. 5.2.1918 Torpedoed and damaged by U53 18 miles
NNE of Kish L.V. o.v. Clyde to Gibraltar with coal. Beached at
Whitesand Bay,total loss.

F199. FORT HAMILTON   (1919 - 1925) 5530g 2889n   425' x 50'
Two T 3-cyl by G. Clark Ltd,Sunderland. 2-screw.
11.1904 Completed by Sir James Laing & Son,Sunderland for Quebec
S.S. Co. Ltd. as BERMUDIAN. 1919 Purchased by Bermuda & West
Indies S.S. Co. Ltd(Furness, Withy & Co. Ltd) ren. FORT HAMILTON.
1925 Sold to Cosulich Triestina di Nav,Trieste ren. STELLA
D'ITALIA. 1930 Reg. under Lloyd Triestino. 1934 B/U.

F200. FORT ST. GEORGE   (1919 - 1935) 7785g 4539n   411' x 57'
Two Q 4-cyl by bldrs. 2-screw.
1912 Completed by W. Beardmore & Co. Ltd,Glasgow for Adelaide
S.S. Co. Ltd,Port Adelaide as WANDILLA. 1919 Purchased by Bermuda
& West Indies S.S. Co. Ltd(Furness,Withy & Co. Ltd) ren. FORT ST.
GEORGE. 1935 Sold to Lloyd Triestino,Trieste ren. CESAREA. 1938
Ren. ARNO. 10.9.1942 Bombed and sunk by British torpedo bombers
40 miles from Tobruk.

F201. FORT VICTORIA   (1919 - 1929) 7784g 4532n   411' x 57'
Two Q 4-cyl by bldrs. 2-screw.
1913 Completed by W. Beardmore & Co. Ltd,Glasgow for Adelaide
S.S. Co. Ltd,Port Adelaide as WILLOCHRA. 1919 Purchased by
Bermuda & West Indies S.S. Co. Ltd(Furness, Withy & Co. Ltd) ren.
FORT VICTORIA. 12.1929 In collision with s.s. ALGONQUIN in
Ambrose Channel,New York. Sank and subsequently blown up.

F202. WENDLAND   (1920 - 1921) 11445g 7167n   520' x 64'
Two T 3-cyl by bldrs. 2-screw.
1919 Completed by Bremer Vulkan,Vegesack but taken over as a
prize by Britain. 1920 Purchased by Furness,Withy & Co. Ltd. 1921
Sold to Federal S.N. Co. Ltd ren. CUMBERLAND. 23.8.1940 Torpedoed
and sunk by U57 in posn. 55-43 N, 7-33 W o.v. Glasgow & Liverpool
for Curacao and Dunedin with metal and general.

F203. SAUERLAND   (1920 - 1921) 10868g 6889n   520' x 64'
Two T 3-cyl by bldrs. 2-screw.
1919 Completed by Bremer Vulkan,Vegesack but taken over as a
prize by Britain. 1920 Purchased by Furness,Withy & Co. Ltd. 1921
Sold to Federal S.N. Co. Ltd ren. NORFOLK. 18.6.1941 Torpedoed
and sunk by U552 in posn. 57-17 N, 11-14 W o.v. Newport to New
York and New Zealand with steel plates and general.

F204. MARAVAL   (1920 - 1934) 5144g 3329n   395' x 50'
T 3-cyl by bldrs.

1903 Completed by W. Denny Bros.,Dumbarton as IRRAWADDY for P. Henderson & Co.,Glasgow. 1914 Sold to Trinidad Shipping & Trading Co. Ltd,Trinidad ren. MARAVAL. 1920 Purchased by Furness,Withy & Co. Ltd name u/ch. 1934 Sold for B/U.

F205. MATURA (1920 - 1929) 4556g 2923n 376' x 48'
T 3-cyl by bldrs.
1901 Completed by Denny & Co.,Dumbarton as AMARAPOORA for P. Henderson & Co.,Glasgow. 1913 Sold to Trinidad Shipping & Trading Co. Ltd,Trinidad ren. MATURA. 1920 Purchased by Furness,Withy & Co. Ltd name u/ch. 1929 Sold for B/U.

F206. MAYARO (1920 - 1929) 3896g 2511n 360' x 45'
T 3-cyl by bldrs.
1900 Completed by Denny & Co.,Dumbarton as PEGU for P. Henderson & Co.,Glasgow. 1910 Sold to Trinidad Shipping & Trading Co. Ltd, Trinidad ren. MAYARO. 1920 Purchased by Furness,Withy & Co. Ltd name u/ch. 1929 Sold for B/U.

F207.TUNISIANA(2) (1921 - 1922) See LANCASTRIAN PRINCE

F208.PERSIANA(3) (1921 - 1922) See CORSICAN PRINCE

F209.ITALIANA(2) (1921) See LANCASTRIAN/ITALIAN PRINCE
(Nos 126,R13 and 124 in 'PRIDE OF THE PRINCES')

F210.PERUVIANA(2) (1921 - 1923) See JESSMORE FJ36

F211. LONDON EXCHANGE (1921 - 1938) 5415g 2862n 420' x 55'
3 Steam turbines by Richardson,Westgarth & Co. Ltd,Hartlepool.
3.1921 Completed by Irvines SB & DD Co. Ltd,Hartlepool as PARISIANA for Neptune S.N. Co. Ltd(Furness,Withy & Co. Ltd). 1922 Ren. LONDON EXCHANGE,same owners. 1934 Transferred to Johnston Warren Lines Ltd name u/ch. 11.1938 Sold to Ben Line Steamers Ltd,Leith ren. BENRINNES. 12.1949 Sold to East & West S.S. Co., Pakistan ren. FATAKADA. 1955 Ren. MINOCHER COWASJEE same owners. 24.1.1957 Reported SE of Mauritius in posn 25-30 S, 68 E but then disappeared.

F212. LONDON CORPORATION (1922 - 1937) 5411g 2921n 420' x 55'
T 3-cyl by Richardson,Westgarth & Co. Ltd,Hartlepool.
1.1922 Completed by Irvines SB & DD Co. Ltd,Hartlepool as CYNTHIANA for Furness,Withy & Co. Ltd. 2.1922 Ren. HOOSAC under Warren Line. 11.1922 Ren. LONDON CORPORATION under Furness,Withy & Co. Ltd. 3.1925 Transferred to Warren Line name u/ch. 12.1928 Reverted to Furness,Withy & Co. Ltd. 12.1937 Sold to Goulandis Bros.,Greece ren. MARIONGA J. GOULANDRIS. 5.1938 Sold to Ben Line,Leith ren. BENLOMOND. 23.11.1942 Torpedoed & Sunk by U172 750 miles E of Amazon o.v. Port Said to Paramaribo via Cape of Good Hope in ballast. 45 crew lost.

F213. LONDON MARINER (1922 - 1935) 8022g 5075n 450' x 58'
2 Steam turbines SR geared to single screw shaft by J. Brown & Co. Ltd,Clydebank.

5.1922 Completed by Furness SB Co. Ltd,Haverton Hill as FELICIANA
for Furness,Withy & Co. Ltd. 1923 Transferred to Gulf Line Ltd
ren. LONDON MARINER. 1928 Ren. IMPERIAL PRINCE. 1935 Sold to
Charente S.S. Co. Ltd(T.& J. Harrison),Liverpool ren. CRAFTSMAN.
9.4.1941 Sunk in Central Atlantic 800 miles W of Dakar by raider
KORMORAN in posn. 5 N, 23-30 W o.v. Rosyth & Oban for Table Bay &
Ismit with general,6 lost.

F214. LONDON SHIPPER   (1922 - 1935) 7939g 4947n 450' x 58'
2 Steam turbines SR geared to single screw shaft by Richardson,
Westgarth & Co. Ltd,Middlesbrough.
8.1923 Completed by Furness SB Co. Ltd,Haverton Hill as LONDON
SHIPPER for Norfolk & North American S.S. Co. Ltd(Furness,Withy &
Co. Ltd). 1928 Ren. BRITISH PRINCE. 1935 Sold to T.& J. Harrison,
Liverpol ren. STATESMAN. 17.5.1941 Sunk by air attack in posn.
56-44 N, 13-45 W o.v. New Orleans for Belfast & Liverpool with
general and steel,1 lost.

F215. LONDON MERCHANT   (1923 - 1935) 7939g 4977n 450' x 58'
2 Steam turbines SR geared to single screw shaft by Richardson,
Westgarth & Co. Ltd,Middlesbrough.
1923 Completed by Furness SB Co. Ltd,Haverton Hill for Neptune
S.N. Co. Ltd(Furness,Withy & Co. Ltd). 1935 Sold to T.& J.
Harrison Ltd,Liverpool ren. POLITICIAN. 4.2.1941 Wrecked on Isle
of Eriskay,Scotland.

F216. LONDON COMMERCE   (1923 - 1935) 7886g 4934n 450' x 58'
2 Steam turbines SR geared to single screw shaft by Richardson,
Westgarth & Co. Ltd,Middlesbrough.
1.1923 Completed by Furness SB Co. Ltd,Haverton Hill for Furness,
Withy & Co. Ltd. 1928 Ren. ROYAL PRINCE. 1935 Sold to Charente
S.S. Co. Ltd(T.& J. Harrison),Liverpool ren. COLLEGIAN. 12.1947
Sold for scrapping at Milford Haven,arriving on 1.1.1948.

F217. LONDON IMPORTER   (1923 - 1933) 7928g 4962n 450' x 58'
2 Steam turbines SR geared to single screw shaft by Richardson,
Westgarth & Co. Ltd,Middlesbrough.
1923 Completed by Furness SB Co. Ltd,Haverton Hill for Furness,
Withy & Co. Ltd. 1933 Sold to The Admiralty ren. RELIANT. 1948
Sold, ren. ANTHONY G. 1949 Sold to East & West S.S. Co.,Karachi
ren. FIRDAUSA. 1962 B/U.

F218. PERUVIANA(3)   (1923 - 1924) 4477g 2792n 355' x 51'
T 3-cyl by N.E. Marine Eng. Co. Ltd,Newcastle.
1923 Completed by Northumberland SB Co. Ltd,Howdon-on-Tyne for
Furness,Withy & Co. Ltd as a tanker. 1924 Sold to Astra Cia
Argentina de Petroleo Soc. Anon.(F. Leitch), Buenos Aires ren.
ASTRA II. 1966 B/U.

F219. THROCKLEY   (1923 - 1928) 2916g 1572n 307' x 45'
T 3-cyl by Richardson,Westgarth & Co. Ltd,Hartlepool.
12.1923 Completed by Furness SB Co. Ltd,Haverton Hill for Furness,Withy & Co. Ltd. Self-trimming collier managed by Newcastle

office. 1928 Sold to Continent Reederei A.G.(Max Murck),Hamburg
ren. MELITA. 1933 Sold to U.S.S.R. ren. JANA. 1960 Deleted.

F220. ELDON (1923 - 1928) 2917g 1579n 307' x 45'
T 3-cyl by Richardson,Westgarth & Co. Ltd,Hartlepool.
11.1923 Completed by Furness SB Co. Ltd,Haverton Hill for Furness,Withy & Co. Ltd. Self-trimming collier managed by Newcastle
office. 1928 Sold to Continent Reederei A.G.(Max Murck),Hamburg
ren. JAPIX. 1933 Sold to U.S.S.R. ren. AMUR. 1960 Deleted.

F221. CYNTHIANA(4) (1927 - 1928) 6903g 4345n 431' x 57'
Two 6-cyl oil engines by W. Beardmore Ltd,Glasgow. 2-screw.
29.5.1924 Launched and 30.10.1924 completed by Blythswood SB Co.
Ltd,Glasgow as SILURIAN for O.& W. Williams,Cardiff. 1927 Purchased
by Furness,Withy & Co. Ltd ren. CYNTHIANA. 23.6.1928 Wrecked at
Cape Mala,Panama Bay o.v. Bellingham to Grangemouth with timber.

F222. PACIFIC SHIPPER (1924 - 1950) 6304g 3850n 420' x 58'
4-cyl 2SCSA oil engine by bldrs.
3.1924 Completed by W. Doxford & Sons Ltd,Sunderland for Furness,
Withy & Co. Ltd for U.S.A/Canada Pacific coast trade. 1950 Sold
for B/U in U.K.

F223. PACIFIC TRADER (1924 - 1938) 6327g 3935n 420' x 58'
4-cyl 2SCSA oil engine by bldrs.
20.2.1924 Launched and 5.1924 completed by W. Doxford & Sons
Ltd,Sunderland for Furness, Withy & Co. Ltd. 1938 Sold to A/S
Braganza(L.G. Braathen),Oslo ren. BRAGANZA. 12.10.1944 Abandoned
after an explosion in engine room 150 miles off Uruguay.

F224. PACIFIC COMMERCE (1925 - 1936) 5089g 3143n 420' x 54'
4-cyl 2SCSA oil engine by bldrs.
2.1922 Completed by W. Doxford & Sons Ltd,Sunderland as DOMINION
MILLER for Norfolk & North American S.S. Co. Ltd(Furness,Withy &
Co. Ltd). 23.5.1923 First arrival at Los Angeles on Pacific
service. 1925 Ren. PACIFIC COMMERCE. 1936 Sold to Brynmos S.S.
Co. Ltd,London(Ambrose,Davies & Matthews,Swansea name u/ch. 1937
Sold to A/S Viking later A/S Lundegaard(Lundegaard & Sonner),
Farsund ren. NORBRYN. 14.1.1959 Arrived Grimstad for B/U.

F225. PACIFIC ENTERPRISE (1927 - 1949) 6722g 4125n 436' x 60'
Two 8-cyl 4SCSA oil engines by J.G. Kincaid Ltd,Glasgow. 2-screw.
12.1927 Completed by Blythswood SB Co. Ltd,Glasgow for Norfolk &
North American S.S. Co. Ltd(Furness,Withy & Co. Ltd). 8.9.1949
Stranded at Point Arena,California.

F226. PACIFIC RELIANCE (1927 - 1940) 6717g 4120n 436' x 60'
Two 8-cyl 4SCSA oil engines by J.G. Kincaid Ltd,Glasgow. 2-screw.
28.6.1927 Launched and 9.1927 completed by Blythswood SB Co. Ltd,
Glasgow for Norfolk & North American S.S. Co. Ltd(Furness, Withy &
Co. Ltd). 4.3.1940 Torpedoed and sunk by U29 in posn. 50-23 N,
5-49 W o.v. London to Liverpool.

F227. BERMUDA   (1927 - 1931)   19066g 11281n   526' x 74'
Two 8-cyl 2SCSA Doxford oil engines,4-screw.
28.7.1927 Launched and 14.12.1937 completed by Workman,Clark &
Co. Ltd,Belfast for Bermuda & West Indies S.S. Co. Ltd(Furness,
Withy & Co. Ltd). 14.1.1928 Maiden voyage New York - Bermuda.
6.1931 Superstructure completely destroyed by fire at Hamilton,
sent to Belfast for repairs. 19.11.1931 Shortly before completion
fire broke out again, completely gutting her and she sank. Raised
on 24.12.1931 the wreck was purchased by her builders, engines
were removed,and set off under tow by SEAMAN for Rosyth breakers.
6.1932 Tow lost and wreck ran aground on Badcall Islands in Eddrachilles Bay,Sutherland. Total loss.

F228. PACIFIC EXPORTER (1928 - 1951) 6723g 4125n 436' x 60'
Two 8-cyl 4SCSA oil engines by J.G. Kincaid Ltd,Glasgow. 2-screw.
22.3.1928 Launched and 5.1928 completed by Blythswood SB Co. Ltd,
Glasgow for Norfolk & North American S.S. Co. Ltd(Furness,Withy &
Co. Ltd). 1951 Sold to G. Costa,Genoa ren. GIACOMO C. 20.10.1958
Arrived Savona for demolition.

F229. PACIFIC PIONEER (1928 - 1942) 6723g 4126n 436' x 60'
Two 8-cyl 4SCSA oil engines by J.G. Kincaid Ltd,Glasgow. 2-screw.
2.1928 Completed by Blythswod SB Co. Ltd,Glasgow for Norfolk
& North American S.S. Co. Ltd(Furness,Withy & Co. Ltd).
29.7.1942 Torpedoed and sunk by U132 in 43-30 N, 60-35 W
o.v. Cardiff & Belfast Lough to Halifax in ballast.

F230. PACIFIC GROVE (1928 - 1943) 7114g 4316n   450' x 61'
Two 6-cyl 4SCSA oil engines by Deutsche Werke,Kiel.2-screw.
4.1928 Completed by Deutsche Werke,Kiel for Furness,Withy &
Co. Ltd. 12.4.1943 Torpedoed and sunk by U563 in 54-10 N, 30
W o.v. New York to Glasgow with general,11 lost.

F231. PACIFIC PRESIDENT (1928 - 1940) 7114g 4316n 450' x 61'
Two 6-cyl 4SCSA oil engines by Deutsche Werke,Kiel.2-screw.
6.1928 Completed by Deutsche Werft,Kiel for Furness,Withy &
Co. Ltd. 2.12.1940 Torpedoed and sunk by U43 in 56-04N, 18-
45 W o.v. Leith & Oban to New York in ballast,all crew lost.

F232. PACIFIC RANGER (1929 - 1940) 6866g 4186n 436' x 60'
Two 8-cyl 4SCSA oil engines by bldrs. 2-screw.
1929 Completed by Burmeister & Wain Ltd,Copenhagen for Furness,
Withy & Co. Ltd. 12.10.1940 Torpedoed and sunk by U59 in 56-20 N,
11-43 W o.v. Seattle for Manchester with lumber and metal.

F233. NERISSA   (1929 - 1941) 5583g 3116n   350' x 54'
T 4-cyl by D. Rowan & Co. Ltd,Glasgow.
6.1926 Completed by W. Hamilton & Co. Ltd,Port Glasgow for C.T.
Bowring & Co. Ltd,London. Red Cross Line service. 1929 Purchased
by Bermuda & West Indies S.S. Co. Ltd(Furness, Withy & Co. Ltd).
30.4.1941 Torpedoed and sunk by U552 in 55-57N,10-08 W o.v.
Halifax & St. John's(NF) for U.K. with general, aluminium,shells
and trucks. 83 crew and 124 passengers lost.

F234. ROSALIND   (1929 - 1936) 2390g 1563n   300' x 40'
T 3-cyl by bldrs.
9.1911 Completed by Clyde SB & Eng. Co.,Glasgow as LADY GWENDOLEN
for British & Irish Steam Packet Co. Ltd,Dublin. 1919 Purchased
by C.T. Bowring & Co. Ltd,London ren. ROSALIND. 1929 Purchased by
Bermuda & West Indies S.S. Co. Ltd(Furness,Withy & Co. Ltd) name
u/ch. 1936 Sold to Zetska Plovidba A.D.,Kotor ren. LOVCEN. 1942
Sold to Cia Centro Americana,Panama ren. COLUMBIA. 1946 Sold to
Chan Kin Cheong,Canton ren. WAH CHING. 1950 Sold to Grande Shpg.
Corp. ren. TERESA. 1953 Deleted from Register.

F235. SILVIA   (1929 - 1934) 3589g 1431n   337' x 45'
T 3-cyl by bldrs.
1909 Completed by Schichau,Danzig as OREL for Russian Volunteer
Fleet Association. 1921 Purchased by C.T. Bowring & Co. Ltd,
London ren. SILVIA. 1929 Purchased by Bermuda & West Indies S.S.
Co. Ltd(Furness,Withy & Co. Ltd) name uch. 1934 Sold to Douglas
S.S. Co. Ltd,Hong Kong. 1935 Sold to Williamson & Co.,Hong Kong
ren. HAITAN. 11.1941 Depot ship at Rangoon and Trincomalee.
6.1946 Returned to Douglas S.S. Co. Ltd and laid-up at Hong Kong.
23.12.1950 Sold for B/U at Hong Kong.

F236. CASTLE HARBOUR (1929 - 1942) 730g 294n   176' x 34'
Two T 3-cyl by J.G. Kincaid,Glasgow. 2-screw.
1929 Completed by Blythswood SB Co. Ltd,Glasgow as MID OCEAN for
Bermuda & West Indies S.S. Co. Ltd (Furness,Withy & Co. Ltd).
1930 Ren. CASTLE HARBOUR. 16.10.1942 Torpedoed and sunk by U160
in posn. 11 N, 61-10 W o.v. Trinidad for Pernambuco in ballast, 9
lost.

F237. LONGBIRD   (1930 - 1935) 636g 244n   170' x 30'
T 3-cyl by bldrs.
1919 Completed by Smiths Dock Co. Ltd,Middlesbrough as H.M.S.
KILMUCKRIDGE. 1919 Sold to Acacia Shpg. Co. Ltd,Halifax(NS) ren.
NEWTON BAY. 1930 Purchased by Bermuda & West Indies S.S. Co.
Ltd(Furness,Withy & Co. Ltd). ren. LONGBIRD. 1935 Sold to Viking
S.S. Co. Ltd,Nassau name u/ch. 1939 Sold to W.A. Wilson,Nassau.
1940 Sold to Derwent Steam Shipping Co Ltd(Anthony & Bainbridge),
Newcastle name u/ch. 16.1.1943 Sunk in collision with s.s. BELTOY
off Blyth o.v. Clyde to Hull with oilseed.

F238. MONARCH OF BERMUDA (1931 - 1947) 22424g 12876n 553' x 77'
2 Fraser & Chalmers turbines driving Gen. Electric motors,4-screw.
17.3.1931 Launched and 7.11.1931 completed by Vickers Armstrong
Ltd,Newcastle for Furness Bermuda Ltd,Hamilton. 8.9.1934 Saved 71
passengers from burning MORRO CASTLE off New Jersey. 1937 Reg. at
London. 11.1939 Converted to troop transport. 24.3.1947 During
renovation work at Newcastle for return to passenger service her
passenger accomodation was destroyed by fire; purchased by
Ministry of Transport,rebuilt by Thorneycroft at Southampton as
Australian emigrant carrier with Shaw,Savill as mgrs, renamed NEW
AUSTRALIA and left 15.8.1950 Southampton on first voyage. 1.1958
Sold to Arcadia S.S. Co(Greek Line),Andros ren. ARKADIA and

modernised by Blohm & Voss at Hamburg. 22.5.1958 First voyage
Bremerhaven - Montreal. 18.12.1966 Arrived Valencia for B/U.

F239. QUEEN OF BERMUDA   (1933 - 1967) 22575g 12777n 553' x 77'
2 Fraser & Chalmers turbines driving Gen. Electric motors,4-screw.
1.9.1932 Launched and 14.2.1933 completed by Vickers Armstrong
Ltd,Barrow for Furness Bermuda Ltd,Hamilton. 1937 Reg. at London.
10.1939 Converted to Armed Merchant Cruiser and third (dummy)
funnel removed. 1943 Troop transport. 1947 Handed back to company
and 2.1949 resumed Bermuda service with three funnels. 10.1961
Reconstruction by Harland & Wolff Ltd,Belfast with new single
funnel and bow. 4.1962 Resumed Bermuda service. 6.12.1966 Arrived
Faslane for B/U.

F240. FORT AMHERST   (1936 - 1951) 3489g 1946n 315' x 45'
T 3-cyl & L.P. exhaust turbine by D.Rowan & Co. Ltd,Glasgow.
1.1936 Completed by Blythswood SB Co. Ltd,Glasgow for Furness,
Withy & Co. Ltd. 12.1951 Sold to Admiralty ren. AMHERST. 1964 B/U
in Belgium.

F241. FORT TOWNSHEND   (1936 - 1952) 3488g 1944n 315' x 45'
T 3-cyl & L.P. exhaust turbine by D.Rowan & Co. Ltd,Glasgow.
4.1936 Completed by Blythswood SB Co. Ltd,Glasgow for Furness,
Withy & Co. Ltd. 10.1952 Sold to Mohammed Abdullah Alireza,
Jeddah ren. AL AMIR SAUD. 1956 Ren. MANSOUR. 1960 Sold to Mari-
fortuna S.A.,Piraeus(Chandris) ren. ROMANTICA. 8.1982 B/U at
Aliaga.

F242. MANAQUI   (1937 - 1942) 2802g 1522n   303' x 47'
T 3-cyl by bldrs.
1921 Completed by Workman,Clark & Co. Ltd,Belfast for Unifruitco
S.S. Co. Ltd(Clark & Service,mgr),Glasgow, later to United Fruit
Co. Ltd,Balboa. 1937 Purchased by Furness,Withy & Co. Ltd name
u/ch. 3.1942 Torpedoed and sunk in posn. 17-15 N, 61 W o.v. Loch
Ewe for Kingston, having left Loch Ewe on 18.2.1942. Reported
missing on 15.3.1942.

F243. PACIFIC IMPORTER   (1947 - 1953) 7176g 4380n 441' x 57'
T 3-cyl by Joshua Hendy Ironworks,Sunnyvale(Cal.).
9.1943 Completed as SAMTREDY for Ministry of War Transport by
California SB Corporation,having been launched as JOHN TIPTON.
1947 Purchased by Furness,Withy & Co. Ltd ren. PACIFIC IMPORTER.
1953 Sold to Ditta Luigi Pittaluga,Genoa ren. AQUITANIA. 1965 Sold
to Akrotiri S.S. Co,Liberia ren. AYIA MARINA. 2.1969 Arrested for
debt at Rio de Janeiro and 12.1969 sold to local breakers.

F244. PACIFIC LIBERTY   (1947 - 1954) 7176g 4380n 441' x 57'
T 3-cyl by Joshua Hendy Ironworks,Sunnyvale(Cal.).
9.1943 Completed as SAMCALIA for Ministry of War Transport
(Furness,Withy & Co. Ltd,mgr) by California SB Corporation,
having been launched as LORRIN A. THURSTON. 1947 Purchased by
Furness,Withy & Co. Ltd ren. PACIFIC LIBERTY. 1954 Sold to Febo
Amedeo Bertorello,Genoa ren. PHOEBUS. 1963 Sold to Seatide

Shipping Co,Liberia ren. BAYHORSE. 1970 Ren. SAN GABRIEL.
21.1.1971 Arrived for B/U at Split.

F245. PACIFIC NOMAD (1947 - 1954) 7176g 4380n 441' x 57'
T 3-cyl by Vulcan Ironworks,Wilkes-Barre(Penn.).
12.1943 Completed as SAMAVON for Ministry of War Transport by New
England SB Corporation,Portland(Me), having been launched as
BRONSON ALCOTT. 1947 Sold to Furness,Withy & Co. Ltd ren. PACIFIC
NOMAD. 1954 Sold to Panama S.S. Co. Ltd,Liberia ren. NIKOLOS.
1960 Sold to Diana Maritime Corp,Liberia ren. STAMATIS. 3.11.1966
Grounded 4 miles south of Madras harbour in typhoon o.v. Madras
to Calcutta with wheat,total loss.

F246. PACIFIC RANGER(2) (1947 - 1952) 7176g 4380n 441' x 57'
T 3-cyl by Harrisburg Mach. Corp,Harrisburg(Penn.).
3.1944 Completed as SAMDARING for Ministry of War Transport by
New England SB Corporation,Portland(Me). 1947 Purchased by
Furness,Withy & Co. Ltd ren. PACIFIC RANGER. 1952 Sold to Cia Nav
Somelga SA,Panama ren. SAN DIMITRIS. 1958 Sold to Albaro Soc.
Italiana di Nav,Genoa ren. PRIARUGGIA. 1960 Forepart joined at
Genoa to aftpart of ALBARO ex JOSEPHINE SHAW LOWELL, resultant
vessel had length 551' 8481g ren. ALBARO. 1963 Sold to Aegean
Cia Nav SA,Piraeus ren. AIGAION. 9.1968 Scrapped at Osaka.

F247. PACIFIC STRONGHOLD (1947 - 1954) See MALAYAN PRINCE
(No. R27 in 'PRIDE OF THE PRINCES')
SOLD 1959 -VARIOUS NAMES. BROKEN UP 1970.

F248. PACIFIC FORTUNE (1948 - 1965) 9400g 5598n 499' x 63'
3 Steam turbines DR & SR geared to 1 shaft by J. Brown & Co. Ltd.
2.1948 Completed by Blythswood SB Co. Ltd for Norfolk & N.
American S.S. Co. Ltd(Furness,Withy & Co. Ltd). 1965 Sold to
Malaysia Marine Corp.(C.Y. Tung),Liberia ren. MALAYSIA FORTUNE.
15.5.1974 Arrived Kaohsiung for B/U.

F249. PACIFIC UNITY (1948 - 1964) 9511g 5610n 499' x 63'
3 Parsons Marine turbines DR & SR geared to 1 shaft.
10.1948 Completed by Sir James Laing & Sons Ltd,Sunderland
for Furness,Withy & Co. Ltd. 1964 Sold to Astroleal Cia Nav
SA,Liberia ren. LAVRENTIOS. 15.4.1970 Left Saigon for
Shanghai for B/U.

F250. FORT AVALON (1949 - 1960) 3484g 1807n 363' x 49'
2 Steam turbines SR geared to 1 shaft by bldrs.
7.1949 Completed by Scotts SB & Eng. Co. Ltd,Greenock for
Furness,Withy & Co. Ltd. 1960 Sold to Comp. Mar. Med Ltda,
Beirut ren. AZUR MED. 27.4.1974 Arrived Burriana for B/U.

F251. FORT HAMILTON(2) (1951 - 1958) See STUART PRINCE
(No. 148 in 'PRIDE OF THE PRINCES')

F252. OCEAN MONARCH (1951 - 1967) 13654g 7135n 516' x 72'
4 Parsons Marine DR geared turbines by builders,2-screw.
27.7.1950 Launched and 23.3.1951 completed trials by Vickers
Armstrong Ltd,Newcastle for Furness,Withy & Co. Ltd. 3.5.1951

Maiden voyage New York - Bermuda. 22.9.1966 Laid-up in Fal.
8.1967 Sold to Balkanturist(Bulgaria),Varna ren. VARNA for
crusing. 1975 Laid-up at Perama by Nav. Maritime Bulgare. 1977
Ren. VENUS. 1978 Sold to Dolphin(Hellas) Shipping SA,Greece ren.
RIVIERA, and operated a series of 15-day crusises from 6.1979 out
of Venice in Trans-Tirreno Express colours. 28.5.1981 Gutted by
fire which broke out in boiler room while lying at Ambelaki for
modifications for the summer season. Towed to a position off Kynosoura she capsized on 1.6.1981 and sank on her side.

F253. PACIFIC RELIANCE(2) (1951 - 1971) 9442g 5528n   501' x 63'
3 Parsons Marine turbines DR & SR geared to 1 shaft.
22.5.1951 Launched and 12.1951 completed by Vickers Armstrong
Ltd,Newcastle for Furness,Withy & Co. Ltd. 26.3.1971 Arrived
Bruges for B/U.

F254. PACIFIC NORTHWEST (1954 - 1971) 9442g 5529n   501' x 63'
3 Parsons Marine turbines DR & SR geared to 1 shaft.
3.1954 Completed by Vickers Armstrong Ltd,Newcastle for Furness,
Withy & Co. Ltd. 1971 Sold to Deltape Nav SA,Panama ren. AEGIS
POWER. 1974 B/U at Whampoa 4.3.1974 Left Singapore Roads for
Shanghai for B/U.

F255. PACFIC ENVOY   (1958 - 1971) 9439g 5572n   501' x 63'
2 Parsons Marine turbines DR geared to 1 shaft.
4.1958 Completed by Vickers Armstrong Ltd,Newcastle for Furness,
Withy & Co. Ltd. 1965 Transferred to Royal Mail Line Ltd ren.
LOCH RYAN. 1970 Ren. PACIFIC ENVOY. 1971 Sold to Amon Shipping
Co. Ltd,Famagusta ren. AEGIS STRENGTH. 29.1.1974 Sailed from
Singapore Roads for Whampoa for B/U.

F256. PACIFIC STRONGHOLD(2)   (1958 - 1971) 9439g 5572n 501' x 63'
2 Parsons Marine turbines DR geared to 1 shaft.
7.1958 Completed by Vickers Armstrong Ltd,Newcastle for Furness,
Withy & Co. Ltd. 1971 Sold to Aspis Shipping Co. Ltd(N. Papalios),
Famagusta ren. AEGIS HONOR. 1.3.1974 Delivered at Whampoa for B/U.

F257. SAGAMORE   (1957 - 1975) 10792g 5686n   505' x 65'
4-cyl 2SCSA Doxford oil engine by D. Rowan & Co. Ltd,Glasgow.
12.1957 Completed by Blythswood SB Co. Ltd,Glasgow for Furness,
Withy & Co. Ltd as an ore-carrier on charter to BISCO. 1974
Transferred to Pacific Maritime Services Ltd(Houlder Bros). 1975
Sold to Soc. Riuniti di Nav srl,Cagliari ren. CAPITAN ALBERTO.
1989 Sold to Sivilla Maritime,St. Vincent ren. TANIA. 9.4.1990
Arrived Malaga from Split for B/U.

F258. EDENMORE   (1958 - 1975) 10792g 5686n   505' x 65'
4-cyl 2SCSA Doxford oil engine by D. Rowan & Co. Ltd,Glasgow.
4.1958 Completed by Blythswood SB Co. Ltd,Glasgow for Furness,
Withy & Co. Ltd as an ore-carrier on charter to BISCO. 1974 Transferred to Pacific Maritime Services Ltd(Houlder Bros). 1975 Sold
to Attlich Inc,Panama ren. WELCOME. 1976 Sold to Cala Pira spA di
Nav,Cagliari ren. DUGLASIA. 15.9.1983 Arrived Savona for B/U. Dem.
commenced at Vado during 1.1984.

F259. BOTANY BAY (1969 - 1982) 26876g 14597n 745' x 101'
2 Steam turbines by Stal-Laval,Finspong.
1969 Completed by Howaldtswerke D.W.,Hamburg for Furness,Withy &
Co. Ltd for operation in Overseas Containers Ltd. 1982 Sold to
Camperdown Ltd(P & O Containers Ltd) name u/ch. 23.4.1983 Arrived
Uno to be re-engined as a motor vessel. 1989 Ren. NEDLLOYD
TASMAN. 9.1991 Still in service.

F260. FURNESS BRIDGE (1971 - 1976) 77316g 65547n 964' x 144'
8-cyl Harland - B&W oil engine.
1971 Completed by Swan Hunter SB Ltd,Haverton Hill for Furness,
Withy & Co. Ltd(Houlder Bros). 1976 Sold to Utah Transport Inc,
Liberia ren. LAKE ARROWHEAD. 1982 Sold to Marcona Carriers Ltd,
Liberia ren. MARCONA PATHFINDER. 1983 Sold to Paramount Transport
Inc,Liberia ren. WORLD PATHFINDER. 1986 Sold to Nerice Maritime
Co. Ltd,Cyprus ren. OCEAN SOVEREIGN. 9.1991 Still in service.

F261. MOUNT NEWMAN (1973 - 1982) 54481g 43099n 856' x 133'
9-cyl 2SCSA B&W oil engine by bldrs.
1.10.1973 Launched as WINSFORD BRIDGE and 11.1973 completed by
Harland & Wolff Ltd,Belfast as MOUNT NEWMAN for Pacific Maritime
Services Ltd(Furness,Withy & Co. Ltd) for 7-year charter to
Australian National Line. 1982 Sold to Nan Fung Development Ltd,
Hong Kong ren. SOUTH VICTOR. 1987 Sold to Queens Gate Shipping
Corp(Ugland),Philippines ren. COLITA. 1990 Sold to Pan Ocean
Shpg. Co. Ltd,Seoul ren. PAN CEDAR. 9.1990 Sold to Orwell Shpg.
Co.,Piraeus ren. IAPETOS. 9.1991 Still in service.

F262. ROEBUCK (1976 - 1982) 6802g 3485n 410' x 62'
6-cyl 2SCSA Mitsubishi oil engine.
1976 Completed by Dae Sun SB & Eng. Co. Ltd,Busan for Dee Navigation Ltd(Furness,Withy & Co. Ltd). 1982 Sold to Transatlantic
Maritime Co. Ltd,Cyprus ren. SOUTH COUNTY. 9.1991 Still in service.

F263. RIVERINA (1977 - 1982) 6802g 3485n 410' x 62'
6-cyl 2SCSA Mitsubishi oil engine.
1977 Completed by Dae Sun SB & Eng. Co. Ltd,Busan for Dee Navigation Ltd(Furness,Withy(Shipping) Ltd). 1982 Sold to P/R Falkon,
Sweden ren. FALKON. 1989 Sold to Apollonia Shpg. Co. Ltd,Cyprus
ren. APOLLONIA FAITH. 9.1991 Still in service.

F264. RAVENSWOOD (1977 - 1982) 6802g 3485n 410' x 62'
6-cyl 2SCSA Mitsubishi oil engine.
1977 Completed by Dae Sun SB & Eng. Co. Ltd,Busan for Dee Navigation Ltd(Furness,Withy(Shipping) Ltd). 1982 Sold to South Faith
Shipping Inc,Liberia ren. SOUTH FAITH. 1987 Sold to Reederei A.
Hartmann,Leer ren. ST.PAUL RIVER. 1988 Sold to Panamar Carriers
SA,Piraeus ren. AFRICAN GLORY. 9,1991 Still in service.

F265. ANDES (1984 - 19) 32150g 18016n 664' x 106'
5-cyl 2SCSA B&W oil engine by bldrs.
4.1984 Completed by Hyundai H.I. Co. Ltd,Ulsan for Furness,Withy
(Shipping) Ltd for Eurosal service to West Coast S. America.
9.1991 Still in service.

FB1.STRAITS OF MENAI   (1896 - 1901) 2870 1849n 314' x 40'
T 3-cyl by W. Allan & Co. Ltd,Sunderland.
9.1894 Completed by Furness,Withy & Co. Ltd,Hartlepool for N.
Maclean & Co.,Glasgow. 1896 Purchased by British Maritime Trust
Ltd(R.B. Stoker,mgr),Glasgow name u/ch. 1901 Sold to Straits of
Menai S.S. Co. Ltd(Williams & Mordey),Glasgow name u/ch. 1913
Sold to Bank of Athens (J. Arvan-itidi & Son,mgr),Syra ren.
CHALKYDON. 14.7.1917 Torpedoed and sunk off Madeira o.v. from New
York.

FB2.CYNTHIANA   (1896 - 1899) 2923g 1934n 311' x 41'
T 3-cyl by Blackwood & Gordon,Glasgow.
4.1891 Completed by Russell & Co.,Pt. Glasgow for Cynthiana S.S.
Co.,(McLean & Sutherland),Glasgow. 1896 Purchased by British
Maritime Trust Ltd(R.B. Stoker,mgr),Glasgow. 1899 Sold to T. Ron-
aldson & Co. Ltd,Glasgow ren. SAXON KING. 1904 Sold to Ellerman
Lines Ltd(Westcott & Laurance) ren. EGYPTIAN. 1912 Wrecked at
Great Yarmouth.

FB3.MEDIANA   (1897 - 1901) 2440g 1591n 315' x 43'
T 3-cyl by Furness,Withy & Co. Ltd,Middlesbrough.
1897 Completed by Sir Raylton Dixon & Co.,Middlesbrough for
British Maritime Tust Ltd(R.B. Stoker,mgr),London. 1901 Sold to
Mediana S.S. Co. Ltd(I. Crocker),Hartlepool name u/ch. 1912 Sold
to A/B Kattegat(H.Swensson),Helsingborg ren SIGNE. 1923 Sold to
Aug. Bolten(W. Muller),Hamburg ren. ROBERT. 1937 Sold to G.H.
Kokotis, Corfu ren. MYDOL. 1938 Ren. ANNITA,same owner. 1939 Sold
to P.G. Cottaropoulos,Tunis ren. CARTHAGE. 2.2.1953 Aground on
the Dutch coast at Scheveningen o.v. Dunkirk to Hartlepool in
ballast. Refloated and scrapped at Leith, dem. commenced
27.3.1954.

FB4.GLORIANA   (1898 - 1901) 2768g 1775n 316' x 42'
T 3-cyl by J. Dickinson & Sons Ltd,Sunderland.
10.1898 Completed by Short Brothers Ltd,Sunderland for British
Maritime Trust Ltd(Furness,Withy & Co. Ltd,mgrs),London. 1901 Sold
to Russische-Baltische D/S Ges.(Helmsing & Grimm,mgrs),Riga ren.
BETTY. 10.6.1917 Torpedoed and sunk in posn. 59-30 N, 6-15 W o.v.
Cardiff to Murmansk with coal.

FB5.ITALIANA   (1898 - 1900) 2663g 1706n 305' x 44'
T 3-cyl by Hall-Brown,Buttery & Co.,Glasgow.
10.1898 Completed by R.Duncan & Co.,Pt. Glasgow for British
Maritime Trust Ltd(Furness,Withy & Co. Ltd,mgrs),London. 5.9.1900
Sold to Italiana S.S. Co. Ltd(Jenkins,Williams & Co),Cardiff name
u/ch. 11.1904 Mgrs. became Jenkins Brothers,Cardiff. 14.9.1916
Torpedoed and sunk by UB43 112 miles E of Malta o.v. Rocas Bay &
Tarragona to Salonica with hay.

FB6.CEBRIANA   (1899 - 1902) & (1904 - 1906) 4221g 2736n 360' x 48'
T 3-cyl by W. Allan & Co. Ltd,Sunderland.

11.1899 Completed by Short Brothers Ltd,Sunderland for British
Maritime Trust Ltd,(Furness,Withy & Co. Ltd,mgrs)London. 1902
Chartered to Britain Steamship Co. Ltd(Watts,Watts & Co. Ltd,
mgrs), London ren. TWICKENHAM. 1902 Returned to B.M.T. ren.
CEBRIANA. 1906 Sold to Agincourt S.S. Co. Ltd,London ren.
DETTINGEN. 1912 Taken over by Furness,Withy & Co. Ltd and
chartered to Lamport & Holt. 1914 Ren. ALGERIANA. 1917 Sold to
B.J. Sutherland,Newcastle. 21.9.1917 Wrecked at Cape Cantia.

FB7.BOLIVIANA (1900 - 1903) & (1906 - 1909) 4573g 2962n 370' x 51'
T 3-cyl by Furness,Westgarth & Co. Ltd,Middlesbrough.
6.1900 Completed by Furness,Withy & Co.,Hartlepool for British
Maritime Trust Ltd(Furness,Withy & Co. Ltd,mgrs),London. 1903
Transferred to Gulf Line Ltd (Furness,Withy & Co. Ltd,mgrs) ren.
LUGANO. 1906 Transferred back to B.M.T. Ltd ren. BOLIVIANA.
24.11.1909 Transferred to Furness,Withy & Co. Ltd. 1920 Sold to
D/S A/S Union(E.G. Lea),Bergen ren. ATLANTIS. 1924 Sold to A/S
Lotus(J. Henschien),Lillesand ren. LOTUS. 1924 Sold to A/S Oddero
(A.I. Langfeldt & Co),Christiania ren. ASMUND. 1931 B/U.

FB8.WYANDOTTE   (1900 - 1909) 4204g 2712n   375' x 48'
T 3-cyl by Muir & Huston Ltd,Glasgow.
4.1900 Completed by A.McMillan & Sons Ltd,Dumbarton as LORD ROBERTS
for Irish Shipowners Co. Ltd(T. Dixon & Sons),Belfast. 1900 Purch-
ased by British Maritime Trust Ltd (Furness,Withy & Co. Ltd,mgrs),
London. 24.11.1909 Transferred to Furness, Withy & Co. Ltd. 1912
Transferred to British & Argentine S.N. Co. Ltd. 1914 Sold to Union
S.S. Co. Ltd of New Zealand ren. WAIMARINO. 1926 Sold to C. Young
Zan, Shanghai ren. KING SING. 1930 Sold to N. Moller,Shanghai ren.
DAISY MOLLER. 1934 B/U.

FB9.AUSTRIANA   (1901 - 1909) 4025g 2579n 345' x 48'
T 3-cyl by Richardson,Westgarth & Co. Ltd,Hartlepool.
9.1901 Completed by Irvines SB & DD Co. Ltd,Hartlepool for British Maritime Trust Ltd(Furness,Withy & Co. Ltd,mgrs),London.
24.11.1909 Transferred to Furness,Withy & Co. Ltd. 11.2.1915 Sold
to London American Maritime Trading Co. Ltd(Petersen & Co. Ltd),
London ren. RIO VERDE. 21.2.1918 Torpedoed and sunk 4 miles W of
Crammock Head,Mull of Galloway.

FB10.BIRMINGHAM   (1901 - 1909) 4025g 2612n   345' x 48'
T 3-cyl by Richardson,Westgarth & Co. Ltd,Hartlepool.
10.1901 Completed by Irvines SB & DD CO. Ltd,Hartlepool for British Maritime Trust Ltd(Furness,Withy & Co. Ltd,mgrs),London.
24.11.1909 Transferred to Furness,Withy & Co. Ltd. 11.2.1915 Sold
to London American Maritime Trading Co. Ltd(Petersen & Co. Ltd),
London ren. RIO PRETO. 1920 Sold to S. Lewis,London name u/ch.
18.12.1922 Stranded 6 miles N of St. Valery o.v. Poti to Boulogne
with manganese ore.

FB11.POTOMAC   (1902 - 1909) 3590g 2355n   348' x 45'
T 3-cyl by Richardson,Westgarth & Co. Ltd,Sunderland
4.1902 Completed by C.S. Swan & Hunter,Wallsend for British
Maritime Trust Ltd(Furness,Withy & Co. Ltd,mgrs),London.

24.11.1909 Transferred to Furness,Withy & Co. Ltd. 1914 Sold to
Sale & Co, London name u/ch. 1916 Sold to Potomac S.S. Co.
Ltd(M.C. Piggott),London name u/ch. 1920 Sold to Soc Anon di Nav
Lloyd Meridionale,Palermo ren. ROVIGNO. 5.10.1922 Wrecked 60
miles S of Rio Grande o.v. Gulfport to Buenos Aires with timber.

FB12.EGYPTIANA   (1902)   See RAPALLO Gulf Line FG8

FB13.ATHENIANA   (1902 - 1907) 2300g 1399n 302' x 43'
T 3-cyl by Central Marine Eng. Works,Hartlepool.
5.1902 Completed by W. Gray & Co. Ltd,Hartlepool for British Marit-
ime Trust Ltd(Furness,Withy & Co Ltd,mgrs),London. 1907 Transferred
to Furness,Withy & Co. Ltd. 1909 Sold to Anglo-Hellenic S.S. Co.
Ltd(A.A. Embiricos),Greece ren. ATHINAIA. 1911 Returned to Furness,
Withy & Co. Ltd ren. ATHENIANA. 1913 Sold to Rederi A/B Urania(B.O.
Borjesson),Helsingborg ren. ALIDA. 1918 Sold to Norrkopings Rederi
A/B(V. Schriel),Norrkoping. 7.1919 Ren. KARLSVIK. 1934 Sold to
Rederi A/B Activ(J. Gorthon),Helsingborg ren. ALIDA GORTHON.
29.8.1940 Torpedoed & sunk 250 miles NW of Inishtrahull by U100
o.v. London to St. John's(NF) via Scotland. 11 crew lost plus 18
survivors from DALBLAIR 4608/26.

FB14.COMO   (1902) See Gulf Line Ltd FG9

FB15.INDIANA   (1902 - 1909) 3869g 2508n 340' x 47'
T 3-cyl by Richardsons,Westgarth & Co. Ltd,Middlesbrough.
5.1902 Completed by R.Stephenson & Co.,Hebburn for British Maritime
Trust Ltd(Furness,Withy & Co. Ltd,mgrs),London. 24.11.1909 Trans-
ferred to Furness,Withy & Co. Ltd. 1919 Sold to K.C.H. Saliaris &
A. Negropontos,Chios ren. NORA SALIARI. 19.5.1924 Foundered off
Cape Carbon near Bougie o.v. Poti to Dunkirk with manganese ore.

FB16.ORIANA   (1902 - 1909) 4418g 2875n   382' x 48'
T 3-cyl by Richardson,Westgarth & Co. Ltd,Sunderland.
8.1902 Completed by Northumberland SB Co. Ltd,Howdon-on-Tyne for
British Maritime Trust Ltd(Furness,Withy & Co. Ltd,mgrs),London.
24.11.1909 Transferred to Furness,Withy & Co. Ltd. 1912 Transferred to British & Argentine S.N. Co. Ltd. 1913 Transferred back
to Furness,Withy & Co. Ltd. 1914 Sold to Osaka Shosen Kabushiki
Kaisha, Osaka ren. JAVA MARU. 1931 Under Tachibana K.K.   1933
B/U.

FB17.PERSIANA   (1902 - 1909) 4032g 2605n 345' x 48'
T 3-cyl by Richardson,Westgarth & Co. Ltd,Hartlepool.
10.1902 Completed by Irvines SB & DD Co. Ltd,Hartlepool for British Maritime Trust Ltd(Furness,Withy & Co. Ltd,mgrs),London.
24.11.1909 Transferred to Furness,Withy & Co. Ltd. 11.2.1915 Sold
to Leander S.S. Co. Ltd(Petersen & Co. Ltd),London ren. RIO
PARANA. 24.2.1915 Torpedoed and sunk 4 miles SE of Beachy Head by
U8 o.v. Tyne to Portoferrajo with coal.

FB18. COMO   (1904 - 1907) See Gulf Line FG9

FB19.BEAUMONT   (1904) 5864g 3797n 400' x 52' TANKER
T 3-cyl by Richardson,Westgarth & Co. Ltd,Hartlepool.
6.1903 Completed by Furness,Withy & Co.,Hartlepool as BEAUMONT
for British Maritime Trust Ltd(Furness,Withy & Co. Ltd,mgrs),
London but retained by builders until 1904 when sold to Anglo-
American Oil Co. Ltd,London ren. SEMINOLE. 1912 Sold to Tank
Storage & Carriage Co. Ltd(W.J. Smith,mgr),Newcastle ren.
WABASHA. 1916 Sold to Standard Transportation Co. Ltd,Hong Kong.
6.7.1917 Damaged by submarine torpedo in English Channel but
reached port. 1924 Sold to Oil & Molasses Tankers Ltd(John I.
Jacobs & Co),London name u/ch. 1926 Sold to Oil Transport
Gmbh,Hamburg. 1929 Ren. NORDSEE. 1932 B/U.

FB20.CYNTHIANA(2)   (1905 - 1909) 3184g 2046n   350' x 46'
T 3-cyl by Central Marine Eng. Works,Hartlepool.
1905 Completed by W. Gray & Co. Ltd,Hartlepool for British Mar-
itime Trust Ltd(Furness,Withy & Co. Ltd,mgrs),London. 24.11.1909
Transferred to Furness,Withy & Co. Ltd. 1913 Sold to West Russian
S.S. Co. Ltd,St. Petersburg,Russia ren. EGRET. 28.1.1917 Mined
and sunk 5 miles SW of Inner Dowsing L.V. o.v. Archangel to
London with timber.

FB21.SANDOWN   (1905 - 1909) 3153g 2476n 340' x 47'
T 3-cyl by Richardson,Westgarth & Co. Ltd,Hartlepool.
7.1905 Completed by Furness,Withy & Co. Ltd,Hartlepool for British Maritime Trust Ltd(Furness,Withy & Co. Ltd,mgrs),London.
24.11.1909 Transferred to Furness,Withy & Co. Ltd. 1910 Renamed
EGYPTIANA. 9.6.1917 Torpedoed and sunk by U70 120 miles WSW of
Scillies o.v. London to Halifax with a part cargo.

FB22.PERUVIANA   (1905 - 1909) 3153g 2006n 350' x 46'
T 3-cyl by Blair & Co. Ltd,Stockton.
9.1905 Completed by Ropner & Sons Ltd,Stockton for British
Maritime Trust Ltd(Furness,Withy & Co. Ltd,mgrs),London.
24.11.1909 Transferred to Furness,Withy & Co. Ltd. 1913 Sold to
West Russian S.S. Co. Ltd,St. Petersburg ren. JOULAN and used as
a Russian Imperial Hospital ship during WWI. 1919 Under Finnish
Government as JOULAN. 1922 Sold to Russian Govt. Baltic S.S.
Co,Leningrad ren. KAMO later Sovtorgflot. 9.12.1936 Wrecked in
Bering Sea on Karagin Island after steering gear failure o.v. to
Kamchatka with furs and supplies.

FB23.CROXDALE   (1906 - 1907) 1283g 806n 230' x 36' Collier
T 3-cyl by N.E. Marine Eng. Co. Ltd,Sunderland.
10.1906 Completed by John Crown & Sons Ltd,Sunderland for British
Maritime Trust Ltd(Furness,Withy & Co. Ltd,mgrs),London. 1907
Transferred to Furness,Withy & Co. Ltd. 1926 Sold to J. Rang,
Estonia ren. URANUS. 1.6.1940 Captured by Germany o.v. Gothenburg
to Methil with cellulose, taken to Bergen. Crew returned to
Tallinn via Stockholm. Ren. HOCHMEISTER. 1947 Ministry of Trans-
port(Neil & Hannan Ltd) ren. URANUS. 1951 Sold to Cia Mar Asta
SA,Panama ren. ASTRA. 1958 B/U.

FB24.TUDHOE (1906 - 1907) 1286g 809n 230' x 36' Collier
T 3-cyl by J. Dickinson & Sons Ltd,Sunderland.
12.1906 Completed by John Crown & Sons Ltd,Sunderland for British
Maritime Trust Ltd(Furness,Withy & Co. Ltd,mgrs),London. 1907
Transferred to Furness,Withy & Co. Ltd. 1913 Sold to Rederi A/B
Groveland (J.P. Jonsson,mgr),Landskrona ren. GROVEMONT. 23.2.1915
Purchased by Gas,Light & Coke Company,London ren. CAPITOL. 1925
Sold to D/S A/S Vilma (K.S. Nordgreen,mgr),Bergen ren. VILMA.
1945 Mgrs. became Jacob Kjode A/S,Bergen. 1947 Sold to Laiva O/Y
Merihelmi (H.Liljestrand,mgr),Helsingfors ren. INGA L. 1954 Ren.
AIRA. 1955 Sold to W. Rostedt,Turku ren. LISBET. 7.1957 B/U at
Hamburg.

FB25.MALINCHE (1906 - 1907) 1868g 1165n 279' x 40' Collier
T 3-cyl by Richardsons,Westgarth & Co. Ltd,Sunderland.
1906 Completed by Osbourne,Graham & Co.,Sunderland for British
Maritime Trust Ltd(Furness,Withy & Co. Ltd,mgrs),London. 1907
Transferred to Furness,Withy & Co. Ltd. 1913 Sold to J. Gaff &
Co. Ltd,Glasgow name u/ch. 29.11.1915 Torpedoed and sunk by U33
50 miles E of Malta o.v. Piraeus to New York with general.

FB26.WESTHAMPTON (1907) 1860g 1162n 279' x 40' Collier
T 3-cyl by Richardsons,Westgarth & Co. Ltd,Sunderland.
1.1907 Completed by Osbourne,Graham & Co.,Sunderland for British
Maritime Trust Ltd(Furness,Withy & Co. Ltd,mgrs),London. 1907
Transferred to Furness,Withy & Co. Ltd. 1909 Sold to Anglo-
Hellenic S.S. Co. Ltd(A.A. Embiticos,mgr),Greece ren. ELLI. 1910
Returned to Furness,Withy & Co. Ltd ren. WESTHAMPTON. 1913 Sold to
J. Gaff & Co.,Glasgow ren. AMPHION. 1915 Purchased by Kelvin
Shipping Co. Ltd(H. Hogarth),Glasgow ren. BARON CATHCART. 1924
Sold to Seed Shipping Co. Ltd,Newcastle ren. MARJORIE SEED.
25.12.1924 Wrecked on NE side of Lady Island o.v. Glasgow to
Huelva with coal and coke.

FB27.ADRIANA (1907) 5420g 3540n 411' x 53'
T 3-cyl by bldrs.
1907 Launched as ADRIANA for British Maritime Trust Ltd and
completed as MEINAM for Messageries Maritime,Marseilles by
Palmers Ltd,Jarrow. 1934 B/U.

FB28.THORNLEY (1907) 1327g 684n 235' x 36' Collier
T 3-cyl by Richardsons,Westgarth & Co. Ltd.
1907 Completed by Blyth SB Co. Ltd,Blyth for British Maritime
Trust(Furness,Withy & Co. Ltd,mgrs),London. 1907 Transferred to
Furness, Withy & Co. Ltd. 1928 Sold to A. Lauro,Genoa ren
PENELOPE. 19.5.1943 War loss in Mediterranean.

FB29.ARABIANA (1907) 3001g 1871n 325' x 47'
T 3-cyl by Richardsons,Westgarth & Co. Ltd,Hartlepool.
12.1907 Completed by Irvines SB & DD Co. Ltd,Hartlepool for
British Maritime Trust Ltd(Furness,Withy & Co. Ltd,mgrs),London.
1907 Transferred to Furness,Withy & Co. Ltd. 1912 Sold to
Mercantile Shpg. Co. Ltd,Antwerp ren. TREVIER. 1916 Reg. under

Lloyd Royal Belge,Antwerp. 4.4.1917 Torpedoed and sunk near Scheveningen o.v. New York to Rotterdam with grain.

FB30.BRAZILIANA (1907) 3826g 2439n 350' x 50' Turret
T 3-cyl by bldrs.
15.1.1907 Launched by W. Doxford & Sons Ltd,Sunderland for J. Sunley,London as BILLITER AVENUE and 3.1907 completed for British Maritime Trust Ltd,London(Furness,Withy & Co. Ltd,mgrs) as BRAZILIANA. 1907 Transferred to Furness,Withy & Co. Ltd. 1914 Sold to Sutherland S.S. Co. Ltd(A.M. Sutherland),Newcastle ren. FORFAR. 4.12.1917 Torpedoed and sunk by UC17 115 miles WSW of Lizard o.v. Blyth to Gibraltar with Admiralty cargo, 3 lost.

FB31.GRACIANA (1907) 4265g 2713n 380' x 49'
T 3-cyl by Richardsons,Westgarth & Co. Ltd,Sunderland.
12.1907 Completed by Northumberland SB Co. Ltd,Howdon-on-Tyne for British Maritime Trust Ltd,London(Furness,Withy & Co. Ltd,mgrs). 1907 Transferred to Furness,Withy & Co. Ltd. 1908 Sold to Cie Royale Belgo-Argentine(Armement Adolf Deppe,mgr),Antwerp ren. MINISTRE BEERNAERT. 26.12.1915 Torpedoed and sunk by U25 40 miles SW of Lundy Island.

FB32.GUARDIANA (1907) See SUTHERLAND GRANGE H18

FB33. ROTTERDAM (1907) 6216g 4026n 410' x 52'
T 3-cyl by Richardsons,Westgarth & Co. Ltd,Sunderland.
4.1907 Completed by Northumberland SB Co. Ltd,Howdon-on-Tyne for British Maritime Trust Ltd(Furness,Withy & Co. Ltd). 1909 Transferred to Holland-America Line ren. SOMMELSDIJK. 21.4.1910 Burnt out while loading at Rotterdam.

APPENDIX FC   CHESAPEAKE & OHIO S.S. CO. LTD

FC1.APPOMATTOX (1893 - 1902) 3338g 2140n 345' x 41'
T 3-cyl by T. Richardson,Hartlepool.
9.1893 Completed by Furness,Withy & Co. Ltd for Chesapeake & Ohio S.S. Co. Ltd(Furness,Withy & Co. Ltd,mgrs),London. 1902 Sold to Elders & Fyffes name u/ch. 1910 Sold to M. Gumuchdjian,Constantinople ren. SEYER. 1916 Sunk by Russian warships off Zongduldak, Turkey.

FC2.CHICKAHOMINY (1893 - 1902) 3332g 2140n 345' x 41'
T 3-cyl by T. Richardson,Hartlepool.
1893 Completed by Furness,Withy & Co. Ltd for Chesapeake & Ohio S.S. Co. Ltd(Furness,Withy & Co. Ltd,mgrs),London. 1902 Sold to Elders & Fyffes name u/ch. 1910 B/U.

FC3.GREENBRIER (1893 - 1902) 3332g 2139n 345' x 41'
T 3-cyl by T. Richardson,Hartlepool.
1893 Completed by Furness,Withy & Co. Ltd for Chesapeake & Ohio S.S. Co. Ltd(Furness,Withy & Co. Ltd,mgrs),London. 1902 Sold to

Elders & Fyffes name u/ch. 1910 Sold to Tropical Fruits S.S. Co.
Ltd, U.S.A. 2.4.1915 Mined and sunk off Frisian Islands to SW of
Amrum near Bremen o.v. Bremerhaven to New York with general.

FC4.RAPPAHANNOCK (1893 - 1907) 3884g 2490 370' x 44'
T 3-cyl by bldrs.
8.1893 Completed by A.Stephen & Sons Ltd,Glasgow for Chesapeake &
Ohio S.S. Co. Ltd(Furness,Withy & Co. Ltd,mgrs),London. 1907 Transferred to Furness,Withy & Co. Ltd. 26.10.1916 Torpedoed and
sunk by U69 70 miles from Scillies o.v. Halifax to London with
grain,deals and general, 37 lost.

FC5.SHENANDOAH (1893 - 1907) 3886g 2492n 370' x 44'
T 3-cyl by bldrs.
10.1893 Completed by A.Stephen & Sons Ltd,Glasgow for Chesapeake
& Ohio S.S. Co. Ltd(Furness,Withy & Co. Ltd,mgrs),London. 1907
Transferred to Furness,Withy & Co. Ltd. 14.4.1916 Mined and sunk
1.5 miles W of Folkestone Gate o.v. St. John(NB)/Halifax to
London with general.

FC6.KANAWHA (1893 - 1907) 3886g 2488n 370' x 44'
T 3-cyl by bldrs.
12.1893 Completed by A. Stephen & Sons Ltd,Glasgow for Chesapeake
& Ohio S.S. Co. Ltd(Furness,Withy & Co. Ltd,mgrs),London. 1907
Transferred to Furness,Withy & Co. Ltd. 1922 Sold to J. Laborie,
Cherbourg ren. GEORGETTE. 1924 Sold to Ditta Galli &
Bertola,Italy name u/ch. 1925 B/U.

FC7.RAPIDAN (1898 - 1901) See HAVERSHAM GRANGE H13

FC8.POWHATAN (1900 - 1909) 4262g 3311n 354' x 50'
T 3-cyl by Furness,Westgarth & Co. Ltd,Middlesbrough.
1900 Completed by Furness,Withy & Co. Ltd for Chesapeake & Ohio
S.S. Co. Ltd(Furness,Withy & Co. Ltd,mgrs),London. 24.11.1909
Transferred to Furness,Withy & Co. Ltd. 1912 Sold to Goshi Kaisha
Tatsuma Shokai,Dairen ren. SENJU MARU. 11.1915 Missing on a
voyage Philadelphia to Vladivostock with railway material, sailed
from Oran on 15.11.1915, presumed sunk by submarine.

FC9.ALLEGHANY (1901 - 1909) 4262g 3311n 354' x 50'
T 3-cyl by Furness,Westgarth & Co. Ltd,Middlesbrough.
3.1901 Completed by Furness,Withy & Co. Ltd for Chesapeake & Ohio
S.S. Co. Ltd(Furness,Withy & Co. Ltd,mgrs),London. 24.11.1909
Transferred to Furness,Withy & Co. Ltd. 1912 Sold to Osaka Shosen
Kabushiki Kaisha,Osaka ren. SAIGON MARU. 23.5.1929 Wrecked on W
coast Hokkaido o.v. Otaru to Karafuto.

FC10.ALBIANA (1905 - 1907) 4221g 2778n 360' x 48'
T 3-cyl by Richardson,Westgarth & Co. Ltd,Sunderland.
1905 Completed by Northumberland SB Co. Ltd,Howdon-on-Tyne for
Chesapeake & Ohio S.S. Co. Ltd(Furness,Withy & Co. Ltd,mgrs),
London. 1907 Transferred to Furness,Withy & Co. Ltd. 1908 Sold to
Agincourt S.S. Co. Ltd,London ren. EVESHAM. 1912 Taken over by
Furness,Withy & Co. Ltd and chartered to Lamport & Holt. 1914

Transferred to Furness Shipping & Agency,Rotterdam ren. VEEN-
BERGEN. 1920 Sold to C. Goudriaan & Co,Rotterdam ren. VOORBURG.
1922 Sold to Emder Reederei,Hamburg ren. KARL HANS. 1924 Sold to
Seereederei Gmbh,Hamburg ren. TEJA. 1928 Sold to Transoceanica
Hungarian Shpg. Co. Ltd(C.Barta,mgr),Budapest ren. TISZA. 1934
B/U.

FC12.MARIANA   (1905 - 1907) 4147g 2667n   360' x 48'
T 3-cyl by bldrs.
1905 Completed by A. Rodger & Co. Ltd,Port Glasgow for Chesapeake
& Ohio S.S. Co. Ltd(Furness,Withy & Co. Ltd,mgrs),London. 1907
Transferred to Furness,Withy & Co. Ltd. 1908 Sold to Cie Royale
Belgo-Argentine(Armement Adolf Deppe,mgr),Antwerp ren. GOUVERNEUR
DE LANTSHEERE. 1934 B/U.

FC13.ROANOKE   (1906 - 1907) 3755g 2442n   368' x 49'
T 3-cyl by Richardsons,Westgarth & Co. Ltd,Hartlepool.
28.12.1906 Launched and 1907 completed by Furness,Withy & Co. Ltd,
Hartlepool as ROANOKE for Chesapeake & Ohio S.S. Co. Ltd(Furness,
Withy & Co. Ltd,mgr),London. 1907 Sold to The Clan Line Steamers
Ltd,Glasgow ren. CLAN MACINNES. 1914 Repurchased by Furness,Withy
& Co. Ltd ren. ROANOKE. 11.2.1917 Torpedoed and damaged 4 miles SE
of Girdleness o.v. Dundee to New York with general. Towed to
Dundee and subsequently repaired. 12.8.1917 Captured by UB48 and
sunk by bombs 100 miles WNW of Butt of Lewis o.v. Leith to
Philadelphia with general.

FC14.RAPIDAN(2)   (1907 - 1907) 3760g 2418n   368' x 49'
T 3-cyl by Richardsons,Westgarth & Co. Ltd,Hartlepool.
20.2.1907 Launched and 1907 completed by Furness,Withy & Co. Ltd,
Hartlepool as RAPIDAN for Chesapeake & Ohio S.S. Co. Ltd(Furness,
Withy & Co. Ltd,mgr),London. 1907 Sold to The Clan Line Steamers
Ltd,Glasgow ren. CLAN MACIVER. 1914 Repurchased by Furness,Withy &
Co. Ltd ren. RAPIDAN. 1924 Sold to Charles G. Dunn Shipping Co.
Ltd,Liverpool ren. DOVENBY HALL. 1927 Sold to P.M. Hadoulis &
partners,Greece ren. PANAGHIS M. HADOULIS. 21.1.1933 Sold to
Meesrs. Olivier & Co.,Panama ren. MIREILLE. 1934 Sold to Italian
breakers and broken up at Genoa.

FC15.RICHMOND   (1907) 2921g 1859n   325' x 47'
T 3-cyl by Richardsons,Westgarth & Co. Ltd,Hartlepool.
4.1907 Completed by Irvines SB & DD CO. Ltd,Hartlepool for Chesapeake & Ohio S.S. Co. Ltd(Furness,Withy & Co. Ltd,mgrs),London.
1907 Transferred to Furness,Withy & Co. Ltd. 1914 Sold to West
Russian S.S. Co. Ltd,St. Petersburg ren. DRONT. 1.9.1917 Torpedoed and sunk by U28 in the Arctic.

FC16.WASHINGTON   (1907) 3031g 2059n   325' x 47'
T 3-cyl by Richardsons,Westgarth & Co. Ltd,Hartlepool.
1907 Completed by Irvines SB & DD Co. Ltd,Hartlepool for Chesapeake & Ohio S.S. Co. Ltd(Furness,Withy & Co. Ltd,mgrs),London.
1907 Transferred to Furness,Withy & Co. Ltd. 1913 Sold to Scheeps
Maats Gylsen (Mercantile & Shipping Co. Ltd,mgr),Antwerp ren.
ERTSHANDEL, then under Lloyd Royal Belge(Brys & Gylsen,mgr),

Antwerp ren. CHILIER. 22.6.1918 Torpedoed and sunk in Atlantic in position 39-30 N, 53-40 W o.v. Barry to Sandy Hook.

FC17.NEWPORT NEWS   (1907) 3031g 2023n   325' x 47'
T 3-cyl by Richardsons,Westgarth & Co. Ltd,Hartlepool.
1907 Completed by Irvines SB & DD Co. Ltd,Hartlepool for Chesapeake & Ohio S.S. Co. Ltd(Furness,Withy & Co. Ltd,mgrs),London.
1907 Transferred to Furness,Withy & Co. Ltd. 1913 Sold to Scheeps Maats Gylsen (Mercantile & Shipping Co. Ltd,mgr),Antwerp ren. IJZERHANDEL, then under Lloyd Royal Belge(Brys & Glysen,mgr), Antwerp ren. SIBERIER. 5.4.1917 Torpedoed and sunk by U86 in position 52-18 N 11-40 W.

FC18.NORFOLK   (1907) 3838g 2504n   360' x 50'
T 3-cyl by G. Clark Ltd,Sunderland.
3.1907 Completed by Northumberland SB Co. Ltd,Howdon-on-Tyne for Chesapeake & Ohio S.S. Co. Ltd(Furness,Withy & Co. Ltd,mgrs), London. 1907 Transferred to Furness,Withy & Co. Ltd. 1914 Sold to N.E. Ambatielos,Greece name u/ch. 1919 Sold to Kloster,Norway same name. 1921 Sold to A/S Selmerske Rederi,Trondhjeim ren. ROWENA. 1939 Sold to Moller Line Ltd,Shanghai ren. NANCY MOLLER. 18.3.1944 Torpedoed & sunk in posn 2-14 N, 78-25 E by Japanese submarine I-165 o.v. Durban to Colombo with coal, 32 lost.

APPENDIX FG   GULF LINE LTD.

FG1.GULF OF ANCUD   (1902 - 1911) 2716g 1734n   314' x 42'
T 3-cyl by Blair & Co.,Stockton.
6.1890 Completed by Hawthorn,Leslie & Co. Ltd,Hebburn for Gulf Line Association Ltd,Greenock. 1902 Purchased by Furness,Withy & Co. Ltd. 1911 Sold to Anglo-Hellenic S.S. Co. Ltd(A.A.Embiricos), Andros ren. VOSTIZZA. 1912 Sold to Ligne Cettoise de Nav(F.Puech & Son),Cette ren. MONT AIGOUAL. 1912 Ren. GENERAL LYAUTEY, same owner. 1916 Sold to Cie Generale Transatlantique,Marseilles ren. ARDECHE. 1925 B/U.

FG2.GULF OF BOTHNIA (1902 - 1903) 3452g 2443n   349' x 42'
T 3-cyl by bldrs.
1891 Completed by Caird & Co.,Greenock for Gulf Line Association Ltd,Greenock. 1902 Purchased by Furness,Withy & Co. Ltd. 1903 Sold to Hamburg America Line ren. SCHWARZBURG. 1916 Seized by Portugal at Punta Delgada,Azores ren. PONTA DELGARDA, chartered to British Government and managed by Furness,Withy & Co. Ltd. 14.7.1918 Sunk off Oran by UC54 o.v. Buenos Aires for Salerno.

FG3.GULF OF GENOA   (1902 - 1903) 3448g 2440n   349' x 42'
T 3-cyl by bldrs.
1891 Completed by Caird & Co.,Greenock for Gulf Line Association, Greenock. 1902 Purchased by Furness,Withy & Co. Ltd. 1903 Sold to Hamburg America Line ren. ALTENBURG. 23.9.1909 Destroyed by fire at Havana and 2.1910 scrapped at Philadelphia.

FG4.GULF OF SIAM (1902 - 1903) 3433g 2145n   349' x 42'
T 3-cyl by bldrs.
1892 Completed by Caird & Co.,Greenock for Gulf Line Association,
Greenock. 1902 Purchased by Furness,Withy & Co. Ltd. 1903 Sold to
Hamburg America Line ren. SCHAUMBURG. 1916 Seized by Portugal
ren. HORTA, chartered to British Government and managed by
Furness,Withy & Co. Ltd. 8.7.1918 Sunk by UC73 near Malta on
French service o.v. from Salonica.

FG5.GULF OF TARANTO (1902 - 1903) 3431g 2193n   349' x 42'
T 3-cyl by bldrs.
1892 Completed by Caird & Co.,Greenock for Gulf Line Association,
Greenock. 1902 Purchased by Furness,Withy & Co. Ltd. 1903 Sold to
Hamburg America Line ren. MECKLENBURG. 1919 Ceded to Britain.
1922 Sold to David de Llano-Ponte y Rosendo Muniz,Aviles ren.
ANTOLINA PONTE. 1924 B/U.

FG6.GULF OF VENICE (1902 - 1913) 3022g 1700n   331' x 42'
C 2-cyl by Blair & Co.,Stockton. Tripled in 1890.
6.1883 Completed by W. Gray & Co.,Hartlepool for Gulf Line Association Ltd,Greenock. 1902 Purchased by Furness,Withy & Co. Ltd.
1913 Sold to V. Sabia,Naples ren. ANNA. 1.12.1914 Lost by fire 10
miles S of Wolf Rock o.v. Marseilles to London with general.

FG7.GULF OF MARTABAN   (1902) 2793g 1725n   320' x 40'
T 3-cyl by Blair & Co. Ltd,Stockton.
2.1889 Completed by Hawthorn,Leslie & Co. Ltd,Hebburn for Gulf
Line Association Ltd,Greenock. 1902 Purchased by Furness,Withy &
Co. Ltd. 1902 Sold to A.C. de Freitas,Hamburg ren. LUSITANIA.
2.4.1909 Stranded at Porer o.v. Trieste to Fiume, refloated and
B/U at Monfalcone.

FG8.RAPALLO   (1902) & (1904 - 1906) & (1908 - 1909) 6511g 4172n
401' x 52'. T 3-cyl by Richardsons,Westgarth & Co Ltd,Hartlepool.
12.3.1902 Launched as EGYPTIANA for British Maritime Trust Ltd,
(Furness,Withy & Co. Ltd,mgr),London and 5.1902 completed as
RAPALLO for Gulf Line Ltd(Furness,Withy & Co. Ltd),Liverpool by
Furness,Withy & Co. Ltd,Hartlepool. Immediately on completion
chartered to R.M. Sloman & Co.,Germany name u/ch. 8.1904 Returned
to Gulf Line Ltd. 3.1906 Chartered to Hamburg-America Line name
u/ch. 3.1908 Returned to Gulf Line Ltd. 5.1909 Sold to Holland-
America Line,Netherlands ren. MAARTENSDIJK. 12.1923 Sold to The
Ben Line Steamers Ltd,Leith ren. BENVRACKIE. 2.1927 Sold to Cie
Internationale de Commerce et d'Armement,Belgium ren. ANI. 1933
Sold to Italy and broken up.

FG9.COMO   (1902) 5137g 3313n   401' x 52'
T 3-cyl by Richardsons,Westgarth & Co. Ltd,Hartlepool.
7.1902 Completed as COMO for Gulf Line Ltd(Furness,Withy & Co.
Ltd,mgr),Liverpool having been laid down for British Maritime
Trust Ltd. Immediately on completion chartered to R.M. Sloman &
Co.,Germany name u/ch. 11.1904 Returned to British Maritime Trust
Ltd. 3.1909 Sold to Holland-America Line,Netherlands ren.

GORREDIJK. 10.1923 Sold to The Ben Line Steamers Ltd,Leith ren. BENMACDHUI. 6.1931 B/U in Japan.

FG10.LUGANO   (1903 - 1906)   See BOLIVIANA   FB7

FG11.SICILY   (1903 - 1906) 18189 1197n   286' x 34'
C 2-cyl by J. Howden,Glasgow.
1880 Completed by Dobie & Co.,Govan as RHENANIA for Hamburg America Line,Hamburg. 1903 Purchased by Gulf Line Ltd(Furness, Withy & Co. Ltd),Liverpool ren. SICILY. 1906 Sold to Fratelli Degregori,Italy ren. LOURDES. 1907 Sold to Soc. Anon. Nazionale di Servizi Maritimi ren. EGEO. 31.3.1916 Torpedoed and sunk 20 miles off Punta Alice in Mediterranean.

FG12.TUSCANY   (1908 - 1913) 3000g 1872n   325' x 47'
T 3-cyl by Richardsons,Westgarth & Co. Ltd,Hartlepool.
2.1908 Completed by Irvines SB & DD Co. Ltd,Hartlepool for Gulf Line Ltd,London(Furness,Withy & Co. Ltd). 1913 Sold to Cia de Nav Olazarri(Garteiz y Mendiadaldua,mgr),Bilbao ren. OQUENDO then to Cia Nav La Blanca,Bilbao name u/ch. 1922 Sold to Cia Vasco Cantabrica de Nav(U. de la Torre),Bilbao ren. LUCHANA. 1939 Sold to Cia Mar del Nervion(Urquijo v Aldecoa),Bilbao ren. MAR TIRRENO. 1955 Sold to Transportes Petroliferos SA(TRAPESA),Bilbao ren. MUNI. 1964 B/U.

FG13.CROSSBY   (1909 - 1915) 3893g 2531n   341' x 47'
T 3-cyl by Blair & Co. Ltd,Stockton.
2.1907 Completed by R. Stephenson & Co. Ltd,Hebburn for Asolvesby S.S. Co. Ltd(R.Harrowing),Whitby. 1909 Purchased by Gulf Line Ltd,London(Furness,Withy & Co. Ltd. 1915 Sold to Bay S.S. Co Ltd (Sale & Co),London ren. BAYCROSS. 1921 Sold to French Government ren. PORT DE BAYONNE. 1922 Sold to Germany ren. TURCKHEIM. 1923 Sold to D.A. Kydoniefs,Andros ren. ANTONIOS D. KYDONIEFS. 1935 Sold to T.W. Ward Ltd and 19.7.1935 arrived Jarrow for B/U.

FG14.FELICIANA   (1911 - 1916) See Furness F142.

FG15.ORISTANO   (1911 - 1922) 4253g 2708n   380' x 49'
T 3-cyl by Richardsons,Westgarth & Co. Ltd,Sunderland.
1911 Completed by Northumberland SB Co. Ltd,Howdon-on-Tyne for Gulf Line Ltd,London(Furness,Withy & Co. Ltd). 1914 First Furness,Withy Group ship to pass through Panama Canal. 1922 Sold to Yamamoto Kisen K.K.,Kobe ren. RYOKAI MARU. 22.8.1943 Torpedoed and sunk by U.S.S. PLUNGER in posn. 42-40 N, 139-48 E.

FG16.APPENINE   (1912 - 1919)   See Furness F137.

FG17.CATERINO   (1912 - 1921) 3723g 2366n   346' x 51'
T 3-cyl by Central Marine Eng. Works,Hartlepool.
1909 Completed by W. Gray & Co. Ltd,Hartlepool for Furness, Withy & Co. Ltd. 1912 Transferred to Gulf Line Ltd. 1921 Sold to N.P. Roussos & Co.,Piraeus ren. MARIA N. ROUSSOS. 1935 Sold to Frano Petrinovic,Split ren. SUPETAR. 12.6.1942 Torpedoed and sunk by

Japanese submarine I-16 in 21-50 S, 35-50 E o.v. Durban to Aden with coal,all crew saved.

FG18.ROSSANO (1912 - 1921) 3744g 2365n 346' x 51'
T 3-cyl by Central Marine Eng. Works,Hartlepool.
1909 Completed by W. Gray & Co. Ltd,Hartlepool for Furness, Withy & Co. Ltd. 1912 Transferred to Gulf Line Ltd. 1921
Sold to N.P. Roussos & Co.,Piraeus ren. POSSIDON. 8.9.1940
Torpedoed and sunk by U47 in posn. 56-40 N 8-50 W o.v. New Orleans to Glasgow with sulphur phosphate,17 killed.

FG19.MESSINA (1912 - 1919) See Furness F168

FG20.SANTERAMO (1914 - 1915) 4670g 3099n 385' x 52'
T 3-cyl by Richardsons,Westgarth & Co. Ltd,Hartlepool.
7.1914 Completed by Irvines SB & DD Co. Ltd as SANTERAMO for Gulf Line Ltd(Furness,Withy & Co. Ltd). 1.1915 Sold to Great City S.S. Co. Ltd(W. Reardon Smith & Sons Ltd),Cardiff ren. JERSEY CITY.
24.5.1917 Torpedoed and sunk by U46 35 miles NW of Flannan Isles o.v. Pensacola to Hull with wheat.

FG21.SALERNO (1915 - 1921) 3667g 2292n 360' x 49'
T 3-cyl by G. Clark Ltd,Sunderland.
1909 Completed by Richardson,Duck & Co.,Stockton as EDENMORE for Barnesmore S.S. Co. Ltd(W.Johnston Ltd),Liverpool. 1915 Purchased by Gulf Line Ltd (Furness,Withy & Co. Ltd) ren. SALERNO. 1921
EVELPIS(Gr) then to D.J. Dambassir,Piraeus ren.JOANNIS(Gr) in 1926. 16.9.1942 Torpedoed and sunk by U165 in St. Lawrence Estuary o.v. Swansea & Sydney(NS) to Montreal with coal,all saved.

FG22.SANTERAMO(2) (1915 - 1922) 3045g 1934n 346' x 45'
T 3-cyl by Blair & Co. Ltd,Stockton.
1904 Completed by Richardson,Duck & Co. Ltd,Stockton as ARRANMORE for Oakmore S.S. Co. Ltd(W. Johnston),Liverpool. 1915 Purchased by Gulf Line Ltd (Furness,Withy & Co. Ltd) ren. SANTERAMO. 192
Sold to C.N. Vassilakis,Chios ren. ANNA VASSILAKIS. 1935 B/U.

FG23.TURINO (1916 - 1917) 4241g 2702n 370' x 51'
T 3-cyl by bldrs.
10.1914 Completed by John Readhead & Sons Ltd,South Shields as WESTOE HALL for Nicholl S.S. Co. Ltd(E. Nicholl & Co),London.
1916 Purchased by Gulf Line Ltd(Furness,Withy & Co. Ltd) ren. TURINO. 4.2.1917 Torpedoed and sunk by U43 174 miles W of Fastnet o.v. Norfolk(VA) to London with general, 4 lost.

FG24.ORTONA (1916 - 1917) 5524g 3530n 385' x 54'
T 3-cyl by J. Dickinson & Sons Ltd,Sunderland.
12.1916 Completed by J.L. Thompson & Sons Ltd,Sunderland for Gulf Line Ltd(Furness,Withy & Co. Ltd). 21.6.1917 Torpedoed and sunk by U50 140 miles SSW of Fastnet o.v. Philadelphia to London with general.

FG25.MODESTA   (1917 - 1922) 3832g 2409n   346' x 51'
T 3-cyl by N.E. Marine Eng. Co. Ltd,Sunderland.
1.1917 Completed by J. Priestman & Co.,Sunderland for Gulf Line
Ltd (Furness, Withy & Co. Ltd). 1922 Sold to A/S Ivarans
Rederi(I. Christensen,mgr),Christiania name u/ch. Later to J.W.
Paulin,Wiborg(Fi) name u/ch. 25.4.1942 Torpedoed and sunk by U108
110 miles NE of Bermuda o.v. Trinidad & St. Thomas for New York
with bauxite,17 lost.

FG26.LUGANO(2)   (1917) 3810g 2385n   350' x 51'
T 3-cyl by Richardsons,Westgarth & Co. Ltd,Hartlepool.
1917 Completed by Irvines SB & DD Co. Ltd,Hartlepool for Gulf
Line Ltd (Furness, Withy & Co. Ltd). 2.10.1917 Struck mine laid
by U79 2 miles SW of Bull Point,Co. Antrim o.v. Newport News to
London with general.

FG27.RAPALLO(2)   (1917 - 1918) 3811g 2385n   350' x 51'
T 3-cyl by Richardsons,Westgarth & Co. Ltd,Hartlepool.
1917 Completed by Irvines SB & DD Co. Ltd,Hartlepool for Gulf
Line Ltd (Furness,Withy & Co. Ltd). 13.1.1918 Torpedoed and sunk
1.5 miles S of Cape Peloro in the Mediterranean by U28 o.v.
Taranto to Messina in ballast.

FG28.ARIANO   (1919 - 1929) 5155g 3124n   400' x 52'
T 3-cyl by bldrs.
29.12.1917 Launched and 24.1.1918 completed by Harland & Wolff
Ltd,Belfast as WAR PYTHON for The Shipping Controller(G. Heyn &
Sons,mgrs). 29.1.1919 Purchased by Gulf Line Ltd(Furness,Withy &
Co. Ltd) ren. ARIANO. 1929 Sold to Chargeurs Reunis,France ren.
FORT ARCHAMBAULT. 1951 Sold to Lauro & Montella,Italy ren.
SILVANO. 17.2.1958 Arrived Spezia for B/U.

FG29.CASTELLANO   (1919 - 1922) 5227g 3253n   400' x 52'
T 3-cyl by N.E. Marine Eng. Co. Ltd,Sunderland.
1.1918 Completed by Short Brothers Ltd,Sunderland as WAR SPANIEL
for The Shipping Controller. 3.1919 Purchased by Gulf Line Ltd
(Furness,Withy & Co. Ltd) ren. CASTELLANO. 1922 Sold to Yamashita
Kisen Goshi Kaisha,Dairen ren. HOKKOH MARU. 1929 Restyled HOKKO
MARU. 28.11.1943 Torpedoed and sunk by U.S.S. RATON off New
Guinea in position 1-40N, 141-45 E.

FG30.COMINO   (1919 - 1929) 4618g 2932n   385' x 52'
T 3-cyl by Rankin & Blackmore Ltd,Glasgow.
27.4.1918 Launched and 7.1918 completed by Russell & Co.,Port
Glasgow as ARDGORM for S.S. Ardgarry Co. Ltd(Lang & Fulton),
Greenock. 1919 Purchased by Gulf Line Ltd (Furness,Withy & Co.
Ltd) ren. COMINO. 1929 Sold to Deutsche Tankreederi A.G.(Max
Morck),Hamburg ren. DORIS. 6.7.1929 Sold to Hamburg America Line
ren. EIFEL. 3.12.1934 Chartered to Hamburg Sud-Amerika D/S
Ges.,Hamburg. 30.6.1936 Purchased by Hamburg-Sud. 11.1937 Ren.
TUCUMAN. 11.1939 Employed as a Barrage breaker. 17.4.1945 Bombed
and sunk at Kiel by Allied aircraft.

APPENDIX FH   HESSLER SHIPPING CO. LTD.

FH1.JUNO   (1907 - 191) 2416g 1546n   300' x 38'
T 3-cyl by T. Richardson & Co.,Hartlepool.
1888 Completed by E. Withy & Co.,Hartlepool for T. Robinson & Co.
1900 Sold to A/S Juno(Blom & Ohlsen),Larvik. 1906 Purchased by
Hessler Shipping Co. Ltd(Jacob Hessler & Co),Hartlepool. 1907
Taken over by Furness,Withy & Co. Ltd. 18.2.1917 Torpedoed and
sunk 15 miles SSW of Start Point o.v. New York to Havre with
general.

FH2.JUPITER   (1907 - 1914) 2124g 1361n   286' x 43'
T 3-cyl by D. Rowan & Co. Ltd,Glasgow.
9.1901 Completed by Grangemouth & Greenock Dockyard Co. Ltd,
Greenock for Hessler Shipping Co. Ltd(Jacob Hessler & Co),Hart-
lepool. 1907 Taken over by Furness,Withy & Co. Ltd. 1914 Sold to
W.C. Bradley & Sons,Hull name u/ch. 21.5.1917 Torpedoed and sunk
15 miles W of Beachy Head, 17 lost including the master.

FH3.LINDA FELL (1907 - 1915) 3025g 1924n   325' x 47'
T 3-cyl by Richardsons,Westgarth & Co. Ltd,Hartlepool.
11.1906 Completed by Irvines SB & DD Co. Ltd,Hartlepool for Hessler
Shipping Co. Ltd,Hartlepool. 1907 Taken over by Furness,Withy & Co.
Ltd. 20.9.1915 Sailed from Philadelphia for Cienfuegos with coal
and disappeared.

FH4.MASCOT   (1907 - 1911) 1705g 1072n   250' x 36'
C 2-cyl by Blair & Co. Ltd.
1883 Completed by Richardson,Duck & Co.,Stockton as ELMFIELD for
F. Binnington,Stockton. 1897 Sold to A/S Mascot(Blom & Ohlsen),
Larvik ren. MASCOT. 1906 Purchased by Hessler Shipping Co. Ltd
(Jacob Hessler),Hartlepool. 1907 Taken over by Furness,Withy &
Co. Ltd. 1911 B/U.

FH5.MYRA FELL   (1907 - 1916) 3024g 1919n   325' x 47'
T 3-cyl by Richardsons,Westgarth & Co. Ltd,Hartlepool.
1.1907 Completed by Irvines SB & DD Co. Ltd,Hartlepool for Hessler
Shpg. Co. Ltd(Jacob Hessler & Co),Hartlepool. 1907 Taken over by
Furness,Withy & Co. Ltd. 1916 Sold to Globe Shipping Co. Ltd
(Humphries(Cardiff) Ltd) ren. GLODALE. 1.1.1918 Wrecked at Pogam
Point o.v. White Sea to Tees with timber.

FH6.NORMAN   (1907 - 1919) 1840g 1156n   275' x 40'
T 3-cyl by N.E. Marine Eng. Co. Ltd,Sunderland.
8.1901 Completed by Osborne,Graham & Co.,Sunderland for Hessler
Shpg. Co. Ltd(Jacob Hessler & Co),Hartlepool. 1907 Taken over by
Furness,Withy & Co. Ltd. 1914 Ren. SALTBURN. 1919 Seized at
Petrograd. 1923 Sold to Rederi A/B Arild(J.A. Thore),Arild ren.
SCANIA. 11.9.1941 Torpedoed and sunk in posn. 63-14 N, 37-12 W
o.v. Sydney(NS) to Hull with timber.

FH7.THRIFT   (1907 - 1911) 2136g 1358n   275' x 37'
T 3-cyl by Blair & Co. Ltd,Stockton.

4.1886 Completed by E. Withy & Co.,Hartlepool as MERCEDES for
Christie & Co.,Cardiff. 1900 Sold to A/S Thrift(Blom & Ohlsen),
Larvik ren. THRIFT. 1906 Purchased by Hessler Shpg. Co. Ltd(Jacob
Hessler & Co),Hartlepool. 1907 Taken over by Furness, Withy & Co.
Ltd. 1911 Sold to Rederi A/B Groveland (J.P. Jonsson),Landskrona
ren. GROVEDALE. 1912 Sold to Rederi A/B Torleif(H.Persson),
Landskrona ren. TORGERD. 1922 Sold to Rederi A/B Iris (C.Abrahan-
sen),Stockholm ren. IRIS. 15.7.1941 Sunk by collision 4 miles from
Pladda,Arran o.v. Cardiff to London with coal, having sailed from
Milford Haven on 11.7.1941.

FH8.URANIA   (1907 - 1911) 2460g 1579n   300' x 39'
T 3-cyl by Central Marine Eng. Works.
1888 Completed by W. Gray & Co. Ltd,Hartlepool for Gladstone &
Cornforth,Hartlepool as URANIA. 1900 Sold to A/S Urania(Blom &
Ohlsen),Larvik. 1906 Purchased by Hessler Shpg. Co. Ltd(Jacob
Hessler & Co),Hartlepool. 1907 Taken over by Furness,Withy & Co.
Ltd. 1911 B/U.

FH9.SEATONIA   (1915 - 1916) 3533g 2287n   338' x 51'
T 3-cyl by Central Marine Engine Works.
1898 Completed by W. Gray & Co. Ltd,Hartlepool as MANCUNIA for
Manchester & Salford S.S. Co. Ltd(Sivewright,Bacon & Co),Manch-
ester. 1915 Sold to Seatonia S.S. Co. Ltd(Hessler & Co),West
Hartlepool ren SEATONIA. 1.11.1916 Captured and torpedoed by U49
80 miles NW1/2N of Fastnet o.v. Musgrave to Barry Roads with pit
props.

FH10.WEARSIDE   (1915 - 1917) 3560g 2299n   338' x 51'
T 3-cyl by Central Marine Engine Works.
1899 Completed by W. Gray & Co. Ltd,West Hartlepool for J. & E.
Kish,Sunderland. 1915 Purchased by Seatonia S.S. Co. Ltd(Hessler
& Co),West Hartlepool. 25.10.1917 Mined and sunk in the Thames 3
miles SW of Sunk L.V. o.v. Tyne to Genoa with coal.

APPENDIX FJ   JOHNSTON LINE LTD & JOHNSTON WARREN LINES LTD

FJ1.BARROWMORE (1916 - 1918) 3832g 2367n   360' x 50'
T 3-cyl by G. Clark Ltd,Sunderland.
1911 Completed by Richardson,Duck & Co. Ltd,Stockton for Lochmore
S.S. Co. Ltd(W. Johnston & Co. Ltd),Liverpool. 1916 Taken over by
Furness,Withy & Co. Ltd. 19.2.1918 Torpedoed and sunk by U94 53
miles NW by W1/4W from Bishop Rock o.v. Huelva to Port Talbot
with copper ore and precipitate, 25 lost.

FJ2.DROMORE   (1916 - 1917) 4450g 2714n   375' x 52'
T 3-cyl by G. Clark Ltd,Sunderland.
1913 Completed by Richardson,Duck & Co. Ltd,Stockton for W.
Johnston & Co Ltd,Liverpool. 1916 Taken over by Furness,Withy &
Co. Ltd. 27.4.1917 Torpedoed and sunk by U58 200 miles from Tory
Island o.v. Liverpool to Baltimore with general.

FJ3.FOYLEMORE (1916 - 1917) 3831g 2371n   360' x 50'
T 3-cyl by G. Clark Ltd,Sunderland.
1911 Completed by J.L. Thompson & Sons Ltd,Sunderland for
Vedamore S.S. Co. Ltd(W. Johnston & Co Ltd),Liverpool. 1916 Taken
over by Furness,Withy & Co. Ltd. 16.12.1917 Sunk off Eddystone by
UB55 o.v. Calais to Manchester in ballast.

FJ4.GORSEMORE (1916 - 1918) 3079g 1980n   331' x 46'
T 3-cyl by Blair & Co. Ltd,Stockton.
1899 Completed by Richardson,Duck & Co.,Stockton for Templemore
S.S. Co. Ltd(W. Johnston & Co Ltd),Liverpool. 1916 Taken over by
Furness,Withy & Co. Ltd. 22.9.1918 Torpedoed and sunk by UC53 44
miles SE1/2E from Cape Colonne,Gulf of Taranto o.v. Barry to
Taranto with coal.

FJ5.INCEMORE (1916 - 1917) 3059g 1973n   331' x 46'
T 3-cyl by Blair & Co. Ltd,Stockton.
1898 Completed by Richardson,Duck & Co.,Stockton for Rowanmore
S.S. Co. Ltd(W. Johnston & Co Ltd),Liverpool. 1916 Taken over by
Furness,Withy & Co. Ltd. 20.8.1917 Torpedoed and sunk 52 miles SE
by S1/2E from Pantellaria by U38 o.v. Malta to Toulon in ballast.

FJ6.JESSMORE (1916 - 1917) 3911g 2414n   360' x 50'
T 3-cyl by G. Clark Ltd,Sunderland.
1911 Completed by Richardson,Duck & Co. Ltd,Stockton for Rowanmore S.S. Co. Ltd(W. Johnston & Co Ltd),Liverpool. 1916 Taken
over by Furness,Withy & Co. Ltd. 13.5.1917 Torpedoed and sunk 180
miles WNW of Fastnet by U48 o.v. Baltimore to Manchester with
general.

FJ7.KENMORE (1916 - 1917) 3919g 2429n   360' x 50'
T 3-cyl by G. Clark Ltd,Sunderland.
1912 Completed by Richardson,Duck & Co. Ltd,Stockton for Blairmore
S.S. Co. Ltd(W. Johnston & Co Ltd),Liverpool. 1916 Taken over by
Furness,Withy & Co. Ltd. 26.8.1917 Torpedoed and sunk 30 miles N
of Inistrahull by U53 o.v. Liverpool to Boston with general.

FJ8.MAPLEMORE (1916 - 1921) 4330g 2680n   365' x 51'
T 3-cyl by G. Clark Ltd,Sunderland.
1916 Completed by W. Pickersgill & Sons Ltd,Sunderland for
Johnston Line Ltd(Furness,Withy & Co. Ltd). 1921 Sold to Glasgow
Shipowners Co. Ltd(Glen & Co),Glasgow ren. GIBRALTAR. 1938 Sold
to Apex Shipping Co. Ltd,London ren. MEOPHAM. 1939 Sold to J.
Fritzen,Stettin ren. ANTJE FRITZEN. 9.1943 Lost due to war
reasons.

FJ9.PINEMORE (1916 - 1922) 5980g 2849n   388' x 54'
T 3-cyl by J. Dickinson & Sons Ltd,Sunderland.
11.1913 Completed by J.L. Thompson & Sons Ltd,Sunderland as DEN
OF EWNIE for Barrie. 1916 Purchased by Johnston Line Ltd
(Furness, Withy & Co. Ltd) ren. PINEMORE. 1922 Sold to Morel
Ltd,Cardiff ren. LESREAULX. 1928 Sold to N.V. Scheep v.Maats
Milingen (G.A. Spliethoff),Rotterdam ren. CALANDPLEIN. 1935 Sold
to J.C. & A.C. Hadjipateras,Chios ren. KONSTANTINOS HADJIPATERAS.

24.10.1939 Sunk by mine off Harwich o.v. Boston for Tyne with scrap iron, 4 lost.

FJ10.QUERNMORE   (1916 - 1917) 7302g 4783n   480' x 52'
T 3-cyl by bldrs.
1898 Completed by Workman,Clark & Co. Ltd,Belfast for Queensmore S.S. Co. Ltd(W. Johnston & Co Ltd),Liverpool. 1916 Taken over by Furness,Withy & Co. Ltd. 31.7.1917 Torpedoed and sunk by U82 160 miles NW3/4W of Tory Island o.v. Liverpool to Baltimore with general.

FJ11.ROWANMORE   (1916) 9455g 6745n   521' x 59'
T 3-cyl by D. Rowan & Co. Ltd.
7.1900 Completed by C. Connell & Co. Ltd,Glasgow for Johnston Line Ltd,Liverpool. 1916 Taken over by Furness,Withy & Co. Ltd. 26.10.1916 Torpedoed and sunk by U57 128 miles WNW of Fastnet o.v. Baltimore to Liverpool with copper,cotton,maize and oil.

FJ12.SWANMORE   (1916 - 1917) 6373g 3938n   405' x 53'
T 3-cyl by G. Clark Ltd,Sunderland.
10.1913 Completed by J.L. Thompson & Sons Ltd,Sunderland for Johnston Line Ltd,Liverpool. 1916 Taken over by Furness,Withy & Co. Ltd. 25.4.1917 Torpedoed and sunk by gunfire from U50 230 miles WNW of Fastnet o.v. Baltimore to Liverpool with ordnance, 11 lost.

FJ13.VEDAMORE   (1916 - 1917) 6329g 4122n   451' x 48'
T 3-cyl by bldrs.
3.1896 Completed by Harland & Wolff Ltd,Belfast for Johnston Line Ltd,Liverpool. 1916 Taken over by Furness,Withy & Co. Ltd. 7.2.1917 Torpedoed and sunk 20 miles W of Fastnet by U85 o.v. Baltimore to Liverpool with general,23 lost.

FJ14.SYCAMORE   (1917) 6550g 4211n   445' x 58'
T 3-cyl by Rankin & Blackmore Ltd,Glasgow.
1917 Completed by R. Duncan & Co. Ltd,Pt. Glasgow for Johnston Line Ltd(Furness, Withy & Co. Ltd),Liverpool. 25.8.1917 Torpedoed and sunk 125 miles NW of Tory Island by UB61 o.v. Baltimore to Liverpool with general including cotton and copper,11 lost.

FJ15.COTTESMORE   (1917 - 1920) 4240g 2661n   390' x 53'
T 3-cyl by J. Dickinson & Sons Ltd,Sunderland.
3.1917 Completed by W. Pickersgill & Sons Ltd,Sunderland as SWINDON for Evan Thomas Radcliffe Ltd,Cardiff. 1917 Purchased by Johnston Line Ltd(Furness,Withy & Co. Ltd) ren. COTTESMORE. 1920 Sold to D. & T.C. Adams,Liverpool ren. AVONMEDE. 1924 Sold to J.& C. Harrison Ltd,London ren. HARPALION. 1931 Sold to N.G.Livanos, Greece ren. THEOFANO. 1937 Sold to V.J. Pateras,Chios ren. DIRPHYS. 8.6.1941 Torpedoed and sunk NE of St. John(NF) by U108 o.v. Swansea to Montreal with anthracite, 6 lost.

FJ16.LINMORE   (1917 - 1920) 4274g 2671n   390' x 53'
T 3-cyl by Richardsons,Westgarth & Co. Ltd,Hartlepool.

1917 Completed by W. Pickersgill & Sons Ltd,Sunderland as
LLANOVER for Evan Thomas Radcliffe Ltd,Cardiff. 1917 Purchased by
Johnston Line Ltd(Furness,Withy & Co. Ltd) ren. LINMORE. 1920
Sold to D. & T.C. Adams,Liverpool ren. SHANNONMEDE. 1924 Sold to
J. & C. Harrison Ltd,London ren. HARPALYCE. 1928 Sold to E.
Nichol ren. LITTLETON. 1931 Sold to Heirs of L.Z. Cambanis,Andros
ren. LEONIDAS Z. CAMBANIS. 3.4.1941 Torpedoed and sunk SE of Cape
Farewell by U74 o.v. Halifax to Swansea with wheat,2 lost.

FJ17.OAKMORE   (1917 - 1920) 4269g 2670n   390' x 53'
T 3-cyl by J. Dickinson & Sons Ltd,Sunderland.
12.1917 Completed by W. Pickersgill & Sons Ltd,Sunderland for
Johnston Line Ltd(Furness,Withy & Co. Ltd) 1920 Sold to D.& T.C.
Adams,Liverpool ren. CLYDEMEDE. 1924 Sold to J.&C. Harrison Ltd,
London ren. HARPAGUS. 1928 Sold to D.A. Pateras,Chios ren.
MAROUKO PATERAS. 3.11.1941 Stranded in foggy weather on Double
Island,Labrador o.v. Probolingo to Loch Ewe via Table Bay &
Sydney(NS) with sugar.

FJ18.THISTLEMORE   (1917 - 1927) 5019g 3135n   420' x 53'
T 3-cyl by Blair & Co. Ltd,Stockton.
1917 Completed by Irvines SB & DD Co. Ltd,Hartlepool for Johnston
Line Ltd(Furness,Withy & Co. Ltd). 7.1922 Aground at Cape Cod,
refloated. 1923 Renamed WHEATMORE. 1927 Sold to Rickmers Reederi
A.G,Hamburg ren. URSULA RICKMERS. 1941 Transferred to Japan ren.
TEISEN MARU. 3.5.1944 Sunk by U.S.S. FLASHER in China Sea.

FJ19.VALEMORE   (1918 - 1930) 5388g 3048n   420' x 55'
T 3-cyl by N.E. Marine Eng. Co. Ltd,Newcastle.
7.1918 Completed by Sir Raylton Dixon & Co.,Middlesbrough for
Johnston Line Ltd(Furness,Withy & Co. Ltd) having been laid down
as DOMINION MILLER. 1930 Transferred to Norfolk & North American
S.S. Co. Ltd(Furness,Withy & Co. Ltd) ren. LONDON CITIZEN. 1936
Sold to James Chambers & Co. Ltd,Liverpool and resold to Rosyth
breakers under Scrap & Build. 10.1936 B/U at Rosyth.

FJ20.REXMORE   (1918 - 1929) 5277g 2897n   420' x 55'
T 3-cyl by Richardsons,Westgarth & Co. Ltd,Middlesbrough.
1918 Completed by Sir James Laing & Sons Ltd,Sunderland for
Johnston Line Ltd(Furness,Withy & Co. Ltd). 1929 Transferred to
Manchester Liners Ltd(Furness,Withy & Co. Ltd) ren. MANCHESTER
EXPORTER. 1947 Sold to Yu Tung S.S. Co. Ltd,Shanghai ren.
NICARAGUA. 1948 Ren. YU TUNG,same owner. 1950 Sold to Wallem &
Co,Panama ren. RIO BAMBA. 1952 Ren. PRECILA. 18.5.1958 Arrived
Osaka for B/U.

FJ21.ERNEMORE   (1919 - 1923) 4593g 2930n   385' x 52'
T 3-cyl by Rankin & Blackmore Ltd,Glasgow.
1.1918 Completed as ARDGAY by Russell & Co.,Pt Glasgow for S.S.
Ardgay Co. Ltd(Lang & Fulton Ltd),Greenock. 1919 Purchased by
Johnston Line Ltd(Furness, Withy & Co. Ltd) ren. ERNEMORE. 1923
Sold to Yamashita Kisen Goshi Kaisha,Dairen ren. TOHKOH MARU.
1931 Ren. TOHO MARU. 1.6.1944 Torpedoed and sunk 250 miles W of

Ladrome Island in the Pacific in posn. 19-45 N, 120-40 E by U.S.
submarine PINTADO.

FJ22.HARTMORE (1919 - 1922) 5131g 3287n 405' x 53'
T 3-cyl by J.G. Kincaid Ltd,Greenock.
12.1913 Completed as ARDMORE by R.Duncan & Co. Ltd,Pt. Glasgow
for S.S. Ardmore Co. Ltd(Lang & Fulton Ltd),Greenock. 1917 Purch-
ased by Norfolk & North American S.S. Co. Ltd(Furness,Withy & Co.
Ltd) ren. HARTLAND POINT. 1919 Transferred to Johnston Line
Ltd(Furness,Withy & Co. Ltd) ren. HARTMORE. 1922 Sold to Anglo-
Oriental Nav. Co. Ltd (Yule, Catto & Co. Ltd),Liverpool ren.
SUREWAY. 1926 Sold to Sanyo Sha Goshi Kaisha,Takasago ren. JUNYO
MARU. 1928 Sold to Kabafuto Kisen K.K.,Tokyo name u/ch. 1938 Sold
to Nissan Kisen K.K.Tokyo ren. ZYUNYO MARU. 1939 Sold to Baba
Shoji K.K.,Tokyo name u/ch. 18.9.1944 Torpedoed and sunk by
British submarine off Indrapura,Sumatra.

FJ23.STANMORE (1919 - 1923) 4527g 2893n 385' x 52'
T 3-cyl by Rankin & Blackmore Ltd,Glasgow.
2.1914 Completed as ARDGARRY by Russell & Co.,Pt. Glasgow for
S.S. Ardgarry Co. Ltd(Lang & Fulton Ltd),Greenock having been
launched as LOCH NA TORREN. 1919 Purchased by Johnston Line
Ltd(Furness,Withy & Co. Ltd) ren. STANMORE. 1923 Sold to 'K' S.S.
Co. Ltd(Kaye,Son & Co. Ltd,mgr),London ren. KEMMEL. 6.1934 Sold
to Lithgows Ltd and B/U at Port Glasgow.

FJ24.TULLAMORE (1919 - 1922)) 4882g 3104n 385' x 52'
T 3-cyl by Rankin & Blackmore Ltd,Glasgow.
10.1918 Completed as ARDGROOM by Russell & Co.,Pt. Glasgow for
S.S. Ardgroom Co. Ltd(Lang & Fultron Ltd),Greenock. 1919
Purchased by Johnston Line Ltd(Furness,Withy & Co. Ltd) ren.
TULLAMORE. 1922 Sold to Dairen Kisen K.K.,Dairen ren SAIKOH MARU
later amended to SAIHO MARU. 11.11.1944 Bombed and sunk by
aircraft in posn. 10-50 N, 124-35 E.

FJ25.WIGMORE(2) (1919 - 1922) 4543g 2950n 385' x 52'
T 3-cyl by Clyde SB & Eng. Co. Ltd,Pt. Glasgow.
11.1916 Completed as ARDGRANGE by Russell & Co.,Pt. Glasgow for
S.S. Ardgrange Co. Ltd(Lang & Fulton Ltd),Greenock. 1919
Purchased by Johnston Line Ltd(Furness,Withy & Co. Ltd) ren.
WIGMORE. 1922 Sold to Yamashita Kisen Goshi Kaisha ren. NANKOH
MARU. 1940 Ren. NANKO MARU for Ichibana Goshi Kaisha,Dairen. 1948
B/U.

FJ26.GALTYMORE (1919 - 1927) 4565g 2802n 385' x 52'
T 3-cyl by Rankin & Blackmore Ltd,Glasgow.
15.3.1919 Launched as WAR SABLE for The Shipping Controller and
5.1919 completed by Lithgows Ltd,Pt. Glasgow for Johnston Line
Ltd(Furness,Withy & Co. Ltd). 1927 Sold to Deutsche Tankreederei
A.G(Max Murck),Hamburg ren. LISA. 19.1.1929 Sold to Hamburg
America Line ren. TAUNUS. 2.1.1935 Chartered by Hamburg-Sud.
30.6.1936 Purchased by Hamburg Sud-Amerika D/S Ges.,Hamburg. 1937
Ren. CORDOBA. 11.9.1940 Severely damaged by mine off Le Havre and

laid up there. 9.1944 Scuttled by retreating German forces.
Raised and scrapped after WWII.

FJ27.AVIEMORE   (1920 - 1939) 4060g 2318n   360' x 52'
T 3-cyl by Richardsons,Westgarth & Co. Ltd,Hartlepool.
1920 Completed by Irvines SB & DD Co. Ltd,Hartlepool for Johnston
Line Ltd(Furness,Withy & Co. Ltd). 16.9.1939 Torpedoed and sunk
by U31 in Western Approaches o.v. Swansea to Buenos Aires with
tin plate and black sheets.

FJ28.BARRYMORE   (1920 - 1924) 5415g 3001n   420' x 55'
T 3-cyl by Richardsons,Westgarth & Co. Ltd,Middlesbrough.
1920 Completed by Sir James Laing & Sons Ltd,Sunderland for
Johnston Line Ltd(Furness,Withy & Co. Ltd). 1924 Sold to Indo-
China S.N. Co. Ltd ren. KUMSANG. 30.9.1942 Torpedoed and sunk in
posn. 47 N, 13-40 W o.v. Colombo,Table Bay,Walvis Bay and
Freetown to U.K.

FJ29.DROMORE(2)   (1920 - 1955) 4096g 2358n   360' x 52'
T 3-cyl by Richardsons,Westgarth & Co. Ltd,Hartlepool.
17.6.1920 Launched and 1920 completed by Irvines SB & DD Co. Ltd,
Hartlepool for Johnston Line Ltd(Furness,Withy & Co. Ltd). 1955
Sold to Cia Estrella Blanca Ltda,Costa Rica ren. MICTRIC. 1956
Sold to Union Meridiana de Nav SA,Panama ren. CHA. 10.7.1959
Arrived Ghent for B/U.

FJ30.INCEMORE(2)   (1920 - 1940) 4098g 2356n   360' x 52'
T 3-cyl by Richardsons,Westgarth & Co. Ltd,Hartlepool.
1920 Completed by Irvines SB & DD Co. Ltd,Hartlepool for Johnston
Line Ltd(Furness,Withy & Co. Ltd). 16.9.1940 Wrecked on Heath
Point, E side of Anticosti Island,Gulf of St. Lawrence o.v.
Manchester to Montreal with general.

FJ31.VEDAMORE(2)   (1922)   See WINGATE F177

FJ32.WESTMORE   (1922)   See PORTINGLIS   F142

FJ33.WIGMORE(2)   (1922)   See VENICE   F175

FJ34.WRAYMORE   (1922)   See POMARON F132

FJ35.WILLOWMORE   (1922)   See CUNDALL F140

FJ36.JESSMORE(2)   (1923 - 1941) 4099g 2357n   360' x 52'
T 3-cyl by Richardsons,Westgarth & Co. Ltd,Hartlepool.
1921 Completed as PERUVIANA by Irvines SB & DD Co. Ltd,Hartlepool
for Furness,Withy & Co. Ltd. 1923 Transferred to Johnston Line
Ltd(Furness,Withy & Co. Ltd) ren. JESSMORE. 19.2.1941 Sunk in
collision with BARON HAIG 300 miles W of Ireland, taken in tow
but sank on 21.2.1941 o.v. Hull to Table Bay,Piraeus and Turkey.

FJ37.KENMORE(2)   (1923 - 1937) 3783g 2085n   363' x 52'
T 3-cyl by Richardsons,Westgarth & Co. Ltd,Hartlepool.

1923 Completed by Furness SB Co. Ltd,Haverton Hill for Johnston
Line Ltd(Furness,Withy & Co. Ltd). 1937 Sold to Cie des Bateaux a
Vapeurs du Nord,Dunkirk ren. LORRAIN. 8.11.1942 Scuttled at Oran.

FJ38.QUERNMORE(2)   (1923 - 1937) 3787g 2117n   363' x 52'
T 3-cyl by Richardsons,Westgarth & Co. Ltd,Hartlepool.
5.1923 Completed by Furness SB Co. Ltd,Haverton Hill for Johnston
Line Ltd(Furness,Withy & Co. Ltd). 1937 Sold to Cie des Bateaux a
Vapeurs du Nord,Dunkirk ren. ALSACIEN. 24.1.1940 Torpedoed and
sunk by U44 off Portuguese coast to SW of Lisbon in posn 38 N, 9-
55 W o.v. Tunis to Rouen.

FJ39.SYCAMORE(2)   (1923 - 1925) 3908g See CASTILIAN PRINCE

FJ40.TRAMORE   (1924 - 1925) 3907g See BRAZILIAN PRINCE
(Nos 127 & 128 'PRIDE OF THE PRINCES')

FJ41.JESSMORE(3)   (1946 - 1958) 7061g 4311n   418' x 57'
4-cyl 2SCSA Oil engine by bldrs.
4.3.1941 Launched and 6.1941 completed by Barclay,Curle & Co.
Ltd,Glasgow as EMPIRE FAITH for Ministry of War Transport. 1946
Purchased by Johnston Warren Lines Ltd(Furness,Withy & Co. Ltd)
ren. JESSMORE. 1958 Sold to Maritime & Commercial Corp Inc,Panama
ren. ANTIOPE. 1964 Sold to Global Nav. Co. Inc,Panama(Wah Kwong &
Co,H/Kong) ren. GLOBAL VENTURE. 6.1971 Arrived Kaohsiung for B/U.

FJ42.OAKMORE(2)   (1947 - 1967) 4769g 2735n   408' x 56'
7-cyl 2SCSA oil engine by F. Krupp A.G.,Kiel.
1939 Completed by Nordseeweke Gmbh,Emden as LEVANTE for Deutsche
Levant Line,Bremen. 1945 Taken as a prize by Ministry of War
Transport. Prince Line Ltd appointed managers. 1947 Mgmt. taken
over by T.& J. Harrison. 1947 Purchased by Johnston-Warren Lines
Ltd ren. OAKMORE. 13.4.1957 Arrived Aviles for B/U.

FJ43.NOVA SCOTIA(2) (1947 - 1962) 7438g 4241n   440' x 61'
3 Steam turbines SR geared by Vickers-Armstrong Ltd,Barrow.
1947 Completed by Vickers Armstrong Ltd,Newcastle for Johnston
Warren Lines Ltd(Furness,Withy & Co. Ltd). 1962 Sold en-bloc for
£650,000 to Dominion Nav. Co. Ltd(H.C.Sleigh),Nassau ren. FRANCIS
DRAKE. 16.3.1971 Arrived Kaohsiung for B/U..

FJ44.NEWFOUNDLAND(2) (1948 - 1962) 7438g 4236n   440' x 61'
3 Steam turbines SR geared by Vickers-Armstrong Ltd,Barrow.
1948 Completed by Vickers Armstrong Ltd,Newcastle for Johnston
Warren Lines Ltd(Furness,Withy & Co. Ltd). 1962 Sold en-bloc for
£650,000 to Dominion Nav. Co. Ltd(H.C.Sleigh),Liverpool ren.
GEORGE ANSON. 15.2.1971 Arrived Kaohsiung for B/U.

FJ45.HEATHMORE   (1948 - 1961) 3825g 2165n   326' x 50'
6-cyl Nordberg oil engine.
1945 Completed by Consolidated Steel,Wilmington,California as
HICKORY MOUNT for U.S. War Shipping Administration. 1948 Purchased by Johnston Warren Lines Ltd(Furness,Withy & Co. Ltd) ren.
HEATHMORE. 1961 Sold to Cia Mar Med Ltda,Piraeus ren. GRECIAN

MED. 1969 Sold to Comp Anon Nav Orinoco,Venezuela ren. IMATACA.
2711.1971 Arrived at Bilbao for B/U.

FJ46.SYCAMORE(3)　　(1950 - 1968) 3343g 1519n　　363' x 51'
4-cyl 2SCSA Doxford oil engine by D. Rowan & Co. Ltd,Glasgow.
2.1950 Completed by Burntisland SB Co. Ltd as SYCAMORE for
Johnston-Warren Lines Ltd. 1955 On charter, ren. WALSINGHAM. 1957
Ren. SYCAMORE. 1965 Ren. MERCHANT PRINCE. 1968 Sold to Kaldelion
Shpg. Co. Ltd,Cyprus ren. ELIAS L. 1973 Sold to Maccomar Shpg.
Co. Ltd,Cyprus ren. JARA. 1975 Sold to Melteco Nav. Ltd,Cyprus
ren. MELTEMI. 1977 Sold to Green Spirit Inc,Cyprus ren. TEMI.
10.5.1979 Arrived Gadani Beach for B/U.

FJ47.BEECHMORE　　　(1954 - 1969) See ENGLISH PRINCE

FJ48.PINEMORE(3)　　(1955 - 1971) See AFRICAN PRINCE
　　　　　　　　　　　(Nos 170 & 171 'PRIDE OF THE PRINCES')

FJ49.ROWANMORE　　　(1956 - 1973) 8492g 4818n　　467' x 61'
5-cyl 2SCSA B&W oil engine by bldrs.
27.3.1956 Launched and 27.6.1956 completed by Harland & Wolff
Ltd,Govan as ROWANMORE for Johnston Warren Lines Ltd (Furness,
Withy & Co. Ltd). 1958 On charter ren. MADULSIMA. 1960 Ren.
ROWANMORE. 1973 Sold to Leo Maritime Co. Ltd,Cyprus ren. ANDRIANA
I. 1977 Sold to Navieros Valientes Nav SA,Greece ren. MARJORIE Y.
9.1978 Laid-up at Piraeus with stranding damage. 22.11.1979 Left
Piraeus in tow and 3.12.1979 arrived Gandia,Spain for B/U.

FJ50.MYSTIC　　　　(1959 - 1975)　6656g 3648n　　407' x 55'
5-cyl 2SCSA oil engine by Hawthorn,Leslie & Co. Ltd,Newcastle.
1959 Completed by Burntisland SB Co. Ltd,Burntisland on charter
to Shaw,Savill & Albion Co. Ltd for Johnston-Warren Lines Ltd,
Liverpool. 1975 Sold to Liberty S.S. Corp. Ltd,Liberia ren. SEA
SWALLOW. 1977 Sold to North Sea Transport Corp,Panama ren. NORTH
SEA. 1978 Sold to Siam Venture Shpg. Co. SA,Panama ren. GOLDEN
RAYS. 4.10.1982 Passed Suez en-route to Karachi for B/U.

FJ51. NEWFOUNDLAND(3) (1964 - 1977) 6905g 3660n　　429' x 61'
6-cyl 2SCSA B&W oil engine by Harland & Wolff Ltd,Belfast.
11.1964 Completed by Burntisland SB CO. Ltd,Burntisland for
Johnston-Warren Lines Ltd. 10.1973 Chartered by Shaw,Savill &
Albion Co. Ltd ren. CUFIC. 1974 Ren. NEWFOUNDLAND. 1976 Chartered
by Shaw,Savill & Albion Co. Ltd ren. CUFIC. 1977 Sold to Golden
City Maritime Corp SA,Panama ren. GAIETY. 10.1985 B/U.

FJ52. NOVA SCOTIA(3) (1965 - 1978) 6905g 3660n　　429' x 61'
6-cyl 2SCSA B&W oil engine by Harland & Wolff Ltd,Belfast.
4.1965 Completed by Burntisland SB Co. Ltd,Burntisland for
Johnston-Warren Lines Ltd. 31.1.1973 Chartered by Shaw,Savill &
Albion Co. Ltd ren. TROPIC. 1974 Ren. NOVA SCOTIA. 1976 Chartered
by Shaw,Savill & Albion Co. Ltd ren. TROPIC. 1978 Sold to Booker
LIne Ltd,Liverpool ren. BOOKER VALIANT. 1980 Sold to Saudi Arabia
Shipping,Jeddah ren. ARAB DABOR. 1986 Ren. ARAB HIND. 9.1991 Still
in service.

APPENDIX FM. MANCHESTER LINERS LTD.

FM1. MANCHESTER TRADER (1898 - 1912) 3318g 2136n 340' x 43'
T 3-cyl by McIlwaine & McColl Ltd,Belfast.
16.8.1890 Launched and 12.1890 completed as PARKMORE for S.S.
Parkmore Ltd(W. Johnston & Co. Ltd),Liverpool by C.J. Bigger,
Londonderry. 1.1897 Sold to Elder,Dempster & Co. name u/ch.
5.5.1898 Purchased by Manchester Liners Ltd(Furness,Withy & Co.
Ltd) ren. MANCHESTER TRADER. 27.8.1903 Struck breakwater entering
Ayr harbour, holed port side and sank alongside quay, refloated
and repaired. 1912 Sold to A/S Ferdinand Melsom(J.Johanson),
Christiania ren. FERDINAND MELSOM. 1914 Sold to H. Westfal
Larsen,Bergen ren. KAUPANGER. 1915 Registered Christiania.
13.12.1916 Torpedoed and sunk off Cartagena by U38 o.v. Cardiff
to Spezia with coal.

FM2. MANCHESTER ENTERPRISE (1898 - 1899) 3792g 2488n 360' x 46'
T 3-cyl by bldrs.
26.6.1889 Launched and 1.1890 completed by Gourlay Bros & Co.,
Dundee as QUEENSMORE for S.S. Queensmore Ltd(W. Johnston & Co.
Ltd),Liverpool. 10.1896 Sold to Elder,Dempster & Co name u/ch.
5.5.1898 Purchased by Manchester Liners Ltd(Furness,Withy & Co.
Ltd) ren. MANCHESTER ENTERPRISE. 18.11.1899 Foundered in posn.
50-25 N, 42-25 W o.v. Mersey to Montreal.

FM3. MANCHESTER CITY (1898 - 1929) 7696g 4992n   445' x 52'
T 3-cyl by Furness,Westgarth & Co. Ltd,Middlesbrough.
10.1898 Completed by Raylton,Dixon & Co. Ltd,Middlesbrough for
Manchester Liners Ltd(Furness,Withy & Co. Ltd). 6.1929 B/U at
Stavanger.

FM4. MANCHESTER PORT (1899 - 1900) 5658g 3684n   452' x 52'
T 3-cyl by bldrs.
4.1899 Launched and 7.1899 completed by Palmers Ltd,Jarrow for
Manchester Liners Ltd(Furness,Withy & Co. Ltd). 1900 Sold to R.P.
Houston & Co. Ltd ren. HYDASPES. 1930 B/U in Italy.

FM5. MANCHESTER IMPORTER (1899 - 1927) 4028g 2538n 370' x 48'
T 3-cyl by W. Allan & Co. Ltd,Sunderland.
5.1899 Launched and 8.1899 completed by Irvines SB & DD Co. Ltd,
Hartlepool for Manchester Liners Ltd(Furness,Withy & Co. Ltd).
1927 Sold to Greece ren. ALEXANDRIA. 1933 B/U at Venice.

FM6. MANCHESTER SHIPPER (1899 - 1930) 4038g 2542n 370' x 48'
T 3-cyl by W. Allan & Co. Ltd,Sunderland.
7.1899 Launched and 2.1900 completed by Irvines SB & DD Co. Ltd,
Hartlepool for Manchester Liners Ltd(Furness,Withy & Co. Ltd).
7.1930 B/U at Briton Ferry.

FM7. MANCHESTER CORPORATION (1899 - 1929) 5400g 3467n 431' x 48'
T 3-cyl by Furness,Westgarth & Co. Ltd,Middlesbrough.
6.1899 Launched and 9.1899 completed by Furness,Withy & Co. Ltd,
Hartlepool for Manchester Liners Ltd(Furness,Withy & Co. Ltd).
7.1929 B/U at Barrow.

FM8. MANCHESTER COMMERCE (1899 - 1914) 5363g 3444n   431' x 38'
T 3-cyl by Furness,Westgarth & Co. Ltd,Middlesbrough.
8.1899 Launched and 11.1899 completed by Furness,Withy & Co. Ltd,
Hartlepool for Manchester Liners Ltd(Furness,Withy & Co. Ltd).
27.10.1914 Mined and sunk off Tory Island.

FM9. MANCHESTER MERCHANT (1900 - 1903) 5657g 3634n   452' x 52'
T 3-cyl by bldrs.
7.1899 Launched and 2.1900 completed by Palmers Ltd,Jarrow for
Manchester Liners Ltd(Furness,Withy & Co. Ltd).15.1.1903 Scuttled
on fire in Dingle Bay o.v. New Orleans to Manchester.

FM10.MANCHESTER EXCHANGE (1901 - 1925) 4091g 2649n   360' x 48'
T 3-cyl by Richardsons,Westgarth & Co. Ltd,Hartlepool.
11.1901 Completed by Furness,Withy & Co. Ltd,Hartlepool for
Manchester Liners Ltd(Furness,Withy & Co. Ltd). 1925 Sold to
Finland ren. EQUATEUR. 1939 B/U in Italy.

FM11.MANCHESTER ENGINEER (1902 - 1916) 4302g 2813n   360' x 48'
T 3-cyl by Richardsons,Westgarth & Co. Ltd,Sunderland.
4.1902 Completed by Northumberland SB Co. Ltd,Willington-on-Tyne
for Manchester Liners Ltd(Furness,Withy & Co. Ltd). 27.3.1916
Torpedoed and sunk in St. George's Channel 20 miles SW of
Coningbeg L.V. by U44 o.v. Philadelphia to Manchester with
general.

FM12.MANCHESTER INVENTOR (1902 - 1917) 4247g 2775n   360' x 48'
T 3-cyl by Richardsons,Westgarth & Co. Ltd,Sunderland.
6.1902 Completed by Northumberland SB Co. Ltd,Willington-on-Tyne
for Manchester Liners Ltd(Furness,Withy & Co. Ltd). 18.1.1917
Captured and sunk by gunfire from U57 50 miles NW by W1/2W of
Fastnet o.v. St John(NB) to Manchester with general.

FM13.MANCHESTER MARKET (1902 - 1903) 4901g 2650n   360' x 48'
T 3-cyl by Richardsons,Westgarth & Co. Ltd,Hartlepool.
23.1.1902 Completed by Furness,Withy & Co. Ltd,Hartlepool for
Manchester Liners Ltd (Furness,Withy & Co. Ltd). 26.4.1903
Wrecked near Tuskar Rock o.v. Manchester to Philadelphia with
general.

FM14.MANCHESTER SPINNER (1903 - 1918) 4227g 2760n   360' x 48'
T 3-cyl by Richardsons,Westgarth & Co. Ltd,Sunderland.
7.1903 Completed by Northumberland SB Co. Ltd,Willington-on-Tyne
for Manchester Liners Ltd(Furness,Withy & Co. Ltd). 22.1.1918
Torpedoed and sunk 33 miles SE of Malta by U27 o.v. Java to U.K.
with sugar.

FM15.MANCHESTER MILLER (1903 - 1917) 4234g 2766n   360' x 48'
T 3-cyl by Richardsons,Westgarth & Co. Ltd,Sunderland.
8.1903 Completed by Northumberland SB Co. Ltd,Willington-on-Tyne
for Manchester Liners Ltd(Furness,Withy & Co. Ltd). 5.6.1917
Torpedoed and sunk by U66 190 miles NW1/2N of Fastnet o.v.
Philadelphia to Manchester with general, 8 lost.

FM16.MANCHESTER MERCHANT(2) (1904 - 1933) 4152g 2707n 360' x 48'
T 3-cyl by Richardsons,Westgarth & Co. Ltd,Sunderland.
1.1904 Completed by Northumberland SB Co. Ltd,Willington-on-Tyne
for Manchester Liners Ltd(Furness,Withy & Co. Ltd). 10.1933 Sold
for B/U in Italy.

FM17.MANCHESTER PORT(2) (1904 - 1925) 4093g 2662n 360' x 48'
T 3-cyl by Richardsons,Westgarth & Co. Ltd,Sunderland.
11.1.1904 Completed by Furness,Withy & Co. Ltd,Hartlepool for
Manchester Liners Ltd(Furness,Withy & Co. Ltd). 1925 Sold to H.
Vogemann,Hamburg ren. VOGESEN. 7.5.1940 Mined and sunk off Vinga.

FM18.MANCHESTER MARINER (1904 - 1925) 4106g 2672n 360' x 48'
T 3-cyl by Richardsons,Westgarth & Co. Ltd,Hartlepool.
2.1904 Completed by Furness,Withy & Co. Ltd,Hartlepool for Manchester Liners Ltd(Furness,Withy & Co. Ltd). 4.12.1917 Mined in
English Channel, towed in. 1925 Sold to Finland ren. MERCATOR.
1.12.1939 Mined and sunk SE of Buchan Ness.

FM19.MANCHESTER CITIZEN (1912 - 1917) 4251g 2725n 380' x 49'
T 3-cyl by Richardsons,Westgarth & Co. Ltd,Sunderland.
8.1912 Completed by Northumberland SB Co. Ltd,Willington-on-Tyne
for Manchester Liners Ltd(Furness,Withy & Co. Ltd). 27.4.1917
Torpedoed and sunk 240 miles NW of Fastnet by U70 o.v. St.
John(NB) to Manchester with general.

FM20.MANCHESTER CIVILIAN (1913 - 1933) 4706g 2927n 385' x 52'
T 3-cyl by Richardsons,Westgarth & Co. Ltd,Hartlepool.
28.8.1913 Completed by Irvines SB & DD Co. Ltd,Hartlepool for
Manchester Liners Ltd(Furness,Withy & Co. Ltd). 1933 Sold to
Greece ren. TASIS. 6.1940 Taken at Dakar by Vichy France ren.
EQUATEUR. 1942 Taken over by Italy ren. BARI. 1.8.1943 Bombed and
sunk at Naples.

FM21.MANCHESTER HERO   (1916 - 1937) 5738g 3672n 400' x 53'
T 3-cyl by Blair & Co. Ltd,Stockton.
1.1916 Completed by Northumberland SB Co. Ltd,Willington-on-Tyne
for Manchester Liners Ltd(Furness,Withy & Co. Ltd) having been
laid down for Lloyd Austriaco and seized. 1937 Sold to Barry
Shipping Co. Ltd(B. & S. Shipping Co. Ltd) ren. ST. WINIFRED.
5.1938 Bombed by Franco aircraft in Spanish Civil War at Alicante
with the loss of 5 crew when bombed again in 6.1938. 8.1938 Towed
to Marseilles for repair and sold to Cia Genovese di Nav a Vap,
Genoa ren. CAPO VITA. 9.3.1941 Torpedoed and sunk by HMS UTMOST
to W of Lampedusa Island.

FM22.MANCHESTER TRADER   (1916 - 1917) 3938g 2597n 345' x 50'
T 3-cyl by Rankin & Blackmore Ltd,Glasgow.
11.1902 Completed by Russell & Co.,Port Glasgow for Auchen S.S.
Co. Ltd(Purdie,Glen & Co),Glasgow as AUCHENBLAE. 1916 Purchased
by Manchester Liners Ltd(Furness,Withy & Co. Ltd) ren. MANCHESTER
TRADER. 4.6.1917 Captured and sunk by gunfire from U65 8 miles SE
of Pantellaria Island o.v. Suda Bay to Algiers in ballast.

FM23.MANCHESTER ENGINEER(2) (1917) 4415g 2874n   378' x 50'
T 3-cyl by bldrs.
9.1905 Completed by D.& W. Henderson & Sons Ltd,Port Glasgow as
CRAIGVAR for West of Scotland SS Co Ltd(Biggart,Fulton & Grier),
Glasgow. 1910 Sold to W. Thaner & Co. Ltd,Liverpool ren. NATION.
1917 Purchased by Manchester Liners Ltd(Furness,Withy & Co. Ltd)
ren. MANCHESTER ENGINEER. 16.8.1917 Torpedoed and sunk 4.5 miles
SE of Flamborough Head o.v. Tyne to St. Nazaire with coal.

FM24.MANCHESTER INVENTOR(2) (1917) 4112g 2589n 382' x 51'
T 3-cyl by Dunsmuir & Jackson Ltd,Glasgow.
8.1907 Completed by A.McMillan & Sons Ltd,Dumbarton as CELTIC
KING for R. Hughes-Jones & Co,Liverpool. 1917 Purchased by
Manchester Liners Ltd(Furness,Withy & Co. Ltd) ren. MANCHESTER
INVENTOR. 30.7.1917 Captured and sunk by gunfire 80 miles NNE of
Muckle Flugga by U94 o.v. Archangel to Belfast with flax.

FM25.MANCHESTER COMMERCE(2) (1916 - 1917) 4144g 2687n 385' x 50'
T 3-cyl by Dunsmuir & Jackson Ltd,Glasgow.
8.1906 Completed by Russell & Co.,Port Glasgow as KING for State
S.S. Co. Ltd(W. Thomas),Liverpool. 1916 Purchased by Manchester
Liners Ltd(Furness,Withy & Co. Ltd) ren. MANCHESTER COMMERCE.
29.7.1917 Torpedoed and sunk in Strait of Gibraltar 15 miles NNW
of Cape Spartel by U39 o.v. Cardiff to Gibraltar with coal and
Govt. stores.

FM26.MANCHESTER BRIGADE (1918 - 1940) 6021g 3771n   418' x 53'
T 3-cyl by Richardsons,Westgarth & Co. Ltd,Hartlepool.
8.1918 Completed by Irvines SB & DD Co. Ltd,Hartlepool for Manchester Liners Ltd(Furness,Withy & Co. Ltd). 26.9.1940 Torpedoed
and sunk by U137 o.v. Manchester to Montreal with general, 58
lost.

FM27.MANCHESTER DIVISION (1918 - 1953) 6027g 3774n   418' x 53'
T 3-cyl by Richardsons,Westgarth & Co. Ltd,Hartlepool.
28.9.1918 Completed by Irvines SB & DD Co. Ltd,Hartlepool for
Manchester Liners Ltd(Furness,Withy & Co. Ltd). 30.9.1918 Rammed
and sank a U-boat off Flamborough Head on her maiden voyage from
Hartlepool to Plymouth. 2.12.1953 Arrived Briton Ferry for B/U.

FM28.MANCHESTER PRODUCER (1921 - 1939) See START POINT FP16.

FM29.MANCHESTER SPINNER(2) (1921 - 1944) 4767g 2968n 385' x 52'
T 3-cyl by Richardsons,Westgarth & Co. Ltd,Hartlepool.
1918 Completed by Irvines SB & DD Co. Ltd,Hartlepool as GRAMPIAN
RANGE for Neptune S.N. Co. Ltd(Furness,Withy & Co. Ltd). 4.4.1921
Transferred to Manchester Liners Ltd(Furness,Withy & Co. Ltd) ren
MANCHESTER SPINNER. 9.6.1944 Sunk at Normandy as blockship for
Mulberry Harbour.

FM30.MANCHESTER REGIMENT (1923 - 1939) 5989g 3199n   450' x 58'
2 Steam turbines SR geared to 1 screw shaft by Richardsons,West-
garth & Co. Ltd,Middlesbrough.

15.9.1922 Launched and 3.1923 Completed by Furness SB Co. Ltd,
Haverton Hill for Manchester Liners Ltd(Furness,Withy & Co. Ltd).
4.12.1939 Lost in collision with s.s. OROPESA to SW of Cape Race.

FM31.MANCHESTER COMMERCE(3) (1925 - 1952) 5342g 3068n 418' x 57'
T 3-cyl by Richardsons,Westgarth & Co. Ltd,Hartlepool.
26.7.1925 Completed by Furness SB Co. Ltd,Haverton Hill for Man-
chester Liners Ltd(Furness,Withy & Co. Ltd). 1.1952 Sold to Camel
Lines ren. CORBITA. 1952 Sold to East & West S.S. Co. Ltd,Karachi
ren. FAKIRJEE COWASJEE. 31.10.1960 Suffered serious damage at
Chittagong during cyclone. 11.2.1967 Laid-up at Karachi and 6.1967
B/U there.

FM32.MANCHESTER CITIZEN(2) (1925 - 1943) 5328g 3009n 418' x 57'
T 3-cyl by Richardsons,Westgarth & Co. Ltd,Hartlepool.
26.8.1925 Completed by Furness SB Co. Ltd,Haverton Hill for Manchester Liners Ltd(Furness,Withy & Co. Ltd). 9.7.1943 Torpedoed and
sunk by U508 o.v. Freetown for Lagos in ballast, 15 lost.

FM33.MANCHESTER EXPORTER (1929 - 1947) See REXMORE FJ20.

FM34.MANCHESTER PORT(3) (1935 - 1964) 5649g 3287n   422' x 57'
3 Steam turbines SR geared to 1 shaft by D.Rowan & Co. Ltd,Glasgow.
7.10.1935 Completed by Blythswood SB Co. Ltd,Glasgow for Manchester
Liners Ltd(Furness,Withy & Co. Ltd). 22.12.1964 Arrived Bilbao for
B/U.

FM35.MANCHESTER CITY(2) (1937 - 1964) 5600g 3329n   431' x 57'
3 Steam turbines SR geared to 1 shaft by D.Rowan & Co. Ltd,Glasgow.
8.1937 Completed by Blythswood SB Co. Ltd,Glasgow for Manchester
Liners Ltd(Furness,Withy & Co. Ltd). 1939 Taken over by Admiralty.
1945 Returned to service. 9.2.1960 Aground in Cape Fear River near
Wilmington(NC),refloated on 18.2.1960. 15.5.1964 Arrived at Faslane
for B/U.

FM36.MANCHESTER PROGRESS (1938 - 1966) 5620g 3343n   431' x 57'
3 Steam turbines SR geared to 1 shaft by D.Rowan & Co. Ltd,Glasgow.
17.9.1938 Completed by Blythswood SB Co. Ltd,Glasgow for Manchester
Liners Ltd(Furness,Withy & Co. Ltd). 15.1.1966 Arrived at Split for
B/U.

FM37.MANCHESTER MERCHANT(3) (1940 - 1943) 7264g 4436n 447' x 57'
3 Steam turbines SR geared to 1 shaft by D.Rowan & Co. Ltd,Glasgow.
10.2.1940 Launched and 4.1940 completed by Blythswood SB Co. Ltd,
Glasgow for Manchester Liners Ltd(Furness,Withy & Co. Ltd). 25.2.1943
Torpedoed and sunk by U628 in mid-Atlantic in posn. 45-10 N, 43-23W
o.v. U.K. to U.S.A.

FM38.MANCHESTER TRADER(3) (1941 - 1963) 7363g 4436n   447' x 57'
3 Steam turbines SR geared to 1 shaft by D.Rowan & Co. Ltd,Glasgow.
15.2.1941 Launched and 5.1941 completed by Blythswood SB Co. Ltd,
Glasgow for Manchester Liners Ltd(Furness,Withy & Co. Ltd). 24.1.1963
Arrived Split for B/U.

FM39.MANCHESTER SHIPPER(2) (1943 - 1969) 7881g 4662n 461' x 58'
3 Steam turbines SR geared to 1 shaft by D.Rowan & Co. Ltd,Glasgow.
30.6.1943 Launched and 10.1943 completed by Blythswood SB Co. Ltd,
Glasgow for Manchester Liners Ltd(Furness,Withy & Co. Ltd). 10.7.1969
Arrived Trieste for B/U.

FM40.MANCHESTER REGIMENT(2) (1947 - 1967) 7638g 4652n 461' x 58'
3 Steam turbines SR geared to 1 shaft by D.Rowan & Co. Ltd,Glasgow.
16.10.1946 Launched and 27.2.1947 completed by Blythswood SB Co.
Ltd,Glasgow for Manchester Liners Ltd(Furness,Withy & Co. Ltd). 1967
Sold to Panama owners ren. AZURE COAST II. 1971 Sold to Singapore
owners ren. PU GOR. 24.11.1971 Arrived at Kaohsiung for B/U.

FM41.MANCHESTER MERCHANT(4) (1951 - 1967) 7651g 4621n 465' x 59'
3 Steam turbines SR geared to 1 shaft by D.Rowan & Co. Ltd,Glasgow.
18.1.1951 Completed by Blythswood SB Co. Ltd,Glasgow for Manchester
Liners Ltd(Furness,Withy & Co. Ltd). 1967 Sold to Liberian owners ren.
CLIO. 14.2.1972 Sank after fire 700 miles off Angola o.v. Chittagong
to Continent.

FM42.MANCHESTER PIONEER (1952 - 1963) 1805g 707n 258' x 43'
2 Steam turbines DR geared to 1 shaft by bldrs.
2.4.1952 Completed by Cammell,Laird & Co. Ltd,Birkenhead for Manchester Liners Ltd(Furness,Withy & Co. Ltd). 2.1960 Lengthened to
290'. 1963 Sold to Greek owners ren. CYPRIAN MED. 1970 Ren. SAN
ANTONIO. 8.1971 B/U at Perama as ELENITSA S.

FM43.MANCHESTER EXPLORER (1952 - 1963) 1805g 707n 258' x 43'
2 Steam turbines DR geared to 1 shaft by bldrs.
15.5.1952 Completed by Cammell,Laird & Co. Ltd,Birkenhead for Manchester Liners Ltd(Furness,Withy & Co. Ltd). 1963 Sold to Crosbie
Shipping Co,Canada ren. C.A. CROSBIE. 1965 Ren. P.M. CROSBIE. 1968
Sold to Pamagos Shpg. Co,Cyprus ren. PANEGIOUS. 1971 Ren. YPERMACHOS
1973 Sold to Argolis Shipping Co. Ltd,Cyprus ren. EMILIA. 6.2.1974
Laid-up at Piraeus. 1980 Ren. TASSOS. 12.1980 Arrived Salamis Island
for B/U.

FM44.MANCHESTER SPINNER(3) (1952 - 1968) 7814g 4588n 466' x 60'
2 Steam turbines DR geared to 1 shaft by bldrs.
1952 Completed by Cammell,Laird & Co. Ltd,Birkenhead for Manchester
Liners Ltd(Furness,Withy & Co. Ltd). 1968 Sold to Estia Cia Nav SA,
Panama ren. ESTIA. 25.11.1971 Sank after engine room explosion in
position 6-10 N, 53-54 W.

FM45.MANCHESTER PROSPECTOR (1953 - 1960) 1400g 665n 258' x 42'
C 2-cyl and L.P. turbine by bldrs.
1948 Completed by Langesunds M.V.,Langesund as VIGOR for S. Ugelstad,
Oslo. 1953 Purchased by Manchester Liners Ltd(Furness,Withy & Co. Ltd)
ren. MANCHESTER PROSPECTOR. 1960 Sold to C.M. Salvis & Co,Greece ren.
GEORGIOS. 1973 Sold to Lassa Special Shpg. SA,Panama ren. AGHIOS
NEKTARIOS L. 1980 To Nikolaou Nikolaos,Piraeus name u/ch.

FM46.MANCHESTER MARINER(2) (1955 - 1968) 7580g 4588n 466' x 60'
2 Steam turbines DR geared to 1 shaft by bldrs.

3.3.1955 Completed by Cammell,Laird & Co. Ltd,Birkenhead for Manchester Liners Ltd(Furness,Withy & Co. Ltd). 1968 Sold to Mira Cia Nav
SA,Panama ren. IRA. 1974 Sold to Philippine National Steel Corporation
ren. PANDAY IRA. 10.1975 Sustained boiler damage at Singapore.
5.5.1977 Demolition commenced at Iligan.

FM47.MANCHESTER VANGUARD (1956 - 1963) 1662g 704n   258' x 43'
Two 8-cyl 4SCSA oil engines by Klockner-Humboldt-Deutz.
19.4.1956 Completed by A.G. Weser,Bremerhaven for Manchester Liners
Ltd (Furness,Withy & Co. Ltd). 1959 First vessel into St. Lawrence
Seaway. 1963 Sold to General Steam Nav. Co. Ltd,London ren. SHELDRAKE.
1968 Sold to Israel ren. BAT GOLAN. 1974 Sold ren WOOCHUCK. 1975 Sold
to Singapore ren. SELATAN MAJU. 1982 WIHAR I. 5.1985 B/U at Hong Kong.

FM48.MANCHESTER VENTURE (1956 - 1961) 1662g 704n   258' x 43'
Two 8-cyl 4SCSA oil engines by Klockner-Humboldt-Deutz.
4.1956 Completed by A.G. Weser,Bremerhaven for Manchester Liners Ltd
(Furness,Withy & Co. Ltd). 1961 Sold to General Steam Nav. Co. Ltd,
London ren. PHILOMEL. 1968 Sold to Israel ren. BAT TIRAN. 8.1972
Beached after explosion and fire in cargo o.v. Rijeka to Haifa.
12.9.1972 Arrived Piraeus for B/U.

FM49.MANCHESTER FAITH (1959 - 1970) See CAIRNESK FT14.

FM50.MANCHESTER FAME (1959 - 1970) See CAIRNGLEN FT15.

FM51.MANCHESTER MILLER (1959 - 1976) 8378g 4654n   468' x 62'
2 Steam turbines DR geared to 1 shaft by bldrs.
12.12.1958 Launched and 3.1959 completed by Harland & Wolff Ltd,
Belfast for Manchester Liners Ltd(Furness,Withy & Co. Ltd). 1970
Rebuilt by Smiths Dock Co. Ltd, Middlesbrough as a container vessel
ren. MANCHESTER QUEST. 29.1.1976 Arrived Kaohsiung for B/U.

FM52.MANCHESTER COMMERCE(4) (1963 - 1971) 8724g 4998n 470' x 62'
6-cyl 2SCSA Sulzer oil engine by G. Clark Ltd,Sunderland.
6.1963 Completed by Smiths Dock Co. Ltd,Middlesbrough for Manchester
Liners Ltd(Furness,Withy & Co. Ltd). 1971 Sold to W.L. Suan,Hong Kong
ren. BER SEA. 1975 Sold to China ren. YANG CHUN. 10.1980 Destroyed by
fire after shelling in Shatt el Arab,Khorramshahr.

FM53.MANCHESTER CITY(3) (1964 - 1971) 8734g 5014n   470' x 62'
6-cyl 2SCSA Sulzer oil engine by G. Clark Ltd,Sunderland.
7.1964 Completed by Smiths Dock Co. Ltd,Middlesbrough for Manchester
Liners Ltd,Middlesbrough(Furness,Withy & Co. Ltd). 1971 Sold to Korean
Shipping Corporation ren. KOREAN WINNER. 1978 Sold to Jin Yang Shpg.
Co. Ltd,Busan ren. ONE WEST NO. 8. 11.1985 B/U at Busan.

FM54.MANCHESTER RENOWN (1964 - 1971) 8742g 5017n   470' x 62'
6-cyl 2SCSA Sulzer oil engine by G. Clark Ltd,Sunderland.
4.1964 Completed by Smiths Dock Co. Ltd,Middlesbrough for Manchester
Liners Ltd(Furness,Withy & Co. Ltd). 1971 Sold to Korean Shipping
Corporation ren. KOREAN CHALLENGER. 1978 Sold to Whitney Shpg. Co.,
Liberia ren. EDESSA. 13.2.1983 Laid-up at Trincomalee. 4.2.1984 Major
fire damage while being reactivated. 1.5.1984 Arrived Kaohsiung B/U.

FM55.MANCHESTER PORT(4) (1966 - 1971) 8138g 5284n   470' x 62'
Two 14-cyl 4SCSA Vee Pielstick oil engines by Crossley.
11.1966 Completed by Smiths Dock Co. Ltd,Middlesbrough for Manchester
Liners Ltd(Furness,Withy & Co. Ltd). 1971 Sold to Jadranska Slobodna
Plovidba,Yugoslavia ren. BIOKOVO. 28.8.1980 Considerable bridge damage
when fire broke out at Civitavecchia. 1.11.1980 Arrived Piraeus in tow
abandoned to insurers. 1980 Sold to Vroulidia Cia Nav SA,Greece ren.
YDRA. 21.1.1983 Aground 1 mile E of Bizerta after engine room fire,
total loss.

FM56.MANCHESTER PROGRESS(2) (1967 - 1980) 8176g 5229n   470' x 62'
Two 14-cyl 4SCSA Vee Pielstick oil engines by Crossley.
2.1967 Completed by Smiths Dock Co. Ltd,Middlesbrough for Manchester
Liners Ltd(Furness,Withy & Co. Ltd). 1971 Rebuilt at Amsterdam as a
container vessel ren. MANCHESTER CONCEPT. 1980 Sold to Singapore ren.
CHERRY BUNGA. 31.5.1985 Arrived Esteban de Pravia for B/U.

FM57.MANCHESTER CHALLENGE (1968 - 1979) 12039g 7260n   498' x 63'
Two 18-cyl 4SCSA Vee Pielstick oil engines by Crossley.
10.1968 Completed by Smiths Dock Co. Ltd,Middlesbrough for Manchester
Liners Ltd(Furness,Withy & Co. Ltd). First company container ship.
1979 Sold to Hong Kong Ocean Shipping Co. Ltd,Liberia ren. OCEAN
CONTAINER. 1989 HANG FU. 1989 MSC SUSANNA.

FM58.MANCHESTER COURAGE (1968 - 1979) 12039g 7295n   498' x 63'
Two 18-cyl 4SCSA Vee Pielstick oil engines by Crossley.
2.1969 Completed by Smiths Dock Co. Ltd,Middlesbrough for Manchester
Liners Ltd(Furness,Withy & Co. Ltd). 1979 Sold to Hong Kong Island
Shipping Co,Liberia ren. PACIFIC CONTAINER. 1989 HANG KWAI. 1989 MSC
MARINA.

FM59.MANCHESTER CONCORDE (1969 - 1982) 12039g 7295n   498' x 63'
Two 18-cyl 4SCSA Vee Pielstick oil engines by Crossley.
5.1969 Completed by Smiths Dock Co. Ltd,Middlesbrough for Manchester
Liners Ltd(Furness,Withy & Co. Ltd). 1982 Sold to Char Lian Marine SA,
Panama ren. CHAR LIAN. 10.12.1983 Arrived Kaohsiung for B/U.

FM60.MANCHESTER MERIT (1970 - 1975) 3414g 2208n   350' x 44'
5-cyl 4SCSA BArreras-Deutz oil engine.
1970 Completed by Basse Sambre-Corco SA,Santander for Manchester
Liners Ltd(Furness,Withy & Co. Ltd) as MANCHESTER MERIT having been
launched as CATALINA DEL MAR. 1972 Demise chartered to Plumbton
Shipping Co. Ltd,Bermuda ren. FORTUNA. 1975 Sold to Chelwood Shpg. Co,
Liberia ren. KATHLEEN. 1987 Ren. KUDU, same owner. 1990 CEMENT TWO.

FM61.MANCHESTER CRUSADE (1971 - 1982) 12039g 7295n   498' x 63'
Two 18-cyl 4SCSA Vee Pielstick oil engines by Crossley.
1971 Completed by Smiths Dock Co. Ltd,Middlesbrough for Manchester
Liners Ltd(Furness,Withy & Co. Ltd). 1982 Sold to Char Lian Marine SA,
Panama ren. CHAR CHE. 2.12.1983 Arrived Kaohsiung for B/U.

FM62.MANCHESTER VIGOUR (1973 - 1980) 5310g 2413n   378' x 51'
12-cyl 4SCSA Pielstick by Crossley Premier Ltd.

1973 Completed by Appledore SB Ltd,Appledore for Manchester Liners Ltd
(Furness,Withy & Co. Ltd). 1980 Sold to Cie Maritime d'Affretement,
Marseilles ren. VILLE D'ORIENT. 1984 Sold to Islamic Development Bank,
Istanbul ren. BENWALID. 1990 Sold to Tanto Line,Sourabaya ren. SEA
LEOPARD.

FM63.MANCHESTER ZEAL   (1973 - 1980) 5310g 2413n   378' x 51'
12-cyl 4SCSA Pielstick by Crossley Premier Ltd.
1973 Completed by Appledore SB Ltd,Appledore for Manchester Liners Ltd
(Furness,Withy & Co. Ltd). 1981 Sold to Pacific International Line
(Pte) Ltd,Singapore ren. SEA HAWK. 1990 SEA LEOPARD.

FM64.MANCHESTER RENOWN (1974 - 1982) 12577g 7755n   499' x 63'
Two 18-cyl 4SCSA Vee Pielstick oil engines by Crossley.
5.1974 Completed by Smiths Dock Co. Ltd,Middlesbrough for Manchester
Liners Ltd(Furness,Withy & Co. Ltd). 1974 Ren. ASIA RENOWN. 1978 Ren.
MANCHESTER RENOWN. 1982 Transferred to P.T. Perusahaan Pelayaran
Karana Line(OOCL),Jakarta ren. RATIH. 1990 Ren. OOCL AMITY. 9.1991
Still in service.

FM65.MANCHESTER REWARD   (1974 - 1982) 12577g 7755n   499' x 63'
Two 18-cyl 4SCSA Vee Pielstick oil engines by Crossley.
10.1974 Completed by Smiths Dock Co. Ltd,Middlesbrough for Manchester
Liners Ltd(Furness,Withy & Co. Ltd). 1974 Ren. ASIA REWARD. 1978 Ren.
MANCHESTER REWARD. 1979 Ren. SEATRAIN NORFOLK. 1982 Transferred to
Overseas Nav. Co. Ltd(OOCL),Hong Kong ren. R.R. RATNA. 9.1991 Still in
service.

FM66.MANCHESTER VANGUARD(2) (1977 - 1983) 17385g 9231n 527' x 82'
7-cyl 2SCSA Sulzer oil engine by Scotts Eng. Co. Ltd,Greenock.
5.1977 Completed by Smiths Dock Co. Ltd,Middlesbrough for Manchester
Liners Ltd(Furness,Withy & Co. Ltd). 1977 Ren. SEATRAIN TRENTON. 1979
Ren. MANCHESTER VANGUARD. 1979 Ren. KEELUNG. 1980 Ren. MANCHESTER
VANGUARD. 1980 Ren. ORIENTAL VANGUARD. 1981 Ren. MANCHESTER VANGUARD
1982 Ren. IBN MAJID. 1983 Ren. ORIENTAL EXPERT. 9.1991 Still in
service.

FM67.MANCHESTER VENTURE(2)   (1977 - 1983) 17385g 9231n 527' x 82'
7-cyl 2SCSA Sulzer oil engine by Scotts Eng. Co. Ltd,Greenock.
10.1977 Completed by Smiths Dock Co. Ltd,Middlesbrough for Manchester
Liners Ltd(Furness,Withy & Co. Ltd). 1977 Ren. SEATRAIN BENNINGTON.
1979 Ren. MANCHESTER VENTURE. 1979 Ren. MARSEILLE. 1980 Ren.
MANCHESTER VENTURE. 1980 Ren. ORIENTAL VENTURE. 1981 Ren. RHEIN
EXPRESS. 1983 Ren. ORIENTAL VENTURE. 1984 Ren. ORIENTAL AMBASSADOR.
1989 Ren. OOCL ALLIANCE. 9.1991 Still in service.

FM68.MANCHESTER CHALLENGE(2) (1981 - 1988) 30817g 13384n 719' x 100'
10-cyl 2SCSA Sulzer oil engine by G. Clark & N.E.M.,Wallsend.
11.1970 Completed by Swan Hunter SB Ltd,Walker as DART AMERICA for
Dart Container Line Co. Ltd(Bristol City Line). 1981 Purchased by
Manchester Liners Ltd(Furness,Withy & Co. Ltd) ren. MANCHESTER
CHALLENGE. 1988 Transferred to Tynedale Shpg. Co. Ltd(OOCL), Hong Kong
ren. OOCL CHALLENGE. 9.1991 Still in service.

FN1.WEST POINT   (1910) 4812g 3100n 375' x 50'
T 3-cyl by bldrs.
6.1899 Completed by R.Stephenson & Co. Ltd,Newcastle for Norfolk
& North American S.S. Co. Ltd(Simpson,Spence & Young,mgrs),
London. 1910 Taken over by Furness,Withy & Co. Ltd. 29.8.1910
Abandoned on fire 600 miles E of Cape Race o.v. Glasgow to
Charleston.

FN2.MONTAUK POINT   (1910 - 1912) 4809g 3100n   375' x 50'
T 3-cyl by bldrs.
11.1899 Completed by R. Stephenson & Co. Ltd,Newcastle for
Norfolk & North American S.S. Co. Ltd(Simpson,Spence & Young,
mgrs), London. 1910 Taken over by Furness,Withy & Co. Ltd. 1912
Sold to Scotia S.S. Co. Ltd(Shankland,Russell & Co),Liverpool
name u/ch. 8.1914 Seized at Hamburg. 1915 - 1918 German Navy
store ship ren. BERGFRIED. 1919 Purchased by Sigval Bergesen,
Stavanger ren. SNEFOND. 1919 Sold to D/S Atlanterhavet A/S(O.J.
Eskildsen), Copenhagen ren. STILLEHAVET. 1922 Purchased by
Continental Rhederei A.G.,Hamburg ren. CARLSFELD. 1924 Sold to
Reederei A.G. von 1896,Hamburg ren. OMEGA. 1926 Sold to
S.Censini,Genoa name u/ch. 1928 Sold to I.N.S.A.(Industrie Navali
Soc. Anon.),Genoa ren. JOHNNY. 10.1929 Sustained grounding
damage. 1930 B/U in Italy.

FN3.CROWN POINT   (1910 - 1917) 5219g 3301n   390' x 51'
T 3-cyl by J. Dickinson & Sons Ltd,Sunderland.
4.1900 Completed by J.L. Thompson & Sons Ltd,Sunderland for
Norfolk & North American S.S. Co. Ltd(Simpson,Spence & Young,
mgrs),London. 1910 Taken over by Furness,Withy & Co. Ltd.
6.2.1917 Torpedoed and sunk by U83 55 miles W of Scillies o.v.
London to Philadelphia with general and chalk. 7 lost including
the Master.

FN4.EAGLE POINT   (1910 - 1916) 5222g 3307n   390' x 51'
T 3-cyl by J. Dickinson & Sons Ltd,Sunderland.
6.1900 Completed by J.L. Thompson & Sons Ltd,Sunderland for
Norfolk & North American S.S. Co. Ltd(Simpson,Spence & Young,
mgrs),London. 1910 Taken over by Furness,Withy & Co. Ltd.
28.3.1916 Captured,torpedoed and sunk by U70 100 miles WNW of
Bishop Rock o.v. St. John(NB) to Le Havre with hay and oats.

FN5.NORTH POINT   (1910 - 1920) 5216g 3300n   390' x 51'
T 3-cyl by J. Dickinson & Sons Ltd,Sunderland.
12.1900 Completed by J.L. THompson & Sons Ltd,Sunderland for
Norfolk & North American S.S. Co. Ltd(Simpson,Spence & Young,
mgrs),London. 1910 Taken over by Furness,Withy & Co. Ltd. 1920
Sold to Soc. Maritime Francaise,La Rochelle ren. GENERAL LYAUTEY.
11.1923 B/U.

FN6.EAST POINT   (1910 - 1917) 5234g 3300n   390' x 51'
T 3-cyl by J. Dickinson & Sons Ltd,Sunderland.

2.1901 Completed by J.L. Thompson & Sons Ltd,Sunderland for
Norfolk & North American S.S. Co. Ltd(Simpson,Spence & Young,
mgrs),London. 1910 Taken over by Furness,Withy & Co. Ltd.
9.3.1917 Torpedoed and sunk by U48 9 miles SE 1/2S of Eddystone
o.v. London to Philadelphia with general.

FN7.SOUTH POINT   (1912 - 1915) 3837g 2429n   375' x 50'
T 3-cyl by Richardsons,Westgarth & Co. Ltd,Hartlepool.
1912 Completed by Irvines SB & DD Co. Ltd,Hartlepool for Norfolk
& North American S.S. Co. Ltd(Furness,Withy & Co. Ltd). 27.3.1915
Captured,torpedoed,shelled and sunk by U28 60 miles W of Lundy
Island o.v. Cardiff to Philadelphia with china clay.

FN8.WEST POINT(2)   (1912 - 1916) 3847g 2413n   375' x 50'
T 3-cyl by Richardsons,Westgarth & Co. Ltd,Hartlepool.
1912 Completed by Irvines SB & DD Co. Ltd,Hartlepool for Norfolk &
North American S.S. Co. Ltd(Furness,Withy & Co. Ltd). 8.10.1916
Captured and sunk with time bombs by U53 46 miles ESE of Nantucket
L.V. o.v. London to Newport News with general.

FN9.START POINT   (1912 - 1915) 3840g 2410n   375' x 50'
T 3-cyl by Richardsons,Westgarth & Co. Ltd,Hartlepool.
1912 Completed by Irvines SB & DD Co. Ltd,Hartlepool for Norfolk
& North American S.S. Co. Ltd(Furness,Withy & Co. Ltd). 1915
Transferred to Furness,Withy & Co. Ltd ren. MAXTON. 28.12.1917
Torpedoed and sunk by U19 28 miles N 1/4W of Malin Head o.v.
Clyde to Philadelphia with general. 1 lost.

FN10.EAVESTONE   (1912 - 1917) 1858g 1104n   276' x 40'
4-cyl 2SCSA oil engine by Richardsons,Westgarth & Co. Ltd,M'bro.
1912 Completed by Sir Raylton Dixon & Co.,Middlesbrough as first
British motor ship for Norfolk & North American S.S. Co. Ltd
(Furness,Withy & Co. Ltd). 1915 Converted to coal-fired T 3-cyl
by Richardsons,Westgarth & Co. Ltd,M'bro. 3.2.1917 Sunk by gunfire from U45 95 miles W of Fastnet o.v. Barry to Gibraltar with
coal.

FN11.NORTHWESTERN MILLER (1915 - 1927) 6504g 4161n   420' x 53'
T 3-cyl by Richardsons,Westgarth & Co. Ltd,Hartlepool.
5.1915 Completed by Northumberland SB Co. Ltd,Howdon-on-Tyne for
Norfolk & North American S.S. Co. Ltd(Furness,Withy & Co. Ltd).
1927 Sold to Norddeutscher Lloyd,Bremen ren. AUGSBURG. 1940 Sold
to Teikoku Senpaku K.K.,Tokyo ren. TEIRYU MARU. 19.7.1944 Torpedoed and sunk by U.S.S. GUARDFISH 200 miles off NW Luzon.

FN12.SOUTHWESTERN MILLER (1915 - 1927) 6514g 4161n   420' x 53'
T 3-cyl by Richardsons,Westgarth & Co. Ltd,Hartlepool.
6.1915 Completed by Northumberland SB Co. Ltd,Howdon-on-Tyne for
Norfolk & North American S.S. Co. Ltd(Furness,Withy & Co. Ltd).
1927 Sold to Norddeutscher Loyd,Bremen ren. GIESSEN. 12.3.1929
Wrecked on Button Rock,Saddle Island in Chekiang Province o.v.
Rotterdam to Shanghai & Yokohama.

FN13.DOMINION MILLER   (1916) See ELSTREE GRANGE(2) H28

FN14.CORNISH POINT (1916 - 1926) 4259g 2706n 390' x 52'
T 3-cyl by bldrs.
1914 Completed as BLAND HALL by W. Doxford & Sons Ltd,Sunderland
for Nicholl S.S. Ltd(E.Nicholl & Co),London. 1916 Purchased by
Norfolk & North American S.S. Co. Ltd(Furness,Withy & Co. Ltd)
ren. CORNISH POINT. 1926 Sold to Unterweser Reed.A.G.,Bremen ren.
GONZENHEIM. 1933 Sold to Atlantic Tank Rhederei Gmbh,Hamburg(J.T.
Essberger) ren. LISA. 1937 Sold to H.Vogemann,Hamburg ren.
WALKURE. 22.12.1942 Wrecked near Kristiansand.

FN15.SOUTH POINT(2) (1916 - 1917) 4258g 2706n 390' x 52'
T 3-cyl by bldrs.
1914 Completed as ALBERT HALL by W. Doxford & Sons Ltd,Sunderland
for Nicholl S.S. Ltd(E.Nicholl & Co),London. 1916 Purchased by
Norfolk & North American S.S. Co. Ltd(Furness,Withy & Co. Ltd)
ren. SOUTH POINT. 11.6.1917 Torpedoed and sunk by UB32 30 miles
SW1/2S of Bishop Rock o.v. London to Newport News in ballast.

FN16.START POINT(2) (1916 - 1921) 6540g 4162n 420' x 53'
T 3-cyl by Richardsons,Westgarth & Co. Ltd,Sunderland.
5.1916 Completed by Sir J. Laing & Sons Ltd,Sunderland for
Norfolk & North American S.S. Co. Ltd(Furness,Withy & Co. Ltd).
1921 Transferred to Manchester Liners Ltd ren. MANCHESTER
PRODUCER. 1939 Purchased by Board of Trade(P.Henderson & Co.,
mgrs) ren. BOTWEY. 26.7.1941 Torpedoed and sunk by U141 in OS1
60 miles N of Tory Island o.v. Ellesmere Port to Port Sulphur in
ballast.

FN17.HARTLAND POINT (1917 - 1919) See HARTMORE FJ27

FN18.GLASTONBURY (1917 - 1920) 6031g 3821n 405' x 53'
T 3-cyl by J. Dickinson & Sons Ltd,Sunderland.
6.1917 Completed by Sir James Laing & Sons Ltd,Sunderland for The
Shipping Controller having been taken over for the war and reg.
under Norfolk & North American S.S. Co. Ltd although the actual
owners were Den Norske Afrika og Australie Linie(W. Wilhelmsen).
1920 Ren. SIMLA. 22.9.1940 Torpedoed and sunk by U100 in HX72
o.v. Philadelphia to Tees with steel billets and scrap iron.

FN19.ABERCORN (1917 - 1920) 5424g 3469n 385' x 54'
T 3-cyl by N.E. Marine Eng. Co. Ltd,Sunderland.
6.1917 Completed by J.L. Thompson & Sons Ltd,Sunderland for The
Shipping Controller having been taken over for the war and reg.
under Norfolk & North American S.S Co. Ltd although the actual
owners were Den Norske Afrika og Australie Linie(W. Wilhelmsen).
1920 Ren. MESNA. 4.9.1924 Wrecked near Nukualofa,Tonga Island in
posn. 20-09 S, 174-55 E o.v. Haiphong to U.K. & Continent with
zinc ore and copper.

FN20.TENTERDEN (1917 - 1920) 4127g 2589n 352' x 51'
T 3-cyl by J. Dickinson & Sons Ltd,Sunderland.
10.1917 Completed by J.L. Thompson & Sons Ltd,Sunderland for The
Shipping Controller having been taken over for the war and reg.
under Norfolk & North American S.S. Co. Ltd although the actual

owners were A/S Gro(J.R. Olsen),Bergen. 1920 Ren. GRO. 1923 Mgrs
became O.Grolle Olsen & I.Hysing Olsen.7.9.1940 Torpedoed and
sunk by U47 in SC2 in posn. 58-30 N, 16-10W o.v. Sydney(CB) to
Manchester with wheat.

FN21.APPLEBY (1917 - 1920) 6030g 3839n 405' x 53'
T 3-cyl by J. Dickinson & Sons Ltd,Sunderland.
12.1917 Completed by Sir James Laing & Sons Ltd,Sunderland for
The Shipping Controller having been taken over for the war and
reg. under Norfolk & North American S.S. Co. Ltd although the
actual owners were Den Norske Afrika og Australie Linie(W. Wilhelmsen). 1920 Ren. RINDA. 30.5.1941 Torpedoed and sunk by U38 in
posn. 6-52 N, 16-25 W o.v. Haifa to U.K. via Cape Town with
general.

FN22.DOMINION MILLER(2) (1918) See VALEMORE FJ19

FN23.DOMINION MILLER(3) (1922 - 1925) See PACIFIC COMMERCE F224

APPENDIX FO   NEPTUNE S.N. CO. LTD

FO1.QUEEN WILHELMINA (1906 - 1915) 3590g 2307n 363' x 46'
T 3-cyl by G. Clark Ltd,Sunderland.
10.1898 Completed by James Laing & Sons Ltd,Sunderland for
Neptune S.N. Co. Ltd(W. & T.W. Pinkney),Sunderland. 1904 Mgrs.
became F.W. Bolam & Swinhoe. 1906 Taken over by Furness,Withy &
Co. Ltd. 8.5.1915 Torpedoed and sunk by U9 20 miles SE of
Longstone Light o.v. Leith to Fowey in ballast. Beached at
Bondicar,1.5 miles SSE of Amble,total loss.

FO2.OHIO (1906 - 1909) 4006g 2575n 393' x 46'
T 3-cyl by G. Clark Ltd,Sunderland.
1899 Completed by Bartram & Son,Sunderland for Neptune S.N. Co.
Ltd(W. & T.W. Pinkney),Sunderland. 1904 Mgrs. became F.W. Bolam &
Swinhoe. 1906 Taken over by Furness,Withy & Co. Ltd. 1909 Sold to
Holland America Line ren. ZAANDIJK. 11.3.1916 Mined 4 miles ENE
Kentish Knock o.v. Philadelphia to Rotterdam with general, put
into London 2 days later. 22.2.1917 Torpedoed and sunk by German
submarine off Scillies o.v. Rotterdam to Philadelphia in ballast.

FO3.RUNO (1906 - 1909) 4016g 2621n 391' x 47'
T 3-cyl by T. Richardson & Co.,Hartlepool.
1900 Completed by James Laing & Son,Sunderland for Neptune S.N.
Co. Ltd(W. & T.W. Pinkney),Sunderloand. 1904 Mgrs. became F.W.
Bolam & Swinhoe. 1906 Taken over by Furness,Withy & Co. Ltd. 1909
Sold to Holland America Line ren. ZILDIJK. 1927 Sold to Stoomship
Eenambt,Rotterdam ren. HOFLAAN. 1930 B/U.

FO4.DURANGO (1906 - 1917) 3008g 1927n 332' x 42'
T 3-cyl by J. Dickinson & Sons Ltd,Sunderland.
3.1895 Completed by Bartram & Son,Sunderland for Neptune S.N. Co.
Ltd(W. & T.W. Pinkney),Sunderland. 1904 Mgrs. became F.W. Bolam &
Swinhoe. 1906 Taken over by Furness,Withy & Co. Ltd. 26.8.1917

Captured by U53 and sunk by gunfire 50 miles NW of Barra Head in position 57-8 N, 8-55 W o.v. Liverpool to St. John's(NF) and Halifax with general.

FO5.TABASCO (1906 - 1917) 2987g 1910n 331' x 42'
T 3-cyl by G. Clark Ltd,Sunderland.
7.1895 Completed by James Laing & Son,Sunderland for Neptune S.N. Co. Ltd(W. & T.W. Pinkney),Sunderland. 1904 Mgrs. became F.W. Bolam & Swinhoe. 1906 Taken over by Furness,Withy & Co. Ltd. 26.1.1917 Captured and sunk by U45 55 miles WNW of Skelligs o.v. Halifax(NS) to Liverpool with general.

FO6.VENANGO (1906 - 1913) 2938g 1910n 309' x 41'
T 3-cyl by G. Clark Ltd,Sunderland.
5.1891 Completed by James Laing & Son,Sunderland for Neptune S.N. Co. Ltd(W. & T.W. Pinkney),Sunderland. 1904 Mgrs. became F.W. Bolam & Swinhoe. 1906 Taken over by Furness,Withy & Co. Ltd. 1913 Sold to Cie des Vapeurs Francais(J.Stern),Rouen ren. ROUENNAIS. 1916 Sold to Cie Generale d'Armements Maritime(J.Lasry),Bordeaux ren. WILFRED. 1927 B/U.

FO7.TAMPICO (1906 - 1907) 2968g 1908n 332' x 42'
T 3-cyl by G. Clark Ltd,Sunderland.
2.1895 Completed by James Laing & Son,Sunderland for Neptune S.N. Co. Ltd(W. & T.W. Pinkney),Sunderland. 1904 Mgrs. became F.W. Bolam & Swinhoe. 1906 Taken over by Furness,Withy & Co. Ltd. 10.1907 Abandoned in posn. 38 N, 33 W o.v. Baltimore to Rotterdam crew all picked up by INDIANA.

FO8.BRANTFORD (1908 -1909) 6292g 4037n 410' x 52'
T 3-cyl by Richardsons,Westgarth & Co. Ltd,Sunderland.
1908 Completed by Northumberland SB Co. Ltd for Neptune S.N. Co. Ltd(Furness,Withy & Co. Ltd). 1909 Sold to Holland America Line ren. ANDIJK. 4.3.1930 Arrived Hendrik Ido Ambacht for B/U.

FO9.GRAMPIAN RANGE (1910 - 1913) 3148g 2017n 330' x 46'
T 3-cyl by Clyde SB & Eng. Co. Ltd,Pt. Glasgow.
8.1905 Completed by W. Hamilton & Co.,Port Glasgow for Neptune S.N. Co. Ltd(F.W. Bolam),Sunderland. 1910 Taken over by Furness, Withy & Co. Ltd. 1913 Sold to West Russian S.S. Co. Ltd,St. Petersburg ren. BERKUT. 8.1914 War loss.

FO10.LOWTHER RANGE (1910 - 1918) 3926g 2465n 340' x 47'
T 3-cyl by Richardsons,Westgarth & Co. Ltd,Hartlepool.
6.1906 Completed by Furness,Withy & Co. Ltd,Hartlepool for Neptune S.N. Co. Ltd(F.W. Bolam),Sunderland. 1910 Taken over by Furness,Withy & Co. Ltd. 20.4.1918 Torpedoed and sunk 20 miles NW1/2W of South Stack Rock by U91 o.v. Cartagena to Clyde with iron ore.

FO11.MALVERN RANGE (1910 - 1913) 3573g 2326n 347' x 47'
T 3-cyl by Richardsons,Westgarth & Co. Ltd,Hartlepool.
5.1906 Completed by Furness,Withy & Co. Ltd,Hartlepool for Neptune S.N. Co. Ltd(F.W. Bolam),Sunderland. 1910 Taken over by

Furness, Withy & Co. Ltd. 1913 Sold to West Russian S.S. Co. Ltd,St. Petersburg ren. ZIMORODOK. WWI under The Shipping Controller(Ellermans Wilson Line,mgr). 1920 Sold to Ornis S.S. Co. Ltd(Glover Bros) name u/ch. 1930 Sold to E.N. Vassilikos, Syra ren. ERMOUPOLIS. 9.1931 Stranded,refloated and B/U.

FO12.NORFOLK RANGE (1910 - 1913) 3054g 1936n   325' x 47'
T 3-cyl by Richardsons,Westgarth & Co. Ltd,Hartlepool.
10.1905 Completed by Irvines SB & DD Co. Ltd,Hartlepool for Neptune S.N. Co. Ltd(F.W. Bolam),Sunderland. 1910 Taken over by Furness, Withy & Co. Ltd). 1913 Sold to Tempus S.S. Co. Ltd(W. Seager), Cardiff ren. CAMPUS. 1919 Sold to St. David's Nav. Co. Ltd(E.L. & F.P. Williams),Cardiff ren. MARSHAL PLUMER. 1921 Sold to St. Mary S.S. Co. Ltd(Williams Bros),Cardiff ren. BROOKWAY. 1924 Sold to Awanokuni Kyodo Kisen K.K. ren. TSURUGISAN MARU. 1938 Respelt TURUGISAN MARU. 27.10.1942 Sunk by U.S. aircraft in position 4-13 S, 152-11 E off Bougainville.

FO13.PENNINE RANGE (1910 - 1913) 3397g 2214n   345' x 47'
T 3-cyl by G. Clark Ltd,Sunderland.
10.1903 Completed by J.L. Thompson & Sons Ltd,Sunderland for Neptune S.N. Co. Ltd(F.W. Bolam),Sunderland. 1910 Taken over by Furness, Withy & Co. Ltd. 1913 Sold to Tempus S.S. Co. Ltd(W. Seager), Cardiff ren. DARIUS. 13.6.1917 Torpedoed and sunk by U54 210 miles SW of Fastnet o.v. Villaricos to Tyne with iron ore,15 lost.

FO14.SNOWDON RANGE (1910 - 1913) 3060g 1939n   325' x 47'
T 3-cyl by Richardsons,Westgarth & Co. Ltd,Hartlepool.
1906 Completed by Irvines SB & DD Co. Ltd,Hartlepool for Neptune S.N. Co. Ltd(F.W. Bolam),Sunderland. 1910 Taken over by Furness, Withy & Co. Ltd. 1913 Sold to West Russian S.S. Co. Ltd,St. Petersburg ren. WORON. 24.10.1917 Torpedoed and sunk in North Sea.

FO15.BRANTFORD(2) (1910 - 1915) 4113g 2656n   365' x 51'
T 3-cyl by Richardsons,Westgarth & Co. Ltd,Sunderland.
4.1910 Completed by Northumberland SB Co. Ltd,Howdon-on-Tyne for Neptune S.N. Co. Ltd(Furness,Withy & Co. Ltd). 1915 Sold to Bay S.S. Co. Ltd,London ren. BAYFORD. 1920 Sold to French Govt. name u/ch. 1921 Sold to Cie Maritime de Nav a Vapeurs ren. PORT DE LA PALLICE. 1925 Sold to M.D. Diacakis,Syra ren. MARIA M. DIACAKIS. 1934 Ren. PENTE ADELPHI. 1935 Sold to C.N. & E.N. Pateras,Chios ren. NICOLAS PATERAS. 25.6.1941 Torpedoed and sunk by U108 to S of Greenland in posn. 55N, 38W o.v. Liverpool to Father Point in ballast.

FO16.CHEVIOT RANGE (1910 - 1913) 3458g 2178n   345' x 47'
T 3-cyl by N.E. Marine Eng. Co. Ltd,Sunderland.
11.1903 Completed by Sunderland SB Co. Ltd,Sunderland for Neptune S.N. Co. Ltd(F.W. Bolam),Newcastle. 1910 Purchased by Furness, Withy & Co. Ltd. 1913 Sold to M.U.Martinolich & Co,Lusinpicio, Italy,ren. FEDORA. 1931 B/U.

FO17.CLEVELAND RANGE (1910 - 1913) 3534g 2228n   340' x 46'
T 3-cyl by T. Richardson & Co.,Hartlepool.
1898 Completed by Hawthorn,Leslie & Co. Ltd,Hebburn as HEATHDENE
for J.T. Lunn & Co.,Newcastle. 1898 Sold to the Forest Oak Steam
Shipping Co. Ltd(H.Sherwood,mgr),Newcastle ren. FOREST DALE. 1910
Purchased by Neptune S.N. Co. Ltd(Furness,Withy & Co. Ltd,mgr)
ren. CLEVELAND RANGE. 1913 Sold to Fratelli Gavarone,Italy ren.
GIUSEPPE G. 1917 Sold to Soc. Anon. Ilva,Italy. 1918 Sold to
Lloyd Mediterranean Soc. Italiana di Nav,Italy. 24.7.1918 Sunk by
explosion,cause unknown, off Cape Polonio,Uruguay o.v. Buenos
Aires to Rio de Janeiro with wheat and oats.

FO18.CHILTERN RANGE (1911 - 1914) 4346g 2718n   380' x 49'
T 3-cyl by Richardsons,Westgarth & Co. Ltd,Sunderland.
12.1911 Completed by Northumberland SB Co. Ltd,Howdon-on-Tyne for
Neptune S.N. Co. Ltd(Furness,Withy & Co. Ltd). 1914 Sold to
Norwegian America Line ren. DRAMMENSFJORD. 1924 Sold to Turnbull
Coal & Shipping Co. Ltd,Cardiff ren. RAISDALE. 1933 Sold to L.A.
Embiricos,Andros ren. RINOS. 1937 Sold to V.K. Song,Tsingtao ren.
YONG SHJANG. 1938 Sold to Kyodo Kaiun K.K,Tokyo ren. EISYO MARU.
5.6.1940 Sunk after collision near Muroran in dense fog o.v.
Muroran to Tokyo.

FO19.COTSWOLD RANGE (1912 - 1914) 4248g 2777n   380' x 49'
T 3-cyl by N.E. Marine Eng. Co. Ltd,Newcastle.
3.1912 Completed by Northumberland SB Co. Ltd,Howdon-on-Tyne
for Neptune S.N. Co. Ltd(Furness,Withy & Co. Ltd). 1914 Sold
to Norwegian America Line ren. TRONDHJEMSFJORD. 28.7.1915
Torpedoed and sunk in posn. 61-08 N, 3-27 W o.v. New York to
Bergen with general.

FO20.CHEVIOT RANGE(2) (1914 - 1918) 3691g 2303n   350' x 51'
T 3-cyl by Richardsons,Westgarth & Co. Ltd,Hartlepool.
10.1914 Completed by Irvines SB & DD Co. Ltd,Hartlepool for Neptune
S.N. Co. Ltd(Furness,Withy & Co. Ltd). 21.2.1918 Torpedoed and sunk 25
miles S of Lizard by U102 o.v. Tuticorin to U.K. with general,all
lost.

FO21.HAMBLETON RANGE (1914 - 1923) 4779g 3580n   350' x 51'
T 3-cyl by Richardsons,Westgarth & Co. Ltd,Hartlepool.
7.1914 Completed by Irvines SB & DD Co. Ltd,Hartlepool for Neptune
S.N. Co. Ltd(Furness,Withy & Co. Ltd). 1923 Sold to E.J. Leslie,
Hartlepool. 1926 Ren. SCOTSCRAIG,same owner. B/U in 1933.

FO22.MENDIP RANGE   (1914 - 1920) 4495g 2866n   385' x 52'
T 3-cyl by Richardsons,Westgarth & Co. Ltd,Sunderland.
1914 Completed by Northumberland SB Co. Ltd,Howdon-on-Tyne for Neptune
S.N. Co. Ltd(Furness,Withy & Co. Ltd). 1920 Sold to Anglo-Celtic
Shipping Co. Ltd(Griffiths,Payne & Co),London ren. ARCHMEL. 1935 Sold
to Cardigan Shpg. Co. Ltd(Walter T. Gould),Cardiff ren.GRELROSA.
28.4.1941 Bombed and sunk off N.W. Ireland in posn. 55-12 N,15-41W
o.v. New York and Halifax to Tyne with wheat,5 lost.

FO23.PENTLAND RANGE (1915) 4500g 2850n   400' x 52'
T 3-cyl by Richardsons,Westgarth & Co. Ltd,Sunderland
1915 Completed by Northumberland SB Co. Ltd,Howdon-on-Tyne for
Neptune S.N. Co. Ltd(Furness,Withy & Co. Ltd). 1915 Sold to
Russian Volunteer Fleet ren. KRASNOIARSK. 1916 To The Shipping
Controller(Royal Mail,mgr). 1922 Sold to St. Mary S.S. Co.
Ltd(Williams Bros),Cardiff ren. EASTWAY. 22.10.1926 Foundered in
Atlantic o.v. Norfolk(VA) to Pernambuco with coal.

FO24.CLEVELAND RANGE(2) (1915 - 1916) 3580g 2275n 344' x 45'
T 3-cyl by J. Dickinson & Sons Ltd,Sunderland.
1897 Completed by Bartram & Son,Sunderland as KIRKLEE for Kirklee
S.S. Co. Ltd(J.R. Cuthbertson),Glasgow. 1915 Purchased by Neptune
S.N. Co. Ltd(Furness, Withy & Co. Ltd. ren. CLEVELAND RANGE. 1916
Sold to Anglo-Belgique Shipping Co. Ltd(Owen & Williams), Liver-
pool ren. CYMRIC VALE. 7.3.1923 Stranded at Naeroeen near Floro
o.v. Rotterdam to Narvik in ballast.

FO25.MALVERN RANGE(2)   (1915 - 1922) 4523g 2839n   380' x 50'
T 3-cyl by Richardsons,Westgarth & Co. Ltd,Sunderland.
7.1915 Completed by J. Priestman & Co. Ltd,Sunderland for Neptune S.N.
Co. Ltd(Furness,Withy & Co. Ltd). 1922 Sold to 'K' S.S. Co. Ltd(Kaye,
Son & Co. Ltd,mgr) ren. KAMBOLE. 29.4.1937 Sold to Barry Shipping Co.
Ltd,Cardiff. 30.4.1937 Sold to Stanhope S.S. Co. Ltd(J.A. Billmeir),
London ren. STANTHORPE. 1938 Sold to O.E. Bertin,China ren. YOLANDE
BERTIN. 1941 Sold to Panamanian Freighters(Wallem & Co),Panama ren.
HONDURAS. 1946 Sold to Cargueros Panamenos S.A(Wallem & Co). 1947 Sold
to E-Hsiang S.S. Co.,China ren FOO HSIANG. 9.11.1953 Arrived Osaka for
B/U.

FO26.SNOWDON RANGE(2)   (1916 - 1917) 4662g 2999n   390' x 52'
T 3-cyl by bldrs.
10.1906 Completed by Scotts SB & Eng. Co. Ltd,Greenock as DALHANNA for
S.S. Dalhanna Co. Ltd(J.M. Campbell & Son),Glasgow. 1915 Sold to C.
Barrie & Sons,Dundee ren. DEN OF KELLY. 1916 Purchased by Neptune S.N.
Co. Ltd(Furness,Withy & Co. Ltd) ren. SNOWDON RANGE. 28.3.1917 Torp-
edoed and sunk 28 miles W of Bardsey Island by UC65 o.v. Philadelphia
to London with wheat and foodstuffs,4 lost.

FO27.KERRY RANGE   (1916 - 1919) 5875g 3798n   400' x 52'
T 3-cyl by Richardsons,Westgarth & Co. Ltd,Sunderland.
2.1916 Completed by Northumberland SB Co. Ltd,Howdon-on-Tyne for
Neptune S.N. Co. Ltd(Furness,Withy & Co. Ltd). 1919 Sold to Steam Nav.
Co. Ltd of Canada,Montreal ren. BLOSSOM HEATH. 1922 Sold to Jugoslov-
ensko Amerikaniska Plovidba,Split ren. VOJVODA PUTNIK. 12.4.1942
Struck bottom and beached 2 miles E of Hen & Chickens L.V.,Buzzards
Bay o.v. New York to Hull with general. 27.4.1942 Refloated and dry-
docked in New York for repairs. 23.2.1943 Sailed from New York for
Loch Ewe o.v. Bahia Blanca to London and disappeared.

FO28.CAMBRIAN RANGE   (1916) 4234g 2740n   385' x 50'
T 3-cyl by Dunsmuir & Jackson Ltd,Glasgow.
10.1906 Completed by A. Rodger & Co.,Port Glasgow as CROWN for William
Thomas Liverpool S.S. Co. Ltd(W.Thomas,Sons & Co. Ltd),Liverpool. 1916

Purchased by Neptune S.N. Co. Ltd(Furness,Withy & Co. Ltd) ren.
CAMBRIAN RANGE. 9.12.1916 Captured and sunk by bombs by raider MOEWE
610 miles SE of Cape Race, crew taken prisoner.

FO29.ALPINE RANGE (1917 - 1924) 3621g 2252n   349' x 46'
T 3-cyl by Dunsmuir & Jackson Ltd,Glasgow.
12.1907 Completed by C.Connell & Co.,Glasgow as KINTAIL for S.S.
Kincraig Co. Ltd(J. Gardiner),Glasgow. 1917 Purchased by Neptune
S.N. Co. Ltd(Furness,Withy & Co. Ltd) ren. ALPINE RANGE. 1924
Sold to B.Bruskos,Hydra ren. AKROPOLIS. 1925 Sold to Cie Dens-
Ocean S.A., Antwerp ren. COMTE DE FLANDRE. 1936 B/U at Hendrik-
Ido-Ambacht.

FO30.PENTLAND RANGE(2)   (1917 - 1918) 3707g 2382n 349' x 46'
T 3-cyl by Dunsmuir & Jackson Ltd,Glasgow.
11.1901 Completed by C. Connell & Co.,Glasgow as KINCRAIG for
S.S. Kincraig Co. Ltd(J. Gardiner),Glasgow. 1917 Purchased by
Neptune S.N. Co. Ltd(Furness,Withy & Co. Ltd) ren. PENTLAND
RANGE. 4.9.1918 Foundered off River Plate o.v. from Rosario to
U.K. with grain.

FO31.NORFOLK RANGE(2)   (1918 - 1923) 5120g 3017n   375' x 51'
T 3-cyl by N.E. Marine Eng. Co. Ltd,Sunderland.
1.1918 Completed by Northumberland SB Co. Ltd,Howdon-on-Tyne for
Neptune S.N. Co. Ltd(Furness,Withy & Co. Ltd). 1923 Sold to
Stockholms Rederi A/B Svea(H.Ericson),Stockholm ren. SVEADROTT.
11.1924 Stranded, refloated and scrapped.

FO32.GRAMPIAN RANGE(2) (1918 - 1921) 4767g See MANCHESTER SPINNER

FO33.SIDLAW RANGE   (1918 - 1922) 4407g 2705n   371' x 50'
T 3-cyl by bldrs.
1.1918 Completed by New Waterway SB Co.,Schiedam for Neptune S.N. Co.
Ltd(Furness,Withy & Co. Ltd). 1922 Sold to 'K' S.S. Co. Ltd(Kaye, Son
& Co. Ltd),London ren. KAMIR. 1934 Sold to Tramp Shipping Development
Co. Ltd and Lemos & Co.(Rethymnis & Kulukundis,mgr),Greece ren.
KYRIAKOULA. 26.2.1941 Sunk during an air attack SW of Rockall o.v.
Liverpool to Halifax in ballast. Crew of 28 saved.

APPENDIX FP. PACIFIC STEAM NAVIGATION CO. LTD

FP1. SARMIENTO   (1965 - 1969) 6393g 3743n   448' x 62'
8-cyl 2SCDA oil engine by bldr.
10.1945 Completed by Harland & Wolff Ltd,Belfast for Pacific Steam
Navigation Company,Liverpool. 1965 P.S.N.C. purchased by Furness,
Withy & Co. Ltd. 1969 Sold to Monomachos Cia Nav SA,Greece ren.
MONOMACHOS. 1970 Sold to Eagle Ocean Shpg.Co, Famagusta ren.
GLADIATOR. 28.2.1971 Left Havana for Shanghai for B/U.

FP2. SALAMANCA   (1965 - 1967) 6704g 3923n   440' x 62'
8-cyl 2SCDA oil engine by bldr.
1948 Completed by Harland & Wolff Ltd,Belfast for Pacific Steam
Navigation Company,Liverpool. 1965 P.S.N.C. purchased by Furness,

Withy & Co. Ltd. 1967 Sold to El Chaco Cia Nav SA,Panama ren.
KRONOS. 17.10.1972 Left Singapore for Shanghai for B/U.

FP3. SALINAS　　　　(1965 - 1967) 6705g 3923n　　440' x 62'
8-cyl 2SCDA oil engine by bldr.
11.1947 Completed by Harland & Wolff Ltd,Belfast for Pacific Steam
Navigation Company,Liverpool. 1956 Store ship at Suez during Canal
crisis. 1965 P.S.N.C purchased by Furness,Withy & Co. Ltd. 1967
Sold to Polyfimos Cia Nav SA,Piraeus ren. POLYFIMOS. 6.12.1972
Left Singapore for Shanghai for B/U.

FP4. SALAVERRY　　　　(1965 - 1967) 6647g 3879n　　440' x 62'
8-cyl 2SCDA oil engine by bldr.
8.1946 Completed by Harland & Wolff Ltd,Belfast for Pacfic Steam
Navigation Company,Liverpool. 1965 P.S.N.C. purchased by Furness,
Withy & Co. Ltd. 1967 Sold to Detabi Cia Nav SA, Piraeus ren.
PELIAS. 12.12.1972 Sank 250 miles S of Durban after engine room
leak o.v. Maceio to Saigon,crew saved.

FP5. SANTANDER　　　　(1965 - 1967) 6648g 3879n　　440' x 62'
8-cyl 2SCDA oil engine by bldr.
5.1946 Completed by Harland & Wolff Ltd,Belfast for Pacific Steam
Navigation Company,Liverpool. 1965 P.S.N.C. purchased by Furness,
Withy & Co. Ltd. 1967 Sold to Navmachos S.S. Co., Famagusta ren.
NAVMACHOS. 9.12.1971 Sold for B/U at Villaneuva y Geltru,Spain.

FP6. REINA DEL MAR　(1965 - 1973) 20750g 8260n　　560' x 78'
2 Parsons turbines DR geared to 2 screws by bldr.
7.6.1955 Launched and 4.1956 completed by Harland & Wolff Ltd,
Belfast for Pacific Steam Navigation Company,Liverpool. 10.3.1964
Arrived Belfast for conversion into cruise liner, painted in
Union-Castle colours and under their management. 9.1973 Sold to
Union-Castle Mail S.S. Co. Ltd. 30.7.1975 Arrived Kaohsiung for
B/U.

FP7. KENUTA　　　　(1965 - 1971) 8494g 4501n　　489' x 66'
3 Steam turbines DR geared to 1 shaft by Parsons Marine.
8.1950 Completed by Greenock Dockyard Co. Ltd,Greenock for Pacific
Steam Navigation Company,Liverpool. 1965 P.S.N.C. purchased by
Furness,Withy & Co. Ltd. 1971 B/U at Antwerp.

FP8. FLAMENCO　　　　(1965 - 1966) 8491g 4504n　　489' x 66'
3 Steam turbines DR geared to 1 shaft by Parsons Marine.
12.1950 Completed by Greenock Dockyard Co. Ltd,Greenock for Pacific
Steam Navigation Company,Liverpool. 1965 P.S.N.C. purchased by
Furness,Withy & Co. Ltd. 1966 Sold to Cia de Nav Abeto SA ren.
PACIFIC ABETO. 31.8.1976 Laid-up at Jakarta by P.T. Perusahaan
Pelarayan Arafat. 22.8.1981 Arrived Chittagong for B/U.

FP9. POTOSI　　　　(1965 - 1972) 8564g 4556n　　489' x 66'
3 Steam turbines DR geared to 1 shaft by Parsons Marine.
23.2.1955 Launched and 1955 completed by Greenock Dockyard Co. Ltd,
Greenock for Pacific Steam Navigation Company,Liverpool. 1965

P.S.N.C. purchased by Furness,Withy & Co. Ltd. 1972 Sold to Gran-
vias Oceanicos Armadora SA,Piraeus ren. KAVO PIERATIS. 10.1976 Sold
for B/U at Santander.

FP10. PIZARRO   (1965 - 1972) 8564g 4556n   489' x 66'
3 Steam turbines DR geared to 1 shaft by Parsons Marine.
10.1955 Completed by Greenock Dockyard Co. Ltd,Greenock for Pacific
Steam Navigation Company,Liverpool. 1965 P.S.N.C. purchased by
Furness,Withy & Co. Ltd. 1972 Sold to Nav Progesivos SA,Piraeus
ren. KAVO MALEAS. 11.1974 B/U at Kaohsiung.

FP11. COTOPAXI   (1965 - 1972) 8559g 4552n   489' x 66'
3 Steam turbines DR geared to 1 shaft by Parsons Marine.
4.1954 Completed by Greenock Dockyard Co. Ltd,Greenock for Pacific
Steam Navigation Company,Liverpool. 1965 P.S.N.C. purchased by
Furness,Withy & Co. Ltd. 1972 Sold to Transportes Mundiales
Armadora SA,Piraeus ren. KAVO LONGOS. 11.1975 B/U in China.

FP12. ELEUTHERA   (1965 - 1971) 5407g 2760n   360' x 54'
4-cyl 2SCSA oil engine by Harland & Wolff Ltd,Glasgow.
1959 Completed by Hall,Russell & Co. Ltd,Aberdeen for Pacific
Steam Navigation Company,Liverpool. 1965 P.S.N.C. purchased by
Furness,Withy & Co. Ltd. 1970 Laid-up in Fal. 1971 Sold to
Seahunter Shpg. Co,Famagusta ren. MIMI M. 1974 Sold to Valient Bay
Shpg. Co,Piraeus ren. MARIA. 1.11.1984 Arrived Gadani Beach B/U.

FP13. SOMERS ISLE   (1965 - 1971) 5684g 2995n   360' x 54'
4-cyl 2SCSA oil engine by Harland & Wolff Ltd,Glasgow.
1959 Completed by Harland & Wolff Ltd,Belfast for Pacific Steam
Navigation Company,Liverpool. 1965 P.S.N.C. purchased by Furness,
Withy & Co. Ltd. 1970 Laid-up in Fal. 1971 Sold to Sealord Shpg.
Co,Famagusta ren. ELDINA. 1975 Sold to Commencement Cia Nav SA,
Famagusta ren. COMMENCEMENT. 1982 Ren. CARIBBEAN. 1983 Ren MELPOL.
12.1983 Damaged by fire in English Channel o.v. Lisbon to
Bremen, towed to Le Havre. 12.1983 Arrived Ghent for B/U.

FP14. CIENFUEGOS   (1965 - 1971) 5224g 2760n   360' x 54'
4-cyl 2SCSA oil engine by Harland & Wolff Ltd,Glasgow.
11.1959 Completed by Hall,Russell & Co. Ltd,Aberdeen for Pacific
Steam Navigation Company,Liverpool. 1965 P.S.N.C. purchased by
Furness,Withy & Co. Ltd. 1968 Ren. CHANDELEUR. 1970 Laid-up in
Fal. 1971 Sold to Seacomber Shpg. Co,Famagusta ren. EMMA M. 1974
Sold to Green Bay Shpg. Co,Piraeus ren. LELA. 1981 Sold to West
Asia Shpg. Co,Singapore ren. JETPUR VICEROY. 11.1982 Arrived
Chittagong for B/U.

FP15. OROYA   (1968 - 1970) See ARABIC FS55

FP16. ORITA   (1968 - 1972) See AFRIC FS56

FP17. OROPESA   (1968 - 1970) See ARAMAIC FS57

FP18. WILLIAM WHEELWRIGHT (1965 - 1976) 31320g 16872n   718' x 98'
2 Steam turbines DR geared to 1 shaft by bldr.

7.1960 Completed by Harland & Wolff Ltd,Belfast as a tanker for Pacific Maritime Services Ltd,Liverpool. 1965 Taken over by Furness,Withy & Co. Ltd. 26.12.1975 Aground off Sinoe to S of Monrovia in ballast. 29.12.1975 Refloated,towed to Lisbon. CTL. 10.1976 Arrived Santander for B/U.

FP19. GEORGE PEACOCK   (1965 - 1969) 19153g 11307n 611' x 81'
7-cyl 2SCSA oil engine by bldr.
7.1961 Completed by Harland & Wolff Ltd,Belfast as a tanker for Pacific Maritime Services Ltd,Liverpool. 1965 Taken over by Furness,Withy & Co. Ltd. 1969 Sold to V.J. Vardinoyannis,Piraeus ren. GEORGIOS V. 1981 Sold to Varnicos,Piraeus name u/ch. 9.1991 Still in service.

FP20. ORCOMA   (1966 - 1979) 10300g 6024n   480' x 70'
8-cyl 2SCSA B&W oil engine by bldr.
1966 Completed by Harland & Wolff Ltd,Belfast for Nile S.S. Co. Ltd and chartered to P.S.N.C.(Furness,Withy & Co. Ltd) for 20 years. 1970 British Exhibition ship. 10.1979 Sold to P.T. Samudera Indonesia ren. EK DAYA SAMUDERA. 31.3.1984 Arrived Kaohsiung for B/U.

FP21. ORBITA   (1972 - 1980) 12321g 6798n   530' x 73'
8-cyl 2SCSA B&W oil engine by J.G. Kincaid & Co. Ltd,Greenock.
1972 Completed by Cammell,Laird & Co. Ltd,Birkenhead for Royal Mail Line(P.S.N.C,mgr),Liverpool. 4.1980 Sold to Cia Sud Amer-icana de Vapores,Valparaiso ren. ANDALIEN. 1980 Sold to Wallem & Co,Hong Kong ren. MORNING SUN. 1980 Returned to Sud Americana ren. RUBENS. 9.1991 Still in service.

FP22. ORDUNA   (1973 - 1982) See BEACON GRANGE H60

FP23. ORTEGA   (1973 - 1982) 12321g 6798n   530' x 73'
8-cyl 2SCSA B&W oil engine by J.G. Kincaid & Co. Ltd,Greenock.
7.1973 Completed by Cammell,Laird & Co. Ltd,Birkenhead for Royal Mail Line(P.S.N.C,mgr),Liverpool. 4.1980 Ren. ANDES. 8.1982 Sold to Blue Haven Co. Ltd,Hong Kong ren. OCEANHAVEN. 1987 Sold to Pacific International Lines,Singapore ren. KOTA AKBAR. 8.3.1989 Beached on fire at Singapore. 11.6.1989 Towed to Singapore and repaired. 9.1991 Still in service.

FP24. OROYA(2)   (1978 - 1986) 14275g 7971n 535' x 75'
6-cyl 2SCSA Sulzer oil engine by Scotts Eng. Co. Ltd,Greenock.
4.1978 Completed by Lithgows Ltd,Port Glasgow for Ardgowan Shpg. Co. Ltd(Furness,Withy(Shipping) Ltd) for P.S.N.C. route. 9.9.1986 Sold to Nigerian Green Line ren. YINKA FOLAWAYO. 8.1989 Sold to Cenargo Ltd,London ren. MERCHANT PREMIER. 9.1991 Still in service.

FP25. OROPESA(2)   (1978 - 1984) 14124g 8753n   535' x 75'
6-cyl 2SCSA Sulzer oil engine by Scotts Eng. Co. Ltd,Greenock.
4.1978 Completed by Lithgows Ltd,Port Glasgow for Blackhall Shpg. Co. Ltd(Furness,Withy(Shipping) Ltd) for P.S.N.C. route. 25.5.1984 Sold to Cenargo Ltd,London ren. MERCHANT PRINCIPAL. 9.1991 Still in service.

FR1. ANDES   (1965 - 1971) 26689g 14787n   669' x 83'
6 Steam turbines SR geared to 2 screw shafts by bldr.
7.3.1939 Launched and 9.1939 completed by Harland & Wolff Ltd,
Belfast for Royal Mail Line,London. Immediately converted to
troopship, first voyage to Halifax(NS). 9.1945 Returned to Oslo
the Norwegian Government in exile. 22.1.1948 First voyage to
Buenos Aires from Southampton after reconditioning at Belfast.
1959/60 Rebuilt by De Schelde at Flushing as a cruise ship. 1965
Taken over by Furness,Withy & Co. Ltd. 7.5.1971 Arrived Ghent for
B/U.

FR2. DESEADO   (1965 - 1968) 9641g 5773n   470' x 65'
Two 6-cyl 2SCDA oil engines by bldr,2-screw.
17.3.1942 Launched and 11.1942 completed by Harland & Wolff Ltd,
Belfast for Royal Mail Line,London. 1965 Royal Mail purchased by
Furness,Withy & Co. Ltd. 7.1967 Laid-up at Belfast. 1968 B/U at
Hamburg.

FR3. DARRO   (1965 - 1967) 9733g 5725n   470' x 65'
Two 6-cyl 2SCDA oil engines by bldr,2-screw.
21.11.1942 Launched and 6.1943 completed by Harland & Wolff Ltd,
Belfast for Royal Mail Line,London. 1965 Royal Mail purchased by
Furness,Withy & Co. Ltd. 1967 Sold to Embajada Cia Nav SA,Piraeus
ren. SURREY. 22.11.1967 Left Hong Kong in tow for Kaohsiung B/U.

FR4. DRINA   (1965 - 1966) See ROMANIC FS67

FR5. DURANGO(2)   (1965 - 1967) See RUTHENIC FS70

FR6. LOCH AVON   (1965 - 1967) 8617g 5132n   498' x 66'
3 Steam turbines DR geared to 1 screw shaft by bldr.
27.11.1946 Launched and 9.1947 completed by Harland & Wolff Ltd,
Belfast for Royal Mail Line N. Pacific service. 1965 Royal Mail
purchased by Furness,Withy & Co. Ltd. 1967 Sold to Singapore
Malaysia Overseas Line ren. HONGKONG OBSERVER. 27.5.1973 Arrived
Kaohsiung for B/U.

FR7. LOCH GARTH   (1965 - 1968) 8617g 5132n   498' x 66'
3 Steam turbines DR geared to 1 screw shaft by bldr.
24.9.1946 Launched and 5.1947 completed by Harland & Wolff Ltd,
Belfast for Royal Mail Line N. Pacific service. 1965 Royal Mail
purchased by Furness,Withy & Co. Ltd. 1968 Sold for B/U.

FR8. EBRO   (1965 - 1969) 7784g 4506n   444' x 57'
6-cyl 2SCSA oil engine by bldr.
29.11.1951 Launched and 6.1952 completed by Harland & Wolff Ltd,
Govan for Royal Mail Line. 1965 Royal Mail purchased by Furness,
Withy & Co. Ltd. 1969 Sold to Fortune Maritime,Hong Kong ren.
FORTUNE VICTORY. 1970 Sold to Union of Burma Five Star Line,
Rangoon ren. KALEMYO. 12.1978 B/U at Tsingtao.

FR9. ESSEQUIBO   (1965 - 1968) 7791g 4513n   444' x 57'
6-cyl 2SCSA oil engine by bldr.
25.3.1952 Launched and 9.1952 completed by Harland & Wolff Ltd,
Govan for Royal Mail Line. 1965 Royal Mail purchased by Furness,
Withy & Co. Ltd. 1968 Sold to China Nav. Co. Ltd,Hong Kong ren.
NINGPO. 1970 Sold to Union of Burma Five Star Line,Rangoon ren.
KALEWA. 15.3.1976 Arrived Shanghai for B/U.

FR10. ESCALANTE   (1965 - 1970) 7791g 4483n   444' x 57'
6-cyl 2SCSA oil engine by bldr.
5.7.1955 Launched and 12.1955 completed by Harland & Wolff Ltd,
Govan for Royal Mail Line. 1965 Royal Mail purchased by Furness,
Withy & Co. Ltd. 1970 Sold to Marescencia Cia de Nav SA,Panama
ren. MANES P. 2.2.1970 Grounded on rock breakwater at St. John
(NB). Total loss.

FR11. EDEN   (1965 - 1969) 7791g 4464n   444' x 57'
6-cyl 2SCSA oil engine by bldr.
19.10.1955 Launched and 2.1956 completed by Harland & Wolff Ltd,
Belfast for Royal Mail Line. 1965 Royal Mail purchased by Furness,
Withy & Co. Ltd. 1969 Sold to Neptune Orient Lines, Singapore ren.
NEPTUNE GARNET. 24.6.1979 Left Bangkok for Kaohsiung B/U.

FR12. LOCH GOWAN   (1965 - 1970) 9718g 5549n   503' x 68'
Steam turbine DR geared to 1 screw shaft by bldr.
19.1.1954 Launched and 6.1954 completed by Harland & Wolff Ltd,
Belfast for Royal Mail Line on joint service to N. Pacific ports
with Holland America Line. 1965 Royal Mail purchased by Furness,
Withy & Co. Ltd. 1970 B/U at Kaohsiung.

FR13. LOCH LOYAL   (1965 - 1971) 11035g 6447n   503' x 68
Steam turbine DR geared to 1 screw shaft by bldr.
9.8.1957 Launched and 12.1957 completed by Harland & Wolff Ltd,
Belfast for Royal Mail Line on joint N. Pacific service with
Holland America Line. 1965 Royal Mail purchased by Furness, Withy
& Co. Ltd. 10.1969 Disabled by engine room fire. 1971 Sold to
Aeakos Cia Nav SA(Papalios),Piraeus ren. AEGIS LOYAL. 10.1974
Arrived Shanghai for B/U.

FR14. TUSCANY(2)   (1965 - 1970) 7455g 4102n   440' x 58'
6-cyl 2SCSA oil engine by bldr.
21.6.1956 Launched and 10.1956 completed by Harland & Wolff Ltd,
Govan for Royal Mail Line. 1965 Royal Mail purchased by Furness,
Withy & Co. Ltd. 1970 Sold to Random Ltd(J.& J. Denholm) ren.
FEDERAL HUDSON. 1973 Sold to Goldtopps Nav SA,Panama ren. GOLDEN
KING. 1975 Sold to Chaffinch Shpg. SA,Panama ren. CHAR HSIUNG.
8.1980 Arrived Kaohsiung for B/U.

FR15. THESSALY   (1965 - 1971) 7299g 4036n   440' x 58'
6-cyl 2SCSA oil engine by bldr.
29.5.1957 Launched and 9.1957 completed by Harland & Wolff Ltd,
Govan for Royal Mail Line. 1965 Royal Mail purchased by Furness,
Withy & Co. Ltd. 1971 Sold to Union S.S. Co,Monrovia ren. JAPAN.

1976 Sold to Li-Ta Shpg. Co,Singapore ren. LIHO. 3.1979 Arrived Kaohsiung for B/U.

FR16. PICARDY   (1965 - 1971) 7306g 4028n   440' x 58'
6-cyl 2SCSA oil engine by bldr.
30.4.1957 Launched and 8.1957 completed by Harland & Wolff Ltd, Belfast for Royal Mail Line. 1965 Royal Mail purchased by Furness, Withy & Co. Ltd. 1971 Sold to Union S.S. Co,Monrovia ren. EUROPE. 1976 Sold to Li-Ta Shpg. Co,Singapore ren. LIRA. 18.8.1977 Caught fire and sank in Indian Ocean in posn. 7-30 N, 71-32 E o.v. Penang to Rotterdam.

FR17. ALBANY   (1965 - 1971) 7299g 4026n   440' x 58'
6-cyl 2SCSA oil engine by bldr.
1.11.1956 Launched and 2.1957 completed by Harland & Wolff Ltd, Govan for Royal Mail Line. 1965 Royal Mail purchased by Furness, Withy & Co. Ltd. 1971 Sold to Union S.S. Co,Monrovia ren. TAIWAN. 1976 Sold to Li-Ta Shpg. Co,Singapore ren. LIDO. 29.3.1979 Arrived Kaohsiung for B/U.

FR18. AMAZON   (1965 - 1968) See AKAROA   FS73

FR19. ARAGON   (1965 - 1969) See ARANDA   FS75

FR20. ARLANZA   (1965 - 1969) See ARAWA   FS74

FR21. DOURO   (1969 - 1972) See HORNBY GRANGE H41

FR22. DERWENT   (1969 - 1971) See PERSIC   FS46

FR23. LOMBARDY   (1969 - 1971) See CAIRNFORTH   FT13

FR24. DRINA   (1972 - 1978) See CYMRIC   FS50

FR25. DARRO   (1973 - 1977) See CARNATIC FS54

FR26. DESEADO   (1976 - 1980) See IBERIC   FS63

FS1. KIA ORA   (1933 - 1935) 6558g 4168n   448' x 56'
Two Q 4-cyl by bldrs,2-screw.
11.1907 Completed by Workman,Clark & Co. Ltd,Belfast for Shaw,
Savill & Albion Co. Ltd. 1913 On N.Z. - Canada service. 1919
Regular N.Z. - U.K. service via Panama. 1933 SSA purchased by
Furness, Withy & Co. Ltd. 1935 Sold to Ditta Luigi Pittaluga,
Genoa ren. VERBANIA. 10.6.1940 Detained at Port Said and taken as
a prize at Haifa in 7.1940, ren. EMPIRE TAMAR under mgmt. of J.A.
Billmeir. 1944 Mgr. became J. & J. Denholm. 6.1944 Sunk as a
blockship at Normandy.

FS2. KUMARA   (1933 - 1937) 7926g 4845n   450' x 58'
Two T 3-cyl by bldrs,2-screw.
19.12.1918 Launched as WAR PRIAM and 3.1919 completed by Harland &
Wolff Ltd,Belfast as BARDIC for Oceanic S.N. Co. Ltd(White Star).
1921 - 1925 Operated by Atlantic Transport Line. 31.8.1924
Grounded on Stag Rock,Lizard in fog, refloated on 28.9.1924 and
repaired. 8.1925 Transferred to Aberdeen Line ren. HOSTILIUS.
8.1926 Ren. HORATIUS. 1933 Placed with Shaw,Savill & Albion Co.
Ltd ren. KUMARA. 1937 Sold to Marathon S.S. Co(J. Latsis),Greece
ren. MARATHON. 9.3.1941 Sunk by battlecruiser SCHARNHORST to NE of
Cape Verde Islands o.v. Cardiff & Swansea for Freetown & Alexandria, crew taken prisoner.

FS3. OTIRA   (1933 - 1937) 7995g 4911n   450' x 58'
Two T 3-cyl by bldrs,2-screw.
5.5.1919 Launched as WAR PARIS and 4.1919 completed by Harland &
Wolff Ltd,Belfast as OTIRA for Shaw,Savill & Albion Co. Ltd. 'G'
class standard meat carrier. 5.1919 Damaged in fog in collision in
Thames. 1933 SSA taken over by Furness,Withy & Co. Ltd. 5.1937 B/U
at Pola in Italy.

FS4. TAINUI   (1933 - 1939) 9957g 6298n   478' x 61'
Two T 3-cyl by bldr, 2-screw.
11.1908 Completed by Workman,Clark & Co. Ltd,Belfast as TAINUI for
Shaw,Savill & Albion Co. Ltd. 1913 Collided with INCA owned by
P.S.N.C. 8.4.1918 Torpedoed in Approaches to English Channel,
abandoned but reboarded and steamed stern-first 130 miles to
Falmouth and beached. 1933 SSA purchased by Furness,Withy & Co.
Ltd. 3.1939 Sold to shipbreakers and then purchased by Government
shortly after the start of WWII before much had been done towards
her demolition. Placed under Shaw,Savill mgmt. and ren. EMPIRE
TRADER in 1940. 21.2.1943 Torpedoed by U92 in Atlantic in posn.
48-25 N, 30-10 W o.v. Newport & Belfast Lough for New York with
825 tons of chemicals. Abandoned late on 22nd, all 106 crew saved.

FS5. PAKEHA (1933 - 1939) & (1946 - 1950) 10481g 5029n 494' x 63'
Two Q 4-cyl by bldr, 2-screw.
26.5.1910 Launched and 8.1910 completed as PAKEHA for Shaw,Savill
& Albion Co. Ltd by Harland & Wolff Ltd,Belfast. 1933 SSA purchased by Furness,Withy & Co. Ltd. 9.1939 Purchased by Admiralty and
converted into a decoy battleship disguised as HMS REVENGE. 6.1941

Converted back to merchantman with cruiser stern retained from decoy, placed under Shaw,Savill mgmt. as EMPIRE PAKEHA. 1946 Repurchased by Shaw,Savill & Albion Co. Ltd ren. PAKEHA and chartered to Ministry of Food as a meat storage hulk in the Thames. 5.1950 Arrived Briton Ferry for B/U.

FS6. WAIMANA (1933 - 1939) & (1946 - 1952) 10389g 5020n 494' x 63' Two T 3-cyl by bldr, 2-screw.
11.9.1911 Launched and 11.1911 completed by Workman,Clark & Co. Ltd,Belfast as WAIMANA for Shaw,Savill & Albion Co Ltd. 16.10.1914 Sailed from Wellington with New Zealand troops, landed at Egypt for Gallipoli campaign. 1915 On S. American meat service. 1926 Chartered to Aberdeen Line ren. HERMINIUS. 1932 Reverted to SSA ren. WAIMANA. 1933 SSA purchased by Furness,Withy & Co. Ltd. 9.1939 Purchased by Admiralty while laid-up in Gareloch for conversion into a decoy battleship disguised as HMS RESOLUTION and anchored in Firth of Forth. 1942 Reconverted on the Tyne to merchantman ren. EMPIRE WAIMANA. 1946 Repurchased by Shaw,Savill & Albion Co. Ltd ren. WAIMANA. 2.1951 Towed the disabled propellerless 'Liberty' SAN LEONARDO 300 miles to Melbourne. 27.1.1952 Arrived Milford Haven for B/U.

FS7. MAMARI　　(1933 - 1939) 10098g 5058n　　　　494' x 63' Two Q 4-cyl by bldr, 2-screw.
29.6.1911 Launched and 10.1911 completed by Harland & Wolff Ltd, Belfast as ZEALANDIC for Oceanic S.N. Co. Ltd(White Star). 1926 Chartered to Aberdeen Line ren. MAMILIUS. 1932 Placed with Shaw, Savill & Albion Co. Ltd ren. MAMARI. 1933 SSA purchased by Furness,Withy & Co. Ltd. 9.1939 Purchased by Admiralty while laid-up for conversion into a dummy aircraft carrier disguised as HMS HERMES. 3.6.1941 While still disguised, ran on to the wreck of tanker AHAMO 8621/26 en-route to Chatham Dockyard off Norfolk coast. Salvage attempts failed and she was torpedoed the next day by E-boats settling in an upright position with flight deck above water. Subsequently used by East Coast convoys for target practice and then blown up.

FS8. RARANGA　　(1933 - 1950) 10040g 5010n　　　　494' x 63' Two Q 4-cyl by N.E. Marine Eng. Co. Ltd,Wallsend, 2-screw.
12.1916 Completed by Armstrong,Whitworth & Co. Ltd,Newcastle as RARANGA for Shaw,Savill & Albion Co. Ltd. 26.6.1918 Torpedoed in English Channel but reached port safely. 1933 SSA purchased by Furness,Withy & Co. Ltd. 25.3.1941 Rescued 57 survivors from the Anchor liner BRITANNIA sunk by a raider off W. Africa in posn. 7-24 N, 24-3 W. 1950 B/U at Blyth.

FS9. MAHANA　　(1933 - 1953) 11796g 5422n　　　　521' x 63' 4 Steam turbines SR geared to 2 screw shafts by bldr.
11.1.1917 Launched and 7.1917 completed by Workman,Clark & Co. Ltd,Belfast as MAHANA for Shaw,Savill & Albion Co. Ltd. 1933 SSA purchased by Furness,Withy & Co. Ltd. 1949 Chartered by Ministry of Food as frozen meat store ship. 1.6.1953 Arrived Dalmuir for B/U.

FS10. MAHIA (1933 - 1953) 10835g 4979n   494' x 63'
Two Q 4-cyl by bldr, 2-screw.
8.1917 Completed by Workman,Clark & Co. Ltd,Belfast as MAHIA for
Shaw,Savill & Albion Co. Ltd. 1930 Aground at Port Royal but came
off undamaged. 1933 SSA purchased by Furness,Withy & Co. Ltd.
16.7.1953 Arrived Faslane for B/U.

FS11. TAIROA (1933 - 1939) 10040g 5021n   494' x 63'
Two Q 4-cyl by N.E. Marine Eng. Co. Ltd,Wallsend, 2-screw.
7.1920 Completed by Armstrong,Whitworth & Co. Ltd,Newcastle as
TAIROA for Shaw,Savill & Albion Co. Ltd. 1933 SSA purchased by
Furness,Withy & Co. Ltd. 3.12.1939 Sunk by ADMIRAL GRAF SPEE while
on the return leg of her first wartime voyage to Australia in posn
20-20 S 3 E. She had called at Durban on her way from Brisbane
with meat,wool,lead and general. Crew transferred to ALTMARK.

FS12. MATAKANA (1933 - 1940) 10101g 5022n   494' x 63'
6 Steam turbines DR geared to 2 screw shafts by bldrs.
6.1921 Completed by A. Stephen & Sons Ltd,Glasgow for Shaw,Savill
& Albion Co. Ltd. 1933 SSA purchased by Furness,Withy & Co. Ltd.
5.1939 Laid-up at Falmouth,recommissioned in 9.1939. 1.5.1940
Wrecked in heavy weather on Plana Cays,Bahamas with some cargo
salved.

FS13. MAIMOA (1933 - 1940) 11291g 5011n   494' x 63'
Two Q 4-cyl by bldr, 2-screw.
9.1920 Completed by Palmers Co. Ltd,Jarrow for Shaw,Savill &
Albion Co. Ltd. 1933 SSA purchased by Furness,Withy & Co. Ltd.
20.11.1940 Sunk by raider PINGUIN in Indian Ocean in posn 31-50 S,
100-21 E o.v. Brisbane & Fremantle for Durban & U.K. with meat,
sugar,lead,steel billets and general.

FS14. KARAMEA (1933 - 1960) 11300g 5148n   499' x 64'
Two 6-cyl 2SCSA Sulzer oil engines by bldr,2-screw.
8.1928 Completed by Fairfield SB & Eng. Co. Ltd,Govan for Shaw,
Savill & Albion Co. Ltd. 1933 SSA purchased by Furness,Withy & Co.
Ltd. 14.10.1939 Escaped from attacking submarine by speed. 2.1941
Bombed and damaged on Australian voyage and given an extensive
refit lasting 321 days with increased refrigerated capacity. 1955
Extensively refitted again. 8.12.1960 Arrived Inverkeithing for
B/U.

FS15. COPTIC (1933 - 1965) 10629g 5221n   499' x 64'
Two 6-cyl 2SCSA Sulzer oil engines by Wallsend Slipway,2-screw.
7.1928 Completed by Swan,Hunter & Wigham Richardson Ltd,Wallsend
for Shaw, Savill & Albion Co. Ltd. 1933 SSA purchased by Furness,
Withy & Co. Ltd. 14.7.1965 Arrived Antwerp for B/U.

FS16. ZEALANDIC (1933 - 1941) 11300g 5219n   499' x 64'
Two 6-cyl 2SCSA Sulzer oil engines by Wallsend Slipway,2-screw.
9.1928 Completed by Swan,Hunter & Wigham Richardson Ltd,Wallsend
for Shaw,Savill & Albion Co. Ltd. 1933 SSA purchased by Furness,
Withy & Co. Ltd. 17.1.1941 Torpedoed and sunk 3 days outward bound

in posn. 58-28 N, 20-43 W o.v. Liverpool for Brisbane with
general, 73 lost.

FS17. TARANAKI (1933 - 1963) 10534g 5140n   499' x 64'
Two 6-cyl 2SCSA Sulzer oil engines by bldr,2-screw.
5.1928 Completed by Fairfield SB & Eng. Co. Ltd,Govan for Shaw,
Savill & Albion Co. Ltd. 1933 SSA purchased by Furness,Withy & Co.
Ltd. 1950 Collided with Union S.S. WAIPATA at entrance to Wellington harbour. 11.9.1963 Arrived Aioi for B/U after completing 71
round voyages from New Zealand and Australia to U.K.

FS18. FORDSDALE (1933 - 1952) 11023g 5647n   520' x 63'
Two Q 4-cyl by bldr, 2-screw.
3.1924 Completed by Commonwealth Dockyard,Sudney(NSW) for Common-
wealth Government Line. 1932 Transferred into Aberdeen & Common-
wealth Line and placed with Shaw,Savill & Albion Co. Ltd. 1933 SSA
Purchased by Furness,Withy & Co. Ltd. 1952 Sold to Audax S.S. Co.
Ltd(C.Y. Tung),Hong Kong ren. OCEAN NEPTUNE. 1954 Sold to Pacific
Union Lines ren. PACIFIC TRADER. 1956 Sold to Atlantic Bulk
Carriers Ltd ren. ATLANTIC CONCORD. 1958 Sold to Chinese Maritime
Trust,Taiwan ren. JUI YUNG. 1959 B/U at Osaka.

FS19. AKAROA   (1933 - 1954) 15316g 9461n   570' x 67'
Two T 3-cyl with L.P. exhaust turbine by bldr, 2-screw.
29.1.1914 Launched and 6.1914 completed by Harland & Wolff Ltd,
Belfast for Aberdeen Line as EURIPIDES. 26.8.1914 Taken over at
Brisbane for Australian Expeditionary Force to Middle East.
11.1920 Resumed Aberdeen Line service. 1929 White Star mgmt. 1932
Placed with Shaw, Savill & Albion Co. Ltd,reburbished by Hawthorn,
Leslie & Co. Ltd at Hebburn,ren. AKAROA. 1933 SSA purchased by
Furness,Withy & Co. Ltd. Troop transport during WWII. 1945 Re-
conditioned on the Tyne. 12.5.1954 Sold to J. de Smedt & Co.,
Antwerp for B/U.

FS20. THEMISTOCLES (1933 - 1947) 11230g 7020n   520' x 63'
Two Q 4-cyl by bldr, 2-screw.
22.9.1910 Launched and 1.1911 completed by Harland & Wolff Ltd,
Belfast for Aberdeen Line. 1928 White Star mgmt. 1932 Placed with
Shaw,Savil & Albion Co. Ltd, and remained on Australian service
and for this reason did not receive a Maori name. 1933 SSA purchased by Furness,Withy & Co. Ltd. 7.1943 Beat off a heavy air
attack. 1946 Laid-up in the Fal after 79 round voyages and
22.8.1947 arrived Dalmuir for B/U.

FS21. MATAROA (1933 - 1957) 12390g 7394n   500' x 63'
4 Steam turbines DR geared to 2 screw shafts by bldr.
2.3.1922 Launched and 7.1922 completed by Harland & Wolff Ltd,
Belfast as DIOGENES for Aberdeen Line. 1926 Chartered by Shaw,
Savill & Albion Co. Ltd ren. MATAROA, and converted to oil-firing
with turbines reconditioned by Wallsend Slipway & Eng. Co. Ltd.
1932 Placed with SSA by the receiver. 1933 SSA purchased by
Furness,Withy & Co. Ltd. 1940 Carried Post Office censor staff to
Bermuda, and troop transport to S. Africa and then across to S.

America for meat. 1.1949 On fire in forward stokehold 500 miles from Wellington. 29.3.1957 Arrived Faslane for B/U.

FS22. TAMAROA (1933 - 1957) 12375g 7394n   500' x 63'
4 Steam turbines DR geared to 2 screw shafts by bldr.
22.9.1921 Launched and 2.1922 completed by Harland & Wolff Ltd, Belfast as SOPHOCLES for Aberdeen Line. 1926 Chartered by Shaw, Savill & Albion Co. Ltd ren. TAMAROA, and converted to oil-firing with turbines reconditioned by Wallsend Slipway & Eng. Co. Ltd. 1932 Placed with SSA by the receiver. 1933 SSA purchased by Furness,Withy & Co. Ltd. 25.12.1940 On first voyage as a Troop transport convoy was attacked in Atlantic by heavy cruiser ADMIRAL HIPPER, beaten off by HMS BERWICK. 11.1942 One of the first Transports into Bone during North Africa landings. 5.3.1957 Arrived Blyth for B/U.

FS23. ESPERANCE BAY (1933 - 1955) 14343g 8572n   549' x 68'
4 Steam turbines DR geared to 2 screw shafts by bldr.
1.1922 Completed by Vickers Ltd,Barrow as HOBSONS BAY for Commonwealth Government Line,Australia. 1928 Sold to Aberdeen & Commonwealth Line(G. Thompson),London. 4.1933 Mgmt. taken over by SSA, who became largest shareholder of Aberdeen & Commonwealth Line, London. SSA taken over by Furness,Withy & Co. Ltd. 1936 Ren. ESPERANCE BAY. 9.1939 Equipped at Brisbane as A.M.C., commissioned at Cape Town on 23.11.1939. 7.1941 Converted to Troop Transport. 1946 Returned to Australian emigrant trade. 1951 SSA became sole owner. 6.7.1955 Arrived Faslane for B/U.

FS24. JERVIS BAY   (1933 - 1940) 14164g 8547n   549' x 68'
4 Steam turbines DR geared to 2 screw shafts by bldr.
1922 Completed by Vickers Ltd,Barrow for Commonwealth Government Line,Australia. 1928 Sold to Aberdeen & Commonwealth Line(G. Thompson),London. 4.1933 Mgmt. taken over by SSA, who became largest shareholder of Aberdeen & Commonwealth Line,London. SSA taken over by Furness,Withy & Co. Ltd. 1939 Equipped as an A.M.C. at London. 5.11.1940 Shelled and sunk in gallant defence with her eight 6" guns of convoy HX84 of 38 ships against ADMIRAL SCHEER. Capt. E.S. Fogarty Fegen received posthumous V.C.

FS25. LARGS BAY   (1933 - 1957) 14182g 8477n   549' x 68'
4 Steam turbines DR geared to 2 screw shafts by bldr.
12.1921 Completed by W. Beardmore & Co. Ltd,Dalmuir for Commonwealth Government Line,Australia. 1928 Sold to Aberdeen & Commonwealth Line(G. Thompson),London. 4.1933 Mgmt. taken over by SSA, who became largest shareholder of Aberdeen & Commonwealth Line. SSA taken over by Furness,Withy & Co. Ltd. 8.1941 Converted to Troop Transport, served at North Africa and Italy. 2.1.1944 Mined in Approaches to Naples, repaired. 1948 Returned to Australian emigrant service. 1951 SSA became sole owner. 22.8.1957 Arrived Barrow for B/U.

FS26. MORETON BAY   (1933 - 1957) 14376g 8584n   549' x 68'
4 Steam turbines DR geared to 2 screw shafts by bldr.

11.1921 Completed by Vickers Ltd,Barrow for Commonwealth Government Line,Australia. 1928 Sold to Aberdeen & Commonwealth Line (G.Thompson),London. 4.1933 Mgmt. taken over by SSA, who became largest shareholder of Aberdeen & Commonwealth Line. SSA taken over by Furness,Withy & Co. Ltd. 9.1939 Converted to A.M.C. in Australia. 1940 Captured the French liner CUBA running the blockade for Vichy France. 8.1941 Converted to Troop Transport, served at Madagascar,North Africa and Normandy. 1948 Returned to Australian emigrant service. 1951 SSA became sole owner. 13.4.1957 Arrived Barrow for B/U.

FS27. CERAMIC (1934 - 1942) 18495g 11718n
T 3-cyl with L.P. exhaust turbines by bldr, 3-screw.
11.12.1912 Launched and 7.1913 completed by Harland & Wolff Ltd, Belfast for Oceanic S.N. Co. Ltd(White Star). 8.1914 Australian Expeditionary force to Middle East. 5.1916 Missed by torpedo in Mediterranean. 9.6.1917 Missed by torpedo in English Channel. 18.11.1920 First post-WWI sailing Liverpool - Sydney. 1930 Collided with LAGUNA owned by P.S.N.C. 1934 Purchased by Shaw,Savill & Albion Co. Ltd(Furness,Withy & Co. Ltd). 2.1940 Requisitioned as Troop Transport. 23.11.1942 Sailed from Liverpool after refit for Australia but 6.12.1942 torpedoed and sunk by U515 in posn. 40-30 N, 40-20 W with 656 crew and troops lost.

FS28.IONIC (1934 - 1937) 12352g 7623n   500' x 63'
Two Q 4-cyl by bldrs,2-screw.
22.5.1902 Launched and 12.1902 completed by Harland & Wolff Ltd,Belfast for Oceanic S.N. Co. Ltd(White Star). 8.1914 N.Z. Expeditionary force troopship. 31.12.1915 Missed by torpedo in Mediterranean. 31.1.1919 Resumed N.Z. service via Panama. 1934 Purchased by Shaw,Savill & Albion Co. Ltd(Furness, Withy & Co. Ltd), transferred to Norfolk & North American S.S. Co. Ltd. 9.9.1936 Final sailing for New Zealand. 1.1937 Arrived for B/U at Osaka.

FS29. WAIPAWA (1934 - 1967) 12437g 6538n   535' x 70'
Two 10-cyl 4SCSA B&W oil engines by bldr, 2-screw.
28.6.1934 Launched and 10.1934 completed by Harland & Wolff Ltd, Belfast for Shaw,Savill & Albion Co. Ltd(Furness,Withy & Co. Ltd). WWII service included meat transport to troops in Sicily and Italy from New Zealand. 1967 Sold to Astro Protector Cia Nav SA,Greece ren. ARAMIS. 19.3.1967 Arrived Kaohsiung for B/U.

FS30. WAIWERA (1934 - 1942) 12435g 6538n   535' x 70'
TWo 10-cyl 4SCSA B&W oil engines by bldr, 2-screw.
1.5.1934 Launched and 8.1934 completed by Harland & Wolff Ltd, Belfast for Shaw,Savill & Albion Co. Ltd(Furness,Withy & Co. Ltd). 5.1940 Suffered bomb damage at Liverpool,WWII service included one Malta convoy. 29.6.1942 Torpedoed by U754 450 miles from Azores and started circling, torpedoed again and sank o.v. Auckland & Cristobal for Liverpool with foodstuffs, crew picked up Norwegian OREGON EXPRESS.

FS31. WAIRANGI (1935 - 1942) 12437g 6538n   535' x 70'
Two 10-cyl 4SCSA B&W oil engines by bldr, 2-screw.
9.10.1934 Launched and 1.1935 completed by Harland & Wolff Ltd,
Govan for Shaw,Savill & Albion Co. Ltd(Furness,Withy & Co. Ltd).
WWII service included Malta convoys. 13.8.1942 Sunk by escort
during Operation Pedestal to Malta after hit by torpedo 1 mile
from Cape Bon.

FS32. ARAWA   (1936 - 1955) 14491g 8584n   549' x 68'
4 Steam turbines DR geared to 2 screw shafts by bldr.
15.12.1921 Launched and 7.1922 Completed by W. Beardmore & Co. Ltd,
Dalmuir as ESPERANCE BAY for Commonwealth Government Line, Australia. 1928 Sold to Aberdeen & Commonwealth Line(G. Thompson),
London. 4.1933 Mgmt. taken over by SSA, who became largest shareholder of Aberdeen & Commonwealth Line,London. SSA taken over by
Furness,Withy & Co. Ltd. 1934 Aground in Bitter Lake,Suez Canal.
1936 Purchased outright by SSA ren. ARAWA. 24.8.1939 Requisitioned
as A.M.C. in New Zealand and sent to China station. 3.1940 Returned
home for use on U.K. - Freetown convoys. 8.1941 Converted to Troop
Transport,served at North Africa. 8.1945 Re-patriated P.O.W.s from
Black Sea ports to Marseilles, and arrived in Tyne for refit in
12.1945. 7.2.1946 Returned to New Zealand service from London.
21.5.1955 Arrived Newport for B/U.

FS33. WAIMARAMA   (1938 - 1942) 12843g 6532n   535' x 70'
Two 10-cyl 4SCSA B&W oil engines by bldr, 2-screw.
31.5.1938 Launched and 10.1938 completed by Harland & Wolff Ltd,
Belfast for Shaw,Savill & Albion Co. Ltd(Furness,Withy & Co. Ltd).
12.1940 Ammunition voyage to Middle East from New Zealand. 3.1941
Damaged at Alexandria. 13.8.1942 Sunk after hits from 4 bombs
abaft the bridge on Operation Pedestal to Malta, petrol cargo
caught fire, 83 crew & gunners lost.

FS34. WAIOTIRA   (1939 - 1940) 12823g 6537n   535' x 70'
Two 10-cyl 4SCSA B&W oil engines by bldr, 2-screw.
1.8.1939 Launched and 11.1939 completed by Harland & Wolff Ltd,
Belfast for Shaw,Savill & Albion Co. Ltd(Furness,Withy & Co. Ltd).
25.12.1940 Hit by 3 torpedoes from U95 in N. Atlantic o.v. Sydney
to U.K. via Panama with foodstuffs and general, sank on 27th.

FS35.DOMINION MONARCH (1939 - 1962) 27155g 14963n 682' x 85'
Four 5-cyl 2SCSA Doxford oil engines by W. Doxford(2) & bldrs(2).
27.7.1938 Launched and 1.1939 completed by Swan,Hunter & Wigham
Richardson Ltd,Wallsend for Shaw,Savill & Albion Co. Ltd(Furness,
Withy & Co. Ltd). Largest passenger ship built on the Tyne since
the MAURETANIA. 16.2.1939 Maiden voyage on the new Australia and
N.Z. combined service, and 9.1939 continued on New Zealand - U.K.
service, making 2 voyages. 8.1940 Converted to Troop Transport.
12.1941 Escaped from Singapore after hasty re-assembly of
engines. 7.1943 Present at landings in Augusta,Italy. 7.12.1948
Returned to service after 15-month overhaul on Tyneside by
builder. 5.1962 Sold for service as floating hotel at Seattle
World Fair. 25.11.1962 Arrived Osaka for B/U as DOMINION MONARCH
MARU.

FS36. WAIWERA(2)   (1944 - 1967) 12028g 6187n   521' x 70'
Two 6-cyl 2SCDA B&W oil engines by bldr, 2-screw.
30.9.1943 Launched and 11.1944 completed by Harland & Wolff Ltd,
Belfast for Shaw,Savill & Albion Co. Ltd(Furness,Withy & Co. Ltd).
Accomodation for 100 passengers, reduced to 12 in 1950. 1967 Sold
to Embajada Cia Nav,Greece ren. JULIA. 13.1.1968 Arrived Kaohsiung
for B/U.

FS37. WAIRANGI(2)   (1946 - 1963) 12804g 7554n   521' x 70'
Two 6-cyl 2SCDA B&W oil engines by bldr, 2-screw.
25.8.1941 Launched and 4.1942 completed by Harland & Wolff Ltd,
Belfast for Ministry of War Transport(SSA,mgrs) as EMPIRE GRACE.
1946 Ren. WAIRANGI with accomodation for 100 passengers,reduced to
12 in 1950. 14.8.1963 Aground on island of Kloevholmen, 25 miles
from Stockholm while inward bound from Rio Grande, refloated on
26th after part-discharge with severe bottom damage. 26.10.1963
Arrived Faslane for B/U.

FS38. CUFIC   (1947 - 1953) 7176g 4380n   441' x 57'
T 3-cyl by Springfield Mch. & Foundry Co.
11.1943 Completed by New England SB Co,Portland(Me) as SAMRICH for
Ministry of War Transport(SSA,mgrs) having been launched as WILLIAM
PITT PREBLE. 1947 Purchased by SSA(Furness,Withy & Co. Ltd) ren.
CUFIC. 1953 Sold to Italy ren. SANTA ELISABETTA. 1967 Sold ren.
STAR. 17.3.1968 Arrived Kaohsiung for B/U.

FS39. TROPIC   (1947 - 1952) 7176g 4380n   441' x 57'
T 3-cyl by Worthington Pump & Mchy. Co.
11.1943 Completed by Bethlehem-Fairfield SB,Baltimore as SAMSYLVAN
for Ministry of War Transport(SSA,mgrs) having been launched as J.
WHITRIDGE WILLIAMS. 1947 Purchased by SSA(Furness,Withy & Co. Ltd)
ren. TROPIC. 1952 Sold to Italy ren. SAN FRANCESCO. 30.1.1960
Grounded near Hainan Island o.v. Whampoa to Yulin, refloated badly
damaged. 9.6.1960 Foundered in typhoon at Hong Kong while awaiting
B/U, raised and scrapped.

FS40. CORINTHIC   (1947 - 1969) 15682g 9097n   560' x 71'
6 Steam turbines SR geared to 2 screw shafts by bldr.
30.5.1946 Launched and 4.1947 completed by Cammell,Laird & Co.
Ltd,Birkenhead for Shaw, Savill & Albion Co. Ltd(Furness,Withy &
Co. Ltd) after fire damage caused a heavy list on 4.i.1947.
18.2.1965 Final passenger sailing,accomodation removed at Schiedam
cargo-only. 23.10.1969 Arrived Kaohsiung for B/U.

FS41. ATHENIC   (1947 - 1969) 15187g 8722n   560' x 71'
6 Steam turbines SR geared to 2 screw shafts by bldr.
26.11.1946 Launched and 7.1947 completed by Harland & Wolff Ltd,
Belfast for Shaw,Savill & Albion Co. Ltd(Furness,Withy & Co. Ltd).
28.1.1965 Final passenger sailing, reduced to cargo-only by Swan,
Hunter & Wigham Richardson Ltd,Wallsend. 25.10.1969 Arrived
Kaohsiung for B/U.

FS42. CERAMIC(2)   (1948 - 1972) 15896g 9162n   560' x 71'
6 Steam turbines SR geared to 2 screw shafts by bldr.

30.12.1947 Launched and 10.1948 completed by Cammell,Laird & Co. Ltd,Birkenhead for Shaw, Savill & Albion Co. Ltd(Furness,Withy & Co. Ltd). 1951 Stand-by Royal yacht with white hull. 13.6.1972 Arrived Tamise in Belgium for B/U.

FS43. GOTHIC   (1948 - 1969) 15911g 9115n   560' x 71'
6 Steam turbines SR geared to 2 screw shafts by Cammell,Laird.
12.12.1947 Launched and 12.1948 completed by Swan,Hunter & Wigham Richardson Ltd,Wallsend for Shaw,Savill & Albion Co. Ltd(Furness, Withy & Co. Ltd). 8.1951 Chartered to Admiralty as Royal Yacht, sent to Birkenhead for alteration,given white hull. 5.2.1952 Arrived Mombasa to embark Princess Elizabeth for tour of Australia and New Zealand, tour cancelled on death of King. Returned to normal service. 21.11.1953 Arrived Jamaica to embark Royal party for tour of Australia and New Zealand, which lasted until Queen disembarked at Aden on 28.4.1954. 9.1954 Resumed normal service after furniture transferred to BRITANNIA at Malta.
1.8.1968 On fire in officers smoke room and bridge 300 miles E of New Zealand o.v. Bluff to Panama, 7 dead. 10.10.1968 Arrived Liverpool where repairs effected to make one more cargo-only round voyage. 13.8.1969 Arrived Kaohsiung for B/U.

FS44. DORIC   (1949 - 1969) 10674g 6215n   509' x 65'
Two 5-cyl 2SCSA Doxford oil engines by bldr.
12.1948 Launched and 7.1949 completed by Fairfield SB & Eng. Co. Ltd,Govan for Shaw, Savill & Albion Co. Ltd(Furness,Withy & Co. Ltd). 3.5.1969 Arrived Tamise for B/U in Belgium.

FS45. DELPHIC   (1949 - 1971) 10691g 6216n   509' x 65'
Two 5-cyl 2SCSA Doxford oil engines by bldr.
11.1949 Completed by Hawthorn,Leslie & Co. Ltd,Hebburn for Shaw, Savill & Albion Co. Ltd(Furness,Withy & Co. Ltd). 14.8.1971 Arrived Kaohsiung for B/U.

FS46. PERSIC   (1949 - 1969) 13594g 7794n   561' x 72'
6 Steam turbines SR geared to 2 screw shafts by bldr.
11.1949 Completed by Cammell,Laird & Co. Ltd,Birkenhead for Shaw, Savill & Albion Co. Ltd(Furness,Withy & Co. Ltd). 9.1969 Transferred to Royal Mail ren. DERWENT. 25.11.1971 Arrived Bilbao for B/U.

FS47. RUNIC   (1950 - 1961) 13587g 7788n   561' x 72'
6 Steam turbines SR geared to 2 screw shafts by bldr.
21.10.1949 Launched and 3.1950 completed by Harland & Wolff Ltd, Belfast for Shaw,Savill & Albion Co. Ltd(Furness,Withy & Co. Ltd). 19.2.1961 Aground on Middleton Reef, 120 miles N of Lord Howe Island o.v. Brisbane to Auckland, BRIGHTON of Chapman & Willan Ltd,Newcastle stood by until tugs arrived, declared CTL in 3.1961.

FS48. SUEVIC   (1950 - 1974) 13587g 7789n   561' x 72'
6 Steam turbines SR geared to 2 screw shafts by bldr.
7.3.1950 Launched and 7.1950 completed by Harland & Wolff Ltd, Belfast for Shaw,Savill & Albion Co. Ltd(Furness,Withy & Co. Ltd).

18.5.1974 Left Lyttelton for Kaohsiung arrived 6.6.1974, having suffered engine trouble since 1.1974.

FS49. CEDRIC (1952 - 1976) 11232g 6557n 512' x 69'
Two 6-cyl 2SCSA B&W oil engines by bldr.
22.5.1952 Launched and 11.1952 completed by Harland & Wolff Ltd, Belfast for Shaw,Savill & Albion Co. Ltd(Furness,Withy & Co. Ltd). 1976 Sold to Fife Shipping Ltd,Panama ren. SEA CONDOR. 23.1.1977 Aground at Mina Khalid,Sharjah while bound inward from Gydnia. 25.8.1977 Arrived Kaohsiung for B/U.

FS50. CYMRIC (1953 - 1973) 11182g 6518n 512' x 69'
Two 6-cyl 2SCSA B&W oil engines by bldr.
5.11.1952 Launched and 5.1953 completed by Harland & Wolff Ltd, Belfast for Shaw,Savill & Albion Co. Ltd(Furness,Withy & Co. Ltd). 1973 Transferred to Royal Mail Line ren. DURANGO. 18.10.1975 Arrived Kaohsiung for B/U.

FS51. CANOPIC (1954 - 1975) 11166g 6350n 512' x 69'
Two 6-cyl 2SCSA B&W oil engines by Harland & Wolff Ltd,Belfast.
12.1954 Completed by Vickers-Armstrong Ltd,Newcastle for Shaw, Savill & Albion Co. Ltd(Furness,Withy & Co. Ltd). 1975 Sold to Roussos Bros,Cyprus ren. CAPETAN NICOLAS. 26.12.1981 Laid-up at Piraeus. 27.9.1986 Arrived Aliaga for B/U.

FS52. CRETIC (1955 - 1973) 11151g 6344n 512' x 69'
Two 6-cyl 2SCSA Doxford oil engines by Wallsend Slipway.
25.1.1955 Launched and 5.1955 completed by Swan,Hunter & Wigham Richardson Ltd,Wallsend for Shaw,Savill & Albion Co. Ltd(Furness, Withy & Co. Ltd). 1973 Transferred to Royal Mail Line ren. DRINA. 1977 Sold to Rotna Maritime Inc,Singapore ren. UNITED VIGOUR. 23.12.1978 Arrived Kaohsiung for B/U.

FS53.SOUTHERN CROSS (1955 - 1973) 20204g 10327n 604' x 78'
4 Steam turbines DR geared to 2 screw shafts by bldr.
17.8.1954 Launched and 3.1955 completed by Harland & Wolff Ltd, Belfast for Shaw,Savill & Albion Co. Ltd(Furness,Withy & Co. Ltd). 29.3.1955 Maiden voyage on new Round the World service. 1969 Hotel ship at Tokyo. 1.1970 First cruises from Sydney to Pacific islands reflecting the growing aircraft competition on Australia & N.Z. route. 6.1970 Summer cruises(7) from Liverpool. 11.1971 Laid-up at Southampton and then in the Fal. 1973 Sold to Cia de Vapores Cerulea SA(N.& J. Vlassopulos),Panama refitted for cruising at Piraeus ren. CALYPSO. 1980 Sold to Gotaas-Larsen Shipping,Bermuda ren. AZURE SEAS. 9.1991 Still in service.

FS54. CARNATIC (1957 - 1973) 11144g 6343n 512' x 69'
Two 6-cyl 2SCSA B&W oil engines by Harland & Wolff Ltd,Belfast.
1.1957 Completed by Cammell,Laird & Co. Ltd,Birkenhead for Shaw, Savill & Albion Co. Ltd(Furness,Withy & Co. Ltd). 1973 Transferred to Royal Mail Line ren. DARRO. 1977 Sold to Ethymar Shipping Co,Cyprus ren. LITSA. 1979 Sold to P. Perimenis,Piraeus ren. DIMITRA. 25.6.1979 Arrived Kaohsiung for B/U.

FS55. ARABIC   (1956 - 1968) 6553g 3372n   475' x 64'
9-cyl 2SCSA MAN oil engine by bldr.
12.1956 Completed by Bremer Vulcan,Vegesack for Shaw,Savill &
Albion Co. Ltd(Furness,Withy & Co. Ltd). 1968 Transferred to
P.S.N.C. ren. OROYA. 1970 Transferred to Furness,Withy & Co. Ltd
ren. PACIFIC RANGER. 1971 Transferred to P.S.N.C. ren. OROYA. 1972
Sold to Hong Kong Islands Shpg. Co, ren. LAMMA ISLAND. 28.5.1983
Arrived Inchon for B/U.

FS56. AFRIC   (1957 - 1968) 6553g 3372n   475' x 64'
9-cyl 2SCSA MAN oil engine by bldr.
2.1957 Completed by Bremer Vulcan,Vegesack for Shaw,Savill &
Albion Co. Ltd(Furness,Withy & Co. Ltd). 1968 Transferred to
P.S.N.C. ren. ORITA. 1972 Sold to Hong Kong Islands Shpg. Co, ren.
HONG KONG ISLAND. 1.5.1983 Arrived Inchon for B/U.

FS57. ARAMAIC   (1957 - 1968) 6553g 3372n   475' x 64'
9-cyl 2SCSA MAN oil engine by bldr.
4.1957 Completed by Bremer Vulcan,Vegesack for Shaw,Savill &
Albion Co. Ltd(Furness,Withy & Co. Ltd). 1968 Transferred to
P.S.N.C. ren. OROPESA. 1970 Transferred to Furness,Withy & Co. Ltd
ren. PACIFIC EXPORTER. 1970 Transferred to P.S.N.C. ren OROPESA.
1972 Sold to Hong Kong Islands Shpg. Co, ren. LANTAO ISLAND.
27.9.1982 Arrived Kaohsiung for B/U.

FS58. ALARIC   (1958 - 1972) 6692g 3501n   473' x 64'
6-cyl 2SCSA B&W oil engine by bldr.
8.10.1957 Launched and 2.1958 completed by Harland & Wolff Ltd,
Belfast for Shaw,Savill & Albion Co. Ltd(Furness,Withy & Co. Ltd).
1972 Sold to Iran Shipping Line ren. IRAN NIRU. 1976 Transferred
to Irano-Hind Shpg. Co, ren. RUMI. 4.6.1979 Arrived Bombay for B/U
with damage.

FS59. IONIC(2)   (1959 - 1978) 11219g 6272n   513' x 70'
8-cyl 2SCSA B&W oil engine by bldr.
3.1959 Completed by Cammell,Laird & Co. Ltd,Birkenhead for Shaw,
Savill & Albion Co. Ltd(Furnes,Withy & Co. Ltd). 1978 Sold to
Panorea Shipping Co,Cyprus ren. GLENPARVA. 18.4.1979 Left Hono-
lulu for Kaohsiung for B/U.

FS60. AMALRIC   (1960 - 1977) 7791g 4090n   457' x 64'
9-cyl 2SCSA MAN oil engine by bldr.
11.1960 Completed by Bremer Vulcan,Vegesack for Shaw,Savill &
Albion Co. Ltd(Furness,Withy & Co. Ltd). 1977 Sold to Afromar Inc,
Greece ren. KYMA. 1985 Sold to Interspirit Maritime Co. Ltd,Hond-
uras ren. MILOS V. 1.3.1986 Dem. commenced at Gadani Beach.

FS61. ILLYRIC   (1960 - 1978) 11256g 6374n   513' x 70'
8-cyl 2SCSA B&W oil engine by Cammell,Laird & Co. Ltd.
7.1959 Launched and 1.1960 completed by Vickers-Armstrong Ltd,
Newcastle for Shaw,Savill & Albion Co. Ltd(Furness,Withy & Co.
Ltd). 1978 Sold to Hanover Marine Co. Ltd,Cyprus ren. CARMILA.
9.3.1979 Arrived Kaohsiung for B/U.

FS62. ICENIC   (1960 - 1978) 11239g 6260n   513' x 70'
8-cyl 2SCSA B&W oil engine by bldr.
23.6.1960 Launched and 12.1960 completed by Harland & Wolff Ltd,
Belfast for Shaw,Savill & Albion Co. Ltd(Furness,Withy & Co. Ltd).
1978 Sold to Atacos Cia Nav SA,Greece ren. AEGEAN UNITY.
12.10.1979 Arrived Kaohsiung for B/U.

FS63. IBERIC   (1961 - 1976) 11248g 6337n   513' x 70'
8-cyl 2SCSA B&W oil engine by Harland & Wolff Ltd,Belfast..
4.1961 Completed by A. Stephen & Sons Ltd,Glasgow for Shaw,Savill
& Albion Co. Ltd(Furness,Withy & Co. Ltd). 1976 Transferred to
Royal Mail Line ren. DESEADO. 1980 Transferred to Metcalfe
Shipping Co. Ltd,Hartlepool name u/ch. 1981 Sold to Maistros Wind
Shipping Co,Cyprus ren. SAN GEORGE. 20.5.1983 Arrived Chittagong
for B/U from the Fal, where she was laid-up from 27.5.1982 to
3.1983.

FS64. NORTHERN STAR (1962 - 1975) 24731g 12567n   650' x 83'
4 Steam turbines DR geared to 2 screw shafts by Parsons,Wallsend.
27.6.1961 Launched by Queen Mother and 6.1962 completed by Vickers-
Armstrong Ltd,Newcastle for Shaw,Savill & Albion Co. Ltd(Furness,
Withy & Co. Ltd). 10.7.1962 Sailed from Southampton on maiden
voyage to New Zealand via Cape Town, suffered turbine trouble with
lubricating oil subsequently changed. 12.1967 Aground at Papeete
harbour,Tahiti. 1969 Cruising out of Southampton. 6.1974 Boiler
trouble in Mediterranean,majority of passengers flown home from
Tunis. 11.12.1975 Arrived Kaohsiung for B/U.

FS65. MEGANTIC   (1962 - 1979) 12226g 6154n   538' x 71'
Two 7-cyl 2SCSA B&W oil engine by bldr.
12.1962 Completed by Swan,Hunter & Wigham Richardson Ltd,Wallsend
for Shaw,Savill & Albion Co. Ltd(Furness,Withy & Co. Ltd). 1979
Sold to Ampney Shipping Co,Greece ren. DEMETRIOS VENTOURIS later
DIMITRIOS VENTOURIS. 18.4.1980 Dem. commenced at Kaohsiung.

FS66. MEDIC   (1963 - 1979) 12220g 6154n   538' x 70'
Two 7-cyl 2SCSA B&W oil engines by bldr.
7.1963 Completed by Swan,Hunter & Wigham Richardson Ltd,Wallsend
for Shaw,Savill & Albion Co. Ltd(Furness,Withy & Co. Ltd). 1979
Sold to A. Bacolitsas,Piraeus ren. ODYSEFS.

FS67. ROMANIC   (1965 - 1968) 9785g 5823n   469' x 65'
Two 6-cyl 2SCDA B&W oil engines by bldr.
30.12.1943 Launched and 7.1944 completed by Harland & Wolff
Ltd,Belfast as DRINA for Royal Mail Line. 1965 Royal Mail purchased
by Furness,Withy & Co. Ltd, transferred to SSA ren. ROMANIC.
22.6.1968 Left Lyttelton for Kaohsiung for B/U.

FS68. ZEALANDIC(2) (1965 - 1980) 7946g 4234n   481' x 65'
8-cyl 2SCSA Sulzer oil engine by G. Clark & NEM Ltd.
3.1965 Completed by A. Stephen & Sons Ltd,Glasgow for Shaw,Savill &
Albion Co. Ltd(Furness,Withy & Co. Ltd). 1980 Sold to Electra Shpg.
Co. SA,Liberia ren. PORT LAUNAY. 1981 Sold to Cobalt Shipping Inc,
Liberia ren. KHALIJ CRYSTAL. 8.11.1984 Arrived Karachi for B/U.

FS69. LAURENTIC   (1965 - 1980) 7751g 4223n   481' x 65'
8-cyl 2SCSA Sulzer oil engine by G. Clark & NEM Ltd.
5.1965 Completed by Vickers-Armstrong Ltd,Newcastle for Shaw,
Savill & Albion Co. Ltd(Furness,Withy & Co. Ltd). 1980 Sold to
National Integrity Cia Nav,Panama ren. SPARTAN REEFER. 28.4.1984
Arrived Karachi from Jeddah for B/U.

FS70. RUTHENIC   (1966 - 1967) 9801g 5786n   469' x 65'
Two 6-cyl 2SCDA B&W oil engines by bldr.
5.9.1944 Launched and 12.1944 completed by Harland & Wolff Ltd,
Belfast for Royal Mail Line as DURANGO. 1965 Royal Mail taken over
by Furness,Withy & Co. Ltd, transferred to SSA in 1966 ren.
RUTHENIC. 7.1967 Sold to Embajada Cia Nav,Greece ren. SUSSEX.
26.12.1967 Arrived Kaohsiung for B/U.

FS71. MAJESTIC   (1967 - 1974) 12591g 6957n   546' x 74'
Two 8-cyl 2SCSA Sulzer oil engines by bldr.
2.1967 Completed by A. Stephen & Sons Ltd,Glasgow for Shaw,Savill &
Albion Co. Ltd(Furness,Withy & Co. Ltd). 1974 Sold to New Zealand
Line(SSA,mgrs) ren. N.Z. AORANGI. 1978 Sold to Vernicos S.S. Co.
Ltd,Piraeus ren. MYKONOS.

FS72. BRITANNIC   (1967 - 1974) 12228g 6941n   546' x 74'
Two 8-cyl 2SCSA Sulzer oil engines by bldr.
12.1967 Completed by A. Stephen & Sons Ltd,Glasgow for Shaw,Savill
& Albion Co. Ltd(Furness,Withy & Co. Ltd). 1974 Sold to New Zealand
Line(SSA,mgrs) ren. N.Z. WAITANGI. 1980 Sold to Vernicos S.S. Co.
Ltd,Piraeus ren. SERIFOS.

FS73. AKAROA(2)   (1968 - 1971) 18565g 11100n   584' x 78'
Two 6-cyl 2SCSA B&W oil engines by bldr.
7.7.1959 Launched by Princess Margaret and 12.1959 completed by
Harland & Wolff Ltd, Belfast for Royal Mail Line as AMAZON for
London - S. America. 1965 Royal Mail taken over by Furness,Withy &
Co. Ltd. 4.1968 Transferred to SSA ren. AKAROA. 1971 Sold to A/S
Ugland Rederi,Norway and converted into a car-carrier ren. AKARITA.
1977 Sold to Ace Autoline Co. Ltd,Liberia ren. HUAL AKARITA. 1980
Ren. AKARITA. 8.1.1982 Arrived Kaosiung for B/U.

FS74. ARAWA(2)   (1968 - 1971) 18595g 11100n   584' x 78'
Two 6-cyl 2SCSA B&W oil engines by bldr.
13.4.1960 Launched and 9.1960 completed by Harland & Wolff Ltd,
Belfast for Royal Mail Line as ARLANZA. 1965 Royal Mail taken over
by Furness,Withy & Co. Ltd. 4.1968 Transferred to SSA ren. ARAWA.
1971 Sold to Leif Hoegh & Co A/S,Norway and converted into a car-
carrier ren. HOEGH TRANSIT. 1972 Ren. HOEGH TROTTER. 1977 Sold to
Ace Autoline Co. Ltd,Liberia ren. HUAL TROTTER. 1980 Ren. TROTTER.
9.12.1981 Arrived Kaohsiung from Kagoshima for B/U.

FS75. ARANDA   (1968 - 1971) 18575g 11100n   584' x 78'
Two 6-cyl 2SCSA B&W oil engines by bldr.
20.10.1959 Launched and 4.1960 completed by Harland & Wolff Ltd,
Belfast for Royal Mail Line as ARAGON. 1965 Royal Mail taken over
by Furness,Withy & Co. Ltd. 4.1968 Transferred to SSA ren ARANDA.

1971 Sold to Leif Hoegh & Co A/S,Norway ren HOEGH TRAVELLER and converted into a car carrier. 1977 Sold to Ace Autoline Co. Ltd,Liberia ren. HUAL TRAVELLER. 1980 Ren. TRAVELLER. 7.11.1981 Arrived Kaohsiung from New Orleans for B/U.

FS76. OCEAN MONARCH(2) (1970 - 1975) 25971g 13993n 640' x 85'
6 Steam turbines DR geared to 2 screw shafts by bldr.
9.5.1956 Launched and 3.1957 completed by Vickers-Armstrong Ltd, Newcastle as EMPRESS OF ENGLAND for Canadian Pacific S.S. Co. Ltd,Liverpool. 18.4.1957 Maiden voyage Liverpool - Quebec - Montreal. 10.1963 Chartered by Travel Savings Association. 2.1970 Purchased by Shaw,Savill & Albion Co. Ltd(Furness,Withy & Co. Ltd) ren. OCEAN MONARCH. 11.4.1970 One sailing Liverpool - Southampton - Australia,then converted for cruising by Cammell,Laird & Co. Ltd. 10.1971 Commenced cruising. 13.6.1975 Left Southampton for Kaohsiung for B/U, arriving on 17.7.1975.

FS77. MAYFIELD   (1973 - 1980) 7898g 3445n   448' x 68'
9-cyl 2SCSA B&W oil engine.
2.1970 Completed by Helsingor Skibs & Mks,Elsinore as CAP COLVILLE for Olau Line A/S,Denmark. 1973 Ren. OLAU PIL. 1973 Purchased by Shaw,Savill & Albion Co. Ltd(Furness,Withy & Co. Ltd) ren. MAYFIELD. 1980 Sold to Friomar Comp. Nav SA,Piraeus ren. SEAFROST.

FS78. LINDFIELD   (1973 - 1980) See LIMPSFIELD FT26

FS79. DERWENT(2)   (1979 - 1982) 9167g 6432n   472' x 73'
4-cyl 2SCSA Sulzer oil engine.
28.2.1979 Launched and 5.1979 completed by Austin & Pickersgill Ltd,Sunderland for Royal Mail Line(Furness,Withy(Shipping) Ltd). 1982 Sold to Toko Co. Ltd,Tokyo ren. MOUNTAIN AZALEA.

FS80. DUNEDIN   (1980 - 1986) 18140g 10080n   578' x 87'
6-cyl 2SCSA B&W oil engine.
15.2.1980 Launched and 7.1980 completed by Swan Hunter SB Ltd, Walker for Shaw,Savill & Albion Co. Ltd(Furness,Withy(Shipping) Ltd). Last ship from Walker Naval Yard, joint service with Bank Line container ship WILLOWBANK. 1986 Sold to Hamburg-Sud ren. MONTE PASCOAL. 1990 Sold to Egon Oldendorff ren. COLUMBUS OLIVOS.

APPENDIX FT   CAIRN LINE OF STEAMSHIPS LTD

FT1. CAIRNMONA(2)   (1928 - 1939) 4666g 2776n   390' x 53'
T 3-cyl by Blair & Co. Ltd,Stockton.
29.11.1917 Launched and 3.1918 completed by Sunderland SB Co. Ltd for Cairn Line of Steamships Ltd(Cairns,Noble & Co,mgrs),Newcastle. 15.6.1918 Torpedoed in North Sea, but reached port safely,3 lives lost. 1928 Cairns,Noble & Co. taken over by Furness,Withy & Co. Ltd. 30.10.1939 Torpedoed and sunk by U13 off Peterhead o.v. Montreal & Halifax to Leith & Tyne with wheat,3 lost.

FT2. CAIRNVALONA   (1928 - 1952) 4929g 2937n   415' x 53'
T 3-cyl by Blair & Co. Ltd,Stockton.

10.4.1918 Launched and 8.1918 completed by Sunderland SB Co. Ltd,
Sunderland for Cairn Line of Steamships Ltd(Cairns,Noble & Co,mgrs),
Newcastle. 8.5.1918 Missed by torpedo while in tow from Wear to Tees
for engine installation. 1928 Cairns,Noble & Co. taken over by
Furness,Withy & Co. Ltd. 1952 Sold to BISCO for scrapping after 180
round Atlantic voyages. 30.6.1952 Moved up to Clayton & Davie Ltd,
Dunston from Newcastle quayside.

FT3. CAIRNDHU(3)   (1928 - 1935) 5250g 3218n   399' x 52'
T 3-cyl by bldrs.
3.1919 Completed by Palmers Co. Ltd,Jarrow for Cairn Line of
Steamships Ltd(Cairns,Noble & Co,mgrs),Newcastle. 1928 Cairns,Noble &
Co. taken over by Furness,Withy & Co. Ltd. 1935 Sold to N.G. Livanos,
Chios ren. STRYMON. 1951 Sold to Cia Maritima International, Liberia
ren. LIBERTY. 17.1.1952 Wrecked near Pendeen L.H., cut up for scrap.

FT4. CAIRNGOWAN(3) (1928 - 1935) 5295g 3257n   399' x 52'
T 3-cyl by Blair & Co. Ltd,Stockton.
4.1919 Completed by Sunderland SB Co. Ltd,Sunderland as CAIRNGOWAN for
Cairn Line of Steamships Ltd(Cairns,Noble & Co,mgrs),Newcastle having
been laid down as WAR ORIOLE for The Shipping Controller. 1928 Cairns,
Noble & Co. taken over by Furness,Withy & Co. Ltd. 1935 Sold to Bright
Navigation Co. Ltd,London ren. BRIGHTORION. 1936 Sold to H.C. Wan,
Tsingtao ren. CHI SING. 1938 Transferred to Yamashita K.K.,Kobe ren.
YAMAHAGI MARU. 12.10.1944 Sunk to SW of Formosa by U.S. Navy carrier-
based aircraft.

FT5. SCATWELL   (1928) 4425g 2763n   385' x 52'
T 3-cyl by J. Dickinson & Sons Ltd,Sunderland.
9.9.1911 Launched and 10.1911 completed as MAISIE by Bartram & Sons,
Sunderland for Laming,D'Ambrumenil & Co(A.Laming & Co,gr),London. 1917
Sold to Harris & Dixon Ltd,London ren. SCATWELL. 1919 Purchased by
Cairn Line of Steamships Ltd(Cairns,Noble & Co,mgrs),Newcastle name
u/ch. 1928 Cairns,Noble & Co. taken over by Furness,Withy & Co. Ltd.
1928 Sold to S.A. & P.A. Lemos,Piraeus ren. ANTONIS G. LEMOS.
24.8.1936 Sunk by collision with HMS KEITH 40 miles S of Portland Bill
o.v. Danzig to Buenos Aires.

FT6. CAIRNROSS(3)   (1928 - 1940) 5494g 3262n   425' x 55'
3 Parsons Marine turbines DR geared to single screw shaft.
25.11.1920 Launched and 8.1921 completed by Sunderland SB Co. Ltd,
Sunderland for Cairn Line of Steamships Ltd(Cairns,Noble & Co,mgrs),
Newcastle. 1928 Cairns,Noble & Co. taken over by Furness,Withy & Co.
Ltd. 17.1.1940 Sunk by mine 8 miles from Mersey Bar L.V. o.v. Tyne,
Leith & Liverpool to St. John(NB) with coal,earthenware & general,
crew saved.

FT7. CAIRNTORR(2)   (1928) 5387g 3206n   425' x 55'
T 3-cyl by N.E. Marine Eng. Co. Ltd,Newcastle.
10.1922 Launched and 11.1922 completed by Sunderland SB Co. Ltd,
Sunderland for Cairn Line of Steamships Ltd(Cairns,Noble & Co,mgrs),
Newcastle. 1928 Cairns,Noble & Co. taken over by Furness,Withy & Co.
Ltd. 23.10.1928 Wrecked at Cape Whittle,Labrador o.v. Montreal to
Leith with general.

FT8. CAIRNESK(3)   (1928 - 1956) 5007g 3015n   402' x 55'
3 Parsons Marine turbines DR geared to single screw shaft.
14.4.1926 Launched and 7.1926 completed by W. Pickersgill & Sons Ltd,
Sunderland for Cairn Line of Steamships Ltd(Cairns,Noble & CO,mgrs),
Newcastle. 1928 Cairns,Noble & Co. taken over by Furness,Withy & Co.
Ltd. 11.1956 Sold to Vamar Cia de Nav,Panama after completing 207
round Atlantic voyages, ren. ZERMATT. 1958 Sold for use as an ore-
carrier ren. AURORA. 9.1959 Sold for £61,000 for B/U in Japan.

FT9. CAIRNGLEN(2)   (1928 - 1940) 5019g 3015n   402' x 55'
3 Parsons Marine turbines DR geared to single screw shaft.
26.7.1926 Launched and 9.1926 completed by W. Pickersgill & Sons Ltd,
Sunderland for Cairn Line of Steamships Ltd(Cairns,Noble & Co,mgrs),
Newcastle. 1928 Cairns,Noble & Co. taken over by Furness,Withy & Co.
Ltd. 22.10.1940 Wrecked at Marsden, 2 miles S of Tyne entrance o.v.
Montreal & Halifax for Leith & Tyne.

FT10. CAIRNAVON(4) (1946 - 1961) 6339g 4010n   407' x 55'
T 3-cyl by D. Rowan & Co. Ltd,Glasgow.
16.12.1940 Launched and 2.1941 completed as EMPIRE SNOW by C. Connell
& Co. Ltd,Glasgow for Ministry of War Transport. 1946 Purchased by
Cairn Line of Steamships Ltd(Cairns,Noble & Co,mgrs),Newcastle ren.
CAIRNAVON. 1961 Sold to Cia Nav Sirikari,Panama ren. VERGOLIVADA,
Lebanese flag. 19.9.1966 Rope round propeller, stranded Doganarslan
Bank in N. Dardanelles o.v. Novorossisk to Persian Gulf with cement.
1.10.1966 Refloated after cargo jettisoned and transhipped,proceeded
to Piraeus. 11.1968 Arrived Shanghai for B/U.

FT11. CAIRNGOWAN(4) (1952 - 1969) 7503g 4631n   429' x 60'
3 Parsons Marine turbines DR geared to single screw shaft.
14.12.1951 Launched and 5.1952 completed by W. Gray & Co. Ltd,
Hartlepool for Cairn Line of Steamships Ltd(Cairns,Noble & Co,
mgrs), Newcastle. 1965 Chartered to Manchester Liners Ltd ren.
MANCHESTER ENGINEER. 1966 Ren. CAIRNGOWAN. 1969 Sold to Mananto
Shipping Co. Ltd,(E.Roussos,mgr),Famagusta ren. GEORGILIS.
10.1973 Demolition began at Gandia near Valencia.

FT12. CAIRNDHU(4)   (1952 - 1969) 7503g 4631n   429' x 60'
3 Parsons Marine turbines DR geared to single screw shaft.
9.4.1952 Launched and 9.1952 completed by W. Gray & Co. Ltd,
Hartlepool for Cairn Line of Steamships Ltd(Cairns,Noble & Co,
mgrs),Newcastle. 1965 Chartered to Manchester Liners Ltd ren.
MANCHESTER EXPORTER. 1969 Sold to   ren. GEMINI
EXPORTER. 2.5.1971 Arrived Kaohsiung for B/U.

FT13. CAIRNFORTH   (1958 - 1969) 8105g 4608n   460' x 60'
4-cyl Doxford 2SCSA oil engine by Hawthorn,Leslie & Co. Ltd,Newcastle.
11.1958 Completed by Burntisland SB Co. Ltd,Burntisland for Cairn
Line of Steamships Ltd(Cairns,Noble & Co,mgrs),Newcastle. 1965
Chartered to Manchester Liners Ltd ren. MANCHESTER FREIGHTER.
1969 Transferred to Royal Mail Line Ltd ren. LOMBARDY. 1971 Sold
to Premier Shipping Co. Inc,Singapore ren. PREMIER PACIFIC. 1975
Sold to Meridian Line SA, Singapore ren. TARA SEA. 1976 Sold to
Sergeant Shipping Co,Liberia ren. GEORGIOS. 1979 Sold to Belcore

Maritime Corp.,Greece ren. MASTRO GIORGIS. 15.9.1979 Grounded at Libreville while bound from Santos, refloated and returned to trading.19.9.1982 Arrived in Greece for B/U.

FT14. CAIRNESK(4)   (1965 - 1966) 4411g 2456n   378' x 50'
Two 5-cyl 2SCSA Sulzer oil engines by G. Clark Ltd,Sunderland.
3.1959 Completed by W. Pickersgill & Sons Ltd,Sunderland as
MANCHESTER FAITH for Manchester Liners Ltd. 1965 Chartered to
Cairn Line of Steamships Ltd,Newcastle ren. CAIRNESK. 1966 Ren.
MANCHESTER FAITH. 1969 Sold to Marlineas Oceanicas SA,Panama ren.
ILKON TAK. 1979 Sold to Yakinthia Shipping Co. SA,Panama ren.
CHRYSEIS. 16.10.1982 Arrived Karachi for B/U.

FT15. CAIRNGLEN(3)   (1965 - 1966) 4412g 2459n   378' x 50'
Two 5-cyl 2SCSA Sulzer oil engines by G. Clark Ltd,Sunderland.
10.1959 Completed by W. Pickersgill & Sons Ltd,Sunderland as
MANCHESTER FAME for Manchester Liners Ltd. 1965 Chartered to
Cairn Line of Steamships Ltd,Newcastle ren. CAIRNGLEN. 1966 Ren.
MANCHESTER FAME. 1969 Sold to Marcaminos Surenos SA,Panama ren.
ILKON NIKI. 1979 Sold to Tranquil Marine Inc,Panama ren. EIFI.
1980 Ren. PANAGIS K. 18.2.1980 Arrived Alexandria, arrested and
laid-up. 1986 B/U at Alexandria.

FT16. CAIRNVENTURE   (1969 - 1974) 1436g 883n   255' x 39'
8-cyl 4SCSA oil engine by Atlas-MaK,Kiel.
1969 Completed by E.J. Smit & Zoon,Westerbroek for Cairn Line of
Steamships Ltd,Newcastle(Shaw,Savill & Albion Co. Ltd,mgr). 1974
Sold to Shipmair N.V.,Rotterdam ren. SHIPMAIR III. 1976 Sold to
Scheeps. Maats. Passaat Santos,Curacao ren. PASSAAT SANTOS. 1977
Sold to Wijdzicht B.V.,Rotterdam ren. ERIC. 1979 Sold to Lifestar
Cia Nav SA (Fereniki Lines,ngr),Piraeus ren. GHADAMES. 1986 Sold
to Brother Hood Shpg. Co. Ltd,Cyprus ren. ALEXIA. 1990 Sold to
A.E. Economides,Thessaloniki ren. STAR QUEEN.

FT17. CAIRNTRADER   (1971 - 1976) 1581g 977n   262' x 39'
8-cyl 4SCSA oil engine by Atlas-MaK,Kiel.
1.1971 Launched as CAIRNTRADER and 3.1971 completed as SAXON
PRINCE for Cairn Line of Steamships Ltd(Shaw,Savill & Albion Co.
Ltd,mgr) by E.J. Smit & Zoon,Westerbroek. 1975 Ren. CAIRNTRADER.
1976 Ren. SAXON PRINCE. 1976 Sold to Van Nievelt,Goudriaan & Co
BV,Rotterdam ren. ADARA. 1986 Sold to Waterdrive Marine
Ltd,Limassol ren. ANDARA.

FT18. CAIRNRANGER   (1971 - 1976) 1598g 1008n   287' x 39'
8-cyl 4SCSA oil engine by Atlas-MaK,Kiel.
1971 Completed by E.J. Smit & Zoon,Westerbroek for Cairn Line of
Steamships Ltd(Shaw,Savill & Albion Co. Ltd,mgr). 1976 Sold to
Denholm Line Steamers Ltd(J.&J. Denholm),Glasgow ren. MOUNTPARK.
1982 Sold to Salverina Varriale,Naples ren. BENEDETTO SCOTTO.
1988 Sold to Sadav spA,Italy ren. MARYLAND.

FT19. CAIRNROVER   (1972 - 1978) 1598g 1008n   287' x 39'
8-cyl 4SCSA oil engine by Atlas-MaK,Kiel.

1972 Completed by Bodewes,Matrenshoek for Cairn Line of Steamships Ltd (Shaw,Savill & Albion Co. Ltd,mgr). 1978 Sold to White Palace Co. SA, Greece ren. GIANNIS. 1983 Sold to Spartohorion Shpg. Co.,Greece ren. ANASTASSIA. 1986 Sold to New Haven Shpg. Co. Ltd,Cyprus ren ANASTASSIA ENA. 1986 Sold to Angelamar di Coppola Tommaso,Italy ren. REIDA.

FT20. CAIRNLEADER (1975 - 1982) 1592g 1050n 261' x 45'
8-cyl 4SCSA oil engine by Atlas-MaK,Kiel.
24.6.1975 Launched and 9.1975 completed by Martin Jansen Schiffswert,Leer for Cairn Line of Steamships Ltd(Shaw,Savill & Albion Co. Ltd). 1982 Sold to H.&P. Holwerda,Holland ren. LINDEWAL. 1987 Ren. BENED. 1988 Ren. MIRFAK 1989 Sold to Hecate Shipping Co., Piraeus ren. FIVI.

FT21. CAIRNFREIGHTER (1975 - 1982) 1592g 1049n 261' x 45'
8-cyl 4SCSA oil engine by Atlas-MaK,Kiel.
29.9.1975 Launched and 11.1975 completed by Martin Jansen Schiffswert,Leer for Cairn Line of Steamships Ltd(Shaw,Savill & Albion Co. Ltd). 1982 Sold to H.& P. Holwerda,Holland ren. TJONGERWAL. 1987 Ren. CENED. 1988 Ren. MEGREZ. 1989 Sold to Italy ren. VILARO.

FT22. CAIRNCARRIER (1976 - 1982) 1592g 1050n 261' x 45'
8-cyl 4SCSA oil engine by Atlas-MaK,Kiel.
5.12.1975 Launched and 1.1976 completed by Martin Jansen Schiffswert, Leer for Cairn Line of Steamships Ltd(Shaw,Savill & Albion Co. Ltd). 1982 Sold to Tequila Maritime SA,Panama ren. TEQUILA SUNSET. 1984 Sold to Arklow Shipping Ltd,Dublin ren. ARKLOW BRIDGE. 1990 Sold to Baterita Shpg SA,Panama ren. WAVE ROSE.

FT23. CAIRNASH (1976 - 1983) 1597g 1169n 276' x 46'
12-cyl 4SCSA oil engine by H. Cegielski,Poznan.
30.9.1976 Launched and 12.1976 completed by Stocznia Gdanska for Cairn Line of Steamships Ltd(Shaw,Savill & Albion Co. Ltd). 1983 Sold to Peter Cremer,Singapore ren. ANDREA and lengthened. 1985 Sold to Minibulk Schiff Gmbh, Vienna ren. ST. ANTON.

FT24. CAIRNELM (1977 - 1983) 1597g 1169n 276' x 46'
12-cyl 4SCSA oil engine by H. Cegielski,Poznan.
19.10.1976 Launched and 1.1977 completed by Stocznia Gdanska for Cairn Line of Steamships Ltd(Shaw,Savill & Albion Co. Ltd). 1983 Sold to Peter Cremer,Singapore ren. CHRISTIANE and lengthened. 1985 Sold to Minibulk Schiff Gmbh,Vienna ren. ST. CHRISTOPH.

FT25. CAIRNOAK (1977 - 1983) 1597g 1169n 276' x 46'
12-cyl 4SCSA oil engine by H. Cegielski,Poznan.
16.11.1976 Launched and 2.1977 completed by Stocznia Gdanska for Cairn Line of Steamships Ltd(Shaw,Savill & Albion Co. Ltd). 1983 Sold to Peter Cremer,Singapore ren. LEONY and lengthened. 1985 Sold to Minibulk Schiff Gmbh, Vienna ren. ST JAKOB.

FT26. LINDFIELD (1977 - 1980) 8219g 3386n 448' x 66'
9-cyl 2SCSA B&W oil engine by bldrs.

10.1970 Completed as CAP MELVILLE for Olau Line A/S,Denmark by Helsin-gor Skibs & Msk,Elsinore. 1973 Ren. OLAU ROLF. 1973 Purchased by 'K' Steamships(Kaye,Son & Co. Ltd) ren. LIMPSFIELD. 1976 Ren. LINDFIELD. 1977 Transferred to Cairn Line of Steamships Ltd(Shaw,Savill & Albion Co. Ltd). 1980 Sold to Cia Argentina de Transportes Maritimos SA,Argentina ren. MARFRIO.

APPENDIX FW   WARREN LINE LTD (WHITE DIAMOND S.S. CO. LTD)

FW1.MICHIGAN   (1912 - 1915) 4982g 3110n   400' x 47'
T 3-cyl by bldrs.
5.7.1887 Launched and 15.10.1887 completed by Harland & Wolff Ltd,Belfast for White Diamond S.S. Co. Ltd(George Warren & Co., mgr). 1912 Purchased by Furness,Withy & Co. Ltd and reg. under George Warren & Co.(Liverpool) Ltd. 1915 Taken over by Admiralty. 1919 Lost on naval service.

FW2.SAGAMORE   (1912 - 1917) 5036g 3305n   430' x 46'
T 3-cyl by bldrs.
8.9.1892 Launched and 30.11.1892 completed by Harland & Wolff Ltd,Belfast for Sagamore S.S. Co.(George Warren & Co., mgr). 1912 Purchased by Furness,Withy & Co. Ltd and reg. under George Warren & Co.(Liverpool) Ltd. 3.3.1917 Torpedoed and sunk 150 miles W of Fastnet by U49 o.v. Boston to Liverpool with general,52 lost.

FW3.SACHEM   (1912 - 1926) 5204g 3414n   445' x 46'
T 3-cyl by bldrs.
29.6.1893 Launched and 28.10.1893 completed by Harland & Wolff Ltd,Belfast for George Warren & Co.,Liverpool. 1912 Purchased by Furness,Withy & Co. Ltd and reg. under George Warren & Co.(Liverpool) Ltd. 1922 Reg. under Warren Line Ltd (Furness,Withy & Co. Ltd). 1926 Sold for B/U.

FW4.IOWA   (1912 - 1913) 8370g 5248n   500' x 58'
Two Q 4-cyl by bldrs. 2-screw.
5.7.1902 Launched and 11.11.1902 completed by Harland & Wolff Ltd,Belfast for White Diamond S.S. Co. Ltd(George Warren & Co.,mgr). 1912 Purchased by Furness,Withy & Co. Ltd and reg. under George Warren & Co.(Liverpool) Ltd. 1913 Sold Hamburg America Line ren. BOHEMIA. 1917 Requisitioned by U.S. Govt. (U.S.S.B.) ren. ARTEMIS. 1940 Taken over by Ministry of War Transport ren. EMPIRE BITTERN. 23.7.1944 Sunk as an additional blockship blockship at Mulberry,Normandy after the gales of 19-22nd June,1944.

FW5.BAY STATE   (1915 - 1917) 6824g 4140n   420' x 53'
T 3-cyl by Blair & Co. Ltd,Stockton.
1915 Completed by Sir J. Laing & Sons Ltd,Sunderland for George Warren & Co.(Liverpool) Ltd(Furness,Withy & Co. Ltd). 10.6.1917 Torpedoed and sunk by U66 250 miles NW of Fastnet o.v. Boston to Liverpool with general.

FW6.RHODE ISLAND   (1918 - 1927) 5655g 3530n   421' x 54'
T 3-cyl by J. Brown & Co. Ltd,Clydebank.

3.1918 Completed by Napier & Miller Ltd,Glasgow as RHODE ISLAND
for White Diamond S.S. Co. Ltd(G.Warren & Co(Liverpool) Ltd
having been laid down to the order of Raeburn & Verel,Glasgow.
1922 Transferred to Warren Line(Liverpool) Ltd. 1927 Sold to
West Hartlepool S.N. Co. Ltd ren. POLAMHALL. 1928 Sold to
A.T. Callinicos,Greece ren. ELENI. 25.6.1946 Wrecked on
Quequen Bar in the Plate o.v. Necochea to U.K. with grain.

FW7.BAY STATE(2)   (1923 - 1928)   See SPARTAN PRINCE No.113

FW8.HOOSAC   (1923 - 1930)   See TROJAN PRINCE   No.114

FW9.SAVANNAH   (1924 - 1927)   See GRECIAN PRINCE No.112
                                             ('PRIDE OF THE PRINCES')

FW10.NEWFOUNDLAND   (1925 - 1943) 6791g 3828n   406' x 55'
Q 4-cyl by bldrs.
6.1925 Completed by Vickers Ltd,Barrow for Warren Line Ltd(Furness,
Withy & Co. Ltd),Liverpool. Hospital ship during WWII. 13.9.1943
Damaged by bomb in position 40-15 N, 14-21 E 60 miles SW of Naples
and sank next day o.v. Bizerta for Salerno, 15 lost.

FW11.NOVA SCOTIA   (1926 - 1942) 6796g 3841n   406' x 55'
Q 4-cyl by bldrs.
5.1926 Completed by Vickers Ltd,Barrow for Warren Line Ltd(Furness,
Withy & Co. Ltd),Liverpool. Troop Transport during WWII. 20.11.1942
Torpedoed and sunk by U177 in posn. 28-30 S, 33-00 E o.v. Aden for
Durban with mail and Italian prisoners, 863 people lost their lives
including 650 prisoners.

HOULDER card showing OSWESTRY GRANGE of 1902.

HOULDER BROTHERS & CO. LTD/HOULDER LINE LTD.

H1. HORNBY GRANGE (1890 - 1919) 2473g 1593n 300' x 40'
T 3-cyl by bldrs.
2.1890 Completed by Wigham Richardson & Co.,Newcastle for Hornby
Grange S.S. Co. Ltd(Houlder Bros. & Co. Ltd). 1899 Transferred to
Houlder Line Ltd. 1919 Sold to Primo Redo Forner,Valencia ren.
AGUSTINA FORNER. 1928 B/U at Barcelona.

H2. OVINGDEAN GRANGE (1890 - 1907) 2413g 1550n 297' x 40'
T 3-cyl by T. Richardson & Sons,Hartlepool.
3.1890 Completed by Raylton Dixon & Co.,Middlesbrough for Ovingdean Grange S.S. Co. Ltd(Houlder Bros. & Co. Ltd). 1899 Transferred to Houlder Line Ltd. 1907 Sold to S. Grooshetzky,Vladi-
vostock ren. ROMAN. 1916 Sold to Japan ren. TAMON MARU. 1917
Disappeared o.v. China to Wakamatsu.

H3. ELSTREE GRANGE (1893 - 1919) 3930g 2487n 365' x 45'
T 3-cyl by G. Clark Ltd,Sunderland.
11.1892 Completed by Short Brothers,Sunderland as CONSTANCE for
J.Y. Short & E.T. Gourley,Sunderland. 1892 Purchased by Furness,
Withy & Co. Ltd. 1893 Purchased by Elstree Grange S.S. Co. Ltd
(Houlder Bros. & Co. Ltd). 1899 Transferred to Houlder Line Ltd.
1919 Sold to L.C. de Zabala,San Sebastian then Suarez & Nunez,San
Sebastian ren. MANU. 1925 B/U in Spain.

H4. URMSTON GRANGE (1894 - 1914) 3444g 2220n 340' x 46'
T 3-cyl by bldrs.
11.1894 Completed by Workman,Clark & Co.,Belfast for Urmston
Grange Co. Ltd(Houlder Bros. & Co. Ltd). 1899 Transferred to
Houlder Line Ltd. 1906 Fitted for cable laying on charter to
Siemens Brothers. 1914 Sunk as a blockship by Admiralty.

H5. LANGTON GRANGE (1896 - 1909) 5851g 3844n 420' x 54'
T 3-cyl by bldrs.
5.1896 Completed by Workman,Clark & Co.,Belfast for Langton
Grange S.S. Co. Ltd(Houlder Bros & Co. Ltd). 1899 Transferred to
Houlder Line Ltd. 5.8.1909 Wrecked off North Bishops o.v. Glasgow
to Newport in ballast.

H6. DENTON GRANGE (1896 - 1899) 5807g 3804n 420' x 54'
T 3-cyl by bldrs.
1896 Completed by Workman,Clark & Co.,Belfast for Denton Grange
S.S. Co. Ltd(Houlder Bros & Co. Ltd). 1899 Transferred to Houlder
Line Ltd. 12.1899 Stranded at Las Palmas while on Government
charter to South Africa during Boer War, refloated. 1901 Sold to
McGregor,Gow & Co. Ltd ren. GLENLOGAN. 31.10.1916 Torpedoed and
sunk 10 miles SE of Stromboli.

H7. ROYSTON GRANGE (1897 - 1928) 4036g 2613n 370' x 47'
T 3-cyl by bldrs.
1897 Completed by Workman,Clark & Co.,Belfast for Royston Grange
S.S. Co. Ltd(Houlder Bros & Co. Ltd). 1899 Transferred to Houlder
Line Ltd. 1928 B/U.

H8. FLORENCE   (1897 - 1900) 2492g 1609n   293' x 40'
T 3-cyl by T. Richardson & Sons,Hartlepool.
10.1889 Completed by Short Brothers,Sunderland for E.R. Gourlay,
Sunderland as FLORENCE. 1897 Purchased by Houlder Bros. & Co.
Ltd. 1900 Sold to Furness,Withy & Co. Ltd. 20.12.1912 Wrecked at
Marine Cove,St. Marys Bay o.v. Halifax(NS) to Liverpool with
general.

H9. RIPPINGHAM GRANGE (1898 - 1912) 5790g 3852n 420' x 54'
T 3-cyl by bldrs.
10.1898 Completed by Workman,Clark & Co.,Belfast for Rippingham
Grange S.S. Co. Ltd(Houlder Bros & Co. Ltd). 1899 Transferred to
Houlder Line Ltd. 4.1912 Sold to New Zealand Shipping Co. Ltd
ren. LIMERICK. 1913 Transferred to Union S.S. Co. Ltd. 28.5.1917
Torpedoed and sunk by U86 140 miles SW of Bishop Rock Lighthouse
o.v. Sydney (NSW) to London with general and frozen meat.

H10. BEACON GRANGE   (1899 - 1921) 4042g 2620n   370' x 47'
T 3-cyl by bldrs.
6.1899 Completed by Workman,Clark & Co.,Belfast for Houlder Line
Ltd. 6.9.1921 Wrecked at entrance to Rio Gallegos in Patagonia
o.v. Newport News to San Julian and Rio Gallegos with coal.

H11. SOUTHERN CROSS (1899 - 1909) 5050g 3311n   400' x 48'
T 3-cyl by bldrs.
9.1892 Completed by Workman,Clark & Co.,Belfast for Southern
Cross S.S. Co. Ltd(Wincott,Cooper & Co.,mgrs). 1899 Purchased by
Houlder Line Ltd. 24.12.1909 Stranded at entrance to Vigo Harbour
o.v. Antwerp and London to Buenos Aires with general,total loss.

H12. MALTESE CROSS   (1900 - 1901) 1490g 956n   240' x 38'
T 3-cyl by J.G. Kincaid & Co.,Greenock.
10.1900 Completed by Londonderry SB Co. Ltd,Londonderry for
Houlder Line Ltd. 5.1901 Sold to W. Howard Smith & Sons Ltd
Proprietary,Australia. 1903 Reg. under Howard Smith Co. Ltd,
Melbourne ren. CHILLAGOE. 1914 Reg. under Australian S.S. Ltd,
(Howard Smith Ltd,mgrs). 1931 Sold to Madrigal & Co.,Philippines
name u/ch. 1935 Deleted from Lloyd's Register. Reported to have
been sold to Chinese owners just prior to WWII.

H13. HAVERSHAM GRANGE (1901 - 1906) 7474g 4877n 475' x 56'
T 3-cyl by N.E. Marine Eng. Co. Ltd,Newcastle.
6.1898 Completed by Furness,Withy & Co. Ltd,Hartlepool as RAPIDAN
for Furness,Withy & Co. Ltd. 1901 Purchased by Houlder Line Ltd
ren. HAVERSHAM GRANGE. 1902 Transferred to Empire Transport Co.
Ltd. 23.10.1906 Abandoned and burnt out at sea 800 miles off Cape
of Good Hope o.v. New York to Australia with general.

H14. THORPE GRANGE (1901 - 1929) 4188g 2720n   400' x 45'
T 3-cyl by bldrs.
5.1889 Completed as INDRAMAYO by London & GLasgow SB Co. Ltd,
Glasgow for McVicar,Marshall & Co. 1901 Purchased by Houlder Line
Ltd ren. THORPE GRANGE. 1929 Scrapped.

H15. DRAYTON GRANGE (1901 - 1912) 6664g 4246n   450' x 55'
Two T 3-cyl by bldrs,2-screw.
12.1901 Completed by Workman,Clark & Co.,Belfast for Houlder Line
Ltd. 4.1912 Sold to New Zealand Shipping Co. Ltd ren. TYRONE.
27.9.1913 Wrecked at Wahine Point,Otago o.v. Lyttelton to Dunedin.

H16. OSWESTRY GRANGE (1902 - 1912) 7381g 4245n   450' x 55'
Two T 3-cyl by bldrs,2-screw.
3.1902 Completed by Workman,Clark & Co.,Belfast for Houlder Line
Ltd. 4.1912 Sold to New Zealand Shipping Co. Ltd ren. ROSCOMMON.
1913 Transferred to Union S.S. Co. Ltd. 21.8.1917 Torpedoed and
sunk 20 miles NE of Tory Island by U53 o.v. Manchester to
Australia with general, all saved.

H17. EVERTON GRANGE (1903 - 1912) 8129g 4565n   475' x 56'
T 3-cyl by Richardsons,Westgarth & Co. Ltd,Hartlepool,2-screw.
8.1903 Completed by Furness,Withy & Co. Ltd,Hartlepool for Empire
Transport Co. Ltd(Houlder Bros,mgrs). 4.1912 Sold to New Zealand
Shipping Co. Ltd ren. WESTMEATH. 1913 Sold to Union S.S. Co. Ltd
of New Zealand. 15.6.1917 Torpedoed in the English Channel but
reached port safely. 1926 Sold to Ditta D. & E. Fratelli Bozzo,
Genoa ren. NORDICO. 1932 Scrapped in Italy.

H18. SUTHERLAND GRANGE (1909 - 1933) 6852g 5158n 411' x 52'
T 3-cyl by bldrs.
1907 Completed by Palmers Co.,Jarrow as GUARDIANA for Furness,
Withy & Co. Ltd. 1909 Purchased by Houlder Line Ltd ren. SUTH-
ERLAND GRANGE. 1933 Scrapped in Italy.

H19. LYNTON GRANGE (1912 - 1933) 4252g 2734n 380' x 49'
T 3-cyl by Richardsons,Westgarth & Co. Ltd,Sunderland.
7.1912 Completed by Northumberland SB Co. Ltd,Howdon-on-Tyne for
Houlder Line Ltd. 1933 Scrapped in Italy.

H20. DENBY GRANGE (1912 - 1917) 4252g 2729n 380' x 49'
T 3-cyl by Richardsons,Westgarth & Co. Ltd,Sunderland.
8.1912 Completed by Northumberland SB Co. Ltd,Howdon-on-Tyne for
Houlder Line Ltd. 24.10.1918 Sunk by collision in convoy with WAR
ISLAND.

H21. OAKLANDS GRANGE (1912 - 1934) 4488g 2853n   385' x 52'
T 3-cyl by Richardsons,Westgarth & Co. Ltd,Sunderland.
9.1912 Completed by Northumberland SB Co. Ltd,Howdon-on-Tyne for
Houlder Line Ltd. 1934 Sold to M.N. Piangos & partners,Greece
ren. NICOLAOS PIANGOS. 31.10.1941 Bombed and set on fire after
sailing from Harwich o.v. London to Tyne and Sydney(NS) with
general.

H22. EL PARAGUAYO (1912 - 1937) 8508g 5161n   440' x 59'
Two T 3-cyl by Richardsons,Westgarth & Co. Ltd,Hartlepool.2-screw.
4.1912 Completed by Irvines SB & DD Co. Ltd,Hartlepool for
Houlder Line Ltd(Houlder Bros). 1937 Sold for B/U.

H23. LA CORRENTINA (1912 - 1914) 8529g 5183n   440' x 59'
Two T 3-cyl by Richardsons,Westgarth & Co. Ltd,Hartlepool,2-screw.
11.1912 Completed by Irvines SB & DD Co. Ltd,Hartlepool for
Houlder Line Ltd(Houlder Bros). 7.10.1914 Capt-ured by German
raider KRONPRINZ WILHELM o.v. Buenos Aires to U.K. with meat, and
sunk 320 miles E of Montevideo.

H24. ROUNTON GRANGE (1913 - 1934) 4487g 2852n   385' x 52'
T 3-cyl by Richardsons,Westgarth & Co. Ltd,Hartlepool.
1913 Completed by Northumberland SB Co. Ltd,Howdon-on-Tyne for
Houlder Line Ltd. 1934 Sold to Atlas Reederi A.G.,Emden ren.
ELISE SCHULTE. 1.1942 Wrecked off Tromso.

H25. OLDFIELD GRANGE   (1913 - 1917) 4653g 2937n 385' x 52'
T 3-cyl by Richardsons,Westgarth & Co. Ltd,Hartlepool.
1913 Completed by Irvines SB & DD Co. Ltd,Hartlepool for Houlder
Line Ltd. 11.12.1917 Torpedoed and sunk by U62 30 miles NE of
Tory Island o.v. New York to Cardiff via Halifax with general.

H26. BOLLINGTON GRANGE (1915 - 1916) 6319g 3403n   420' x 52'
T 3-cyl by bldrs.
10.10.1893 Launched and 12.1893 completed by R.W. Hawthorn,
Leslie & Co. Ltd,Hebburn as BUTESHIRE for Elderslie S.S. Co. Ltd
(Turnbull,Martin & Co.,mgrs),Glasgow. 1910 Sold to Scottish Shire
Line Ltd,London,same mgrs. 1915 Purchased by Houlder Line Ltd ren
BOLLINGTON GRANGE. 1916 Transferred to Furness-Houlder Argentine
Lines Ltd ren. CANONESA. 1.5.1918 Torpedoed and damaged off
Worthing by UB57, reached port safely. 1919 Sold to Brodway S.S.
Co. Ltd(Blue Star Line(1920),mgrs) ren. MAGICSTAR. 1920 Trans-
ferred to Union Cold Storage Co. Ltd(Blue Star Line(1920),mgr).
1930 Sold to T.W. Ward Ltd, scrapped at Inverkeithing.

H27. HARDWICKE GRANGE (1921 - 1942) 9005g 5628n 430' x 61'
Two T-3 cyl by D. Rowan & Co. Ltd,Glasgow. 2-screw.
10.1921 Completed by W. Hamilton & Co. Ltd,Port Glasgow for
Houlder Line Ltd. 12.6.1942 Torpedoed and sunk 450 miles N of San
Juan(PR) by U129 o.v. Newport News for Trinidad & Plate with a
part cargo including 700 tons of refrigerated cargo.

H28. UPWEY GRANGE (1925 - 1940) 9130g 5182n   430' x 61'
Two 12-cyl 2SCSA oil engines by bldrs. 2-screw.
11.1925 Completed by Fairfield SB Co. Ltd,Glasgow for Houlder
Line Ltd. First motorship in the fleet. 8.8.1940 Torpedoed and
sunk 200 miles NW of Donegal by U37 o.v. Buenos Aires to U.K.
with frozen meat,37 lost.

H29. DUNSTER GRANGE (1927 - 1951) 9494g 6011n   431' x 62'
Two 12-cyl 2SCSA oil engines by bldrs. 2-screw.
25.10.1927 Launched by Mrs. W.C. Warwick and 22.1.1928 completed
by Fairfield SB Co. Ltd,Glasgow for Houlder Line Ltd. 1951 Sold
to Vaasan Laiva O/Y(A.Korhonen),Vasa,Finland ren. VAASA. 1958
Sold to Hokuyo Suisan K.K.,Tokyo ren. KINYO MARU. 1963 Sold to
Nippon Suisan Kaisha K.K. converted to a crab fish factory ship
ren. YOKO MARU. 25.5.1974 Arrived Aioi for B/U from Innoshima.

H30. ELSTREE GRANGE(2) (1928 - 1941) 6572g 4223n 420' x 53'
T 3-cyl by Richardsons,Westgarth & Co. Ltd,Middlesbrough.
3.1916 Completed by Sir Raylton Dixon & Co.,Middlesbrough as ABA-
DESA for Furness-Houlder Argentine Lines Ltd, having been laid
down as DOMINION MILLER. 1928 Transferred to Houlder Line Ltd ren.
ELSTREE GRANGE, converted to oil-firing. 3.5.1941 Destroyed by a
land mine at Liverpool.

H31. ROYSTON GRANGE(2) (1935 - 1939) 5144g 3178n 400' x 52'
T 3-cyl by bldrs.
5.1918 Completed by Hawthorn,Leslie & Co. Ltd,Hebburn as WAR
BISON for The Shipping Controller. 1919 Sold to Lloyd Royal
Belge,Antwerp ren. AUSTRALIER. 1927 Sold to Buenos Aires Great
Southern Railway Co. Ltd(A.Holland & Co. Ltd,mgrs) ren. SALADO.
1935 Purchased by Houlder Line Ltd ren. ROYSTON GRANGE.
25.11.1939 Torpedoed and sunk in Western Approaches by U28 o.v.
Buenos Aires for Liverpool with grain and general.

H32. LANGTON GRANGE(2) (1935 - 1939) 5295g 3239n 400' x 52'
T 3-cyl by Blair & Co. Ltd,Stockton.
2.1919 Completed by Richardson,Duck & Co. Ltd,Stockton as WAR
PANSY for The Shipping Controller. 3.1919 Sold to Buenos Aires
Great Southern Railway Co. Ltd(A.Holland & Co. Ltd,mgrs) ren.
SEGURA. 1935 Purchased by Houlder Line Ltd ren. LANGTON GRANGE.
1939 Sold to A.A. Embiricos,Greece ren. NICOLAOS M. EMBIRICOS.
4.11.1939 Mined and sunk 15 miles E of Dover near Sandettie L.V.
o.v. Galveston for U.K. and Antwerp with wheat.

H33. OVINGDEAN GRANGE(2) (1935 - 1936) 4895g 3088n 400' x 52'
T 3-cyl by Rankin & Blackmore Ltd,Glasgow.
5.1924 Completed by Lithgows Ltd,Port Glasgow as ZAPALA for
Buenos Aires Great Southern Railway Co. Ltd(A.Holland & Co. Ltd,
mgrs). 1935 Purchased by Houlder Line Ltd ren. OVINGDEAN GRANGE.
1936 Sold to Campden Hill S.S. Co. Ltd(Nav. & Coal Trade Co Ltd),
London ren. PEARLSTONE. 1939 Sold to Soc. Anon. Sitmar,Genoa ren.
CASTELBIANCO. 1941 Taken over by Argentine Government while at
Buenos Aires; ren. RIO CHUBUT. 11.5.1959 Stranded off Uruguay.
1960 B/U 'as lies'.

H34. OSWESTRY GRANGE(2) (1937 - 1941) 4684g 2825n 407' x 55'
T 3-cyl by D. Rowan & Co. Ltd,Glasgow.
8.1935 Completed by Blythswood SB Co. Ltd,Glasgow as ARGENTINE
TRANSPORT for Empire Transport Co. Ltd(Houlder Bros.,mgrs). 1935
Transferred to Prince Line Ltd ren. RHODESIAN PRINCE. 1937 Transferred to Houlder Line Ltd ren. OSWESTRY GRANGE. 12.2.1941 Sunk
by German cruiser ADMIRAL HIPPER in Atlantic in position 37-10 N,
21-20 W o.v. Rosario for Liverpool with general.

H35. LYNTON GRANGE(2) (1937 - 1942) 5029g 2986n 418' x 56'
T 3-cyl by D. Rowan & Co. Ltd,Glasgow.
1937 Completed by Blythswood SB Co. Ltd,Glasgow for Houlder Line
Ltd. 28.12.1942 Torpedoed and sunk by U628 in Atlantic in position 42-23 N, 27-14 W o.v. Swansea & Belfast Lough for Saldanha

Bay,Table Bay & Middle East with general,Govt. stores and explosives.

H36. BEACON GRANGE(2) (1938 - 1941) 10119g 6221n 448' x 65'
Two 4SCSA Werkspoor oil engines by bldrs. 2-screw.
4.5.1938 Completed by Hawthorn,Leslie & Co. Ltd,Hebburn for
Houlder Line Ltd. 26.4.1941 Torpedoed and sunk by U552 in position 62 N 16-40 W o.v. Tyne for Buenos Aires in ballast.

H37. RIPPINGHAM GRANGE(2) (1943 - 1961) 10365g 6227n 448' x 65'
Two 4SCSA Werkspoor oil engines by bldrs. 2-screw.
6.3.1943 Launched and 9.1943 completed by Hawthorn,Leslie & Co.
Ltd,Hebburn for Houlder Line Ltd. 1961 Sold to Far East Marine
Enterprises Ltd,Hong Kong ren. ABBEY WOOD. 23.4.1962 Arrived
Hakodate for B/U.

H38. OVINGDEAN GRANGE(3) (1946 - 1959) 7070g 4204n 432' x 56'
T 3-cyl by D. Rowan & Co. Ltd,Glasgow.
30.6.1942 Launched and 9.1942 completed by Lithgows Ltd,Port
Glasgow as EMPIRE BUCKLER for Ministry of War Transport. 1946
Purchased by Houlder Line Ltd ren. OVINGDEAN GRANGE. 1959 Sold to
Devon Shipping Co. Ltd,Liberia(Empresa Nav. Proamar,Argentina)
ren. SABRINA. 1961 Sold to Cia Nav Marcasa SA,Lebanon(S. Catsell
& Co. Ltd,London) ren. NOEMI. 27.12.1965 Aground 1 miles SW
of Ras Abu ar Rasas,south of Masirah,Oman o.v. Matanzas in
Cuba to Basra with sugar. Total loss.

H39. URMSTON GRANGE(2) (1946 - 1959) 7046g4192n 432' x 56'
T 3-cyl by Rankin & Blackmore Ltd,Glasgow.
2.9.1942 Launched and 11.1942 completed by Lithgows Ltd,Port
Glasgow as EMPIRE PIBROCH for Ministry of War Transport. 1946
Purchased by Houlder Line Ltd ren. URMSTON GRANGE. 1959 Sold to
Argonaut Shipping & Trading Co. Ltd(A. Lusi),Greece ren. ARGO
GRANGE. 18.12.1959 Arrived Hong Kong for B/U.

H40. LANGTON GRANGE(3) (1946 - 1960) 7069g 4194n 432' x 56'
T 3-cyl by D. Rowan & Co. Ltd,Glasgow.
30.9.1942 Launched and 12.1942 completed as EMPIRE PENNANT for
Ministry of War Transport. 1946 Purchased by Houlder Line Ltd ren.
LANGTON GRANGE. 5.10.1960 Arrived Hong Kong for B/U.

H41. HORNBY GRANGE(2) (1946 - 1969) 10785g 6524n 463' x 66'
Two 8-cyl 2SCSA oil engines by bldrs.
31.5.1946 Launched and 12.1946 completed by Hawthorn,Leslie & Co.
Ltd,Hebburn for Houlder Line Ltd. 1969 Transferred to Royal Mail
Lines Ltd,London ren. DOURO. 1970 Transferred to Prince Line
Ltd(Shaw,Savill & Albion Co. Ltd) name u/ch. 6.6.1972 Arrived
Aviles for B/U.

H42. ELSTREE GRANGE(3) (1947 - 1960) 7176g 4380n 441' x 57'
T 3-cyl by General Machinery Corporation,Hamilton,Ohio.
1.1944 Completed by Bethlehem-Fairfield SB at Baltimore as SAM-
ETTRICK for Ministry of War Transport. 1947 Purchased by Houlder
Line Ltd ren. ELSTREE GRANGE. 1960 Sold to Polish Steamship Lines

ren. KOPALNIA MIECHOWICE. 8.1.1972 Damaged rudder off Portuguese coast o.v. Gdynia to Italy with coal, towed into Lisbon. Later completed voyage and arrived Split 5.1972 for B/U.

H43. BEACON GRANGE(3) (1948 - 1949) 7157g 4282n 441' x 57'
T 3-cyl by Dominion Engineering Works,Montreal.
4.1945 Completed by Burrard DD Co. Ltd,Vancouver as ALBERT PARK for Ministry of War Transport. 1946 Sold to Canadian Transport Co. Ltd,Vancouver ren. HARMAC VICTORIA. 1948 Purchased by Furness(Canada) Ltd(Prince Line & Houlder Bros,mgrs),Montreal ren. BEACON GRANGE. 1949 Sold to Conquistador Cia Nav SA,Piraeus ren. CONSTANTINOS. 1967 B/U.

H44. ROYSTON GRANGE(3) (1948 - 1949) 7158g 4245n 441' x 57'
T 3-cyl by Dominion Engineering Works,Montreal.
1.1944 Completed by Burrard DD Co. Ltd,Vancouver as SAPPERTON PARK for Ministry of War Transport having been laid down as FORT TOULOUSE. 1946 Sold to Canadian Transport Co. Ltd,Vancouver ren. HARMAC ALBERNI. 1948 Purchased by Furness(Canada) Ltd,Montreal (Prince Line & Houlder Bros,mgrs) ren. ROYSTON GRANGE. 1949 Sold to Rio Pardo Cia Nav SA,Panama ren. YIANNIS. 1967 B/U.

H45. BARTON GRANGE (1949 - 1958) 7201g 4982n 433' x 56'
T 3-cyl by Harland & Wolff Ltd,Glasgow.
27.6.1944 Launched and 9.1944 completed by Lithgows Ltd,Port Glasgow as EMPIRE BALFOUR for Ministry of War Transport. 1949 Purchased by Houlder Line Ltd ren. BARTON GRANGE. 1958 Sold to Western S.S. Co. Ltd(Wang Kee & Co. Ltd),Hong Kong ren. SUNLIGHT. 1962 Sold to Pan-Norse S.S. Co. SA,Panama (Wallem & Co) name u/ch. 30.3.1967 Arrived Hong Kong for B/U.

H46. ROYSTON GRANGE(4) (1950 - 1952) 7133g 4245n 441' x 57'
T 3-cyl by Dominion Engineering Works,Montreal.
4.1943 Completed by Burrard DD Co. Ltd,Vancouver as FORT ASH for Ministry of War Transport. 1946 Bare-boat chartered by Houlder Line Ltd for Plate service. 1950 Purchased by Houlder Line Ltd ren. ROYSTON GRANGE. 1952 Sold to Portoria Compania di Nav spA, Genoa ren. GIUAN. 1960 Ren. CINQUETERRE. 1961 Sold to Myrrinella Nav SA,Piraeus ren. TILEMAHOS. 9.1965 Sold to Triton Shipping Ltd, Gibraltar ren. ELICOS. 1967 B/U in Yugoslavia.

H47. OSWESTRY GRANGE(3) (1952 - 1971) 9406g 5516n 459' x 62'
4-cyl 2SCSA Doxford oil engine by bldrs.
4.1952 Completed by Hawthorn,Leslie & Co. Ltd for Houlder Line Ltd. 1972 Sold to Glyfada Seafaring,Greece ren. DINOS METHENITIS. 1979 Sold to Seafreight Holding Corp.,Panama ren. DINOS V. 1.1.1979 Beached at Gadani Beach for B/U.

H48. THORPE GRANGE(2) (1954 - 1973) 8695g 5120n 460' x 62'
4-cyl 2SCSA Doxford oil engine by Wallsend Slipway & Eng. Co. Ltd. 1954 Completed by Bartram & Sons Ltd,Sunderland for Houlder Line Ltd. 1966 Ren. ST. MERRIEL. 1971 Ren. THORPE GRANGE. 1972 Ren. ST. MERRIEL. 1973 Sold to Joo Hong Maritime Nav Pte Ltd,Singapore

ren. JOO HONG. 1975 Sold to Lita Shipping Co. Pte Ltd,Singapore
ren. PAN TECK. 1978 Ren. LIVA,Malaysian flag. 4.4.1979 Arrived
Kaohsiung in tow for B/U, having been laid-up at Colombo from
25.3.1977 to 10.3.1979.

H49. DENBY GRANGE(2) (1958 - 1973) 12572g 7209n 559' x 72' TANKER
2 Steam turbines DR geared to a single screw shaft.
7.1958 Completed by Hawthorn,Leslie & Co. Ltd,Hebburn for Houlder
Line Ltd. 1968 Converted to chemical tanker. 1969 Ren. STOLT
GRANGE. 1973 Sold to Dundee Shipping Inc,Liberia ren. STOLT PUMA.
1976 Sold to Nord Shipping Inc ren. PUMA(Li). 16.9.1976 Arrived
Kaohsiung for B/U.

H50. ROYSTON GRANGE(5) (1959 - 1972) 10261g 5028n 489' x 66'
2 Steam turbines DR geared to a single screw shaft.
1959 Completed by Hawthorn,Leslie & Co. Ltd,Hebburn for Houlder
Line Ltd. 14.2.1966 Rescued all crew of Spanish coaster MORCUERA
on fire near Ile de Batz,France. 11.5.1972 Collided with Liberian
tanker TIEN CHEE of 15595g in the Indio Channel,Plate Estuary
near Montevideo while outward bound from Buenos Aires to London
via Montevideo with a cargo of meat and butter. Crew of 63 including Chief Steward's wife and daughter and 10 passengers and
pilot burnt to death. Vessel towed to Montevideo and B/U in
Spain.

H51. HARDWICKE GRANGE(2) (1960 - 1977) 10337g 5086n 489' x 66'
2 Steam turbines DR geared to a single screw shaft.
1960 Completed by Hawthorn,Leslie & Co. Ltd,Hebburn for Houlder
Line Ltd. 1.1966 Stood by German ore-carrier KREMSERTOR in N.
Atlantic. 1975 Transferred to Shaw,Savill & Albion Co. Ltd. 1977
Sold to Montezillon Nav. Corp.,Liberia ren. JACQUES. 27.3.1979
Arrived Kaohsiung for B/U.

H52. OSWESTRY GRANGE(4) (1974 - 1985) 5440g 2725n 370' x 54'
6-cyl 2SCSA Stork oil engine by NV Werkspoor,Amsterdam.
1964 Completed by Bartram & Sons Ltd,Sunderland as CHELWOOD for
France,Fenwick & Co. Ltd,London. 1972/74 Mgd. by Houlder Bros.
1974 Company purchased by Houlder Brothers ren. OSWESTRY GRANGE,
continued in North East coal trade to London. 1985 Sold to
Oxelosund Hamn A/B,Sweden and hulked at Oxelosund as STEN JOHAN,
having left the Thames on 30.7.1985.

H53. UPWEY GRANGE(2) (1976 - 1982) 15906g 11082n 600' x 74' B26
6-cyl 2SCSA Sulzer oil engine by Hawthorn,Leslie & Co. Ltd,Newcastle.
3.3.1976 Launched and 5.1976 completed by Austin & Pickersgill
Ltd,Sunderland for Alexander Shipping Co. Ltd(Houlder Bros.). 1982
Sold to Ace Pacific Nav Co. SA,Panama ren. LILY VILLAGE. 1986 Sold to
Seama International Shipping Ltd,London ren. PUGGI. 1990 Sold to
Cyprian owners ren. NATALIA. 9.1991 Still in service.

H54. LYNTON GRANGE(3) (1976 - 1982) 15906g 11082n 600' x 74' B26
6-cyl 2SCSA Sulzer oil engine by Hawthorn,Leslie & Co. Ltd,Newcastle.
12.5.1976 Launched and 9.1976 completed by Austin & Pickersgill
Ltd, Sunderland for Alexander Shipping Co. Ltd(Houlder Bros.).

1982 Sold to Central Shipping Holdings Inc,Panama ren. NORTHERN
CHERRY. 2.1990 Sold to Greece ren. CHIOS CHARM. 9.1991 Still in
service.

H55. DUNSTER GRANGE(2) (1977 - 1982) 24024g 16863n 660' x 92'
6-cyl 2SCSA Sulzer oil engine by bldrs.
10.1967 Completed as CLYDESDALE for Hadley Shipping Co. Ltd by
Scotts SB & Eng. Co. Ltd,Greenock on 50/50 basis with Houlder
Bros. 1969 Ren. CLYDE BRIDGE. 1977 Purchased by Houlder Bros.
ren. DUNSTER GRANGE. 1982 Sold to Gulf Shipping Line Ltd ren.
GULF KESTREL. 1983 Sold to Graphite Shpg. Inc,Liberia ren. FIVE
STAR. 31.8.1986 Arrived Kaohsiung breakers.

H56. HORNBY GRANGE(3) (1979 - 1985) 39626g 25730n 749' x 106' TANKER
6-cyl B&W 2SCSA oil engine by bldrs.
6.10.1978 Launched and 20.6.1979 completed by Harland & Wolff Ltd,
Belfast for Alexander Shipping Co. Ltd(Houlder Bros.). 1985 Sold to
Fest Atlantic Co. Ltd,Monrovia(Island Nav. Corp Ltd,mgrs) ren. SANTA
BARBARA. 8.1989 Sold to Transpetrol Services,Brussels ren. AFFINITY.
9.1991 Still in service.

H57. ELSTREE GRANGE(4) (1979 - 1985) 39626g 25730n 749' x 106' TANKER
6-cyl B&W 2SCSA oil engine by bldrs.
27.1.1979 Launched and 24.10.1979 completed by Harland & Wolff Ltd,
Belfast for Alexander Shipping Co. Ltd(Houlder Bros.). 1985 Sold to
Fest Pacific Co. Ltd,Monrovia(Island Nav. Corp Ltd,mgrs) ren. SANTA
LUCIA. 3.1989 Sold to Transpetrol Services,Brussels ren. SPIRIT.
9.1991 Still in service.

H58. RIPON GRANGE (1979 - 1980) 28880g 20614n 716' x 92'
6-cyl 2SCSA Doxford oil engine by bldrs.
3.11.1967 Launched as OROTAVA for Ore Carriers Ltd(Houlder Bros) and
1968 completed by Sunderland Shipbuilders Ltd. 1969 Ren. OROTAVA
BRIDGE. 1974 Ren. OROTAVA. 1979 Ren. RIPON GRANGE. 1980 Sold to Leda
Segundo Cia Nav SA(Stravelakis),Panama ren. LEDA. 1982 Sold to Unity
Enterprises Co. Ltd,Malta ren. UNITY. 1985 Sold to Romneya Shipping
Corp.,Panama ren. LATINI. 20.3.1986 Left Trincomalee for Chinese
breakers and 25.4.1986 arrived in China.

H59. ROUNTON GRANGE(2) (1980 - 1984) 40753g 27867n 800' x 106'
6-cyl 2SCSA oil engine by bldrs.
1972 Completed by Brodogradliste 3 Maj,Rijeka as PACIFIC WASA for
Rederi A/B Disa,Stockholm. 1980 Purchased by Furness,Withy & Co. Ltd
(Houlder Bros) ren. ROUNTON GRANGE. 1984 Sold to Chong Shing Ocean
Enterprise Corp.,Taipei ren. CHINA MARQUIS. 1986 Sold to Nantai Line
Co. Ltd,Keelung ren. OCEAN PEACE. 10.1988 Sold to International Sugar
Transport Inc,Piraeus ren. FORUM GLORY. 9.1991 Still in service.

H60. BEACON GRANGE(4) (1982 - 1984) 12321g 6798n 530' x 73'
8-cyl 2SCSA B&W oil engine by J.G. Kincaid & Co. Ltd,Greenock.
3.1973 Completed as ORDUNA for Royal Mail Lines Ltd(P.S.N.C.,mgr) by
Cammell,Laird & Co. Ltd,Birkenhead. 1982 Ren. BEACON GRANGE. 1984 Sold
to Triport Shipping Co. Ltd(Cenaro Ltd),London ren. MERCHANT PIONEER.
9.1991 Still in service.

APPENDIX HA. ALEXANDER SHIPPING CO. LTD.

HA1. AYLESBURY (1947 - 1948) 6327g 4592n   407' x 55'
T 3-cyl by D. Rowan & Co. Ltd,Glasgow.
24.5.1941 Launched and 7.1941 completed by C. Connell & Co.
Ltd,Glasgow as EMPIRE GLEN for Ministry of War Transport. 1945
Purchased by Alexander Shipping Co. Ltd(Capper,Alexander & Co)
ren. AYLESBURY. 1947 Taken over by Houlder Bros. 1948 Sold to
Gibbs & Co.,Cardiff ren. WEST WALES. 1961 Sold to Iranian Lloyd
Co. Ltd,Iran ren. PERSIAN XERXES. 9.1964 Scrapped at Hendrik Ido
Ambacht.

HA2. BIBURY   (1947 - 1951) 6700g 4821n   416' x 56'
T 3-cyl by N.E. Marine Eng. Co. Ltd,Sunderland.
17.12.1941 Launched and 3.1942 completed as EMPIRE BALLAD by
Bartram & Sons Ltd,Sunderland for Ministry of War Transport. 1946
Purchased by Alexander Shipping Co. Ltd(Capper,Alexander & Co)
ren. BIBURY. 1947 Taken over by Houlder Bros. 1951 Sold to
Halcyon Lijn NV,Holland ren. STAD MAASSLUIS. 1962 Sold to Cia.
Nav. Jaguar (Palomba & Salvatori),Italy ren. JAGUAR. 1966 Reg.
under Olamar SA (Palomba & Salvatori),Italy ren. GOLDFIELD. 1968
Sold to Cia de Nav Sulemar(V.Coccoli),Italy ren POSEIDONE. 9.1969
Grounded on voyage Rouen to Egypt with grain, put into Naples.
Sold and 21.11.1969 Arrived Split in tow for B/U.

HA3. CHARLBURY (1947 - 1958) 7069g 5194n   432' x 56'
T 3-cyl by bldrs.
28.7.1941 Launched and 8.1941 completed by Cammell,Laird & Co.
Ltd,Birkenhead as EMPIRE CLIVE for Ministry of War Transport.
1946 Purchased by Alexander Shipping Co. Ltd(Capper,Alexander &
Co) ren. CHARLBURY. 1947 Taken over by Houlder Bros. 1958 Sold to
Red Anchor Line Ltd,Hong Kong ren. ISABEL ERICA. 1964 Reg. under
St. Merryn Shpg. Co. Ltd(C. Moller),Hong Kong. 8.1969 B/U at Hong
Kong.

HA4. EASTBURY (1947 - 1958) 7066g 4845n   432' x 56'
T 3-cyl by Central Marine Eng. Works,Hartlepool.
23.3.1943 Launched and 5.1943 completed by W. Gray & Co. Ltd,
Hartlepool as EMPIRE STALWART for Ministry of War Transport. 1946
Purchased by Alexander Shipping Co. Ltd(Capper,Alexander & Co)
ren. EASTBURY. 1947 Taken over by Houlder Bros. 1958 Sold to
Transportes Maritimos Mexicanos SA ren. CONSTITUCION. 10.1968 B/U
at Veracruz in Mexico.

HA5. HOLMBURY (1947 - 1960) 7081g 4871n   431' x 56'
T 3-cyl by N.E. Marine Eng. Co. Ltd,Newcastle.
11.11.1943 Launched and 12.1943 completed by Caledon SB & Eng.
Co. Ltd,Dundee for Ministry of War Transport as EMPIRE CANYON.
1947 Purchased by Alexander Shipping Co. Ltd(Capper,Alexander &
Co) ren. HOLMBURY. 1947 Taken over by Houlder Bros. 1960 Sold to
United Oriental Shipping Co,Karachi ren. ILYASBAKSH. 12.8.1965
Arrived Bombay; placed under restraint while undergoing rudder
repairs during Pakistan/India war. 11.1966 Impounded by Indian
Govt. 12.1970 Scrapped at Bombay.

HA6. KINGSBURY (1947 - 1960) 7246g 4382n   441' x 56'
T 3-cyl by General Electric Corp.,Hamilton,Ohio.
6.1944 Completed by Bethlehem-Fairfield SB, Baltimore as SAMLAMU
for Ministry of War Transport. 1947 Purchased by Alexander Shpg.
Co. Ltd(Capper,Alexander & Co) ren. KINGSBURY. 1947 Taken over by
Houlder Bros. 1960 Sold to Polish S.S. Co. Ltd ren. HUTA BEDZIN.
1969 Converted in Poland to a non-seagoing floating warehouse,
ren. M-ZP-GDY-6 later MP-ZP-GDY-6. 7.1982 Arrived Hamina in
Finland for B/U.

HA7. LEDBURY   (1948 - 1961) 7271g 4385n   441' x 56'
T 3-cyl by General Electric Corp.,Hamilton,Ohio.
10.1943 Completed by Bethlehem-Fairfield SB, Baltimore as SAMDAK
for Ministry of War Transport. 1947 Sold to Alpha S. African S.S.
Co. Ltd(Moller Line),London ren. ALPHA VAAL. 1948 Purchased by
Alexander Shipping Co. Ltd(Houlder Bros) ren. LEDBURY. 1961 Sold
to Polish Steamship Co., ren. KOPALNIA CZELADZ. 2.1973 Arrived
Faslane for B/U.

HA8. MALMESBURY (1949 - 1955) 7174g 4272n   425' x 57'
T 3-cyl by General Machinery Corporation,Hamilton.
1.1942 Completed by Todd-California SB, Richmond,California as
OCEAN VALLEY for Ministry of War Transport. 1949 Purchased by
Alexander Shipping Co. Ltd(Houlder Bros). 1955 Sold to Trafalgar
S.S. Co. Ltd(Tsavliris Shipping Ltd),London ren. GRANNY SUZANNE.
1958 Ren. FREE ENTERPRISE(Tsavliris). 1959 Ren. ALEXANDROS
TSAVLIRIS. 1964 Ren. NEWDENE(Tsavliris). 1965 Ren. FREE NAVIGATOR
(Tsavliris). 1969 B/U at La Spezia.

HA9. NEWBURY   (1951 - 1966) 11199g 6482n   530' x 68' TANKER
2SCSA Doxford oil engine by D. Rowan & Co. Ltd,Glasgow.
12.1951 Completed by Lithgows Ltd,Port Glasgow for Alexander
Shipping Co. Ltd(Houlder Bros). 1966 Sold to Angfartygs A/B Alfa
(Lundquist Rederierna),Mariehamn,Finland name u/ch. 20.8.1973
Arrived Faslane for B/U.

HA10. QUEENSBURY   (1953 - 1971) 6175g 3415n   457' x 60'
Two 6-cyl 2SCSA oil engines by Central Marine Eng. Works.
6.1953 Completed by Burntisland SB Co. Ltd,Burntisland for
Alexander Shipping Co. Ltd(Houlder Bros). 1971 Sold to Kyknos
Shipping Co. Ltd,Famagusta ren. SANDRA. 1973 FONG LEE. 1976 Sold
to Lien Chang Nav. Co. Ltd SA,Panama ren. LIEN CHANG. 18.11.1978
Arrived Kaohsiung for B/U.

HA11. SHAFTESBURY   (1958 - 1972) 8532g 4798n   457' x 62'
5-cyl Doxford' 2SCSA oil engine by Hawthorn,Leslie Ltd,Newcastle.
8.1958 Completed by Burntisland SB Co. Ltd,Burntisland for
Alexander Shipping Co. Ltd(Houlder Bros). 1972 Sold to First
United Carriers Inc,Panama ren. PORTLOE. 1973 Ren. ARAUCO. 1978
Sold to Fife Shipping Ltd,Panama ren. JALSEA CONDOR. 3.7.1978
Sprang a leak 25 miles off River Cunene,Angola o.v. Bangkok to
Lagos with general. Sank in tow to NE of Walvis Bay in position
19-10 S, 12-08 E on 6.7.1978.

HA12. TEWKESBURY (1959 - 1972) 8532g 4798n 457' x 62'
5-cyl Doxford 2SCSA oil engine by Hawthorn,Leslie Ltd,Newcastle.
1959 Completed by Burntisland SB Co. Ltd,Burntisland for
Alexander Shipping Co. Ltd(Houlder Bros). 1972 Sold to Del Bene
Ultramar SA,Buenos Aires ren. CAMINITO. 1981 Sold to Colbrook
Shipping Corp.,Panama ren. BRAZIL. 4.6.1983 Left New Orleans for
Busan for B/U.

HA13. WESTBURY (1960 - 1978) 8533g 4727n 457' x 62'
5-cyl Doxford 2SCSA oil engine by Hawthorn,Leslie Ltd,Newcastle.
11.1960 Completed by Burntisland SB Co. Ltd,Burntisland for
Alexander Shipping Co. Ltd(Houlder Bros). 1976 Transferred to
Shaw,Savill & Albion Co. Ltd. 1978 Sold to Celika Shipping Co.,
Greece ren. DIAMANDO. 1981 Sold to Iktinos Shipping Co.,Greece
ren. POLANA. 24.5.1983 Arrived at Gadani Beach for B/U.

HA14. TENBURY (1965 - 1972) 8252g 4600n 462' x 63'
6-cyl 2SCSA Sulzer oil engine by J. Brown & Co. Ltd,Clydebank.
4.10.1965 Completed by Burntisland SB Co. Ltd,Burntisland for
Alexander Shipping Co. Ltd(Houlder Bros). 1972 Sold to Bibby Bulk
Carriers Ltd,Liverpool(Houlder Bros,mgrs). 1974 Sold to Boundary
Bay Shipping Co.,Hong Kong ren. AL-BARAT. 1981 Sold to Arabian
Maritime Transport,Jeddah name u/ch. 1984 Sold to Byron Bay
Shipping Inc(Gulfeast Ship Management) ren. SEA EAGLE. 27.4.1984
Struck by missile near Bandar Khomeini, taken to Bushire and
arrived 3.12.1984 at Alang for B/U.

HA15. BANBURY (1971 - 1982) 11381g 6678n 524' x 75'
7-cyl Sulzer 2SCSA oil engine by bldrs.
1971 Completed by Scotts SB & Eng. Co. Ltd,Greenock as IRON
BANBURY for Alexander Shipping Co. Ltd(Houlder Bros) on bare-boat
charter to Broken Hill Proprietary Co. Ltd,Australia having been
launched as BANBURY. 1975 Ren. BANBURY. 1982 Sold to Wallem Ship
Management Ltd,Hong Kong ren. LADY MARINA. 1989 Sold to Mediterranean Shipping Co,Geneva ren. ARIANE S. 9.1991 Still in service.

APPENDIX HB. BRITISH EMPIRE STEAM NAVIGATION CO. LTD.

HB1. ORANGE RIVER (1914 - 1934) 4708g 2959n 385' x 52'
T 3-cyl by Richardsons,Westgarth & Co. Ltd,Hartlepool.
1914 Completed by Irvines SB & DD Co. Ltd,Hartlepool for British
Empire S.N. Co. Ltd(Houlder Bros). 1934 Sold to Antonis G.
Lemos,Chios ren. GAROUFALIA. 11.12.1939 Torpedoed and sunk by U38
near Namsos o.v. Oslo to Kirkenes in ballast.

HB2. BRISBANE RIVER (1914 - 1917) 4989g 3149n 400' x 52'
T 3-cyl by Richardsons,Westgarth & Co. Ltd,Hartlepool.
11.1914 Completed by Irvines SB & DD Co. Ltd,Hartlepool for
British Empire S.N. Co. Ltd(Houlder Bros). 16.4.1917 Captured and
sunk by bombs by U35 140 miles W of Gibraltar o.v. Malta to
Baltimore in ballast.

HB3. CLUTHA RIVER (1914 - 1933) 4986g 3145n 400' x 52'
T 3-cyl by Richardsons,Westgarth & Co. Ltd,Hartlepool.
12.1914 Completed by Irvines SB & DD Co. Ltd,Hartlepool for
British Empire S.N. Co. Ltd(Houlder Bros). 1915 Transferred to
Empire Transport Co. Ltd(Houlder Bros) ren. RHODESIAN TRANSPORT.
1933 Sold to Moller & Co.,Shanghai ren. ALICE MOLLER. 1946 Sold
to Zui Kong S.S. Co. Ltd,Shanghai ren. LING YUNG. 10.1948
Wrecked.

HB4. SAGAMA RIVER (1915 - 1932) 4728g 2990n 385' x 52'
T 3-cyl by Richardsons,Westgarth & Co. Ltd,Hartlepool.
1915 Completed by Irvines SB & DD Co. Ltd,Hartlepool for British
Empire S.N. Co. Ltd(Houlder Bros). 1932 Sold to Greece ren.
NITSA. 2.12.1943 Torpedoed and sunk by Japanese I-27 100 miles S
of Aden o.v. Calcutta to Aden and Alexandria with coal.

HB5. DERWENT RIVER (1915 - 1932) 4724g 2984n 385' x 52'
T 3-cyl by Richardsons,Westgarth & Co. Ltd,Hartlepool.
1915 Completed by Irvines SB & DD Co. Ltd,Hartlepool for British
Empire S.N. Co. Ltd(Houlder Bros). 1932 Sold to Greece ren.
ILISSOS. 1954 B/U in Japan.

HB6. SWAN RIVER (1915 - 1917) 4724g 2982n 385' x 52'
T 3-cyl by Richardsons,Westgarth & Co. Ltd,Hartlepool.
1915 Completed by Irvines SB & DD Co. Ltd,Hartlepool for British
Empire S.N. Co. Ltd(Houlder Bros), having been launched as VAAL
RIVER. 27.9.1917 Torpedoed and sunk by U39 27 miles NNW of Oran
o.v. Gibraltar to Benisaf in ballast.

HB7. PENNAR RIVER (1915 - 1916) 3801g 2373n 350' x 51'
T 3-cyl by Richardsons,Westgarth & Co. Ltd,Hartlepool.
1915 Completed by Irvines SB & DD Co. Ltd,Hartlepool for British
Empire S.N. Co. Ltd(Houlder Bros). 1916 Sold to Gascony S.S. Co.
Ltd(Leopold Walford),London ren. GASCONIA. 16.11.1917 Torpedoed
and sunk 12 miles NE1/2E of Cape Shershel,Algeria o.v. Barry to
Malta with coal and Govt. stores, 3 lost.

HB8. GAMBIA RIVER (1915 - 1933) 4724g 2984n 385' x 52'
T 3-cyl by Richardsons,Westgarth & Co. Ltd,Hartlepool.
1915 Completed by Irvines SB & DD Co. Ltd,Hartlepool for British
Empire S.N. Co. Ltd(Houlder Bros). 1933 Sold to Greece ren. MOUNT
PENTELIKON. 1934 Sold to Pateras Bros,Piraeus ren. AEAS. 7.9.1942
Torpedoed and sunk in Gulf of St. Lawrence by U165 o.v. Three
Rivers to U.K. with lumber and steel.

HB9. FRASER RIVER (1915 - 1921) 3805g 2350n 350' x 51'
T 3-cyl by Richardsons,Westgarth & Co. Ltd,Hartlepool.
1915 Completed by Irvines SB & DD Co. Ltd,Hartlepool for
British Empire S.N. Co. Ltd(Houlder Bros), having been laid
down as ST. LAWRENCE RIVER. 1921 Sold to Yule,Catto & Co.,
ren. RIVERWAY. 1922 Sold to Japan ren. ANZAN MARU. 3.7.1943
War loss.

HB10. MERSEY RIVER (1915 - 1916) 3805g 2375n   350' x 51'
T 3-cyl by Richardsons,Westgarth & Co. Ltd,Hartlepool.
1915 Completed by Irvines SB & DD Co. Ltd,Hartlepool for British
Empire S.N. Co. Ltd(Houlder Bros). 1916 Sold to James Moss & Co.,
Liverpool ren. MINIEH. 9.1.1917 Captured by German raider MOEWE
170 miles ENE of Pernambuco and sunk by bombs.

HB11. CARONI RIVER (1928 - 1940) 7807g 4844n 456' x 59' TANKER
Two 4SCSA oil engines by J.G. Kincaid & Co. Ltd,Greenock.
1928 Completed by Blythswood SB Co. Ltd,Glasgow for British
Empire S.N. Co. Ltd(Houlder Bros). 20.1.1940 Sunk by mine off
Falmouth while on trials.

HB12. DERWENT RIVER(2) (1945 - 1946) 8602g 4837n 475' x 62' TANKER
T 3-cyl by N.E. Marine Eng. Co. Ltd,Newcastle.
11.2.1941 Launched by Sir James Laing & Sons,Sunderland as EMPIRE
CORAL for Ministry of War Transport(Eagle Oil & Shipping Co Ltd).
1943 Houlder Bros. became mgrs. 1945 Purchased by British Empire
S.N. Co. Ltd(Houlder Bros) ren. DERWENT RIVER. 16.12.1946 Sold to
Northern Petroleum Tank S.S. Co. Ltd(Hunting & Son),Newcastle
ren. DERWENTFIELD. 1.9.1952 Badly damaged by explosion and fire
at Balik Papan and towed to Osaka, survey showed repairs to be
uneconomical and beached in Kitzu river,Osaka for B/U, which
began on 21.8.1953.

HB13. FRASER RIVER(2) (1947 - 1952) 7176g 4380n   441' x 56'
T 3-cyl by General Machinery Corporation,Hamilton,Ohio.
5.1944 Completed by Bethlehem-Fairfield SB, Baltimore as SAM-
SOARING for Ministry of War Transport. Took a heavy list to port
alongside fitting-out quay after engine room explosion blew out
side plating. 10.1944 Struck by heavy seas in a storm, severe
list to port but made Delaware river safely o.v. U.K./America.
1945 Touched bottom near Outer Dowsing Sands o.v. London to Hull,
repaired on Tyneside. 1947 Purchased by British Empire S.N. Co.
Ltd(Houlder Bros) ren. FRASER RIVER. 1952 Sold to Belmonte Cia
Nav SA,Panama ren. NORTH PRINCESS. 1959 Sold to Ermis Mar Co,
Panama ren. GEORGIOS A. 1960 Sold to St.Ioannis Shpg.,Piraeus
ren. IOANNIS K. 3.1.1968 Aground after steering gear damage at
Vung Tau,Vietnam in position 10-14 N,107-05 E o.v. Saigon to
Singapore in ballast,abandoned. 10.1968 Sold to Korean ship-
breakers. 8.1973 Resold to Vietnam breakers, B/U.

HB14. CLUTHA RIVER(2) (1952 - 1966) 12323g 7061n 557' x 70' TANKER
6-cyl oil engine Doxford by bldrs.
1952 Completed by Hawthorn,Leslie & Co. Ltd,Hebburn for British
Empire S.N. Co. Ltd(Houlder Bros). 1966 Sold to Marguardia Cia
Nav SA,Chios ren. ARES III. 24.11.1969 Reported crankshaft damage
o.v. Kandlha to Japan, discharged Chiba. 22.3.1970 Arrived
Shanghai in tow for B/U.

HB15. SWAN RIVER(2) (1959 - 1971) 9637g 5354n 487' x 64'
5-cyl 2SCSA oil engine by Hawthorn,Leslie & Co. Ltd,Newcastle.
1959 Completed by Greenock Dockyard Co. Ltd,Greenock for British
Empire S.N. Co. Ltd(Houlder Bros). 1971 Sold to Premier Shipping

Corp. Inc,Singapore(Maldivian National Trading Corp. Ltd) ren.
PREMIER ATLANTIC.1973 Sold to Weymouth Shipping Co. Ltd,Singapore
ren. CONFIDENCE EXPRESS. 1979 Sold to Strathmure Freighters,Sing-
apore ren. BACHLONG. 7.12.1979 Arrived in tow at Rio de Janeiro
following engine failure and collapse of her tween decks o.v.
Vitoria to Karachi. 1980 Sold to Humber Shipping Co. Ltd,Panama
ren. EASTERN CONCORD. 1981 Reg. under Everjust Shipping Co. Ltd,
Panama. 30.1.1983 Arrived Bombay for B/U.

APPENDIX HE. EMPIRE TRANSPORT CO. LTD.

HE1. EMPIRE TRANSPORT   (1910 - 1912) 4849g 3072n 410' x 52'
T 3-cyl by Richardsons,Westgarth & Co. Ltd,Sunderland.
5.1909 Completed as SAVANNAH by Northumberland SB Co. Ltd,Howdon-
on-Tyne for Furness,Withy & Co. Ltd. 1910 Purchased by Empire
Transport Co. Ltd(Houlder Bros) ren. EMPIRE TRANSPORT. 1912 Sold
to Holland America Line ren. SOMMELSDIJK. 1934 Sold to Atlantide
Soc. per Imprese,Italy ren. ANTIOPE. 1936 Ren. ATLANTIDE.
23.12.1938 Wrecked off Valkenisse in River Scheldt o.v. Antwerp
to Savona with wheat.

HE2. INDIAN TRANSPORT   (1910 - 1929) 4111g 2650n 365' x 51'
T 3-cyl by Richardsons,Westgarth & Co. Ltd,Sunderland.
5.1910 Completed by Northumberland SB Co. Ltd,Howdon-on-Tyne for
Empire Transport Co. Ltd(Houlder Bros). 1929 Sold to Livanos
Bros(N.G. Livanos,mgr),Greece ren. NAGOS. 1934 Sold to Mrs. P.G.
Andrendi,Chios ren. THETIS A. 14.7.1940 Torpedoed and sunk by U52
in Western Approaches o.v. Roasario to Limerick with grain.

HE3. CAPE TRANSPORT   (1910 - 1929) 4130g 2650n 365' x 51'
T 3-cyl by Richardsons,Westgarth & Co. Ltd,Sunderland.
6.1910 Completed by Northumberland SB Co. Ltd,Howdon-on-Tyne for
Empire Transport Co. Ltd(Houlder Bros) having been launched as
GRACIANA for Furness,Withy & Co. Ltd. 1929 Sold to Chios S.S. Co.
Ltd(saliaris Bros),Greece ren. CHRISTOFOROS but seized back due
to non-payment of balance of purchase price on 12.1931. 1932 Sold
to 'K' S.S. Co. Ltd(Kaye,Son & Co),London ren. MARGAY. 4.1933
Sold for B/U in Italy.

HE4. BRITISH TRANSPORT (1910 - 1932) 4143g 2663n 365' x 51'
T 3-cyl by Richardsons,Westgarth & Co. Ltd,Middlesbrough.
6.1910 Completed by Raylton Dixon & Co.,Middlesbrough for Empire
Transport Co. Ltd(Houlder Bros). .191 5-hour action with U-boat
resulting in sinking of U-boat o.v. Brest to Archangel with ammunition and high explosives. Capt. Pope awarded D.S.O. for his
bravery, plus a large monetary prize offered to first merchantman
who sank a submarine. 11.9.1917 Missed by 2 torpedoes and attacked by gunfire in Atlantic. 1932 B/U in Italy.

HE5. NATAL TRANSPORT   (1910 - 1915) 4107g 2648n 365' x 51'
T 3-cyl by Richardsons,Westgarth & Co. Ltd,Sunderland.
6.1910 Completed by Northumberland SB Co. Ltd,Howdon-on-Tyne for
Empire Transort Co. Ltd(Houlder Bros). 4.9.1915 Torpedoed and

sunk by U34 40 miles W of Gavdo Island,S. Crete o.v. Bombay to
Liverpool with general.

HE6. CANADIAN TRANSPORT (1910 - 1932) 4139g 2654n 365' x 51'
T 3-cyl by Richardsons,Westgarth & Co. Ltd,Middlesbrough.
7.1910 Completed by Raylton Dixon & Co.,Middlesbrough for Empire
Transport Co. Ltd(Houlder Bros). 1932 B/U.

HE7. ARGENTINE TRANSPORT (1911 - 1916) 4763g 3024n 385' x 52'
T 3-cyl by Richardsons,Westgarth & Co. Ltd,Hartlepool.
1911 Completed by Irvines SB & DD Co. Ltd,Hartlepool for Empire
Transport Co. Ltd(Houlder Bros). 1916 Transferred to Furness,
Withy & Co. Ltd ren. PARISIANA. 23.4.1916 Captured and torpedoed
82 miles SW of Ushant by U19 o.v. London to Newport News with
manure and Fuller's earth.

HE8. AMERICAN TRANSPORT (1911 - 1929) 4767g 3010n 385' x 52'
T 3-cyl by Richardsons,Westgarth & Co. Ltd,Hartlepool.
1911 Completed by Irvines SB & DD Co. Ltd,Hartlepool for Empire
Transport Co. Ltd(Houlder Bros). 1929 Sold to Hendrik Fisser
A.G.,Emden ren. MARTHA HENDRIK FISSER. 2.1935 Wrecked.

HE9. AUSTRALIAN TRANSPORT (1911 - 1918) 4773g 3030n 385' x 52'
T 3-cyl by Richardsons,Westgarth & Co. Ltd,Hartlepool.
1911 Completed by Irvines SB & DD Co. Ltd,Hartlepool for Empire
Transport Co. Ltd(Houlder Bros). 23.8.1918 Torpedoed and sunk off
Bizerta 40 miles WNW of Marittimo Island o.v. Karachi to Bizerta
with wheat and onions.

HE10. QUEENSLAND TRANSPORT (1913 - 1934) 4663g 2939n 385' x 52'
T 3-cyl by Richardsons,Westgarth & Co. Ltd,Hartlepool.
1913 Completed by Irvines SB & DD Co. Ltd,Hartlepool for Empire
Transport Co. Ltd(Houlder Bros). 1934 Sold to Goulandris Bros.,
Andros ren. MAROUSSIO LOGOTHETIS. 9.7.1940 Seized at Diego
Suarez,Madagascar by Vichy French(Messageries Maritime,mgr) ren.
GENERAL DUQUESNE. 7.1942 Recovered by British forces at Mayotta
Island. 15.5.1943 Torpedoed and sunk by U105 in posn. 5-28 N, 14-
28 W o.v. Rio de Janeiro to Freetown and U.K. with ore.

HE11. VICTORIAN TRANSPORT (1913 - 1932) 4482g 2849n 385' x 52'
T 3-cyl by Richardsons,Westgarth & Co. Ltd,Sunderland.
1913 Completed by Northumberland SB Co. Ltd,Howdon-on-Tyne for
Empire Transport Co. Ltd(Houlder Bros). 1914 Seized by Germany at
Stettin, remaining there until end 1918, when re-entered company
service. 1932 Sold to N.G. Livanos,Piraeus ren. EVI. 1937 Reg.
under Theofano Maritime Co. Ltd(N.G. Livanos,mgr),Piraeus ren.
ALIAKMON. 11.11.1941 Sailed from Loch Ewe in ballast for
Sydney(CB) and disappeared.

HE12. TASMANIAN TRANSPORT (1913 - 1932) 4482g 2850n 385' x 52'
T 3-cyl by Richardsons,Westgarth & Co. Ltd,Sunderland.
1913 Completed by Northumberland SB Co. Ltd,Howdon-on-Tyne for
Empire Transport Co. Ltd(Houlder Bros). 1932 Sold for B/U in
Italy.

HE13. AFRICAN TRANSPORT (1913 - 1918) 4482g 2852n 385' x 52'
T 3-cyl by Richardsons,Westgarth & Co. Ltd,Sunderland.
1913 Completed by Northumberland SB Co. Ltd,Howdon-on-Tyne for
Empire Transport Co. Ltd(Houlder Bros). 25.6.1918 Torpedoed and
sunk by UB88 3 miles N of Whitby o.v. Tyne to Falmouth with coal,
3 lost.

HE14. OCEAN TRANSPORT (1913 - 1928) 4643g 2919n 385' x 52'
T 3-cyl by Richardsons,Westgarth & Co. Ltd,Hartlepool.
1913 Completed by Irvines SB & DD Co. Ltd,Hartlepool for Empire
Transport Co. Ltd(Houlder Bros). 30.1.1928 Wrecked on Ocean
Island in South Pacific in a hurricane.

HE15. IMPERIAL TRANSPORT (1913 - 1917) 4645g 2924n 385' x 52'
T 3-cyl by Richardsons,Westgarth & Co. Ltd,Hartlepool.
1913 Completed by Irvines SB & DD Co. Ltd,Hartlepool for Empire
Transport Co. Ltd(Houlder Bros). 11.4.1917 Torpedoed and sunk by
UC34 140 miles NW1/2W of Alexandria o.v. Port Said to Phillippe-
ville in ballast.

HE16. PACIFIC TRANSPORT (1913 - 1932) 4482g 2848n 385' x 52'
T 3-cyl by Richardsons,Westharth & Co. Ltd,Sunderland.
1913 Completed by Northumberland SB Co. Ltd,Howdon-on-Tyne for
Empire Transport Co. Ltd(Houlder Bros). 1932 Sold for B/U in
Italy.

HE17. NEW ZEALAND TRANSPORT (1913 - 1917) 4481g 2848n 385' x 52'
T 3-cyl by Richardsons,Westgarth & Co. Ltd,Sunderland.
1913 Completed by Northumberland SB Co. Ltd,Howdon-on-Tyne for
Empire Transport Co. Ltd(Houlder Bros). 14.6.1917 Torpedoed and
sunk by UC23 in Aegean 8 miles SE of Serphopulo Island o.v. Port
Talbot to Mudros with coal.

HE18. ROYAL TRANSPORT (1913 - 1929) 4213g 2927n 385' x 52'
T 3-cyl by Richardsons,Westgarth & Co. Ltd,Hartlepool.
1913 Completed by Irvines SB & DD Co. Ltd,Hartlepool for Empire
Transport Co. Ltd(Houlder Bros). 1929 Sold to J. Wessels,Germany
ren. JOHANN WESSELS. 9.1941 Wrecked.

HE19. EGYPTIAN TRANSPORT (1914 - 1933) 4648g 2923n 385' x 52'
T 3-cyl by Richardsons,Westgarth & Co. Ltd,Hartlepool.
1914 Completed by Irvines SB & DD Co. Ltd,Hartlepool for Empire
Transport Co. Ltd(Houlder Bros). 1933 Sold to Moller & Co.,
Shanghai ren. HELEN MOLLER. 1933 Sold to J.Chandris,Greece ren.
RITA CHANDRIS. 1939 Sold to F. Grauds,Riga ren. EVERIGA.
24.5.1945 Reported at Copenhagen; ceded to U.S.S.R. as EVERIGA.
1960 Deleted.

HE20. PANAMA TRANSPORT (1914 - 1933) 4644g 2920n 385' x 52'
T 3-cyl by Richardsons,Westgarth & Co. Ltd,Hartlepool.
1914 Completed by Irvines SB & DD Co. Ltd,Hartlepool for Empire
Transport Co. Ltd(Houlder Bros). 1933 Sold for B/U in Italy.

HE21. RHODESIAN TRANSPORT   See CLUTHA RIVER HB3

HE22. IMPERIAL TRANSPORT(2) (1931 - 1947) 8022g 4830n 460' x 60'
Two 8-cyl 4SCSA oil engines by N.E. Marine Eng. Co Ltd,Newcastle.
1931 Completed by Blythswood SB Co. Ltd,Glasgow for Empire Transport Co. Ltd(Houlder Bros) and laid-up in Holy Loch for two years
due to depressed tanker rates. 11.2.1940 Torpedoed in posn. 59 N,
12 W and broke in two, stern half recovered and new bow built by
W. Hamilton & Co. Ltd. 25.3.1942 Torpedoed off St. John's(NF),
towed in and on to New York where she was repaired. 1947 Sold to
Victor Jensen Rederi A/S (Simonsen & Astrup,mgrs),Oslo ren.
MESNA. 1949 Sold to Skibs A/S Agmes(E. Saanum,mgr),Mandal ren.
RONA. 1958 B/U in Germany.

HE23. ARGENTINE TRANSPORT(2) See OSWESTRY GRANGE(2) H32

HE24. ARGENTINE TRANSPORT(3) (1947 - 1958) 7176g 4380n 441' x 56'
T 3-cyl by Springfield Mch. & Foundry Co.,Springfield,Mass.
2.1944 Completed by New England SB Corp.,Portland(Me) as SAMTYNE
for Ministry of War Transport. 1947 Purchased by Empire Transport
Co. Ltd(Houlder Bros) ren. ARGENTINE TRANSPORT. 1958 Sold to
S. Atlantic Shpg. Co. Ltd,Liberia ren. ARCHANDROS. 1967 Ren.
ZEPHYR. 12.1968 Scrapped at Hirao.

HE25. IMPERIAL TRANSPORT(3) (1953 - 1964) 11365g 6356n 543' x 69'
6-cyl 2SCSA Doxford oil engine by Vickers-Armstrong Ltd,Barrow.
1.1953 Completed by Greenock Dockyard Co. Ltd,Greenock for Empire
Transport Co. Ltd(Houlder Bros) on charter to SHELL. 1964 Sold to
Cia de Athenian de Nav SA,(Fafalios)Liberia ren. ANGELIKI. 1969
B/U at Kaosiung.

HE26. OCEAN TRANSPORT(2) (1962 - 1979) 8608g 4812n 463' x 63'
4-cyl Hawthorn - Doxford (P type) oil engine.
1962 Completed by Hawthorn,Leslie & Co. Ltd,Hebburn for Empire
Transport Co. Ltd(Houlder Bros). 1975 Reg. under Shaw,Savill &
Albion Co. Ltd. 1977 Transferred to Welldeck Shipping Co. Ltd
(Furness,Withy & Co. Ltd). 1979 Sold to Viceroy Maritime Corporation,Liberia ren. ELLION HOPE. 27.2.1983 Arrived Gadani Beach
for B/U.

APPENDIX HF. BRITISH & ARGENTINE S.N. CO. LTD/FURNESS-HOULDER
ARGENTINE LINES

HF1. LA BLANCA   (1911 - 1917) 6813g 4405n   425' x 57'
T 3-cyl by G. Clark Ltd,Sunderland.
1906 Completed by James Laing & Son,Sunderland for Anglo-Argentine
Shipping Co.(J.& E. Hall Ltd). 1908 Purchased by Argentine Cargo
Line(Birt,Potter & Hughes,mgr),Liverpool. 1911 Chartered by
Furness,Withy & Co. Ltd(Houlder Bros,mgr). 23.11.1917 Torpedoed
and sunk 10 miles SSE of Berry Head by U96 o.v. Buenos Aires to Le
Havre with meat and general.

HF2. EL ARGENTINO   (1911 - 1916) 6809g 4411n   425' x 57'
T 3-cyl by G. Clark Ltd,Sunderland.
1907 Completed by James Laing & Son,Sunderland for Anglo-Argentine
Shipping Co.(J.&E. Hall Ltd). 1908 Purchased by Argentine Cargo

Line(Birt,Potter & Hughes,mgr),Liverpool. 1911 Chartered by
Furness,Withy & Co. Ltd(Houlder Bros,mgr). 1912 Transferred to
British & Argentine Steam Nav. Co. Ltd(Furness,Withy & Co. Ltd).
26.5.1916 Struck a mine and sank 7 miles SSE of Southwold laid by
UC1 o.v. Hull and London to Buenos Aires in ballast.

HF3. EL URUGUAYO   (1912 - 1937) 8361g 4967n   440' x 59'
Two T 3-cyl by bldrs,2-screw.
4.1912 Completed by A. Stephen & Sons Ltd,Glasgow for British &
Argentine S.N. Co. Ltd(Furness,Withy & Co. Ltd). 1937 Sold for
scrap.

HF4. LA ROSARINA   (1912 - 1937) 8332g 4948n   440' x 59'
Two T 3-cyl by bldrs,2-screw.
6.1912 Completed by Palmers Co.,Jarrow for British & Argentine
S.N. Co. Ltd(Furness,Withy & Co. Ltd). 1937 Sold for scrap in
Japan, ren. ROSARINA for voyage to breakers.

HF5. EL CORDOBES   (1912 - 1929) 5683g 3792n   421' x 53'
T 3-cyl by J. Dickinson & Sons Ltd,Sunderland.
1900 Completed by James Laing & Son,Sunderland as INDRADEVI for
T.B. Royden & Co.,Liverpool. 1911 Purchased by Furness,Withy &
Co. Ltd ren. CHASESIDE. 1912 Transferred to British & Argentine
S.N. Co. Ltd(Furness,Withy & Co. Ltd) ren. EL CORDOBES. 1929 Sold
to M. Querei & O. Rosini,Genoa ren. PRATOMAGNO. 1931 B/U.

HF6. ORIANA   (1912 - 1913) See B.M.T.   FB16

HF7. WYANDOTTE   (1912 - 1914) See B.M.T.   FB8

HF8. LA NEGRA   (1913 - 1917) 8312g 4949n   440' x 59'
Two T 3-cyl by bldrs,2-screw.
4.1913 Completed by Palmers Co.,Jarrow for British & Argentine
S.N. Co. Ltd(Houlder Bros). 3.9.1917 Torpedoed and sunk by UC50
50 miles SSW of Start Point o.v. Buenos Aires to U.K. with meat,
4 lost.

HF9. ABADESA   (1916 - 1928) See ELSTREE GRANGE(2) H28

HF10. CANONESA (1916 - 1919) See BOLLINGTON GRANGE H24

HF11. CONDESA   (1916 - 1917) 8800g 5146n   430' x 61'
Two T 3-cyl by bldrs,2-screw.
1916 Completed by Earles Co.,Hull for Furness-Houlder Argentine
Line Ltd(Houlder Bros). 7.7.1917 Torpedoed by U84 and sank
following day in Western Approaches on her maiden voyage home
from the Plate with meat.

HF12. DUQUESA   (1918 - 1940) 8651g 5400n   429' x 61'
Two T 3-cyl by Richardson,Westgarth & Co. Ltd,Hartlepool,2-screw.
5.1918 Completed by Irvines SB & DD Co. Ltd,Hartlepool for
Furness-Houlder Argentine Line Ltd(Houlder Bros). 18.12.1940
Captured by German battleship ADMIRAL SCHEER o.v. home from the
Plate with meat. 18.2.1941 Sunk after use as a storeship.

HF 13. BARONESA (1918 - 1946) 8663g 5408n 431' x 61'
Two T 3-cyl by Richardson,Westgarth & Co. Ltd,Hartlepool,2-screw.
4.1918 Completed by Sir Raylton Dixon & Co.,Middlesbrough for
Furness-Houlder Argentine Line Ltd(Houlder Bros). 1946 Sold for
scrap in Belgium.

HF 14. PRINCESA (1918 - 1949) 8731g 5453n 430' x 61'
Two T 3-cyl by J. Brown & Co. Ltd,Clydebank,2-screw.
7.1918 Completed by A. Stephen & Sons Ltd,Glasgow for Furness-
Houlder Argentine Line Ltd(Houlder Bros). 3.1949 Sold for scrap
at Blyth.

HF 15. MARQUESA (1918 - 1947) 8979g 5604n 430' x 61'
Two T 3-cyl by D. Rowan & Co. Ltd,Glasgow,2-screw.
7.1918 Completed by W. Hamilton & Co. Ltd,Port Glasgow for
Furness-Houlder Argentine Line Ltd(Houlder Bros). 1947 Sold for
scrap and B/U at Faslane in 1948.

HF 16. CANONESA(2) (1920 - 1940) 8286g 5102n 450' x 58'
2 Steam turbines DR geared to a single screw shaft by bldrs.
6.3.1920 Launched as a 'WAR' standard G class meat carrier and
4.11.1920 completed as CANONESA by Workman,Clark & Co. Ltd,Belfast
for Furness-Houlder Argentine Line Ltd(Houlder Bros). 21.9.1940
Torpedoed and sunk by U100 in posn. 54-53 N, 18-25 W o.v. Montreal
and Sydney(NS) to Manchester with frozen meat,cheese, and fish.

HF 17. EL ARGENTINO (1929 - 1943) 9501g 6011n 431' x 65'
Two 6-cyl 2SCSA oil engines by bldrs,2-screw.
12.1.1928 Launched and 4.1928 completed by Fairfield SB Co. Ltd,
Glasgow for British & Argentine S.N. Co. Ltd(Furness,Withy & Co.
Ltd). 1936 Transferred to Furness-Houlder Argentine Line Ltd
(Houlder Bros). 26.7.1943 Destroyed by German aircraft off
Portuguese coast while outward bound from Glasgow to the Plate
in ballast.

HF 18. CONDESA(2) (1944 - 1962) 10367g 6251n 465' x 65'
Two 6-cyl 2SCSA Werkspoor oil engines by bldrs,2-screw.
17.8.1943 Launched and 4.1944 completed by Hawthorn,Leslie & Co.
Ltd,Hebburn for Furness-Houlder Argentine Line Ltd(Houlder Bros).
31.10.1960 Chartered by French Govt. and used as a storeship for
frozen meat at Boulogne. 6.1962 Arrived Spezia for B/U.

HF 19. DUQUESA(2) (1949 - 1966) 11007g 6564n 479' x 66'
2 Steam turbines DR geared to a single screw shaft by bldrs.
7.1948 Launched by Mrs. M.C. Houlder and 3.1949 completed by
Hawthorn,Leslie & Co. Ltd,Hebburn for Furness-Houlder Argentine
Line Ltd(Houlder Bros). 1968 Transferred to Royal Mail. 14.8.1969
Arrived Spezia for B/U.

HF 20. ABADESA(2) (1962 - 1973) 13350g 7951n 565.0 x 72' TANKER
6-cyl 2SCSA Doxford oil engine by bldrs.
1962 Completed by Swan,Hunter & Wigham Richardson Ltd,Wallsend
for Furness-Houlder Argentine Lines Ltd. 1968 Transferred to
Royal Mail, retained Houlder funnel. 3.1969 Converted to a chem-

ical tanker at Horten for long-term charter to Stolt Nielsen for
carriage of chemicals,fats etc. ren. STOLT ABADESA. 1971 Reg.
under Pacific Maritime Services Ltd. 1973 Sold to Aberdeen
Shipping Inc,Monrovia,still on charter to Stolt-Nielsen ren.
STOLT TIGER. 1974 Ren. STOLT VIKING. 1983 Sold to Alap Shipping,
Piraeus ren. VIKING. 30.4.1983 Laid-up at Piraeus. 1984 Ren.
TRITON. 1984 Sold to Newstead Shipping Corp,Panama ren. NEW
BRIGHTON. 1986 Sold to Alkona Shpg. SA,Panama ren. EMIR MAN.
6.11.1986 Arrived Dubai after suffering a fire and explosion,
sold to breakers in Pakistan. Arrived Gadani Beach prior to
15.2.1987.

APPENDIX HO.
ORE CARRIERS LTD/HOULDER OFFSHORE LTD/OCEAN GAS TRANSPORT LTD

HO1. ORELIA   (1954 - 1971) 6858g 3268n   427' x 57'
Two 5-cyl 2SCSA Gray-Polar oil engines by Central Marine Eng. Works.
3.1954 Completed by W. Gray & Co. Ltd,Hartlepool for Ore Carriers
Ltd(Houlder Bros). 1971 Sold to Allied Finance SA,Piraeus ren.
ORELIA STAR. 1973 Sold to Orelia Star Shipping Co.,Famagusta ren.
MARISUERTA. 29.4.1974 Arrived Hsinkiang for B/U.

HO2. OREOSA   (1954 - 1971) 6856g 3267n   427' x 57'
Two 5-cyl 2SCSA Gray-Polar oil engines by Central Marine Eng. Works.
5.1954 Completed by W. Gray & Co. Ltd,Hartlepool for Ore Carriers
Ltd(Houlder Bros). 1971 Sold to Allied Finance SA,Piraeus ren.
OREOSA STAR. 1973 Sold to Mariluck Maritime Co. Ltd,Famagusta
ren. MARILUCK. 1974 Sold to Prekookeanska Plovidba,Bar(Yu) ren.
PODGORICA. 1988 Sold to Dabinovic SA,St. Vincent ren. ALMADEN.
25.3.1989 Arrived Alang for B/U.

HO3. OREPTON   (1955 - 1971) 6859g 3219n   427' x 57'
Two 5-cyl 2SCSA Gray-Polar oil engines by Central Marine Eng. Works.
3.1955 Completed by W. Gray & Co. Ltd,Hartlepool for Ore Carriers
Ltd(Houlder Bros). 1971 Sold to Allied Finance SA,Piraeus ren.
OREPTON STAR. 1973 Sold to Orepton Shipping Co. Ltd(Chandris,mgr)
ren. MARITIHI. 5.5.1974 Arrived Hsinkiang for B/U.

HO4. OREDIAN   (1955 - 1971) 6859g 3219n   427' x 57'
Two 5-cyl 2SCSA Gray-Polar oil engines by Central Marine Eng. Works.
7.1955 Completed by W. Gray & Co. Ltd,Hartlepool for Ore Carriers
Ltd(Houlder Bros). 1971 Sold to Allied Finance SA,Piraeus ren.
OREDIAN STAR. 1973 Sold to Oredian Shpg. Co. Ltd(Chandris,mgr)
ren. MARICHANCE. 1974 B/U in China.

HO5. OREGIS   (1955 - 1982) 6858g 3009n   427' x 57'
5-cyl 2SCSA Doxford oil engines by Hawthorn,Leslie & Co. Ltd.
11.1955 Completed by W. Gray & Co. Ltd,Hartlepool for Ore Carriers
Ltd(Houlder Bros). 1974 Sold to Houlder Offshore Ltd. 10.3.1974
Aground at Spanish Battery,Tynemouth while leaving on trials on
completion of conversion to diving main-tenance support ship by
Smiths Dock Co. Ltd,North Shields. Tyne tug NORTHSIDER also aground
during refloating attempts. 8.4.1974 Re-floated with severe bottom
damage,repairs at North Shields took 3 months at a cost of £2M.

1974 Ren. HTS COUPLER 1. 1975 Ren. OREGIS. 11.1982 Left Tyne for breakers at Vigo.

HO6. OREMINA (1956 - 1974) 6858g 3010n 427' x 57'
5-cyl 2SCSA Doxford oil engines by Hawthorn,Leslie & Co. Ltd.
5.1956 Completed by W. Gray & Co. Ltd,Hartlepool for Vallum
Shipping Co. Ltd(Houlder Bros). 1974 Sold to Societa Riunite di
Nav. srl,Italy ren. GENERALE FEDERICO. 8.3.1985 Arrived Savona for
B/U.

HO7. JOYA McCANCE (1960 - 1976) 11871g 4812n 507' x 68'
5-cyl 2SCSA oil engine by Central Marine Eng. Works,Hartlepool.
1960 Completed by W. Gray & Co. Ltd,Hartlepool for Ore Carriers Ltd
(Houlder Bros). 1966 Ren. ST. MARGARET. 1976 Sold to Independent
Carriers Inc,Panama name u/ch. 1978 Sold to Hadiotis Shipping Co.
SA,Piraeus ren. HADIOTIS. 12.7.1986 Suffered damage to intermediate
tailshaft while anchored in R. Orinoco between Smalkalden and
Puerto Ordaz, having arrived there on 26.2.1986. 1987 Sold for use
as a barge on Orinoco ren. MARITIMA VI. 14.4.1989 Arrived Malta in
tow of Russian tug BIZON from Orinoco, left Valetta 25.4.1989 in
tow of BIZON for Iskunderun.

HO8. MABEL WARWICK (1960 - 1976) 11632g 4679n 500' x 68'
5-cyl 2SCSA oil engine by Central Marine Eng. Works,Hartlepool.
1960 Completed by W. Gray & Co. Ltd,Hartlepool for Ore Carriers
Ltd(Houlder Bros). 1976 Sold to Celika Navigation Co. Ltd,Cyprus
ren. NIKOLAOS MALEFAKIS. 1980 Sold to Rubini Shipping Co. Ltd,
Piraeus ren. RUBINI. 12.7.1982 Arrived Piraeus with engine damage
o.v. from Caen, repairs uneconomical & scrapped at Perama during
10.1983.

HO9. BRANDON PRIORY (1960 - 1975) 22735g 12582n 660' x 85'
Steam turbine DR geared to 1 shaft by bldr.
1960 Completed by Hawthorn,Leslie & Co. Ltd,Hebburn for Warwick
Tanker Co. Ltd(Houlder Bros) for charter to BP. 9.6.1975 Arrived
Castellon for B/U.

HO10.BIDFORD PRIORY (1960 - 1975) 22748g 12596n 660' x 85'
Steam turbine DR geared to 1 shaft by bldr.
1960 Completed by Cammell,Laird & Co. Ltd,Birkenhead for Warwick
Tanker Co. Ltd(Houlder Bros) for charter to BP. 29.10.1975 Arrived
Faslane for B/U.

HO11.AVOGADRO (1964 - 1970) 855g 526n 204' x 30'
12-cyl Vee Pielstick oil engine.
1962 Completed by Chants Nav de la Ciotat for Margas spA,Palermo
having been launched as ARAGO. 1964 Purchased by Gazocean,Paris and
transferred to Ocean Gas Transport Co. Ltd(Houlder Bros). 1970 Sold
to Caribgaz Inc, ren.CARIBGAZ. 1971 Sold to Luzon Stevedoring
Co.,Manila ren. LSCO ANZAC. 14.9.1975 On fire at Cebu, total loss.

HO12.JOULE(1) (1964 - 1970) 2291g 1199n 299' x 40'
10-cyl 4SCSA M.A.N. oil engine.

1964 Completed by Dubigeon-Normandie,Nantes for Ocean Gas Transport
Co. Ltd(Houlder Bros). 1970 Sold to Carbrooke Soc di Nav Oceangas
spA,Italy ren. GIAMBATTISTA VENTURI. 10.1.1983 Sold to Ditta
Palermo for demolition at Naples.

HO13. CLERK-MAXWELL (1966 - 1986) 8298g 4642n ⠀⠀461' x 63'
7-cyl Hawthorn-Sulzer oil engine.
1966 Completed by Hawthorn,Leslie & Co. Ltd,Hebburn for Nile S.S.
Co. Ltd(Houlder Bros). Later to Ocean Gas Transport Co. Ltd,London.
1983 Reg. under Stevinson Hardy(Tankers) Ltd. 1984 Reg. under
Shaw,Savill & Albion Co. Ltd. 7.2.1986 Arrived Aviles for B/U.

HO14. JOYA McCANCE(2) (1967 - 1968) 26836g 16822n 699' x 92' TANKER
2 General Electric Steam turbines DR geared to single screw shaft.
1964 Launched as BEAUVAL by Kristiansand M.V. for Bion Biornstad,
Oslo and completed for Ore Carriers Ltd(Houlder Bros). 1966 Ren.
JOYA McCANCE by Houlder Bros. 7.1.1977 Arrived Kaohsiung for B/U.

HO15. OROTAVA ⠀⠀⠀⠀⠀(1967 - 1979) See RIPON GRANGE H58

HO16. HUMBOLDT ⠀⠀⠀⠀(1968 - 1984) 5200g 2666n ⠀⠀383' x 54'
7-cyl 2SCSA M.A.N. oil engine,2-screw.
1968 Completed by Chantiers dela Ciotat,La Ciotat for Ocean Gas
Transport Co. Ltd(Houlder Bros). 1984 Sold to Agada Shipping
SA,Panama(Vlasov) ren. BOLD 1. 1987 Reg. under V Ships,Monaco.
1989 Ren. EUROGAZ TWO. 1989 Sold to Naflumar SA,Piraeus ren.
YUCATAN. 9.1991 Still in service.

HO17. CAVENDISH ⠀⠀⠀⠀(1971 - 199) 26802g 14031n ⠀⠀637' x 95'
6-cyl Fiat oil engine.
1971 Completed by Chantiers de la Ciotat,La Ciotat for Ocean Gas
Transport Co. Ltd(Houlder Bros). 1977 Transferred to Gazocean
(Ocean Gas Transport Co. Ltd,mgr). 4.11.1985 Anchored off
Guayaquil for use as a gas storage tanker. 1989 Returned to
service under Furness,Withy(Shipping) Ltd. 9.1991 Still in
service.

HO18. FARADAY ⠀⠀⠀⠀(1971 - 199) 19754g 12296n ⠀⠀613' x 88'
6-cyl Hawthorn - Doxford oil engine.
1971 Completed by Swan Hunter Shipbuilders Ltd,Hebburn for Nile
S.S. Co. Ltd(Houlder Bros), operated by Ocean Gas Transport Co.
Ltd. 1989 Reg. under Furness,Withy(Shipping) Ltd. 9.1991 Still in
service.

HO19. ORENDA ⠀⠀⠀⠀(1972 - 1978) 69824g 49190n 882' x 140'
9-cyl 2SCSA Doxford oil engine by bldrs.
3.11.1971 Launched and 3.1972 Completed by Doxford & Sunderland
SB & Eng. Ltd,Sunderland as ORENDA BRIDGE for Ore Carriers Ltd
(Houlder Bros) on charter to Seabridge consortium. 1977 Ren.
ORENDA. 1978 Sold to Nathaniel Shipping Inc,Liberia ren. THEO-
DORA. 1983 Ren. SERENA. 12.11.1985 Arrived Valencia in tow from
Gibraltar for B/U.

HO20.JOULE(2)   (1973 - 1984) 8996g 4151n   463' x 63'
7-cyl 2SCSA M.A.N. oil engine by Kockums A/B.
1965 Completed by Moss Vaerft,Moss as HAVGAS for P. Meyer,Norway.
1973 Purchased by Morland Shipping Co. Ltd(Houlder Bros) on charter
to Ocean Gas Transport Ltd,London ren. JOULE. 4.8.1984 Arrived
Shanghai for B/U.

HO21. LORD KELVIN   (1978 - 1987) 21374g 12372n   630' x 85'
6-cyl 2SCSA Sulzer oil engine by H. Cegielski,Poznan.
5.1978 Completed by Nuovi Cantieri Apuania spA,Marina di Carrara
for Ocean Gas Transport Co. Ltd(Houlder Bros). 1987 Sold to Moss
Rosenburg, Norway ren. HELIOS. 9.1991 Still in service.

HO22. ORELIA(2)   (1984 - 1989) 5553g 3080n   469' x 63'
Six 6-cyl 4SCSA Mirlees oil engines DR geared to 3 shafts.
11.12.1982 Launched and 6.1984 completed by Swan Hunter SB Ltd,
Wallsend as a Diving Support ship for Houlder Offshore Ltd. 1989
Sold to Stena Offshore ren. STENA ORELIA. 9.1991 Still in service.

HO23. HUMBOLDT(2)   (1987 - 199) 1844g 905n   271' x 44'
8-cyl 4SCSA M.A.N. oil engine.
1968 Completed by Est. Nav de Viana do Castelo as CIDLA for Soc
Mar Ltda,Lisbon. 1987 Purchased by Furness,Withy(Shipping) Ltd
and registered under Navigas SA, Guayaquil for use on Ecuadorian
feeder service, ren. HUMBOLDT. 9.1991 Still in service.

HO24. JOULE(3)   (1989 - 199) 2527g 1272n   289' x 45'
9-cyl 2SCSA Sulzer oil engine.
1972 Completed by Seutelvens Verksted as LEIV EIRIKSSON for A/S
Leiv Eiriksson(E.Bakkevig),Oslo. 1987 Sold to Bibby Gas Tankers
Ltd,Liverpool ren. LANCASHIRE. 1989 Purchased by Furness,Withy
(Shipping) Ltd ren. JOULE for Mediterranean trading. 9.1991 Still
in service.

Name	Code	Name	Code	Name	Code
PERUVIANA(2)	F209	SALERNO	FG21	TRAMORE	FJ40
(3)	F218	SALINAS	FP3	TROPIC	FS39
PICARDY	FR16	SANDOWN	FB21	TRURO CITY	F27
PINEMORE	FJ9	SANTANDER	FP5	TUDHOE	FB24
(2)	FJ48	SANTERAMO	FG20	TULLAMORE	FJ24
PIZARRO	FP10	(2)	FG22	TUNISIANA	F172
PLATO	F56	SARMIENTO	FP1	(2)	F207
PLEIADES	F22	SARNIA	F63	TUNSTALL	F126
POMARON	F121	SAUERLAND	F203	TURINO	FG23
PORTINGLIS	F131	SAVANNAH	F146	TUSCANY	FG12
POTOMAC	FB11	(2)	FW9	(2)	FR14
POTOSI	FP9	SCANDINAVIA	F23	TYNEDALE	F30
POWHATAN	FC8	SCATWELL	FT5	TYNEHEAD	F32
QUEEN OF BERMUDA	F239	SEATONIA	FH9	ULUNDA	F14
QUEEN WILHELMINA	FO1	SHENANDOAH	FC5	URANIA	FH8
QUERNMORE	FJ10	SICILY	FG11	VALEMORE	FJ19
(2)	FJ38	SIDLAW RANGE	FO33	VEDAMORE	FJ13
RAPALLO	FG8	SILVIA	F235	(2)	FJ31
(2)	FG27	SNOWDON RANGE	FO14	VENANGO	FO6
RAPIDAN	FC7	(2)	FO26	VENICE	F177
(2)	FC14	SOMERS ISLE	FP13	WAIMANA	FS6
RAPPAHANNOCK	FC4	SORRENTO	F59	WAIMARAMA	FS33
RARANGA	FS8	SOUTHERN CROSS	FS53	WAIOTIRA	FS34
RAVENSWOOD	F264	SOUTH POINT	FN7	WAIPAWA	FS29
REINA DEL MAR	FP6	(2)	FN15	WAIRANGI	FS31
REXMORE	FJ20	SOWWELL	F183	(2)	FS37
RHODE ISLAND	FW6	STANMORE	FJ23	WAIWERA	FS30
RICHMOND	FC15	START POINT	FN8	(2)	FS36
RIPON	F88	(2)	FN16	WASHINGTON	FC16
RIPON CITY	F9	STOCKHOLM CITY	F10	WASHINGTON CITY	F15
RIVERINA	F263	SUEVIC	FS48	WATERLAND	F81
ROANOKE	FC13	SULTAN	F24	WEARSIDE	FH10
ROEBUCK	F262	SWALEDALE	F135	WELLDECK	F36
ROMANIC	FS67	SWANMORE	FJ12	WENDLAND	F202
ROSALIND	F234	SYCAMORE	FJ14	WENSLEYDALE	F136
ROSSANO	FG18	(2)	FJ39	WESTHAMPTON	FB26
ROTA	F188	(3)	FJ46	WESTMORE	FJ32
ROTTERDAM	FB33	SYLVIANA	F69	WESTWOOD	F124
ROUEN	F145	TABASCO	FO5	WEST POINT	FN1
ROWANMORE	FJ11	TAINUI	FS4	(2)	FN8
(2)	FJ49	TAIROA	FS11	WETHERBY	F8
RUNIC	FS47	TAMAQUA	F189	WHEATMORE	FJ18
RUNO	FO3	TAMAROA	FS22	WHORLTON	F125
RUTHENIC	FS70	TAMPICO	FO7	WIGMORE	FJ25
RYHOPE	F122	TARANAKI	FS17	(2)	FJ33
SACHEM	FW3	TAYMOUTH CASTLE	F29	WILLOWMORE	FJ35
SAGAMORE	FW2	TENTERDEN	FN20	WINGATE	F179
(2)	F257	THEMISTOCLES	FS20	WRAYMORE	FJ34
ST. JOHN CITY	F51	THESSALY	FR15	WYANDOTTE	FB8
(2)	F78	THIMBLEBY	F123	WYNCOTE	F190
ST. LOUIS	F26	THISTLEMORE	FJ18	YORK CITY	F4
ST. RONANS	F46	THORNLEY	FB28	ZEALANDIC	FS16
SALAMANCA	FP2	THRIFT	FH7	(2)	FS68
SALAVERRY	FP4	THROCKLEY	F219	ZEBRA	F58